NEVER REST ON YOUR ORES

Footprints Series
Jane Errington, Editor

The life stories of individual women and men who were participants in interesting events help nuance larger historical narratives, at times reinforcing those narratives, at other times contradicting them. The Footprints series introduces extraordinary Canadians, past and present, who have led fascinating and important lives at home and throughout the world.

   The series includes primarily original manuscripts but may consider the English-language translation of works that have already appeared in another language. The editor of the series welcomes inquiries from authors. If you are in the process of completing a manuscript that you think might fit into the series, please contact her, care of McGill-Queen's University Press, 1010 Sherbrooke Street West, Suite 1720, Montreal, QC, H3A 2R7.

NEVER REST ON YOUR ORES

Building a Mining Company, One Stone at a Time

Second Edition

NORMAN B. KEEVIL

McGill-Queen's University Press
Montreal & Kingston • London • Chicago

© McGill-Queen's University Press 2023

ISBN 978-0-2280-1778-3 (cloth)
ISBN 978-0-2280-1781-3 (ePDF)
ISBN 978-0-2280-1782-0 (ePUB)

Legal deposit second quarter 2023
Bibliothèque nationale du Québec

First edition 2017

Printed in Canada on acid-free paper that is 100% ancient forest free
(100% post-consumer recycled), processed chlorine free

Funded by the   Financé par le
Government   gouvernement
of Canada   du Canada

Canada Council   Conseil des arts
for the Arts   du Canada

We acknowledge the support of the Canada Council for the Arts.
Nous remercions le Conseil des arts du Canada de son soutien.

Photos and sketches courtesy of Teck and Keevil family archives.
Paintings by Frank Halliday part of Teck and Keevil family archives.
Permission to use David Lee painting granted by his agent, Jim Killett,
owner of Lahaina Galleries, Hawaii.

Library and Archives Canada Cataloguing in Publication

Title: Never rest on your ores : building a mining company, one stone at
    a time / Norman B. Keevil.
Names: Keevil, Norman B., 1938- author.
Series: Footprints series (Montréal, Quebec) ; 26.
Description: Second edition. | Series statement: Footprints series ;
    26 | Includes bibliographical references and index.
Identifiers: Canadiana (print) 2022046281X | Canadiana (ebook)
    20220462852 | ISBN 9780228017783 (cloth) | ISBN 9780228017813 (ePDF)
    | ISBN 9780228017820 (ePUB)
Subjects: LCSH: Keevil, Norman Bell. | LCSH: Keevil, Norman B., 1938- |
    LCSH: Teck Corporation—History. | LCSH: Mining corporations—
    Canada—History. | LCSH: Mines and mineral resources—Canada—
    History. | LCGFT: Autobiographies.
Classification: LCC HD9506.C24 T43 2023 | DDC 338.7/6220971—dc23

For my wife Joan, who has done so much for me and has been my pillar of strength.

All royalties earned from the sale of this book will go to support two charitable organizations that provide programs to raise awareness among students and the general public about the importance of rocks, minerals, metals, and mining. MineralsEd was started in British Columbia in 1991 by Maureen Lipkewich, the wife of one of Teck Corporation's senior mining engineers. The idea was taken up nationally with the leadership of two of Teck's Eastern Canadian geologists in 1994 under the name Mining Matters. Together these organizations now provide mineral resources education programs for teachers, students and the public across Canada.

CONTENTS

PREFACE

You should write a book.

The motivation to write this book arose from a Founders Awards Dinner hosted by the Fraser Institute, a Canadian think tank, at which I was asked to say a few words. They said: "Just tell some stories," so I did.

These seemed to ring a bell, because that night, and for some time after, people came up to me to say: "You should write a book." Never having done that before, and being unlikely to do so again, for the next year or so I jotted down notes as they came to mind, often at the most unlikely times. I checked old files, and tried to confirm that my recollections were correct with people who had shared some of our experiences. As time went on, I began to think it really was a good idea to record some of the part we played in Canada's mining history, and that it could be useful to those who come after. As Cory Sibbald (one of the key engineers who helped build some of those mines that made our Teck Resources what it is) put it: "Somebody has to do it."

I thought of my father, who had been encouraged to write a memoir after he was getting on in years and had retired from active business. He had begun: "For years, people have been saying: 'Why don't you have someone write a book?'" He told of his grandchildren who asked things such as: "Tell us the story about the wolves closing in on your camp." He never got a chance to finish his story, so this is for both of us, as well as for the many others who joined in the journey, and without whose efforts there would be no Teck Resources as we know it today.

My father, also named Norman Keevil, was an avid canoeist, fond of encouraging people onwards by saying: "Never rest on your oars." It must be said that canoeists use paddles, and oars are more likely to be found in rowboats or Viking longboats, but "never rest on your paddles" somehow seems to lack the same bite.

This is a book about some of the people who find and build mines. It may not be widely appreciated, but the lifeblood of all mines, their foundation, is the ore deposits from which they produce metals or minerals. Without ore, there would be no mines, and without mines, and the hard-rock miners that work them, no cars, bicycles, cell phones, radios, televisions, and countless other things that society takes for granted.

I've used a bit of poetic licence in titling this book *Never Rest on Your Ores*. Just as with those Viking oarsmen lined down each side of the ship, rowing as though their very lives depended upon it, and perhaps did, a mine that rests on its ores for too long seems destined not to last for long. Every ore deposit is finite and will eventually be depleted, so no mine, or mining company, can last without discovering and developing new ore reserves to replace the old. It is a challenge from which miners can never rest.

Our story will see prospects that work out and others that don't. It will see mines discovered, opened and, when the time comes, closed. And we will meet people who will go on to find and build the next mine, in the spirit of ongoing, creative construction. Somebody does have to do it.

I hope you enjoy these tales, and that they will encourage others to keep on finding and developing those new mines that society will continue to need. In the process, we may discover the meaning of the owl.

PREFACE TO THE SECOND EDITION

You should write a book.

The first edition of this book, written in 2015 and published in 2017, told a collection of stories over almost 100 years from the start of Teck-Hughes Gold Mines Limited on a gold discovery at Kirkland Lake, Ontario; the contemporaneous birth of my father, also Norman B. Keevil, in a hamlet in Saskatchewan; and how the two threads came together some 50 years later to create Teck Corporation, an adventurous producer of copper, gold, silver, and oil with aspirations to become a major force in Canadian mining.

It told how Teck grew from modest beginnings by finding and developing a succession of new mines, adding niobium, zinc, and metallurgical coal to the portfolio, managed by a C-suite that included the two Keevils, father and son, mining icon Robert Hallbauer, and financial guru David Thompson, with the support of countless colleagues. Between 1975 and 2005 alone Teck developed or acquired 17 new mines, a growth period that culminated in Teck's participation in a major copper and zinc mine in Peru and the consolidation of its Elkview mine with five additional independent Canadian coal mines into the Elk Valley coal partnership, managed and effectively controlled by Teck. In the process, Teck grew from a $25 million company in 1975 into a $12.6 billion company in 2005.

The stories of the first edition essentially ended there, as the author and Thompson retired from their successive CEO roles and Don Lindsay became CEO. Chapter 42, "The Last Decade," touched on some events in the ensuing years that began with the new "China super-cycle," an almost unprecedented commodities boom that began to be noticed around 2005. But, as we observed in that edition, "the tales of the last 10 years have, for the most part, yet to mature, let alone be finished. So I will just note briefly some of the main events and works in progress."

Now, with the passing of seven more years, it seems timely to flesh out the story – at least until the world was disrupted by the Covid-19 pandemic in 2020 and entered a new era of volatility, the outcomes of which will be unclear for a while and gist for another author in perhaps 10 more years.

A revised chapter 42 deals with how the advent of the China super-cycle affected the mining industry at large, leading to three years of booming prices that were then interrupted by a global financial crisis. The boom resumed for a couple more years, after which the inevitable second half of cycles, the decline, began to be felt. As the up-cycle began some adventurous mining companies looked at each other with predatory eyes, while they and other miners dusted off every shovel-ready expansion or new mine development project that had been lying dormant on their books. The result was a major increase in supply just as demand growth slowed, leading to an industry-wide downturn.

A new chapter 43 traces Teck's activities and results over the super-cycle era, beginning with similar predatory eyes, a flirtation with bankruptcy, a peak as the cycle peaked, and a major decline as it waned. The net result was a mixed bag of ups and downs, but the period closed with the successful development of what should be a core Teck copper mine for decades to come.

And as before, this part of the story ends with changes at the top: the new CEO, Jonathan Price, and the incoming president, Red Conger, have accepted the challenge of taking Teck to a new plateau, higher and better than ever before. As part of the founding group, we have high expectations of them and the rest of the Teck team.

Norman B. Keevil
September 2022

ACKNOWLEDGMENTS

This book would not be complete without acknowledging the leaders I had the pleasure of working with and learning from along the way: John Simpson, Stan Ward, Charlie Smith, my father, Bob Hallbauer, Ed Thompson, David Thompson, Moriki Aoyagi, Bob Wright, and others too numerous to name.

Thanks to the many, and especially Joan Keevil, Warren Seyffert, Klaus Zeitler, Peter Brown, and Keith Steeves, who provided editorial and research input, and to Linda Rowe, Peter Dunsford, and Karen Dunfee, who have worked with us for so long that they seem part of the family, and to all of the prospectors, geologists, promoters, engineers, hard-rock miners at the face and in the open pits. They are part of what makes our mining world so fascinating.

And to Gillian Scobie, whose copy editing helped to make this book better.

LIST OF CHARACTERS
(In Order of Appearance)

Princess Mary of Teck: Grandmother of Queen Elizabeth II of England.

James Hughes: Prospector and discoverer of the Teck-Hughes gold mine at Kirkland Lake, Ontario, 1912.

Sandy McIntyre, a.k.a. Oliphant: Prospector and co-discoverer of Teck-Hughes and also of the McIntyre gold mine at Timmins.

Ed Horne: Prospector and discoverer of the Horne mine at Rouyn, the start of the major Canadian mining company Noranda Mines.

Norman B. Keevil Sr, OC, PhD, CMHF (Member of the Canadian Mining Hall of Fame): Entrepreneurial scientist turned mine-finder.

Albert Einstein: Iconic scientist and initiator of the Manhattan Project.

The Right Honourable D. Roland Michener: Governor General of Canada, later chairman of Teck Corporation.

Joe Hirshhorn, CMHF: Multi-millionaire mining promoter.

Norman B. Keevil Jr, OC, PhD, PEng, CMHF: The author and Chairman Emeritus of Teck Resources.

Bill Bergey and Joe Frantz: Key Keevil Mining Group geologists.

Charles H. Smith: Geological Survey of Canada.

Stan Ward and Herb Hawkes: Leaders in geophysics and geochemistry.

Doug Fraser, PhD: Inventor of the DIGHEM airborne electromagnetic survey system.

John D. Simpson, CMHF: Builder of Placer Development, one of the world's leading mining companies in its day.

Ed Thompson, PEng: Geologist and one of the key players in the early days as the Keevil Mining Group (KMG) evolved into Teck Corporation (TMG).

Robert E. Hallbauer, PEng, CMHF: With Teck, one of Canada's leading builders of new mines.

Herman "Spud" Huestis, CMHF: Prospector and discoverer of Bethlehem Copper.

Doug Perigoe: Toronto investment broker.

Roy Jodrey: Major Nova Scotia investor.

Jack Perry: President of Teck-Hughes prior to the KMG takeover, and later board chairman.

John Leishman: Co-discoverer of Canadian Devonian Petroleum's Steelman oil field.

Len Watt: Irascible investment adviser.

Steve Kay: Brought to KMG the prospect that became its new Silverfields mine in Cobalt.

Walter Holyk: Leading geologist involved in Texas Gulf Sulphur's major Kidd Creek copper-zinc discovery at Timmins.

Ken Darke: Project geologist who in 1963 convinced Holyk to authorize drilling one last test hole, the one that resulted in that discovery.

Don McKinnon: Prospector involved in the staking rush after the Kidd Creek discovery and, 20 years later, in the Hemlo gold discovery in Western Ontario.

Viola MacMillan, CMHF: Mining entrepreneur.

Karl Springer, CMHF: Iconic mine-finder and builder.

Harold Geneen: CEO of the International Telephone and Telegraph Company.

Andronico Luksic: Chilean mining entrepreneur in the 1960s; Luksic would eventually establish Antofagasta PLC as a major Chilean mining and transportation company.

John Downing: Petroleum geologist who managed Teck's early oil exploration business.

Alan Keevil: Petroleum geologist and successor to John Downing.

Côme Carbonneau: President of SOQUEM, the Quebec government's mine exploration and development arm.

Bob Falkins: Mining entrepreneur.

Kenjiro Kawakami: President of Sumitomo Metal Mining and financier of Bethlehem Copper.

Keith Steeves, CPA: With Bethlehem when Teck made an unsolicited investment offer in 1969, and later a valued Teck executive.

Bernie Brynelsen, CMHF: Mine developer responsible for developing the Brenda mine, the first large-scale open pit copper mine in British Columbia, before teaming up with a group to found Brameda Resources.

Bob Wright: KMG lawyer and later head of Ontario Securities Commission.

Jacob Austin, lawyer: One of the founders of Brameda Resources, and later Deputy Minister of Mines and chief of staff to Prime Minister Pierre Trudeau.

Earl Joudrie: As president of Ashland Oil Canada, Earl teamed up with Teck in a friendly bid for Home Oil, a major Canadian oil company.

Mike Lipkewich: Mining engineer and successor to Bob Hallbauer in Teck Corporation.

Warren Seyffert: Teck lawyer and later vice-chairman and lead director of Teck Resources.

Chester Millar, CMHF: Mining entrepreneur and discoverer of the Afton copper deposit.

Judge Tom Berger: Ex-leader of British Columbia's NDP party and later a sitting judge.

Dave Barrett: The first NDP premier of British Columbia; Barrett's government lasted for three tumultuous years before being defeated by Bill Bennett.

Karl Gustaf Ratjen: CEO of Metallgesellschaft (Metall) of Germany. Metall became a significant shareholder of Teck and Ratjen joined the board of directors, along with associates *Heinz Schimmelbusch* and *Klaus Zeitler*.

David Thompson, CMHF: CFO of Teck during 1981 recession, later president of TeckCominco.

Harold Keevil: Innovator who came up with the plan to combine Metallgesellschaft and Keevil shareholdings in Teck into a joint holding company.

Ian Rushbrooke: Executive at Edinburgh investment trust Ivory and Sime, from whom Teck acquired a key interest in Lornex Mining Corporation.

George Albino: President of Rio Algom, controlling shareholder of Lornex.

Konrad von Finckenstein: Functionary dealing with Ottawa's Foreign Investment Review Act (FIRA).

The Honourable Jean Chrétien: Minister in charge of FIRA, and later prime minister of Canada.

Tim Nemoto: Managing director of NKK, co-ordinating steel mill for the Japanese coal buyers' consortium.

Dick Drozd, PEng: A key Teck participant in the negotiations with Japanese steel mills on Bullmoose coal.

Robert Andras: Businessman turned politician and back, and a key player in negotiations for the northeast coal project.

Don Phillips: Known as "the mouth that roared," Phillips was Minister of Economic Development in Bill Bennett's British Columbia government.

Deng Xiaoping: A leader in China's emergence as a world superpower once again.

Rong Yiren: A protégé of Deng and co-founder of China International Trust and Investment Corporation.

Jimmy Connacher: Innovative investment banker who rocked the boat of the old Toronto brokerage establishment.

Morton Shulman: Physician, politician, businessman, author, and coroner; editor of the finance magazine *The Money Letter*.

Tim Snider: Chemist and miner who helped Phelps Dodge develop the new SX-EW process to recover copper by leaching and electrowinning, and later became its president.

David Bell: Geologist and discoverer of the first gold mine at Hemlo.

Murray Pezim, a.k.a. "The Pez": Stock promoter who financed Corona Resources' discovery of Hemlo and *Nell Dragovan*, Corona president.

Bob Quartermain, CMHF: Teck geologist at Hemlo and later a highly successful independent mining entrepreneur.

Dennis Sheehan: Geologist for Lac Minerals, the defendant in a major mining lawsuit over a Hemlo gold mine.

Peter Allen: President of Lac Minerals.

Egil Lorntzen, CMHF: Prospector and discoverer of the major Lornex orebody, key to later development of Highland Valley Copper.

Bill Stinson: President of CP Limited, whose Cominco unit was sold to Teck in 1986.

Norm Anderson: President of Cominco Limited prior to the Teck acquisition.

George Tikkanen: Geologist active in acquiring Cominco's interest in Alaska's Red Dog mine, as well as Quebrada Blanca.

Lee Bilheimer: A key member of Teck's new mine construction team.

Jim Gill, CMHF: Discoverer of the Louvicourt copper-zinc mine in Quebec.

Ken Pickering: Built and managed the giant Escondida mine in Chile.

Joe Oppenheimer: Anglo American's manager in Chile and Argentina.

Ed Dowling, PhD: With Cyprus Amax, outbid Teck to acquire Chile's El Abra copper prospect.

Bill James Jr, CMHF: Renowned consultant and executive in the Canadian mining industry.

Akihiko Shinozaki: Fifth president of Sumitomo Metal Mining (SMM).

Moriki Aoyagi: SMM's sixth president, and partner on Pogo gold prospect in Alaska.

Fukushima Koichi: SMM's's seventh president.

Nobumasa Kemori: SMM's eighth president.

Yoshiaki Nakazato: SMM's ninth president.

Robert Friedland, CMHF: Entrepreneur and mine-finder; discoverer of Diamond Fields' Voisey's Bay nickel mine.

Mike Sopko: President of Inco.

David Walsh: President of Bre-X Resources as it became involved in a major salting scandal.

Graham Farquarson, CMHF: Consultant who raised the curtain on the Bre-X scandal.

David Culver: CEO of Alcan and co-founder of the Canada-Japan Businessmen's Conference.

Gary Jones: Teck's principal evaluations engineer for many years.

David Kerr: President of Noranda Mines and partner in the large Antamina mine in Peru.

David Sinclair: Independent director of Cominco during the 2000 merger negotiations with Teck.

Jim Gardiner: President of coal producer Fording Inc. after it was spun off by CP Limited.

Ian Delaney: CEO of Sherritt International; and *Brian Gibson*, executive at the Ontario Teachers Pension Plan: The two jointly made a takeover bid for Fording in 2002.

Jimmy Pattison: Eclectic Vancouver businessman and chairman of Expo 86. Financial partner with Teck in 2003 consolidation of Canadian coal.

Jim Popowich: Co-operative mining engineer with Fording Coal Partnership.

Donald Lindsay: Mining engineer turned investment banker, and president of Teck Resources, 2005–22.

Akira Nozaki: Tenth president of Sumitomo Metal Mining.

Alex Christopher: Key member of Teck's QB2 development team.

Dale Andres: Key member of Teck's QB2 development team.

Karl Hroza: Teck's QB2 project director.

Sheila Murray: Chairperson of Teck and leader of succession committee, 2020–22.

Harold "Red" Conger: President and COO of Teck from September 2022.

Jonathan Price: CEO of Teck from September 2022.

Sir Andrew Mackenzie: CEO of BHP, 2013–20.

David Humphreys: Retired chief economist of Rio Tinto and author.

Bob Dorrance: CEO of TD Securities.

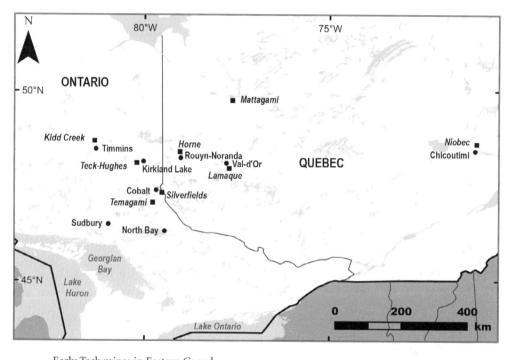

Early Teck mines in Eastern Canada

Parts of Ontario and Quebec: The Teck story began with the Teck-Hughes gold discovery, part of what became the Kirkland Lake gold camp in northern Ontario. This was followed 50 years later by a high-grade copper discovery at Temagami. How the two came together to begin the present-day Teck Resources is part of the story of this book. The map shows some of the mines in Eastern Canada that played a role in the early days.

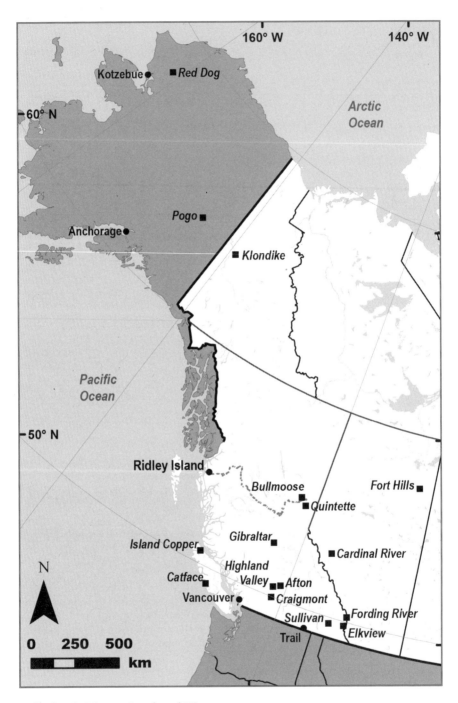

Teck mines in Western Canada and US
Parts of British Columbia, Alberta, and Alaska: From the early 1970s the new Teck Corporation was part of a surge in new mine development in Western Canada, followed by mines in Alaska and elsewhere in the world.

Teck and other mines in Chile and Peru
Parts of Chile and Peru: The Keevil Mining Group had been exploring in Chile 50 years ago, but it wasn't until the 1990s that Teck began building new mines in both Chile and Peru. The region remains a key focus of Teck in the twenty-first century.

NEVER REST ON YOUR ORES

INTRODUCTION

Not everything that can be counted counts, and not everything that counts
can be counted.
Albert Einstein, after William Bruce Cameron

Our story begins about a century ago with two events that were completely unrelated and that would remain so for the next 50 years. Then these two paths would merge, resulting in what became Teck Resources, by early in the twenty-first century the largest diversified mining company in Canada.

The first path begins with prospector James Hughes, who may or may not have been grizzled, since history is silent on the subject. He was certainly adept in the ways of the bush. He was also flexible enough that, when he couldn't find silver during a staking rush in the new silver mining camp of Cobalt, he just went north and found the gold that became the Teck-Hughes gold mine at Kirkland Lake.

The story peripherally involves the British royal family: Queen Mary of Teck, the grandmother of Queen Elizabeth, was a member of German royalty whose family would lend its name to a township in Northern Ontario, and to a mining company.

Contemporaneously, it begins with a family that centuries earlier had migrated to England from Brittany, now part of France. Its name of Chiveles, or perhaps deKevilly, had eventually been Anglicized to Keevil, and by the early twentieth century the family was successfully farming and raising horses in Wiltshire, England. One of these Keevils, Roland, had just immigrated to Canada, homesteaded in the wilds of Saskatchewan, and started a new line that would go on to great accomplishments.

This second path follows an academic from the deKevilly roots who helped establish new scientific exploration techniques and later capitalized upon them himself by making an important copper discovery. Eventually he took a high-risk gamble that paid off, acquiring control of Teck-Hughes Gold by the skin of his teeth, as the two separate journeys came together 50 years after that early gold discovery.

We will see diversions from mining into the oil business. Not many people realize that the historic gold miner, Teck-Hughes, became primarily an oil company in the 1960s. How we got into oil, tried to get out of it as we gradually learned what we did and did not know about that business, and how we were once again involved in it in a much bigger way years later is part of the history to be told.

We will follow the company that eventually diversified into a producer of copper, silver, zinc, lead, niobium, oil, and steelmaking coal, as well as developing more gold mines. How it got there through mineral discoveries, by taking chances, with serendipity and just plain hard work in spite of ever-changing times represents one of the many success stories in the annals of the mining industry.

What is ore anyway? The American Heritage Science Dictionary defines it as: "A naturally occurring mineral or rock from which a valuable or useful substance, especially a metal, can be extracted at a reasonable cost."

A deposit of gold or copper or coal that is uneconomic to mine is not ore, however large. One that can be mined profitably and safely is, no matter how small. Without ore, there can be no successful mine.

Andrew Grove, one of the builders of chip giant Intel, wrote about managing a high-tech business through changing times in an incisive book, *Only the Paranoid Survive*. We miners might add that: "Those who rest on their ores" will not survive either, at least for long. Grove described times of major change as "strategic inflection points," which he defined as "a time in the life of a business when its fundamentals are about to change. That change can mean an opportunity to rise to new heights. But it may just as likely signal the beginning of the end."

We will see a few of these inflection points, as the mining company that got its start with James Hughes evolved into something much larger and different over the years.

This is about people seeing and grasping opportunities, sometimes to good effect, although not always. It covers initiatives that worked out and some others that didn't. In a parallel universe, perhaps those that didn't work here did there, and our future and that of the alternate universe's Teck Resources could have been remarkably different. One never knows, and can only go from chance to chance, without looking back. The decisions people in this business make that turn out to be game changers are seldom obvious at the start. If they were, everyone would be chasing the same tales.

Most of this story takes place in the 50 years from 1955 through 2005. The ten years since have been at least as entertaining, being the most volatile in the memory of most miners around the world, but it is said that history is best written after the effluxion of time. Much will be told of the recent China "super-cycle" and the industry's reactions to it, but this should best be done a decade from now, perhaps in a future edition of *Never Rest on Your Ores*.

The narrative refers at times to technical geological or mining engineering terms that may not be completely familiar to all readers, and an excellent source for further information is a book by W. Scott Dunbar titled *How Mining Works*, published by the Society for Mining, Metallurgical & Exploration Inc.

Finally, a small point as to style: I should note that Canada changed to the metric system in stages over the late 1970s, and this book uses the modern kilometres and other metric units for the most part. However, we will sometimes use tons (from the old Imperial system) in describing the size and milling capacity of mines in the pre-metric era. These were usually reported in round numbers and changing them to metric would result in numbers less round, and unnecessarily confusing. The difference is about 10 per cent and not material to the stories.

As the poet T.S. Eliot wrote: "Let us go and make our visit."

PART ONE

BEGINNINGS

Part 1 starts with the discovery and development of the Teck-Hughes mine at Kirkland Lake, Ontario. It then covers the contemporaneous arrival and early career of Norman Keevil, an academic who would go on to practise as a consulting geophysicist, and eventually make an important copper discovery at Temagami, also in Ontario.

The two paths would come together some 50 years later, and the result would be the creation of Teck Corporation, a new force in Canadian mining. These are just a few of the many stories that brought them to that crossing.

The Teck-Hughes gold mine, ca. 1930

CHAPTER 1

DISCOVERING GOLD

This is the law of the Yukon, and ever she makes it plain:
"Send not your foolish and feeble; send me your strong and your sane –
Strong for the red rage of battle; sane, for I harry them sore;
Send me men girt for the combat, men who are grit to the core."
Robert Service, "The Law of the Yukon"

There is an adage in the mining business that mines are made, not found. History abounds with tales of gold or copper showings that have been known for years, ones that stayed little explored and undeveloped until imaginative entrepreneurs, geologists, or engineers came along and found a way to make them into mines.

But the fact is somebody does have to find the prospects in the first place, whether they will then lie fallow for ages or can be developed quickly. That is the role of the prospector, whether the grizzled bush men of 100 years ago like Sandy McIntyre and Jim Hughes, less grizzled but still entrepreneurial ones of 50 years ago like Egil Lorntzen and Spud Huestis, or the geologists and geophysicists who use the latest science and technology to make their mark.

We will meet these people and others in our stories, but first we have to explain how and why we came to be known as Teck, including how it relates to Queen Elizabeth II.

Queen Mary and the Castle of Teck

It all hails back to Count Conrad von Wirtemberg, a Prussian gentleman who in the year 1080 built a castle for himself near what is now Stuttgart in Germany.

Time passed. The castle was destroyed and rebuilt several times, and by the early 1800s Duke Frederick of "Wurttemberg" (Spelling 101 not yet having been invented) had allied with Napoleon I. This proved useful, the principality soon became part of the Confederation of the Rhine, and in 1806 he was crowned King of Wurttemberg.

Frederick had a son, Francis, the result of a morganatic marriage with a beautiful Transylvanian princess named Claudia Rhedey de Kis-rhede. She was later known more simply as the Countess of Hohenstein. Francis himself was known as the Duke of Teck, and they lived in the modern-day Teck Castle that still stands near Stuttgart, Germany.

Their daughter, Victoria Mary of Teck, was born in England in May 1867. One of her three godparents was Queen Victoria. Princess Mary of Teck eventually became Queen Consort to King George V of England, and was the mother of King George VI. She passed away in 1952, at the beginning of the reign of her granddaughter, Queen Elizabeth II.

A Cartographer that Named Us

Sometime in the nineteenth century, an unknown cartographer was busy putting place names on maps of Northern Ontario, which was being subdivided on paper into square blocks of land known as townships. We can assume that he had never visited the area, then populated mainly by blackflies and the occasional moose, but for some reason he chose to name one of the blocks Teck Township.

This block lay 70 kilometres north of what would become the town of Cobalt, 100 kilometres north of Temagami, 100 kilometres southeast of what would become Timmins, and contained what would eventually become the towns of Swastika and Kirkland Lake, important places in Canada's mining history. Why that cartographer chose the name Teck for this particular township rather than others near it is one of those things we'll never know. As we saw, the name did reflect a part of German and English history, the royal families of which were often intermixed, and perhaps the cartographer was a historian.

While Queen Elizabeth II made many visits to Canada, it is not recorded that she ever visited Teck Township, or for that matter ever came across the names Teck-Hughes Gold Mines Limited or Teck Resources. Some of us have, however, visited the Teck Castle in Stuttgart, in the company of a one-time partner, Metallgesellschaft AG (Metall), and are properly proud of our royal heritage, however inadvertent it may have been.

We are also thankful that the cartographer picked well and didn't name it Beaver Township, in which case our company might now be named Beaver Resources – or even worse, named it Moose Pasture Township. Beavers and moose pasture are still both common in the area. Gold prospectors today are less so.

What does seem likely is that none of this history was in the mind of James Hughes that day in 1912 when, grizzled or not, he walked through the bush near Kirkland Lake looking for outcrops of rock where he might find traces of silver or gold. He was there primarily because there was no more land available to explore at a previous mineral discovery 70 kilometres to the south.

Silver Discoveries in Cobalt

Prospectors' interest in Northern Ontario had been sparked in 1903, after the discovery of rich silver veins by workers building the Temiskaming and Northern Ontario Railway.

The purpose of the railway, later to be known as the Ontario Northland, was to reach an outlier of somewhat fertile farmland in New Liskeard. This was an unusual area of Paleozoic rocks surrounded by the infertile Precambrian Shield, and the railroad was being built to encourage Canadians from the south to go north and homestead.

According to legend, one day Fred La Rose, a blacksmith working on the railroad, threw his hammer at a fox. The fox scampered away and survived, but the hammer struck a rocky ledge and revealed a glittering vein of silver.

Interestingly, the major nickel deposits at Sudbury had been discovered some time earlier in much the same way, when copper mineralization (later found to contain nickel as well) had been exposed in road cuts during railroad construction. It is not clear whether or not those two events spawned a new exploration theory that mines are there to be found wherever railroad contractors go. This does not seem to have much geological merit, but then a number of geological theories over the years have had to be discarded as thinking evolved, some in hindsight being as far-fetched as this. Regardless, with few new railroads being built these days the discussion is somewhat academic.

The silver veins discovered in 1903 also contained cobalt, and the new mining town became known as Cobalt. Development was rapid, and by 1905 there were 16 silver mines in the area. By 1908, it was producing 9 per cent of the world's silver and in 1911 alone, over 30 million ounces. As Michael Barnes reported in his book *More than Free Gold*: "In the silver town's heyday, Toronto was said to be the place where you changed trains for Cobalt."

However, while the silver-bearing veins were high grade, they were of limited vertical extent, all occurring at or near the flat-lying contact between the extensive Nipissing diabase sill and the underlying rocks. By 1917 most of the mines had closed down – in part because of the lack of able-bodied men to work them during the First World War.

The Nipissing Sill was part of a major magmatic intrusion, called the Ungava event, about 2.2 billion years ago, with its explosive centre hundreds of kilometres to the northeast of Cobalt. The relatively flat-lying phase in Cobalt's new silver camp intruded earlier Precambrian rocks, and is particularly extensive.

How and why the silver got deposited in and around its base remains a mystery to all but the most imaginative geologists, but it did. Was the silver related to the Nipissing intrusive event itself or is that just a spatial coincidence? Radiometric age dating has been inconclusive, possibly due to later metamorphism of the vein material. This is one of those little-understood situations we often encounter in mining geology. Given the large regional extent of the diabase sill, there may well be a lot more silver where it came from, but the $64 question has always been how to find it effectively.

The Silver Rush Goes North and Turns to Gold

Encouraged by the success at Cobalt, but with most of the nearby ground already staked, prospectors fanned out farther north, and in 1906 gold was found on the shores of Larder Lake, resulting in the first gold rush of Northern Ontario. That property would eventually become the Kerr-Addison mine, although not until more exploration would finally prove up enough ore to justify building a mine a full 30 years later.

By 1909, prospectors Jack Wilson and Harry Preston had paddled and portaged 200 kilometres northwest of Cobalt and come across spectacular gold mineralization on a large rounded outcrop. They staked four claims that later became known as the Big Dome. These became the heart of the major Dome Mine in what is now Timmins, Ontario. This was followed by the discovery of more gold 6 kilometres to the west by prospectors Benny Hollinger and Alec Gillies, which would become the important Hollinger

Mine. While those two celebrated their discovery, another prospector, Sandy McIntyre, arrived in the area and went a short distance north to stake what would become the McIntyre Mine, the third of the great gold producers in the Timmins camp.

Meanwhile, halfway between Timmins and Cobalt, more discoveries were being made near Larder Lake, in what would become the Kirkland Lake gold camp.

As described in *Kirkland Lake: An Introduction*: "It all began in 1911, when William Wright and Ed Hargreaves began prospecting in the area. Apparently, Mr Hargreaves got lost while the two were hunting rabbit. In order to attract the attention of Mr Wright, he fired a shot. While rushing through the bush, Mr Wright stumbled on a quartz outcrop with visible gold. The two then staked out several claims the following day, marking the discovery of the Kirkland Lake Gold Camp." It is not recorded what happened to the rabbit.

Early results were inconclusive, and the Wright-Hargreaves Mine, while it eventually became the second-largest gold producer in the camp, did not actually achieve production until ten years later, in 1921. Nobody said exploration and mine development was easy.

James Hughes and Sandy McIntyre Discover Gold in Teck Township

Meanwhile, prospector James Hughes had been slogging around in the Northern Ontario bush for months, looking for gold in what is now euphemistically called the boreal forest. This is a term used most often these days by city folk who have little knowledge of it, and even less interest in going there. It is largely a mosquito- and blackfly-infested mixture of mucky swamps and stunted trees known as jack pines, populated primarily by bears, moose, beavers, prospectors, and geologists. It actually takes the latter two to see any beauty in it.

Hughes and Sandy McIntyre, soon to be a serial gold mine discoverer, teamed up, and in 1912 discovered gold on a claim in Teck Township, not far from the earlier find by Wright, Hargreaves, and the rabbit. Wasting no time, and with gold and silver prospects in vogue in those days, they were able to locate financial backers who would form a company to explore the ground.

The Teck-Hughes Gold Mines Limited was formed in early 1913, with a capitalization of 2 million shares. Initial financing included the issuance of 200,000 treasury shares at a price of 18 ½ cents a share. The prospectus stated: "The most important feature in connection with this property is the opening up of a rich and promising vein located on claim No. 1238. This vein shows free gold in large quantities and can be traced nearly across the claim commencing close to the shore of Kirkland Lake and extending in a westerly direction."

In 1913, a shaft was sunk to a depth of 212 feet and initial drifting (tunneling) on the vein system was carried out on the 200-foot level. However, as with many new mines, the early days were fraught with continuous financial problems and the threat of complete shutdown. Following the original financing, a deal was made to issue the remaining treasury shares of the company to Nipissing Mining Company Ltd at 15 cents a share, raising $40,000, and to give Nipissing options on enough early vendors' shares to give it eventual control. By 1915, Nipissing in turn had decided the property was not attractive enough to continue exploring and abandoned its options. No funds remained on hand, and all work was stopped.

But a new US group headed by Charles H. Denison and including A.W. Johnston, a vice-president of International Nickel Company, took an interest in the property. The group agreed to acquire two-thirds of the issued shares and lend the company additional funds to allow it to continue to explore. Further tunneling continued over the next two years, and by 1917 a 50-ton-per-day mill had been built and the mine began producing gold.

The first six years under the new syndicate were frustrating, with a constant flow of funds required to keep Teck-Hughes afloat, but after a capital reorganization in 1922, additional claims were acquired, higher-grade gold was found and the mill capacity was increased to 160 tons per day. This marked a turning point in the mine's history. By 1926, Teck-Hughes was able to pay its first dividend, amounting to 5 cents a share. By 1931, mill capacity had been increased to 1,300 tons per day, and the next year the company paid dividends of 65 cents a share.

James Hughes was not the first to discover gold at Kirkland Lake, and the Teck-Hughes mine was not the largest to be developed, but it was one of the first to be brought into commercial production.

The mine would live for some 50 years until it finally exhausted its ore reserves in 1968. Its workings would extend to 1.8 kilometres below the surface, or over a mile deep. It would produce 3.7 million ounces of gold valued at $104 million, making it the third largest of the seven mines in the Kirkland Lake camp, after the Macassa and Wright-Hargreaves Mines, and pay dividends to its shareholders amounting to $52 million.

During the Depression years, the Kirkland Lake area was one of the most flourishing parts of Canada. In the end, the district would produce 37 million ounces of gold and be the second largest in Canada, after the Timmins camp. In contrast, the more recent Hemlo gold camp, while important and highly profitable, has produced only 22 million ounces to date.

A Second Gold Mine for Teck-Hughes, at Lamaque

In the early 1930s, Teck-Hughes supported the development of a second gold mine 200 kilometres to the East, in the Bourlamaque/Val-d'Or area of northern Quebec.

American prospector Robert C. Clark, along with Gabriel Commandant, an Indigenous guide, had discovered gold at Bourlamaque in 1923. Five years later, Read-Authier Mines Ltd acquired the property and continued exploration. In 1932, Teck-Hughes acquired control of the property from Read-Authier and formed a new company, Lamaque Gold Mines Ltd, to explore it further. This program was successful and production began in 1935 at a milling rate of 250 tons per day. In 1953, this was increased to 2,100 tons per day, a high production rate for Canadian mines in those days.

As with Teck-Hughes, the Lamaque mine would operate for 50 years and produce 4.5 million ounces of gold over its life, making it the largest gold miner in the province of Quebec.

McIntyre

Well-known mining historian George Lonn tells an interesting story about Sandy in *The Mine Finders*: "Near the end of the first decade of the century, Alexander Oliphant was a moulder in Scotland. Unhappily, he did not get along with his wife and, after a particularly violent quarrel, Oliphant decided to move as far from his ancestral home as he could go. He chose Canada for his emigration and lost little time in making his headquarters in Northern Ontario, where there were opportunities for a possible fortune. To make sure that Mrs. Oliphant back home in Glasgow would not find him, the former moulder changed his name to Sandy McIntyre."

Oliphant was right about those opportunities; he took part in two important discoveries in a short time. His new namesake, McIntyre Mines, would go on to become a major gold producer, along with its neighbours in the Timmins/Porcupine camp. McIntyre Mines would later branch out into base metals and even coal, developing one of the first modern coal mines in Western Canada. It became part of Thayer Lindsley's complex Ventures Empire, which included Falconbridge Nickel, and was an important part of the Canadian mining scene for many years.

Meanwhile, Elsewhere in Canadian Gold Mining

Gold was not the only metal being mined in Canada in those years, but, relative to the industrial metals and coal, it held more importance then than it has in recent years. There were three other gold mines built across the country in those days that would indirectly have a bearing on the future of Teck-Hughes.

The great Klondike rush took place in Yukon Territory in 1889, peaking in the 1920s, with the largest producer being the Yukon Consolidated Gold Mining Company. The stories about this gold rush could fill a book, and in fact have filled a number of them, perhaps the best of which is *The Gold Hustlers* by Lewis Green. Yukon Consolidated would play a part in the evolution of Teck much later and with a different metal, when it participated in development of prospector Egil Lorntzen's Lornex Copper mine in the 1970s. This would become the largest metal mine in Canada for a time, and Teck would subsequently acquire control of and merge with Yukon – but that story is for much later in this book.

In addition to Lamaque, the new Pickle Crow mine in northwestern Ontario started production in 1935, led by legendary mining promoter Jack Hammell. Later, in the 1960s, Pickle Crow would play a small role in our evolving story. Similarly, Little Long Lac Gold Mines began producing gold from its new Geraldton mine in 1935, just as Lamaque and Pickle Crow started up. Later known as Lac Minerals, its path would cross that of Teck on a number of occasions over the years ahead. Canada is a large country, but for mining people it often seems to be a small world.

Producing Gold with a Fixed Price Becomes Difficult

Teck-Hughes remained a pure gold company until the late 1950s, and the fact that its two mines would each produce successfully for 50 years was a remarkable achievement.

This future was not at all clear for either mine when they started because, as with most underground mines, it was not possible to drill off reserves for years in advance, even if one had wanted to. Access to places from which to drill holes is generally a problem, and it is usually necessary to sink shafts and drive tunnels well away from the ore veins in order to open up places from which to drill more deeply. For example, it can be hard to explore to a depth of 700 metres until one has already mined to 500 metres. It would have been impossible to drill from the surface to the eventual bottom of the Teck-Hughes mine, more than two kilometres below the surface, in those early days.

Unfortunately, with the price of gold having been fixed at US$35 per ounce since 1933 and with costs increasing each year, it soon became a struggle for any gold company to stay profitable. By 1951, president D.L.H. Forbes reported that shareholders "must expect cessation of Teck-Hughes' gold production about the middle of the current year," and, "the company's continuing existence as a profitable mining enterprise is assured through operation of its subsidiaries, Lamaque Gold Mines and Teck Exploration Co." But, as is often said, good mines die hard, and it would turn out that Teck-Hughes was able to keep mining for another 17 years after that.

Forbes was intent on securing a replacement mine, and Teck did do some drilling on a gold prospect held by Lake Superior Mining Company in 1951. In the end, Teck-Hughes reported: "The grade indicated is too low for profitable operation at present." This was certainly true at the time and the gold mineralization, two kilometres east of the town of Hemlo, Ontario, was left to be rediscovered by Vancouver promoters 30 years later, resulting in the important Hemlo gold camp.

Teck-Hughes did branch out into a limited amount of exploration for base metals in the late 1950s, participating in a syndicated airborne geophysical program run by the legendary explorer and developer Karl Springer. It would result in the discovery of a major copper-zinc ore deposit in northwestern Quebec that would become the Mattagami mine, to be developed eventually by Noranda Mines.

From 1948 until the price of gold was finally freed up in 1971, Canada's gold mines and the communities they worked in were supported by a modest federal government subsidy under the Emergency Gold Mines Assistance Act, allowing some mines that otherwise would have had to close to remain open for a time. However, the cost-price squeeze was such that pure gold

mining was destined to be a declining business until the fixed price was finally abandoned by the Nixon administration in 1971, too late for Teck-
Hughes and many others.

Today, with the price of gold free to be set by the market for the last 45
years, it is easy to forget those more difficult times.

Elsewhere in Canadian Mining

Other mines and mining companies producing different products faced their
own challenges in those days, but none were quite the same as a fixed price
in an inflationary world. As well, in the 1940s it was more important to produce metals and minerals that would help the war effort than old-fashioned
financial commodities such as gold.

The 50 years from 1910 saw the Canadian mining sector grow beyond
what any of the early prospectors could have imagined. It evolved from discoveries by grizzled rock hounds to those made through high-technology
exploration; from people targeting primarily gold to the inclusion of base
metals, coal, and other commodities; from grubstake syndicates funding prospectors to the tune of $200 a field season to larger syndicates of
medium-size companies using airborne geophysics; and it saw a number of
large companies and corporate groups built on new mines and new ideas.

It is not the purpose of this book to try to cover the long and complex history of Canadian mining. Rather, I will just touch on a few small pieces, some
to illustrate the challenges and perseverance that go into success in this business, and others just because they are about people who in one way or another had something to do with where Teck Resources is today.

In 1911, about the time Jim Hughes and Sandy McIntyre/Oliphant were
staking claims in Teck Township, another prospector, Nova Scotia-born Ed
Horne, took his canoe 200 kilometres northeast of Cobalt and across the
border into Quebec. He was convinced that the favourable rocks of northeastern Ontario didn't stop at the border, and he found some interesting volcanic formations on the shores of Tremoy Lake (now Osisko Lake).

Like most prospectors of the day, Ed was looking primarily for gold or silver. Panning didn't show any gold and he moved on, but he kept thinking
about the Tremoy rocks and returned again and again to the area over the
next six years. Convinced that all he needed was a grubstake to keep him
going while he prospected more thoroughly, he went back to New Liskeard,
near Cobalt, to try to line up funding. Eleven locals obliged with the grand

total of $225, and Ed was able to return with another prospector partner. In 1920, nine years after first going to the area, he staked 70 acres of claims and started working on them in earnest.

Two years later, a fire they had lit to ward off blackflies got out of hand and became a small bush fire. When it was put out, they found it had burned off a lot of brush and moss concealing the underlying rocks which, in Horne's words, were full of (copper-bearing) sulphides.

What may be becoming evident to the reader looking for new exploration techniques is that we have encountered four successful ones so far in this chapter: following people excavating for railroads (Sudbury), throwing a blacksmith's hammer at a fox (Cobalt), hunting rabbits (Wright-Hargreaves), and starting a small forest fire. In exploration, the best tool may be "whatever works."

Horne now needed more funding to continue prospecting, and luckily, two businessmen from New York were in nearby Haileybury looking for mining opportunities. They optioned the claims from the Tremoy Grubstake for $320,000 in cash (in installments) and a 10 per cent interest in any company to be formed. The news started a staking rush, and by the end of 1922 all of Rouyn Township had been staked by a variety of prospectors and promoters.

The new syndicate first drilled two other properties that appeared to be better prospects, but struck out. As often happens in this business, perseverance paid off and it would be third time lucky. They returned to Ed's claims and started drilling. The first hole found nothing, but the second hole encountered solid sulphides, with the deepest part containing high-grade copper. As George Lonn wrote: "That was the first indication the Horne property might be a copper rather than a gold mine."

The discovery became the H ore body, for Horne. It was renamed the Upper H after another important copper ore body, the Lower H, was discovered eight years later. These would be the mainstay of what would become Noranda Mines, one of Canada's strongest mining companies for years to come. Noranda would go on to build other new mines in Quebec, New Brunswick, and British Columbia as well as copper smelters* and a zinc

---

* Metal ores such as those bearing a few percentage points of copper, zinc, or nickel are generally upgraded to a higher metal content in a mill, with the product (the "concentrate") then sent to a smelter or refinery for conversion into usable metal. Most mines own their mill, but the smelters and refineries are often located elsewhere and owned independently, and there is a natural conflict of interest between them.

refinery, and to branch into forestry and oil holdings. Noranda would become a household name in Canadian mining.

After 50 Years

Whether because of good management or because it was not inhibited by the difficulties of producing a single commodity with a fixed price, or perhaps both, by 1960, Noranda, as a diversified miner, had far outpaced its older peer, attaining a market capitalization of $220 million, 16 times greater than Teck-Hughes' $14 million.

Consolidated Mining and Smelting Company (later renamed Cominco) had been founded about the same time as Teck-Hughes, based on zinc-lead prospects in eastern British Columbia that would become the Sullivan mine. With sponsorship by the Canadian Pacific Railroad empire and some timely metallurgical breakthroughs, it had grown substantially over the years and by 1960 had a market capitalization of $344 million, more than Noranda and 25 times that of Teck-Hughes.

Inco, started earlier than Teck, and Falconbridge, the result of a series of convoluted manoeuvres led by the inestimable Thayer Lindsley, had also both outpaced Teck-Hughes in value.

The original Teck-Hughes mine was still struggling but its Lamaque mine was trotting along, and the directors had built a fabulous lodge in Bourlamaque that they visited by private train several times a year to "take a look at the operation." As well, it had participated with five other companies in an exploration syndicate that had just discovered the major Mattagami base metal deposit in northern Quebec. While Mattagami would eventually be developed and controlled by Noranda, the shares the six exploration companies retained would prove to be important to Teck-Hughes as time went on.

This was the scene when Norman Keevil, fresh from making a high-grade copper discovery at Lake Temagami in Ontario, entered the picture and acquired control of the venerable old company. If Teck-Hughes had grown as large as Noranda, for example, it wouldn't have been available to him at an achievable price. If it had been seriously unsuccessful, it wouldn't have been of interest. As we will see, if its president, Jack Perry, had been allowed to make a particular telephone call, the future would have been much different.

Of such convergences, opportunities are made to "put a dent in the universe," as Steve Jobs said.

But first let's look at the parallel, independent, 50-year career of my father, Norman Keevil, born around the same time as the Teck-Hughes discovery, and follow that for a while.

CHAPTER 2

THE KEEVILS FROM ENGLAND

Keevil and Keevil are Butchers.
Wikipedia, on Sir Ambrose Keevil

The Horsemen from England

Norman B. Keevil was born in Pike Lake, Saskatchewan in 1910, around the time James Hughes and Sandy McIntyre were nosing about for gold in Teck Township. He was the son of Roland and Sarah Keevil, recent immigrants from England.

Roland's family proudly traced its ancestry to the time of William the Conquerer and the Battle of Hastings in 1066, when, according to the *Domesday Book*, the Chiveles were granted lands in Wiltshire, England. Spellings varied in those medieval times, and his ancestors were variously known as deKevilly, Keevill, Kevell, and Wolff. The family, with the name finally agreed upon to be Keevil, seems to have lived within a few miles of Camelay for generations after, many prospering as farmers and traders of produce, and by 1911 Keevil and Keevil was one of the largest poultry and game suppliers in England.

Sir Ambrose Keevil, Roland's younger brother, would run the company until the end of the Second World War and be knighted for his role in persuading other producers to join him in keeping a lid on scarce food prices. The firm was then sold to Fitch and Lovell, and Ambrose's *The Story of Fitch Lovell* is required reading for all members of the family still living in the United Kingdom. Resold by Fitch and recovering its old name in 1991, Keevil and Keevil claims to be Smithfield Market's oldest butchers, and recently advertised "a free pack of our Cumberland sausages with orders over 60 pounds."

According to a less authorized version of history, some of the other branches of the centuries-old family had names other than deKevilly or its Anglicized offshoot. This included Wolff, who was thought to have been a highwayman. Exactly what sort of highwayman that might have been is unclear.

Roland's father Clement was said to have been "a stern and slightly autocratic figure whose austere religious upbringing instilled in him the virtues of hard work and honesty." Clement, however, had one love greater than business. This was the raising of Shire horses, a hobby which, according to Ambrose, became almost an obsession with him. Also according to Ambrose, Roland was Clement's favourite and was expected to join the family business.

But Roland had other ideas, and in 1905 at the age of 20 he and a groom were sent to Canada in a tramp steamer, along with a number of thoroughbred horses. Among them was one of Clement's best Shire stallions, which was to be shown at the Royal Canadian Winter Fair. As the family story from our side of the Atlantic goes, Roland got so seasick that he sent the horses back to England with the groom but vowed never to return himself. He instead went on to Saskatchewan, as far from the sea as one can get in Canada, and homesteaded there. What actually became of the horses is not entirely clear. My London investment banker cousin, Philip, who is Ambrose's grandson, suggested to me that Roland had absconded with them, but then investment bankers are wont to tell scandalous stories.

There is still a small town of Keevil with a population of 331 near Camelay in Wiltshire, England. None of the present residents seems to be named Keevil, and where they all went is unknown.

Norman Keevil Arrives on the Scene

Roland homesteaded on two sections of land at Pike Lake, 30 kilometres south of Saskatoon. He built a small home by himself, married one of a family of five beautiful girls that had moved to a nearby homestead, and in 1910 their first son, Norman, was born on the farm. Some years later another son, Alan, joined him, along with several other siblings. Both Norman and Alan would go on to success in the natural resources business, Norman as a leader in the new science of geophysics and later as a mining entrepreneur, and Alan as a senior geologist with California Standard in the expanding oil patch of Saskatchewan and Alberta.

After eight years, the family gathered its belongings in a covered wagon and moved to Saskatoon, where Roland lived until he passed away in 1963.

On retiring from the real estate business at the age of 74 he took up painting and became one of Western Canada's prominent artists of the day, using a version of the Grandma Moses style that was unique to him. Some two dozen of his descendants currently hold and treasure one or more of his paintings, most of them scenes from the Prairies of mid-century Canada. It is said that Princess Margaret had one in her collection as well.

Norman's childhood was the usual one for an industrious farm boy, and later in the big city of Saskatoon. He told stories about catching rabbits, fishing for goldeye and selling these to the neighbours, raising pigeons and keeping the cats away from them, chasing groundhogs, and playing hockey. Like Gordie Howe, who hailed from nearby Delisle, Saskatchewan, most Prairie boys grew up playing the game and many became pretty good, including Norman, who turned into a star centre at the University of Saskatchewan. Years later he would captain the Keevil Mining Group team at the annual Prospectors and Developers Association Hockey Game at Maple Leaf Gardens, challenged by a ragtag bunch known as "The Prospectors All-Stars." A highlight of this later career was scoring a hat trick while playing on a line with the retired Eddie Shack, on a team coached by Red Kelly.

Discovering Geology in the GSC

Norman developed an interest in chemistry and geology while at the University of Saskatchewan in the mid-1930s, and as he put it: "It was during that period that we took these trips to the coast. Coming from the flat prairies where there were no hills and no water to speak of, the mountains were an impressive sight. I was interested in all the various shapes and forms, and on reading the university calendar I noticed that in Geology 1, part of the description of the course was the scientific interpretation of scenery. So I took the geology course and the next year after that specialized in geology as well."

He started doing field geology with the Geological Survey of Canada (a.k.a. The GSC or The Survey), first as a student assistant in Saskatchewan and Manitoba, then for two summers in and around Great Slave Lake, and finally in 1935 with his own field party in Western Ontario.

In his words after the second GSC summer, when he worked with the renowned Dr Clifford Stockwell: "My second job in The GSC was with a survey party going up to Great Slave Lake, which was probably one of the great experiences of my life. I learned more geology that summer than I learned in all the years of university. All the geology is laid out in front of you with very little overburden, and most of the rocks were well exposed."

Harvard Days

In his last year at Saskatchewan Norman was looking for postgraduate opportunities.

I had applied for geochemistry scholarships and for whatever I could get, to some of the larger universities such as California, Minnesota, Wisconsin, and a couple of others. I never thought of applying to any of the Ivy League colleges such as Harvard, Yale or Princeton. I finally was awarded a studentship, which is one of the highest National Research Council scholarships that you can get, to study physical chemistry under a professor at McGill University, not that I wanted to do that in particular, but it was the only thing around. Then in the first week of September I received a telegram asking if I would take a teaching position at Harvard. I quickly wired back, accepting it, and on September 13th I boarded the train for Montreal and Boston.

I met the Harvard professor. He told me that I had to start teaching in two weeks, and the first thing I had to do was teach a class of 100 students how to blow glass. At Canadian universities everything is done for you, there are glass blowers and machine shops. At Harvard, where of all places one would expect that, you had to learn how to do things yourself. The machine shop had a threading machine and lathe, which you had to learn how to use, and you had to learn how to blow glass. I don't consider myself the most mechanically inclined person in the world, but I learned how to blow glass in two weeks and got up in front of the class, blowing one piece and making t-joints, and then teaching them in the lab how to do it.

The position at Harvard was probably the best break I ever had. I was appointed to the faculty of Harvard University at a magnificent salary of $85/month, which compares today (1988) to something like $3,000/month. This was long before the Second World War. The Depression on the prairies was so bad of course that if you raised eggs you couldn't sell them, and you could buy them for 3 cents a dozen.

Norman went on:

I was so active and busy all the time that I don't think it really sunk in how badly the Depression hurt my father Roland and so many other people. I would come back from surveying late, as the field season usually extended until after the university one began, so I started right in on my master's degree, and no matter what hour I came in at night my father was always up and running his fingers through his hair, which was starting to turn grey.

After I got to Harvard I didn't turn down my studentship at McGill until some time late in October. At that time, it was particularly difficult for Canadians to accept any position in the States, due to the Depression, and I thought there might be trouble. Sure enough, by the middle of October I got a letter from the Department of Immigration saying that I had to leave the country and I wasn't allowed to work there, so I took the letter over to the secretary of the board of overseers who was a great, corpulent fellow, everybody's picture of a typical head of a major corporation, puffing away on his pipe and very important. He read the letter and said, 'Leave this with me.' I left, and the next morning he called me over to his office and, sitting in his chair, he read proudly his letter to the Department of Immigration that nobody in the government tells Harvard what to do! That was the essence of it and he said not to worry. I notified McGill, much to their chagrin and continued at Harvard.

It was at Harvard that Norman met a young chemist named Verna Bond, who was studying at Radcliffe College, Harvard's sister school at the time, and was working her way through school by serving coffee in the morning to itinerant people such as Albert Einstein. They were soon married, Verna and Norman that is, and she went on to bear him five children, three of whom would work with him in the business in later years.

The Manhattan Project, and Back to Canada

Norman's work at Harvard covered the whole spectrum of chemistry and put him in touch with some of the most creative scientific minds of the era. He followed that by being awarded the Royal Society of Canada Fellowship to do post-doctoral research in geological science at MIT (Massachusetts Institute of Technology), studying radioactive decay products and how they could be used in dating the ages of ancient rocks.

Meanwhile, Einstein, who only a few years earlier had ridiculed the prospects of harnessing nuclear energy, had an epiphany about possible nuclear weapons. Learning that the Germans had managed to separate uranium isotope 235, Einstein urged President Roosevelt to mount a project to try to develop an atomic bomb before the Germans did. Roosevelt took up the gauntlet, and the job was assigned to Harold Urey, a Nobel Prize winner a few years earlier. "Your job Dr. Urey, should you decide to accept it, is to discover an atomic bomb before the Germans do."

One of the people Urey tapped was Robert Oppenheimer, a brilliant young physicist at Berkeley who, as chance would have it, had just written a key paper contradicting Einstein on another thing he had deemed impossible. Oppenheimer had used the same relativistic physics to prove that singularities, later dubbed black holes, were in fact possible after all. There was now only one thing for Einstein to do: get Oppenheimer off that project and on to the bomb.

While he was at Harvard, Norman had run across Dr Urey. As he recalled it:

> Urey looked around but there were only two or three other people in North America working on uranium. One had been at Harvard and that was me, so he called me over and asked me to head the Manhattan Project. He had just hired two physicists who were working with computers, which at that time were two adding machines. I was all set to go there when they realized that, being a Canadian, I would have to get clearance, and the FBI had said it would take a year to clear me. Urey put the pressure on and they said they could do it in three months but no quicker. So the job went to Willard Frank Libby, who had been working on similar radioactive age dating studies at the University of California.

Libby joined the Manhattan Project and made major contributions to its success, along with Edward Teller and Oppenheimer, who was actually in charge of building the bomb. Libby received the Nobel Prize in Chemistry in 1960.

Norman returned to Canada shortly after his clearance episode, along with his wife Verna and a newly-born son, who turned out to be me. He took a position as a professor in the new field of geophysics at the University of Toronto (U of T), and planned to continue devoting his time to research and teaching.

During his academic career, Norman's research resulted in the publication of 45 scientific papers in a number of technical journals, covering a wide variety of topics in the fields of chemistry, physics, geology and geophysics. His eclectic research touched on studies of mustard gas during the war years, the importance of Vitamin B2 to vision in bright light, isotopic tracers in explosive reactions and the distribution of uranium and thorium in North America, as well as radioactive age dating of rocks. Despite his protestations about not being too mechanically inclined, at U of T he built the first mass spectrometer in Canada, so he could further research in his new field of geophysics.

The Vitamin B2 project was particularly interesting. It was sponsored by the Royal Canadian Air Force, which had become concerned about the effect of a lack of the vitamin on its pilots' vision. Apparently Vitamin B2 is used up very rapidly in the eyes in bright light, and the Air Force wanted to find a way to supplement it in their pilots, so that on sunny days they could see what they were doing. That did sound like a good plan.

On reading an article in *Nature* magazine, Norman learned there was a considerable amount of Vitamin B2 in British beer, which he thought the pilots might possibly be interested in consuming to improve their vision, even if at the expense of some reaction time. So, as he said: "To get the project going, we persuaded several beer companies to provide samples for us. We only needed a thimbleful for a test, but all of the breweries sent over two or three cases, so that one side of the lab was completely stacked with cases of beer. My students thought this was the best research project they had ever engaged in. We used a small amount out of each lot for the experiment and disposed of the rest in an appropriate manner" (figure 2.1).

These eclectic interests would continue until his dying days. I recall growing up on a rented farm with a barn full of chickens, one goat, and piles of colourful pigments he had invented, and thought could be a breakthrough in something or other. Later we would invest in many things from oyster farming in Hawaii to lithium battery research. There seemed to be no limits to what he could imagine, which is probably a sine qua non for such a natural-born prospector.

Figure 2.1
Norman Keevil doing research for the Royal Canadian Air Force, 1941

As time went on, Norman became the highest paid assistant professor in the Geology Department at U of T, but with four children and counting rapidly, and with heavy wartime taxes, he found it necessary to turn to outside commercial work to supplement that income.

From Academic Research to Consulting

While at U of T, Norman had formed a geophysical consulting firm to carry out surveys for people in the mining exploration business, from operating companies to raw promoters with a dream or a scheme. Mining Geophysics Corporation was incorporated in 1944 by his lawyer friend Roland Michener, who would later go on to a distinguished career in government service, culminating as Canada's governor general, before coming back to business as chairman of the board of Teck Corporation, but those would be many years away.

Unlike today, when academics at most forward-looking universities are encouraged to at least dabble in the real world to broaden their horizons, in the mid-1940s this was not only uncommon, it was even frowned upon. It was frowned upon especially by the head of the department, the well-known Dr Tuzo Wilson, a situation that seemed not to present a particularly career-enhancing situation for Norman.

He soon found that the commercial world and mineral exploration provided a more stimulating challenge. The war news had turned from bad to good, there was more confidence as the community tried to get back to business as usual, and there was a new mining and exploration boom developing. So Norman left teaching in 1946 and took on the consulting and contract geophysical business full time.

My first geophysical consulting during the University of Toronto years was for James & Buffam, the most prominent consulting geologists at the time. Bill James (Sr.) was working for Bert Lang, president of Broulan Mines. I did a couple of surveys for them, and then did some consulting work for Hollinger Mines. It didn't take long for me to become recognized and get a reputation, and soon I got to know dozens of people in the mining business, and in the brokerage mining and financial community, which included of course all sorts of promoters. These were the wild and woolly years with no holds barred, and in a bull market the promoters could raise public money easily, often very little of it going into the ground.

One of the most colourful of these was Joe Hirshhorn. He had once been a Brooklyn newsboy, but by the time I knew him he was on the road to making $50 million from Dr Franc Joubin's uranium discovery at Blind River. Wealthy or not, Joe couldn't resist continuing to be a promoter. In later years he became quite mellow, and as a graying senior took on the air of a successful conservative citizen, but I can recall Joe back in those earlier boom days promoting like mad, buying and selling stock, mainly in his own companies. I guess he respected me, as I used to talk to him frequently over the years, and he would often give me a call just for a chat.

He was always full of surprises. In those days the telephone system was rather clumsy. There were boxes roughly 6 inches square with only 2 lines in each of them, with green and red lights and a hold button. Of course Joe needed at least 20 lines, so he would have a whole desk lined up with these boxes, switches going up and down and green and red lights flashing, and he would sometimes use them all at once, easy to do today, but in those days quite a feat. One day in the middle of all this, as I sat across from him, he suddenly disappeared below his desk, and then popped up with a crazy hat on for no reason at all.

He just felt in the mood to do something silly. I myself got to the point where I had to have several of these boxes too, a lot different from the compact switchboards and automated equipment we have become accustomed to today.

Norman had a favourite story about promoter Brian Newkirk, who would float a new company, complete with his own personal stash of free vendors' shares. He'd issue the first shares to the public at, say, 25 cents. Then he'd make sure it was talked up, and in due course as the market rose he'd issue the next batch of new shares at 50 cents, and so on through 75 cents and up, spreading news and rumours all the way. Then, after it hit a dollar or so, he'd start to believe his own BS, and before you knew it he was in the market trying to buy it all back.

I've met many similar promoters over the years, guys like Bob Falkins and Murray Pezim, not to mention a few well-known geologists, and what most of them share with Newkirk is an optimism that leads them in time to start believing their own stories. You know what? Occasionally they turn out to be right and really create something.

Learning to Sell

Not content to be just an academic, Norman learned from the promoters as well, and told the following story on himself from a few years later, after he'd discovered and built a high-grade copper mine at Temagami.

Another broker I got to know in those early days was Brad Streit, mainly because his nephew Doug was a good fellow and a geologist. Doug decided he would work with Brad's firm, advising him on the mining end of it, and learning something about the brokerage business. With them was a Joe Hackett, who was a businesslike character and was really their hatchet man, doing all their dirty work.

They got interested in Temagami when we made that discovery, and I guess they made a fair amount of money from it. Shortly thereafter I formed a new company, Geoscientific Prospectors, to carry on that same type of work and look for another Temagami. I mentioned this to Joe Hackett, who didn't show any interest at all. But by that time I had learned a few of the tricks of the trade, just by dropping in to their office from time to time, and into the offices of some of the others I was doing consulting work for. Those were the days when there were few stock exchange regulations, I suppose you could say before the Viola MacMillan "Windfall" episode in the 1960s claim-staking rush at Timmins.

At this time there was a bit of a recession. I was down to a staff of two, Peggy and Barbara, and I decided to get a stock issuer's licence for Geoscientific through the Securities Commission. I had that before I talked to Hackett, so I got Peggy and Barbara and all their friends, and all the people I could think of, to call different brokers around town and ask them about Geoscientific Prospectors, and what it was trading at or been quoted at. I made a couple of trades that opened the market at 85 to 90 cents, what you would call wash trades, and not allowed today. A few other trades went through, and all of a sudden I got a call from Joe Hackett, "Come on over! What's all this about Geoscientific Prospectors?" I said, "I told you about that a couple of weeks ago." He said, "Well, I want the deal." He got the deal, put up the money, and Geoscientific Prospectors got started.

Airborne Magnetic Surveys, a Geological Mapping Breakthrough

During the war, a key problem on the Allies' side had been finding a way to detect and track German submarines, and scientists with the Gulf Oil Company and the US Navy had developed a way to do this from airplanes, using a new instrument called an airborne magnetometer.

This geophysical equipment was carried in or behind the tail of a plane and, when flying over nothing but unoccupied ocean water, would just record the normal background magnetic field of the earth in that area. But if there happened to be something made of magnetic steel not too far beneath the water, like a submarine, the magnetometer would pick up an extra signal, known as an anomaly. With a little careful calibration and interpretation, one could guess what was down there under the surface, and begin to do something about it.

Theoretically the same technology might be applied in mining exploration, looking for magnetic bodies beneath the surface soils and rocks rather than under water. At its simplest, if a buried magnetic deposit looking something like a submarine was down there, it too should be discoverable.

In fact, most rocks contain small amounts of an iron mineral called magnetite, some more than others. If an airplane flying low across a swath of land measures the magnetic field below it, that field will vary as the plane flies over different rock beds, and a competent geologist might be able to interpret something about the underlying rocks and geological structures. If a number of parallel lines are flown in this way, the data can be assembled into a map of the magnetic field that may be interpreted to help understand the underlying geology.

Following the declassification of this technology after the war ended, Gulf Oil retained the rights to use it for petroleum exploration. Norman got wind of this and approached Gulf about setting up a partnership to explore for hard-rock minerals in Canada. Under this agreement, Mining Geophysics would organize exploration programs, consult and do the initial interpretations, and would have a 10 per cent interest in any discoveries. Gulf would, of course, put up all of the money. This would be a structure we would later replicate in an agreement with International Telephone and Telegraph (ITT) to explore for copper in Chile.

With the partnership's first survey flight in 1947, it detected an exceptionally strong magnetic anomaly near Emerald Lake, not far northeast of the major Sudbury nickel mining camp, and we will come back to that shortly. Soon after, the Gulf partnership would locate another anomaly over a large iron deposit, which would eventually be developed and become the Adams mine, six kilometres south of Kirkland Lake and the Teck-Hughes gold mine.

The Geological Survey of Canada followed the airborne magnetometer program carefully. Within two years, The Survey realized what a useful tool it could be to assist in geological mapping of the country as a whole. Rock outcroppings that can be seen and mapped on the surface are rare in many parts of Canada, and it is necessary to interpolate between outcrops to assemble a map of the regional geology in any area. Data from airborne magnetometer surveys can be an invaluable aid in this interpretation. This eventually became much more important than its application in direct exploration for iron, nickel, or other magnetic deposits. Today geological maps all over the world owe their accuracy and usefulness to similar aeromagnetic surveys.

The Gulf project suffered from sclerotic management, and Norman eventually sold his interest in it in 1949, but his consulting geophysical business continued, doing ground magnetic and electrical surveys as well as occasional airborne ones over properties held by other mining companies.

These ground-level surveys could detect buried mineralization that was either anomalously magnetic or electrically conductive, but they were also important indirectly, in much the same way as airborne magnetic surveys. Both were helpful in interpreting geological continuities and discontinuities in areas that were covered by gravel, swamps, and other overburden between outcropping rocks. The better a geophysicist could interpret and understand the underlying geology, the better chances there were that exploration would eventually be successful in defining economic mineralization, whether it was itself magnetic or not.

Norman and his field team, led by young geologists Joe Frantz and Bill Bergey, became quite good at this interpretation, and their work was in demand from companies in the industry, both large and small. This demand was of course sporadic, with work for the smaller, promotional companies being dependent upon whether the stock market was strong or weak at any given point in time. It was a good business, professionally satisfying, but economically cyclical.

International Exploration: A Deal with President Batista

With contracts to run surveys hit and miss in the mid-1950s, depending upon the market, John B. McClusky, who'd been hired to run Mining Geophysics, got the bright idea of negotiating a contract to do an airborne magnetometer survey over the entire country of Cuba. Naturally this would take a long time, generate some much-needed revenue, and include some kind of rights to participate in any discoveries. He flew down to Cuba to see what he could negotiate with President Batista.

Of course there was a revolution beginning there, and while it would take the better part of six years before Fidel Castro completely ousted Batista, it was a work in progress. McClusky became excited about the revolution and got onto the Castro bandwagon.

As my father later put it: "He called me at 4 a.m. one morning and ranted for hours about Castro and how he was still going to get airborne survey contracts, just with a different chief. I got quite concerned and called his wife. She went down to Cuba, rescued him and brought him back. I had to get him to resign and then reorganize Mining Geophysics. In fact, I disbanded it shortly after and formed Geophysical Engineering and Surveys to carry on our consulting work."

The Emerald Lake Anomaly

But Norman was a prospector at heart, and was intent on using his technology when he could to try to discover a mine for his own account, so between those third-party jobs he would come back to an area about which he was particularly optimistic.

He had remained intrigued by the Emerald Lake Anomaly (see colour page 2), discovered in that first survey in 1947. Today it is still one of the strongest magnetic anomalies ever found in the world, clearly related to a deep magnetic source. With its proximity to the major Sudbury nickel and copper mining district, now thought to have resulted from a massive meteor impact, it was easy to speculate that the new anomaly could be related to the same geological events that had resulted in the Sudbury mines and could hold the potential for additional discoveries of nickel and copper.

Still not completely explained to this day, the Anomaly was clearly destined to catch the attention of aspiring geophysical exploration people. It would lead Norman to Lake Temagami, and his destiny would take a new direction.

When we were doing consulting work, before there was any significant air travel we used to travel by train, usually on the Ontario Northland which left Toronto at 6 p.m. and got to the north-country (Kirkland Lake) in the morning and Noranda the following noon. At 4 a.m. the steam engines would require water at Temagami, so we had a nice view of the bay during that early morning stop, but we didn't realize what a beautiful lake lay beyond until the first trip following up the results from the Gulf surveys.

As a result of that I took my first vacation in many years, renting at the Rabbit Nose Lodge in the north arm of Lake Temagami. We had a small cottage and so-called dock, which was just two planks extending out to a place where we could tie canoes. I was standing there one day and said, 'Where's my son Harold, I thought he was with us?'

I looked around and his head popped out of the water. We hadn't heard him go down. We got him out the first time he bobbed* up. He was six years old at the time.

I spent most of that vacation going down the west side of the lake doing geochemical surveys with my older son Norman. We did pick up an anomaly on the so-called Temagami fault, which is the extension of the northeast arm and passes through Temagami Island, and then to the west shore through to Skunk Lake and Emerald Lake.

There were two old copper showings on Temagami Island that had been noted by government geologists in the late 1800s, and after getting the geochemical results, my father was about to paddle over to make a deal with the claim owner, Dewey Derosier, who had a tourist camp nearby. However, the wind came up and he had to paddle back to Rabbit Nose. As it happened, Bud Knight, a stockbroker and promoter, beat him to it and made a deal with Dewey the next morning. Bud drilled a few holes in late 1951, encountering low-grade nickel and copper mineralization but nothing approaching economic grades and tonnages.

Lake Temagami, 500 kilometres north of Toronto, could almost have been the Eighth Wonder of the World. It is a pristine lake that in places is as deep as 500 metres, boasts 5,000 kilometres of shoreline and 1,500 islands, and yet on the lake one is never farther than 1,000 metres from shore. On top of that, the water everywhere was good enough to drink, and fish (lake trout, pickerel, and bass) were abundant. It is also surrounded by dozens of other lakes that are an easy portage away. It was in a provincial Forest Reserve and, except for a kilometre or so near the town of Temagami, building on the mainland was not permitted. The only building could be on islands, provided they were at least 0.25 acre in size.

In those days unclaimed islands between 0.25 and 3 acres in size could be purchased from the provincial government for $45 an acre. There were still some of these available and Norman purchased a small one about 8 kilometres north of Temagami Island and built a modest cottage on it. I later did the same with another island some 20 kilometres to the south.

For a prospector/naturalist interested in both the northern woods and geology, this combination of the best of nature with a happy hunting ground

---

* Actually, Harold now claims that he was simply diving for pickerel at the bottom, where they congregate, and would have come up with a tasty fish the next bob, had he been allowed to go back down.

for minerals was nirvana. Years later, these two interests seem to have become incompatible. If the Temagami deposit were to be discovered today, in what is still relatively pristine recreational country, it is questionable whether it could ever be permitted for development. If that, the inability to get an exploration and development permit, had been the case, this whole story would be much different. But wait – at this point in the narrative, the mine has yet to be discovered. That is a compelling story of science, serendipity, and perseverance and deserves a chapter by itself.

CHAPTER 3

DISCOVERING COPPER AT TEMAGAMI

All truths are easy to understand once they are discovered.
The trick is to discover them.
Galileo Galilei

The discovery drill hole at what would become the Temagami mine was spectacular. Chalcopyrite, the copper-iron-sulphur mineral ($CuFeS_2$) that constitutes most copper ores, has a normal chemical content of 34 per cent copper. The grade of long sections of drill core from one of the early holes was an unheard-of 28 per cent. The first Temagami ore deposit turned out to be the largest body of nearly pure chalcopyrite ever discovered in Canada.

Mineral Discoveries Are Seldom Obvious

Mines, once built, may appear to have been reasonably obvious, just waiting for someone to make them happen. But reality is somewhat more complicated, and most discoveries come after a long period of hard work and failed attempts before one turns out to be the real pot of gold under that rainbow. The many years it took from first prospecting to establishing viable mines for both Kerr-Addison and Wright-Hargreaves was noted in chapter 1.

Temagami was no exception. My father was first drawn to the area because of the large Emerald Lake magnetic anomaly, but it would be seven years before he drilled that fateful discovery hole. In between, the property was drilled and re-drilled, and at one point optioned to a major US mining company, Anaconda Mining. Fortunately, it was returned after that company's exploration failed to come up with anything economic.

Those intervening geophysical consulting years before the discovery included boom times with lots of contracting work and other years when it dried up. As a kid I could only sense these changes indirectly, when for some reason we had to sell the goat we kept in the garage, or when a second-hand car replaced my father's Cadillac. One good year we finally stopped renting, although we would always miss that farm, and we actually owned a house in Lorne Park, complete with a nearby community tennis court, woodlands, and real human neighbours.

Sometimes the telltale sign for me would be the hat. When times were good my father would wear his beige Stetson hat, which he was fond of saying was actually a Keevil hat. Apparently the original cowboy hat was known as a Keevil, until William Stetson and Sons took over the company in the Depression years. It is probably just as well, because "John Wayne put on his Keevil and rode off into the sunset" doesn't have quite the right ring to it.

Then we got a cottage in Temagami, on a small island some 25 kilometres up the lake from the town. We'd pick up several weeks of provisions in a small skiff, powered by a 5 HP outboard motor and, loaded to the gunwales, would bounce our way to our little island in the sun. This was after our stream sediment geochemical surveys along the shores of the lake, described in the last chapter, and well before the actual mine discovery.

My father's geophysical contracting and consulting work continued and began to be augmented where possible by the formation of new exploration companies to explore for their own account. These had names like Wabico Minerals, Abex Mines, Geoscientific Prospectors, Inmont Mining, Offshore Mines, and Temagami Mining. Some worked in remote areas, such as in Montbray Township in the Noranda region, some near Emerald Lake, and others in the Lake Temagami area itself.

The Pyritic Zone and the Anaconda Farm-out

But Norman would always return to Dewey Derosier's property on Temagami Island, the one that Bud Knight had scooped from under his nose when the waters were too heavy for him to paddle to Dewey's by canoe.

Through his newly-formed Offshore Mines, he staked claims in the vicinity, carried out geophysical surveys, and did some initial drilling that located other areas of low-grade, nickel-copper mineralization, sparking considerable news interest. This mineralization, later known as the pyritic zone, was at the geologically lower boundary (the footwall) of a steeply inclined, basic intrusive sill that occurs over almost 15 kilometres along the northeast arm of the lake from Temagami Island to near the town. Given the area's proximity to the major Sudbury mining camp to the southwest, which also hosted nickel and copper deposits related to basic intrusive rocks, that considerable news interest was not surprising.

However, funding was not easy to come by at the time and in due course Offshore, Bud Knight's company Derosier Nickel and Copper Mines, and a third company controlled by diamond driller Herb Niemetz combined their claims in the area into a new company called Temagami Mining Co.

In need of financing to carry out further drilling, Temagami reached an agreement to option the property to Anaconda Copper, then the owner of the massive Chuquicamata Copper Mine in Chile and the giant Butte mine in Montana, and one of the world's major mining companies. Anaconda was to carry out ongoing exploration at an agreed upon pace and, at its option, could either return the property to Temagami unencumbered or proceed to develop it and acquire majority control. This was the usual process in the Canadian mining business, in which junior companies with promising prospects either dealt off control or sold outright to larger operating mining companies with the ability to fund advanced exploration or construction financing.

Anaconda did a lot of drilling on the property. By November 1952 *The Northern Miner* newspaper reported: "Dr. Keevil says 66 holes have been drilled on the three optioned properties, 45 of them by Anaconda. No results have yet been issued but a large mass of sulphides has been reported." That large mass was the pyritic zone.

Anaconda Returns the Property

However, Anaconda eventually ran out of enthusiasm and abandoned its option, reckoning that the low-grade zone didn't have sufficient size and grade potential to meet its criteria.

While most attention was being paid to that low-grade nickel-copper zone at the footwall of the basic intrusive sill, my father was also intrigued by the possibilities for higher-grade copper in the underlying felsic volcanic rocks. These were rocks similar to those hosting important copper mines elsewhere in Eastern Canada, such as Noranda's Horne mine. While Anaconda still held and was exploring the property, he carried out additional geophysical surveys on his own over those rocks, using a novel method called SP or self potential, also known then as spontaneous polarization, that is little-known or used anywhere today.

The SP *Geophysical Method*

The SP method measures naturally generated electrical currents, which can measure up to as much as hundreds of millivolts over reasonably short distances, that may result from oxidation of near-surface, sulphide deposits. As with most geophysical tools, anomalies may result from other extraneous things as well, but, properly interpreted, the results can help an explorer discover economic mineralization.

The simple technique involves two field men, each with a porous ceramic pot about 5 centimetres wide and filled with copper sulphate or a similar electrolyte. The pots are placed on the ground some distance apart and the electrolyte seeping through the pots makes electrical contact with the ground. When the two pots are connected by wire with a voltmeter in between, it is possible to measure the naturally occurring voltage or potential difference between the two points.

As with most ground geophysical surveys, the field technicians usually cut a grid of straight lines through the bush, using axes or machetes, and mark out survey stations every so many metres. This might be anywhere from 15 to 30 metres apart in a normal survey, depending what level of detailed information is required.

By taking readings of the potential difference between successive stations along a surveyed line, and along parallel lines, one can generate a map that will show which parts of the surveyed area are underlain by anomalous conditions (possible ore) and which parts appear just electrically flat and uninteresting. This is similar to magnetic surveys done to detect anomalous amounts of magnetite, or buried submarines.

The tools required are cheap and available at almost any hardware store, and where it is applicable the technique has the advantage that it works, is fast, and is very inexpensive. This is quite useful when exploration funding is limited, as it was for Temagami in those days.

Anaconda had not been interested in the mineral potential in the underlying volcanic rocks where Temagami had been doing its SP surveys, although it did drill one exploratory hole in the area. It was drilled right into the middle of the target, a strong, circular SP anomaly, but the drill core returned only a rock known as diabase, a late-stage, post-mineralization, and normally barren intrusive rock that could in no way have caused the anomaly. As it turned out, the Anaconda drill hole missed the first two high-grade copper bodies by only a few metres.

I've always thought this was a classic case of an exploration mistake in principle, because if a geophysical anomaly is worth drilling in the first place, and the results so obviously don't explain it, then it should be worth a follow-up test. However, SP was a relatively new and untried technique and Anaconda was primarily interested in the larger pyritic zone, so it's understandable that they didn't press this anomaly further.

Some of the later, independent survey work we had carried out while Anaconda still held the property included much more closely spaced, detailed SP surveying in that area, hoping to explain why that drill hole encountered only non-conductive rocks. This more detailed survey, illustrated schematically in figure 3.1, showed that instead of one broad anomaly there were actually two separate ones with a gap in between, pretty well where Anaconda had encountered its barren diabase dyke. These would be good drilling targets when and if Anaconda returned the property and funds became available.

The Discovery

Eventually, Anaconda did drop its option and the property was returned to Temagami Mining. It was time to test some of these ideas.

As my father wrote years later:

Work on the property was continued by our group with a small budget under the direction of Bill Bergey. Part of the program was to test local anomalies located in geophysical surveys carried out by me at my own expense during the Anaconda option, and which were largely ignored during their drilling program. On reviewing these results, it was noted that one of the drill holes intersected narrow sections of massive chalcopyrite in felsic volcanic rocks near the footwall of the basic sill. Of additional significance was a new hole drilled to test a footwall resistivity anomaly in Phillips Bay that intersected 2 feet of massive chalcopyrite containing more than an ounce of platinum group metals.

The 1954 drilling program proceeded very slowly, since Herb Niemetz worked full time as a miner at the Falconbridge mine in Sudbury. He would drill a short hole on his long weekend and move the drill the following weekend. I instructed Bergey to lay out a hole for my upcoming visit with some potential financiers in September, with

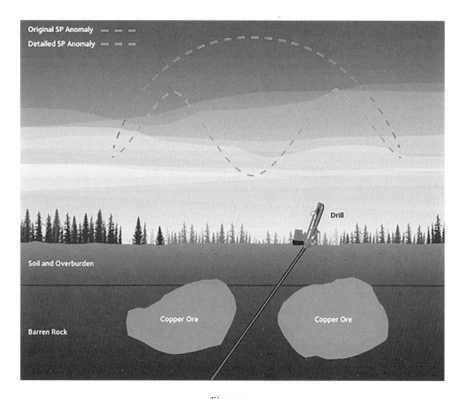

Figure 3.1
Anaconda drilled a hole that missed both high-grade copper zones at Temagami
by just a few metres

the admonition, 'Make it a good one!' With this in mind he decided
to test a small but strong SP anomaly, little more than 100 feet in
length, in the footwall volcanics. The drilling started early on Saturday morning and by the time we arrived the driller had only one foot
of casing* left, bedrock was not in sight, and gloom descended.

Then Herb Neimetz came running up to the core shack where John
Dumbrille, the consulting geologist for the prospective financiers, was
being courteous enough to look at the older Anaconda core, and shouted:
"It's coming out okay. I hit bedrock with my last foot of casing, and it's
coming out green." The group went back to the drill site and saw the green
sludge coming out that is typical of chalcopyrite. "There goes my deal,"
said Dumbrille (see colour pages 2 and 3).

---

* The drill hole started in glacial till, loose gravel that covered the area to various depths, often 30
feet or so. The driller would have to progress through that overburden to reach the bedrock that
may or may not contain mineralization, using casing to hold back the loose material while the drill
rods penetrated inside it to try to reach bedrock.

With an unprecedented 28 per cent copper across 58 feet of core from a subsequent hole, this became the mining industry story of the day. My father was quoted in the Toronto press: "It's hard to tell how big a thing it is."

Years later, Jack McOuat, the respected partner in consulting firm Watts, Griffiths and McOuat, would say this about projects that he was promoting, including the Voisey's Bay nickel discovery in which we were considering investing: "We know how small it is; we just don't know how big it is." It's not clear whether he realized whom he was paraphrasing.

Even with this high grade of copper it was not obvious this discovery was going to turn into an actual mine. Thayer Lindsley, one of the mining greats of the era, sent Bill Gross up to look at it. Bill was a professor of economic geology at U of T and a mentor of mine at the time. He examined the core, and said: "It's very dry country, and you must have drilled down a vein. If it makes a mine, I'll eat my hat."

Bill Gross was wrong, but understandably so, since the intersection was unique in the geological experience of all concerned. He also noted: "Your geophysics was too effective. I don't believe that there's a reasonable chance of making a mine out of a mineralized zone as limited as your results indicate." He was right, from a tonnage point of view, but high grade can occasionally trump pure size.

Bill Bergey was on the job at the time and later wrote: "On receiving the report Thayer Lindsley once again demonstrated his incredible nose for ore, even though the ore was half a continent away from his nose. He rejected Gross's recommendation and, through his Quebec Metallurgical Industries, provided Temagami with $100,000 in cash.

"Using these funds, we drilled off two bodies of massive chalcopyrite prior to Christmas, 1954. Although very small these bodies were extremely rich. I calculated a geological reserve of 35,000 tons at a grade of about 28 per cent copper. We shipped the core from the best hole to Toronto, where it was put on display in the window of one of the city's trust companies."

The Feasibility Study

Bergey later wrote:

During the Prospectors' Convention in March 1955, Dr. Keevil, Joe Frantz and I discussed the situation over a drink in our hospitality suite in the Royal York Hotel. The discussion went something like this:

> Dr. Keevil: What shall we do about Temagami?
> Joe Frantz: Let's put it into production.
> Bill Bergey: Sounds good to me.

The feasibility study thus having been completed, we decided that 1 June, only 2½ months away, was a suitable start-up date for the new mine. Dr Keevil appointed me the interim manager, and I was ordered to take a train to Temagami the following day to hire a crew, purchase equipment, build a mining camp and commence excavation of the open pit."

Building a Mine

Bergey had a certain familiarity with some of the dimly-lit establishments in the town, so the first person he hired to help get the mine going was one Bill Manderstrom. Bill was the bartender at the local Miniwassi Hotel, and thus had some familiarity with rocks. Time was of the essence, and for Bergey it was any port in a storm.

Between the two Bills, they managed to scrounge up some equipment to strip the loose glacial overburden off the first two small copper deposits, and to hire contractors to blast the high-grade copper-bearing rocks so they could be loaded onto trucks to begin transporting them to a smelter. Unfortunately, the 1 June target date for the first shipment of ore could not quite be met. The mine was ready, as was the barge that would take the ore to the railroad loading station, but Temagami hadn't counted on problems at the other end of the shipment. This, interestingly, would be the first and last time for another 30 years that we were not on time and on budget in building a new mine.

Bergey described the small complication that had delayed matters:

I had visited Noranda in April, along with officials from the Ontario Northland Railway, to arrange for transportation and smelting. Since our direct-shipping ore was about the same grade as the usual copper concentrates they bought and processed, there appeared to be no obstacle to having it treated in the Noranda smelter. We agreed to make a test shipment of a carload of ore in order to determine the smelting characteristics of the material.

The results were dismaying. At the last minute, Noranda refused to treat our ore due to what they called excessive amounts of palladium (a platinum group metal). We eventually arranged to send our first ore to the American Metal Co. smelter in Carteret, New Jersey.

The following year the Noranda smelter people changed their minds about accepting our ore and concentrate, claiming that their initial test work was in error and we didn't have too much palladium after all. In fact, the ore did contain a lot of palladium, but of course we weren't paid anything for it. Noranda simply figured out how to get it from us for free.

Over the ensuing years, Noranda to the north and Inco to the south would compete with each other to decide which would purchase and treat our copper. One year Inco might want it more so we would suddenly get paid a bit for our palladium but not as much for our copper. The next year Noranda might offer us a good deal on the copper, but again pay nothing for the palladium. Competition was supposed to be good for us, but we were, somehow, never completely sure.

It was not until years later, with input from our new friends at German smelter and refiner Metallgesellschaft, and then our own Cominco smelter people, that we would learn some of the ropes on that side of the business as well. I can only say that our suspicions back then were not completely allayed by these later revelations.

As fortune would have it, those first two Temagami ore bodies were the highest grade and best of what would turn out to be many separate ore lenses in the mine. With both buried under a few metres of loose glacial overburden, it was just a matter of stripping away that gravel and quarrying them using simple, conventional earth-moving methods. Transportation was by barge from a dock a few metres away, 20 kilometres up the Northeast Arm to where the direct-shipping ore could be loaded onto a train on the Ontario Northland Railway. Later we would build a gravel road from south of the town to a loading station about 1 kilometre across the lake from the mine. Many tourists are still using "the mine road" as their main access to the lake to this day.

With the grade being so high, there was no need to build a mill to concentrate the copper further, as with virtually all other mines, and no need to give up control to a senior company in order to get the financing to go into production. The proceeds from those first two lenses were deployed into further drilling and more, deeper discoveries, albeit of lower grade. Temagami was able to bootstrap itself up from a small exploration company to an important miner largely through these proceeds, sinking a shaft and building a modest, 200-ton-per-day mill to upgrade the ore from these deeper, lower-grade copper ore zones into a saleable copper concentrate.

Bergey tells a story about a meeting between him, Bill Manderstrom, my father, and a well-known shaft-sinking contractor as they were contemplating beginning underground development. The contractor had made a good offer to not only sink the shaft, but to do all of the mining as well. It would have made life simple, with Temagami Mining's only job being to maintain the property in good standing and spend or raise funds from time to time. Manderstrom was recommending this, but Bergey intervened: "Norm, if you're going to build a mining company you have to do the mining part too. Otherwise, what are you?"

As Bill Bergey says today: "I thought then he could turn Temagami into a real mining company. I just never imagined how big or how well."

Keeping the Mine Going

Temagami would eventually mine some 30 separate copper-bearing deposits (ore bodies) to a depth of 700 metres below the surface. All of these pods of ore occurred in the felsic volcanic rocks within a short distance of the basic, metadiorite intrusive sill, and their origin was presumably closely related to the larger tonnage but lower-grade nickel-copper pyritic zone where most of the earlier exploratory work had been focused.

The contact with that large sill dipped almost vertically, so that the mine's vertical shaft tended to remain fairly close to it and to the favourable horizon for the high-grade copper deposits. Once the mine was established and the geological system was well understood, exploration for additional pods of ore was mainly a matter of continuing to drill from the underground workings, and it was quite successful. The geophysics that had led to the first discovery was of less use once we went underground, and ongoing exploration generally involved pattern drilling and following up leads from that.

The Temagami story would not be complete without mentioning Terry Patrick, one of our brilliant, slightly eccentric geologists, who was charged with consulting on exploration at Temagami for many years. We used to hold regular board meetings of what became the Keevil Mining Group companies at a small lodge on an island just across from the mine, and before each visit, my father would instruct Terry that it was time he presented us with another new ore body.

Terry, who appeared to sleep almost 23 hours a day, had some miraculous way of exploring, because it seemed that each time the directors showed up, he was able to oblige with some impressive new drill results. Either he always had a few good holes hidden away in reserve or he had a sixth sense, or perhaps a bit of both.

The end of the mine finally did happen in 1972. As we went deeper and deeper, we found that the geology that had been so consistent from surface to about 700 metres depth had suddenly changed. The metadiorite-felsic volcanic contact we had been following down from the surface was cut off by a fault that displaced it about 1,000 metres, well away from the mine workings. With it, of course, went the favourable ore-bearing horizon. It was a simple calculation to show that, even if there were 30 more similar copper lenses to be discovered in the next 700 vertical metres, to a total depth of 1,400 metres, the cost of driving tunnels over to the displaced contact, sinking a new shaft and exploring to discover the lenses would cost more than they were worth, if in fact they existed.

By then we had other bigger projects on the go, with potential new mines in Newfoundland, Quebec, and British Columbia. Common sense trumped dreaming, but I've often wondered what really is down there, in the favourable rocks below Lake Temagami.

Epilogue

By the time the mine closed, it had become the catalyst, the foundation that would evolve into a much larger business enterprise, eventually becoming Canada's largest diversified mining company.

Serendipity helps to make mines and mining companies. If, instead, the two high-grade ore lenses had been buried much deeper and those occurring at surface been more typical of the normal, lower grades later discovered at depth, the development would never have been self-financing. Control of the Temagami mine would have been lost to a larger company with the necessary capital, and my father might have continued on as a discoverer, consultant, contractor, and explorer – with whatever that future universe decided to unfold.

If Anaconda had discovered the high-grade pods, it would have considered them too small to be of interest, but with who knows what outcome? It might have either kept the property in inventory or sold it off to someone with more funds than Temagami had to buy it.

And did Bill Gross actually eat his hat? We will never know for sure.

While a modest deposit by world standards, Temagami would change our lives, and as a result, the Canadian mining scene would have a different future than might have been the case in one of those alternate universes.

It would now be time to move beyond Temagami. That story will resume in chapter 5, but first I might digress for a few words on my own introduction to geology, geophysics, and the mysterious ways of mining.

CHAPTER 4

WHAT HAPPENED TO THE TRILOBITES?

*The only way of discovering the limits of the possible is to venture
a little way past them into the impossible.*
Arthur C. Clarke

Where Are the Trilobites?

I was a minor participant in prospecting early on in my career, a passenger in a canoe doing stream geochemical sampling on the shores of Lake Temagami when I was 12 years old. I later got involved cutting survey lines and taking SP geophysical readings on Temagami Island, but I was really just an observer in those days in the early 1950s.

How did I get caught up in geology and geophysics? It has been written somewhere that my interest in the science stemmed from walking on the shore of Lake Ontario near Toronto. According to this story there were lots of trilobites in the rocks that were exposed at the time, and I became strangely interested in fossils. Trilobites lived in the Cambrian era some 500 million years ago and are said to have roamed the ocean floors for 270 million years.

I can say that there are no trilobites or their remains roaming that Lake Ontario shore now. In fact, there are no fossils of any kind, perhaps because whatever sedimentary rocks were exposed earlier have since eroded away. Perhaps, even, the trilobites and the story were both imaginary.

Regardless, any interest I might have had in paleontology, the study of fossils, died out when I eventually went to on to take geological engineering at the University of Toronto, where the professor of paleontology was particularly boring. This may have helped me avoid becoming an oil geologist, but by then I'd already become more interested in volcanoes, disruptive faults, and other earth events more dramatic than the roaming of trilobites, anyway.

I remember attending that first day in engineering, when the dean spoke to about 250 of us new students and said that 50 per cent would be failed after the first year. It was their way of weeding out the chaff from the wheat. I'd never had a problem with grades in high school, so I didn't take it too seriously. But there were 39 of us that started in the Engineering Geology subgroup that year, and I ended up 19th. Numbers 20 to 39 all failed, as the dean had predicted. That was a bit of a wakeup call, and in each of the next three years I buckled down and finished first. It helped that, while the first year courses were general engineering subjects, the same for everyone whether they were enrolled in electrical engineering, chemical engineering, physics, or whatever, from that year on, the studies were largely in our own chosen sub-fields. It also helped that, after my first year, I refrained from skipping electrical engineering every morning to play basketball at Hart House.

These studies in our chosen fields became much more interesting, with a strong faculty including the same, generally hatless, Bill Gross, who taught economic geology; Digger Gorman, a spell-binding mineralogist who was eventually inducted into the Canadian Mining Hall of Fame; and F. Gordon Smith, a physical chemist who got me fascinated with fluid inclusions in mineral crystals. These are small bubbles thought to contain the remains of fluids in which the crystals formed zillions of years ago, and we would spend a lot of time analyzing them and pondering their history. It really is strange, the things that interest a geology student.

We had an exceptional class, and I think we kind of fed off each other. Number two was Ed Thompson and number four was John May, each of whom would work with us building mines later; number three was more interested in oil geology, perhaps having seen one of those disappearing trilobites.

Working for "The Survey," Discovering Geochemistry and Zinc

It was the summer jobs that defined most of us, and I was lucky to have been able to spend two summers on mapping parties with the Geological Survey of Canada. As with my father years earlier, I had an outstanding party leader in Charlie Smith, from whom I learned more about geological mapping than from any university courses.

The first summer we were mapping the California Lake area west of Bathurst, New Brunswick. It was an exciting time to be there because of the important zinc and copper discoveries that were being made. One day we were camped on Upsalquitch Lake (well, actually by a stream on the shore of the lake, but that's how geologists speak of their tent camps – we say:

"camped on the lake"). It had rained all day, and we weren't able to do any mapping, but when the sun came out at day's end we decided to try out a new geochemical Quick Test that Charlie had come across.

Using this survey technique, one puts a small sample of soil or sediment from a stream bed into a test tube, adds a mysterious organic liquid called dithizone, caps the tube, and shakes it up. If the liquid turns green there is no "heavy metal" in the sample, but if it turns red, there is. The heavy metal may be copper or zinc, and if the test shows red, it means there may be copper or zinc mineralization upstream. Hope always springs eternal for a geologist.

This was not unlike panning for gold, as prospectors had been doing for years, but it was done chemically and for copper or zinc, rather than looking for visible grains of fine gold. The underlying premise of each survey method is that, as the forces of nature wear down the nearby hills or mountains, the material eroded finds its way into the streams and riverbeds draining the area. If there is, or had been, anomalous gold or copper or zinc in those rocks above, the streams draining them may be anomalous, as well. Upstream would then seem to be a good place to search for mines.

When we tested sediments in the little stream near Upsalquitch Lake, the very first sample we took turned beet red, and we thought there must be something wrong. As we walked further upstream, sampling every 20 metres or so, we kept getting red liquid until, finally, we got a green result, presumably having gone upstream past the source of anomalous metal content. We went back and forth between the last two sample points until we found the cut-off, dug down into the stream bed with our prospectors' picks, and actually found bedrock containing massive zinc sulphides.

It was my first exposure to a discovery, other than peripherally at Temagami, and it was surprising how easy it was. I became a lifelong fan of geochemistry as an exploration tool. It would be some time before I realized it wouldn't always be that easy.

However, this wasn't what we were supposed to be doing. It was not our job, so we covered up the digging, the weather cleared, and we spent the rest of the summer doing our real work of simply mapping the rocks. I was just a rather innocent student with no idea at the time of what you were supposed to do after a discovery.

Charlie was quite concerned though, because another GSC party apparently had let slip news about some mineralization they had seen in

Newfoundland the previous summer, and this had led to local promoters staking claims and playing the markets. As government employees we were not supposed to give anybody advance knowledge of important results. On the other hand, should we tell the property owner, whoever it might be? What if we didn't and they abandoned work without knowing what we had found? It was an interesting question. What Charlie decided to do with the information – probably put a notation in his formal report – I never did find out.

This was in 1956, and I later learned that Selco Exploration had staked the property two years earlier, but had done little or no exploration on it before optioning it to New Jersey Zinc, an American mining company, in 1957. Two years later, New Jersey apparently rediscovered that same mineral deposit using a similar geochemical technique, but analyzing soils rather than stream sediments. The deposit was given the name Restigouche, after a nearby salmon river of some repute.

The New Brunswick bush that year was infested with tent caterpillars, and the local lumber companies were actively spraying from the air to try to control them. They used old biplanes that could fly really slowly just above treetop level, and I remember one day I heard one coming. I ducked, and it sprayed its gunk all over me. This was before Vietnam and the infamous Agent Orange, but when I came back the next summer to work with Charlie Smith in the Gaspé Peninsula and my hairline had receded quite a bit, he insisted it must have been the spray that did it.

Actually, my bald spot is a family trait, with Sir Ambrose having had the same hairline, as well as Roland and my uncle Alan, who called it his "boney Toni." Only my father kept a full head of hair past his teens, or at least that is what he wanted us to believe. It did have a way of changing colour occasionally.

It was also full of blackflies – the Bathurst area bush, not the hair. These seem attracted to certain skin types and didn't bother me too much, but we had another summer assistant named Ian Duncan MacGregor who wasn't as lucky. It was probably his pale, northern Scottish skin, but he would attract any and all blackflies that were in the region, to the point where at times all we could see was a large black swarm walking along beside us. Ian gave up and left to go back to Scotland after three weeks, and we sorely missed him because that swarm of blackflies didn't leave our group and now seemed intent on testing our mettle.

Cutting Lines

Those early field experiences tend to stay with geologists for years, and I was lucky to have been exposed to quite a number of them, starting with pretty rudimentary ones such as carrying supplies and portaging the canoe for the party chief, and line cutting.

Before the advent of GPS, line-cutting was a necessary art in exploration that is not part of the curriculum of the average student from southern Ontario. When plunked down on an unmapped piece of land in the northern bush, the first thing that had to be done was to establish a point of reference to which all future surveying could be tied. This might start with a fixed point X, such as a particular rock beside a lake. Then other observations can be located relative to that point, as in "gold-bearing rock outcrop #12 at X + 100 metres north and X + 300 metres west."

For our geophysical surveys, we would need a surveyed grid from which to take data every 30 metres or so. Usually we would lay out a baseline, perhaps a straight, east-west line 4 kilometres long cut out of the bush. Lacking transits and the like in bush camps we would start by cutting pickets – straight saplings about 1 metre long with the tops cut to fine points – using our axe. We would put the first picket in place vertically in the ground and then start cutting our baseline westerly using our compass, pausing every 20 metres or so to put in a new picket. Once we had a few pickets in place we would set aside the compass, which was affected by local rock variations anyway, and simply rely upon lining up the point on each new picket with the two or three behind it. It was amazing how straight a baseline we could establish in this simple way.

Then, every 100 metres or so along the baseline we would begin to cut north-south cross-lines. The real art came in being able to stand on the baseline with arms outstretched along it, look north, swing those arms together to point north in a perfect right angle, and then plunk down a new picket, starting a cross line at exactly 90 degrees from the baseline. If we did it right, we would have a fine grid from which our colleagues could begin mapping and sampling. Of course, if we did it wrong, the new cross-lines might themselves eventually cross instead of proceeding in parallel, with a serious consequence on the accuracy of our mapping.

My brother Harold and I actually got pretty good at this. The early survey work at Temagami was all laid out this way, as was that for most of our early ground geophysical surveys.

One summer though, after the Geological Survey years, I was asked to go down to Jamaica to help map a copper prospect at Guy's Hill, deep in the Blue Mountains rainforest. Bill Bergey was in charge and, with his own strong nose for ore, had come up with some decent-grade copper mineralization in rocks not unlike those of the major western US porphyry copper mines. That – studying rocks similar to those that contain economic mineralization elsewhere – is often a good place to start.

Bergey was one of those eclectic explorers who used whatever tools were at hand to try to find mines, and we will see him discover another important one for us later in this story. In Jamaica, he developed an effective if not particularly high-tech survey tool. Since copper-bearing rocks in such climates tend to weather into spectacular green and blue secondary minerals, he would travel around the dirt roads with a bag full of such specimens and, whenever he met a local, he'd ask: "Have you ever seen anything like this?" Some had, and would happily lead Bill to the site.

So here I am at the Guy's Hill prospect, ready to start doing real geological mapping, and Bergey says: "We need a baseline." "Unhuh?" I replied, and Bill says: "Here's an axe. Start cutting."

Well, it was a mountainside with vegetation that looked nothing like Ontario's, but I found saplings that could serve as pickets and strutted merrily down the hill and up the other side with my trusty axe. I was humming along, thinking how much easier this bush was than the entanglement that is Canada's enchanted boreal forest, when I came over a rise and there, blocking my nice straight line, was a slightly larger tree than normal. Well, chop chop, carry on. The line must go on.

Then a wild, growling howl emanated from a small hut off to the side, and a large, dark man ran toward us brandishing a machete. To make matters more threatening, if that was necessary, he had no tongue, apparently having lost it in another machete fight some time back.

I had, it appeared, cut down his favourite mango tree.

If I'd been my British cousin Philip Keevil, I might have ended the potential confrontation with a few good "pip pips and jolly fines," but as it was I decided quickly to emulate instead my more cautious American ancestors who, as the song "The Battle of New Orleans" had it, turned tail and "ran through the briars, and they ran through the brambles, and they ran through the bushes where a rabbit couldn't go."

Bergey somehow rectified the situation, and we all remain here to tell the tale.

Choosing Berkeley

When I was about to graduate from U of T, with one child and another on the way, I looked around to see if I could get accepted for PhD studies at one of the prestigious American universities. Given my growing family, it would only work if I could get the university to pay me something to go there. So I applied to Harvard, MIT, Stanford, Chicago, and the University of California at Berkeley, in each case asking for a stipend as either a teaching or research assistant.

All five accepted me, much to my surprise, but the first four offered jobs at $100 a month and Berkeley offered $125 a month. I chose Berkeley, also known to its graduates as "Cal." It is tempting to say that this was because it had the largest number of Nobel Prize winners of any university in the world, but in reality I chose it because it paid the most – and also because a well-known Toronto geophysicist named Stan Ward had helped start up a new program there that made a lot of sense to me.

This new Department of Mineral Technology consisted of Stan Ward; Herb Hawkes, an exploration geochemist who had written the definitive textbook of the day on the subject; Ed Wisser, a structural geologist famous for his work in interpreting complex vein systems at the Pachuca Mine in Mexico; and Lyle Shaffer, a mining engineer, to round out the team. In addition, a nearby building housed the Department of Geology, including one of the exceptional theoretical and field geologists of his time, Charles Meyer. The new department was a good idea with a great team, and they attracted a pretty good bunch of postgraduate students. The idea was to combine all of these exploration sciences or technologies into one department, putting out a new breed of well-rounded geoscientists.

I was Stan's research assistant, and we did some interesting work on a new geophysical technique called induced polarization, or IP. It was unlike the spontaneous polarization, or SP, that we had used at Temagami, which measured naturally occurring electrical fields and was limited in depth penetration. IP worked by introducing an electrical field into the ground and measuring any anomalous responses, ones that might be caused by buried conductive bodies such as economic sulphide deposits. They might also be caused by uneconomic sulphides (pyrite, or fool's gold) or by completely different rocks that would give similar but spurious responses, such as ones containing graphite or clay minerals.

Our research effort was to see if there were ways to recognize differences in the signals from these various sources so we could better interpret anomalies and avoid the spurious ones. I have to say the results were not definitive and do not form a major part of current geophysical practice. In fact, they may not form part of it at all.

I spent a lot of time with Herb Hawkes because after our Upsalquitch Lake discovery in New Brunswick, I was intrigued by the fact that geochemical techniques detected metals directly, as opposed to geophysical ones that measured magnetic or electrical properties that could just as easily be caused by barren sulphides, graphite, clay, or other uninteresting things. If you took a soil or stream sediment sample and it measured anomalously high in copper, that meant there was copper in the vicinity. Maybe it wasn't in sufficient concentration to be economic, but at least it was indicative of copper and not of clay or fool's gold.

Herb was a treasure trove of ideas, an occasionally absent-minded, entrepreneurial scientist who never stopped thinking, and he was eager to share his new thoughts with anyone who would listen. One of our doctoral candidates asked him why he didn't take more care to protect these ideas, and his memorable reply was: "If I ever get to the point where my latest idea is my last, you guys should put me out to pasture."

I've never forgotten that. The willingness to pass ideas and information freely back and forth can often lead, synergistically, to two or more people coming up with even better ones. Hoarding ideas and information is the dystopian practice of the bureaucrat.

While at Cal I became close friends with another PhD candidate from New Brunswick, Doug Fraser. Ironically, Doug had come to Berkeley to work with Herb Hawkes, having been interested first in geochemistry, but PhD students then, as now, needed research funds to keep them going. Herb was as inspirational as anyone there, but he turned out to be pretty poor at raising funds. Stan Ward, on the other hand, was a past master at this. So Doug the putative geochemist, fairly soon became Doug the geophysicist. Of such happenings new careers are made.

As budding scientists, we were very dependent on getting research funding. In those days, the best source for us seemed to be the Office of Naval Research, and its needs determined where we would focus our efforts. If a project appealed to them, we'd promote it; if not, we'd tend to leave that project lying fallow and find other research work that would actually get funded.

While our research was always academically pure and surely must have been highly useful, this did give me a healthy suspicion of scientific motivation.

Scientists, pure or not, naturally need to follow the money. If they don't manage to get access to funds, their ability to attract students and do research dries up. Some of the best scientists get to be quite good at selling their wares, as Stan and I did. It does tend to make one slightly skeptical, and wary of whatever the well-funded, politically scientific mantra of the day may be.

At Berkeley, I also was able to get to know and learn from Chuck Meyer over in Geology. He was a great guy, acknowledged in the field as one of the outstanding geologists of his day, but he had only published one paper in his life. That was the definitive work on wall-rock alteration at the large copper mine at Butte, Montana, co-written with Anaconda's Dr Reno Sales. While many university professors at the time seemed caught up in the publish or perish tradition, Chuck was such a perfectionist that he was never quite sure he had learned enough about any subject to publish on it. There was always more work to be done first. As a result, while he was an exceptional scientist, field geologists, and teacher one had to be there to learn from him, because there was only one paper of his in the literature available to be read and studied.

The Terrors of the PhD Orals

Berkeley was a great place to be in those days, with top faculty and students. They were heady times, but there was a deep abyss that had to be crossed on the way to a doctorate. The dreaded three-hour oral examination was a test of endurance that came before the candidate had even started research on a PhD thesis, and in fact if it was not passed, there would be no more research and no tomorrow at that school.

There being no defined subject, the three professors making up the Orals Tribunal could ask questions on anything under the sun, were expected to do so, and did. They might explore a geologist's understanding of meteorology, a physicist's understanding of the mating habits of hummingbirds, or a rocket scientist's understanding of geology. Preparation was, in a way, impossible, but that didn't stop candidates from cramming on almost any subjects they could imagine in the months before the trial. Some dropped out before even getting to the actual exam, too tired or afraid to stand up to it.

In fact, the examiners didn't expect anyone to have all the right answers to all questions, but wanted to test by fire the way in which each candidate thought about them. We were all well aware of this, but knew we had better have at least some of the answers, so we crammed anyway.

One of our fellow candidates was an experienced geologist who had come back to school to try for a doctorate. Bert, as we will call him, was a bit older than the rest of us and apparently much wiser, being quite the talker. One day he went in for his orals and, three hours later, came out with his tail between his legs. He'd flunked them, and was soon nowhere to be seen.

Doug Fraser was due to take his orals a few months after that, and described his reaction to our friend's experience:

It gave me quite a shock as I had not taken mine yet. It really scared me because I thought Bert knew just about everything under the sun. I spoke to Stan Ward about this, wondering if I would have a chance with my orals. Stan told me not to worry because Bert was full of BS, and his advice was to study a lot. As the weeks went by, Stan could see I wasn't relaxing, and so he exiled me to Lake Tahoe for 10 days (with my family), where we tented. I built a chipmunk trap (reliving my childhood), caught 2 chipmunks and studied like mad. I returned to Berkeley (with the chipmunks) and passed the orals. Stan was certainly a wise man and good at handling students.

Doug did pass with flying colours, and after leaving Cal, he returned to Toronto to join our Geophysical Engineering and Surveys firm as chief geophysicist. With us, he would eventually develop DIGHEM, the most state-of-the-art airborne electromagnetic survey system in the industry.

I had earlier gone up against Stan Ward, Herb Hawkes, and Chuck Meyer in my orals and somehow managed to get through them. In the end, my greatest fear was that one of the examiners would present a rock and ask me to identify it, since, after all that cramming on everything under the sun, I worried that I'd forgotten anything I'd ever known about geology. Fortunately, nobody showed me a rock.

Now, with that out of the way it was time to get on with a thesis, or dissertation, by this time almost an anticlimax. I'd had enough of university life and wanted to get back into the field to do some real geology.

Moving on to the Craigmont Mine

Stan was close to a Vancouver-based mining company named Placer Development, which was just bringing an important new copper mine into production near Merritt, BC. This had been another geophysical discovery. A small exploration company, Craigmont Mines Limited, had drilled a magnetic anomaly, and it turned out to have been caused by a large copper-bearing deposit that also contained a fair amount of magnetite. The seventh drill hole on the property had intersected an amazing 180 metres of 2.2 per cent copper, one of the better discovery holes ever drilled. Placer had taken over financing and management and was the new mine operator, with Noranda Mines also having become a shareholder.

Stan got me a job there as a research geologist and in 1962, just as the new mine started production, I loaded up all my worldly possessions in a small U-Haul and drove with my wife and three kids from Berkeley to Merritt.

The mine operators on site were intent on getting the operation running smoothly, as with all new mines, but to their credit they put up with the research guy that head office had foisted on them, as long as I stayed out of their way. I was hired by and reported to Doug Little, a senior Placer engineer and vice-president from the Vancouver office, and started at a salary of $250 a month. Whether Doug thought I'd signed too cheaply or thought I might actually do some good is unknown, but after three months I got an unsolicited raise to $275 a month, and in another three months they made it $300 a month. I became a Placer Development fan for life.

The company was led by John D. Simpson, an Australian mining engineer who had come to Canada initially to work for McIntyre Mines at Timmins. Later, after stints dredging gold in Columbia and New Guinea, he arrived back in Canada, this time in Vancouver, and in 1957 assumed the presidency of Placer Development. Simpson had led Placer into the Craigmont mine, and would later develop the important Endako molybdenum mine in BC, Cortez gold in Nevada, Marcopper in the Philippines, and Gibraltar copper in BC. He was inducted into the Canadian Mining Hall of Fame in 1991 as one of Canada's foremost mine developers.

Simpson had a favourite Stetson hat he would wear to mine openings, his own and those of other companies, and years later when we opened the David Bell mine at Hemlo in Ontario, John told me that it was the twenty-third mine opening his hat had attended. It was only our seventh since I'd left Placer, so we still had a long way to go.

The Craigmont deposit was fascinating. It wasn't as high grade as Temagami but was much larger, with reserves of over 25 million tons. That was still small by today's standards, when we talk of hundreds of millions or billions of tons (or, in the current metric system, tonnes), but the mine was important in its day. By the time it closed in 1982 it had mined and milled 34 million tons containing an average grade of 1.8 per cent copper.

Craigmont was the first large-scale open pit mine in British Columbia, although it seems a different world when one looks at today's Highland Valley Copper mine only 30 kilometres to the north, which has a current mining and milling rate some 40 times higher at 140,000 tonnes of ore per day.

The copper at Craigmont occurred in what had once been a sequence of limestone and other sediments that had been altered by the heat and fluids from a granitic intrusion, resulting in what is known as a skarn deposit. This contained a number of exotic calcium silicate alteration minerals such as garnet and epidote, along with specular hematite, the magnetite that had led to the discovery, and of course the copper sulphides. The copper source, most likely, was the adjacent Guichon Batholith, a large complex consisting of a number of phases of granitic intrusions, although unlike in the Highland Valley, near Craigmont the granite itself apparently was not mineralized. That inconsistency, given that the adjacent limestones were altered substantially by something, does still seem to suggest room for more work.

Interestingly, another small copper mine was being put into production not far away, the first mine to be developed in the Highland Valley, and it did occur in a phase of that same large, Guichon granite complex. Financed by Sumitomo Metal Mining (SMM) of Japan, Vancouver-based Bethlehem Copper built a modest mill and started mining in 1962. With ore grades only about 0.7 per cent copper in a series of small open pits it was a more difficult and less profitable operation than Craigmont, but it would be the precursor of today's huge Highland Valley Copper mine.

The discoverer of Bethlehem was a New Brunswick-born prospector named Herman "Spud" Huestis, and I recall him saying, as he visited us at Craigmont: "There's a billion tons of copper ore up there." We all smiled politely but, as it turned out, he was understating what would eventually be discovered and built in the Highland Valley.

Meeting Bob Hallbauer, and the Silver Sine Prank

My job was to try to find the next Craigmont ore body, or at least show the way to it, and I delved into the geology and geophysics with alacrity, but sometimes when we weren't discovering or mining ore we would liven things up with the odd prank.

The chief geologist at the Craigmont mine was one Cliff Rennie, and he had organized a weekly pool in which a random sample of copper ore from the pit would be tabled, and everyone in the office was invited to bet on the amount of copper it contained. Once the bets were in, the sample would be assayed, the percentage of copper announced, and the winner determined. Since the mineralization was quite coarse-grained and obvious compared with, say, that from a low-grade gold mine, it seemed likely that a professional geologist could fairly easily estimate the grade. As it happened, the winner was usually from the secretarial pool, was occasionally a mining engineer, and was almost never a geologist. In fact, Cliff never did win the pool.

Despite their occasional inability to recognize ore grades, most of the participants in the Craigmont office played the penny stock market, and they kept in touch with the market through twice-daily Teletype reports sent from Placer's head office in Vancouver. Cliff Rennie was one of them and tended to rely upon stock price charts he would keep to guide his investing. It was Cliff's own version of what today passes as technical analysis.

One of my neighbours and friends in the Craigmont village was Bob Hallbauer, then the open pit superintendent, and later to become a key player in our story. Bob and I played the market a bit, but more on news and rumours than using charts, so we thought up a little trick to play on Rennie.

We assembled a few months of imaginary, future market prices on a fictional stock we invented named Silver Sine, and we sent these off to a co-conspirator at head office who agreed to put them on the Teletype, one quote at a time, twice a day for the next six months. Our imaginary Silver Sine was of course named after a sine wave, a mathematical term describing a regular cyclical pattern of ups and downs, also called a smooth repetitive oscillation. The six months of prearranged, fictional data covered several such cycles, and when plotted up by a technical analyst, the share price pattern would form a perfect sine wave.

We began to comment, within earshot of Rennie, about this fantastic new silver property we'd heard about, and how it was "really going to go." It was like feeding bread to an aquarium full of fish, steak to a dog, or a cliff to lemmings. Sure enough, Cliff the technical analyst started plotting the results, and a while later, after seeing two or three perfect cycles, he had Silver Sine figured out as a buy. The next time it was at the bottom of this perfect pattern, he called his broker to buy big.

Naturally his broker had never heard of it. Cliff turned around and saw Bob and me at the door, smiling. He asked us where it traded and how he could get in on Silver Sine. We both just gave him "the look," and his jaw dropped. Cliff knew immediately how we'd caught him.

The Mysterious Deep Magnetic Anomaly

Fun and games aside, we did actually try to find the next big ore body at or near Craigmont, with our best hope being to find some remote sensing tool to look beneath the later, barren volcanic rocks that covered the favourable horizon to the west of the known mine. These overlying rocks were unmineralized but, coincidentally, also contained variable amounts of magnetite.

Surveys over them would produce magnetic data that was erratic and not easily interpreted, tending to obscure deeper-sourced anomalies from any buried copper ore body below. So, unlike with the discovery a few years earlier, magnetic surveys were thought unlikely to be of much exploration help, even though the underlying geology was permissive of additional ore occurring, on trend of the known ore body, down there beneath those later volcanic rocks.

We did do extensive surveys to the west anyway, and the magnetic numbers were indeed high and erratic. However, we had an ingenious theory that, if we massaged the data through some magical, mathematical filters that would reduce the noise caused by those near-surface, overlying rocks, we might be able to see deeper-sourced anomalies that could lead us to another mine like Craigmont. We did this, and of course actually came up with a beautiful, filtered anomaly that seemingly represented something big buried beneath all that shallow noise. It was under the adjoining Betty Lou mining claims not far to the west of the main mine, claims that had been ignored previously.

We arranged to drill a few holes on the claims but didn't find anything to explain our magic anomaly, and we went on to other projects in other areas. I always wondered whether we had sufficiently followed up the idea or not. Fifty years later, I would run across Neil Hillhouse, an old friend who had been with us at Craigmont, in a parking lot in Vancouver and we reminisced about those Betty Lou claims. It turns out that Cliff Rennie had kept them and held them personally until his death a few years earlier, convinced as well that there could be something there. He had consulted for a company that had done some drilling on them as recently as 2006.

Exploration is like golf in that, as they say, hope springs eternal. Was this a similar case of Cliff's believing in a non-starter like Silver Sine, or is there really some copper there after all? Hmmmmm. Did I miss something?

John Simpson's Placer Development

My couple of years with Placer left an indelible impression of what it was like to be with the best in the business. Everyone on the property thought he or she was part of the top mining company of the day, and was proud of it.

The people there were some of the most impressive I'd ever worked with, and I credited John Simpson for that. He stressed solid engineering, with every capital decision requiring a serious discounted present value analysis as well as careful engineering study of the alternatives. Simpson was at the same time a risk-taker who also knew how to find and capitalize upon mining opportunities such as Craigmont, as well as several later discoveries. He knew how to get them, and then how to build and operate them well.

I thought Simpson was the kind of leader we all should aspire to be. The company's primary strength was in its construction and operating engineering. But in exploration it created a new way of gaining exposure to discoveries through what we called "development contracts." In these it used its engineering and financial capacity to negotiate a major interest in the new prospects found by other, junior explorers. Earning 50 per cent to 80 per cent of a new mine by providing management and financing credibility, as they did in the case of the Endako mine, beat paying through the nose to actually *buy* one at full value. One didn't need to be a rocket scientist to understand that.

Time to Move On

I'd enjoyed both California and the interior of British Columbia. They were good years, but I was just about finished my thesis work and it became time to move on.

In one of my trips back to Berkeley, Stan Ward had raised the idea of my going to the University of Utah as an assistant professor to start up a new

Department of Exploration Geophysics. Apparently the role was on offer, and it had some appeal to me, for reasons that are now obscured by antiquity. I might have become quite a good skier.

But by then I'd begun to appreciate what Simpson had done at Placer Development in the real world, and I had been watching what my father was doing back East. He had been gradually co-opting me with copies of the weekly progress reports from each of his team of geologists – Bill Bergey and Joe Frantz from the Temagami and geophysical contracting days, and others, including Gordon McIntosh, Fred Sharpley, Kevin O'Flaherty, Terry Patrick, and my U of T colleagues Ed Thompson and John May, all first-class exploration people.

Interestingly, I was still resisting joining the new "family business," as my own engineer son Norman III and lawyer brother Brian did years later, and other than sending those weekly reports to whet my appetite, my father never actually asked. However, one day my mother called me up in BC and said: "He's not going to ask you, but he wants you to and needs you, so you'd better come back." Whether true or not, the call probably tilted the balance.

So I packed up my bags and said au revoir to my friends at Placer. We shipped ourselves back to Toronto, with three kids and a German shepherd named Bluff, and didn't become permanent Westerners until Teck moved its head office to British Columbia ten years later.

Epilogue

Those were exciting times for a young geoscientist. Important mines at Temagami, Mattagami, Geco, and Heath Steele had all been discovered using the new geophysical technology, and the biggest of all, Kidd Creek in Timmins, soon would be. Walter Holyk and others had advanced new theories of the volcanogenic origin of certain types of major ore deposits, and the long-debunked concept of continental drift had been proven right after all, and given the newly accepted name of plate tectonics. It was like a toy box of new tools had suddenly been opened and was there for the using. It was time to forget Utah and get on with exploring.

We are all influenced by the places we work and the people we work with. I was fortunate to have worked under Charlie Smith of the GSC and to have studied with Ed Thompson and John May at U of T. Ed and John would work with the Keevil Mining Group, later the Teck Group, and contribute to building our company, as we shall see. Similarly, Doug Fraser from New

Brunswick and Cal would join us as chief geophysicist and be responsible for designing the DIGHEM helicopter-borne electromagnetic survey system that would be used by many in the industry.

Simpson's Placer Development became a model for us and we would emulate his methods in both mining and exploration, and in some ways exceed them. We would also see some of their top people come across to the wild side and join our budding mining group.

Bob Hallbauer had been pit superintendent when I went to the Craigmont mine, and he later became mine manager. We had been neighbours, us with our dog named Bluff and Bob with his horse called Hallbauer, although the horse was generally out of town and appeared more often in conversation than in reality.

When I left Craigmont I'd said to Bob: "See you later," not realizing it was prophetic. He would join Teck as vice-president for mining a few years later and would eventually be inducted into the Canadian Mining Hall of Fame for his contributions to Placer and Teck.

Cory Sibbald had been mill engineer at Craigmont, went on to the Endako molybdenum mine for Placer, and would eventually join Teck as well, along with John Anderson, Mike Lipkewich, Charlie Lightall, and a number of other strong Placer engineers. All would help to make Teck a better company, one that has thrived long after Placer Development disappeared.

CHAPTER 5

FROM TEMAGAMI TO TECK CORPORATION

I'm not interested in preserving the status quo; I want to overthrow it.
Niccolo Machiavelli

Back in Toronto, many things had been happening since the Temagami discovery. Geophysics, previously seen by some of the old hands as one of the more expensive and least understood of the options for an exploration program, was now in vogue. Not only Temagami, but the important new Heath Steele mine in New Brunswick and the even larger Mattagami mine in Quebec owed their discovery purely to geophysics. Everybody now wanted some of what those mines had.

The old Mining Geophysics Corporation that Roland Michener had incorporated was no more, having been shut down after the McClusky saga in Cuba, but the consulting and contracting work would go on. The low days of my father's staff being down to Peggy and Barbara were over, times for the mining industry were picking up, and Geophysical Engineering and Surveys Limited had as much business as it could handle. The Stetson had come out of the closet once again.

The basic consulting-contracting business had never been busier, but increasingly there were other, bigger opportunities arising, or being presented. My father had worked as a geophysical consultant for most of the stock promoters of the day and knew them all, their warts, successes, and failures. Some were admirable scoundrels, some just plain scoundrels, and others were truly dedicated geniuses. This has never changed.

Norman had also worked for many of the larger operating mining companies, and realized the advantage that having established, long-life, mineable ore reserves under their belts gave them in building a sustainable business. He admired and respected people like J.R. Bradfield, who had helped to build Noranda into a major Canadian company, and Thayer Lindsley, who had assembled the important Ventures mining empire, including McIntyre and Falconbridge. My father was determined to achieve similar heights.

So while the Temagami mine was being built and operated, he was always looking for the next big thing, and there was no shortage of people bringing ideas to him. Some would work, to a greater or lesser extent; others would not.

Two Early Acquisitions – Goldfields and Pickle Crow

By 1958, Norman's main interests were in two companies, Geoscientific Prospectors and Mining Geophysics, both offshoots from his exploration and consulting days. These two owned 44 per cent of Temagami Mining Co., and each had a cash position of about $500,000.

In the first of a series of quick moves to expand the Group interests, Geo-scientific and Mining Geophysics jointly purchased control of Goldfields Uranium Mines Ltd, a company trading on the Toronto Stock Exchange, for a price of $540,000. The seller of the control block was international mining giant Rio Tinto, but the inspiration for the deal came from founder Joe Hirshhorn, the mining entrepreneur we met earlier.

Goldfields held a block of shares in a company called New Hosco that had just announced a high-grade drill hole in Quebec, near the recent Mattagami copper-zinc discovery. With New Hosco shares skyrocketing from pennies to over $7 in a few trading days, the new Goldfields control group decided to sell the block and take the profit of over $1 million. The Goldfields/Geo-Scientific/Mining Geophysics team then acquired control of Pickle Crow Gold Mines Ltd from the estate of its founder, bringing its 400-ton-per-day mining and milling operation in northwestern Ontario into the Group.

The *Toronto Star* headlined the story: "Keevil calls Pickle Crow Mine Scientist's Delight," and quoted him as saying: "For the geophysicist, Pickle Crow is a natural." The gold veins were associated with magnetic iron formation, and "a 6,000-foot stretch of known gold-bearing formation has never been more than casually investigated."

It was an interesting property, and I had the pleasure of helping to map it geologically, working with mine geologist Bob Graham and a well-known consultant named Dr McMurchy. The doc was getting on and I think he may have had difficulty seeing some of the more fine-grained parts of the rocks. There was one time when he mumbled: "Isn't that a corker?" before handing me a rock sample and his geologist's magnifying glass. I concurred it was a corker, and from then on Bob and I mapped that particular horizon as corker. (For the non-technical readers, corker is not a common geological term, and definitely does not describe any known rock formations.)

Although deep exploration from underground was fairly successful for a while, we didn't find much new ore from our surface mapping of the rest of the property, away from the mine workings. With costs rising and the price of gold fixed, the mine would eventually shut down in the mid-1960s, after having produced 1.5 million ounces of gold in its 30-year life. Now, in the twenty-first century, a small mining company has announced plans to try to redevelop the property, and one wonders if they will ever know what form of scientific observation led to the "corker formation" that shows up on their old maps.

As the 1950s ended, the new Keevil Mining Group consisted of Geophysical Engineering and Surveys, Geoscientific, Mining Geophysics, Temagami Mining, Goldfields, Pickle Crow, Jamaican Mining, and a number of smaller exploration companies. It operated two mines, Temagami and Pickle Crow, and had a reasonable cash and securities position from which to move on to the next stage, whatever that might be.

Norman Keevil, the academic turned mine builder, was beginning to shake the trees in the old Canadian mining fraternity. Only he, from his consulting days, was on first name terms at the same time with the loose promoters on Bay Street and the illustrious barons of Toronto who were running the old-time, established mining companies. Revered by some and perhaps frightening others, he was on a roll, and in very short order the next acquisition was to come.

The Teck-Hughes Acquisition, and "10 Seconds that Would Change It All"

Norman had formed close friendships with two of the more innovative players in the Toronto brokerage community. One was Len Watt, a charmingly tough financial type who would later found his own firm named Fiscal Consultants, and who became known for his aphorisms such as: "Every rat needs a second hole." That one would serve us in good stead at times in the future, as a wise admonition to hedge our more ambitious schemes with a decent escape route should things go wrong.

The second was Doug Perigoe from George Gardiner's Gardiner, Watson & Co., as soft-spoken a gentleman as Watt was irascible, and devoted to finding good deals and putting the players together. He was a neighbour of my father's in Lorne Park, outside of Toronto, and would often catch a ride to work with him.

The story of how they mused about and then gained control of Teck-Hughes is a classic, and my father's notes from years back describe it:

> Doug being a neighbor and not having a car, I picked him up regularly and we would drive the 18 miles in to Toronto, which usually took about 40 minutes. Doug was on the board of Teck-Hughes, a gold miner in Kirkland Lake headed by J. B. Perry, who only held about 10,000 shares in the company. Four or five others had positions ranging from 25,000 to 250,000 shares, including John McClusky with 100,000, so some very small blocks of shares controlled the company.
>
> Doug wasn't satisfied with the company's operators, as they didn't do anything original, could seldom agree on policy and were sort of led around by the nose by Noranda. Noranda took in partners on exploration deals and later did the financing of the mine to gain control. The Teck-Hughes people were very proud of themselves for making deals of that sort and for being involved with such a big company. Doug was quite disgusted with the management as they paid out large amounts in dividends rather than spending it on exploration. McIntyre, which had started production later than Teck-Hughes, had become a larger and richer company by paying smaller dividends and investing its money wisely.

Although Teck-Hughes was one of the oldest mining companies in Canada, having started around the same time as McIntyre Mines and well before Noranda, by 1959 it had fallen far behind in scale. Rightly or wrongly, it was the antithesis of the kind of growth company Doug and my father admired, or aspired to run and build on.

Norman went on to say:

> Off and on we would discuss how we would get control of Teck-Hughes, and by the end of our drive in to Toronto we would always end up concluding it couldn't be done. The next time we drove in to Toronto we would discuss it again, and so on.
>
> One thing I learned was that Roy Jodrey, 'Mr Nova Scotia,' who was on more boards than anyone else in Canada and had dozens if

not hundreds of investments, was really the leading force, and Mc-Clusky would always vote with him. Jodrey had the reputation of getting the highest price per share when he sold.

I got to know Jodrey fairly well. He was a nice man, self-effacing and modest. He used to come to Toronto regularly for board meetings and I would often meet him at the National Club. We would discuss mining, and I suspect he knew I was interested in buying his shares, and if he did make this guess he would think to himself that he would get the highest price.

One day he was complaining that he couldn't get back to Halifax on Trans-Canada Air Lines (TCA) and he would have to take the train. I was using TCA often at the time and knew quite a few of its operating people, so I suggested that he go to the airport with me. I took him around a long line of standbys and spoke to the chap in charge, saying it was urgent we get on the flight. The two of us got on. Jodrey was quite grateful and drove me to his place across a large inlet in Hansport in western Nova Scotia. I stayed there in his old clapboard house, spent the night and his wife made some poached eggs on toast for breakfast. He then took me out to lunch, for all of 35 cents.

He had a black book with all of his investments, which he looked through for me, and we finally got around to talking about his Teck-Hughes shares. He knew why I was there and was aware that this was a cat and mouse game. The market was around $1.50 a share, and Jodrey finally agreed to sell his block for $1.85 a share.

The problem was I had no way of paying for the shares unless the whole deal went through and I could then convince a bank to lend me the money. I flew back to Toronto and called Paul McCloskey, another director, that night, told him I had purchased Jodrey's shares, and he agreed to sell his at a slightly lower price.

The next morning, I drove in to Toronto and had just crossed the street when I remembered that Jack rode there in a car pool from Oakville, so after passing that street I turned around and went up to his office. There wasn't a soul in the outer office but Jack was there alone, picking up the telephone. I told him I had purchased Jodrey's and McClusky's shares and wanted to know how I could get control of the board. We went through the numbers one by one. We decided we would have to get J.P. Dolan. Perry jumped up and said he would go get him. I said no. Just sit down. I'll call him.

I said: 'JP? It's Norm Keevil. I have just bought Jodrey's and McCloskey's shares and we want control of the board. Would you mind resigning in favour of one of our people?' He said: 'Sure Norm. Would you buy my shares too?' I agreed, paying $1.75 a share.

He came over and resigned and we then had control of the board. I learned later that if I hadn't turned around and backtracked to Jack Perry's office he was picking up his telephone to call Jack Allen, who had been trying to get control of Teck-Hughes for years. He was president of Little Long Lac, another gold mining company, and I'm sure he was willing to pay full price for all of the shares.

Writing in 1988, my father said: "That 10 seconds when I turned around and went up to see Jack Perry changed everything. If I hadn't done it, I probably would have lost the deal. If Jack Allen had the stock it would probably still be trading at $1.50 instead of the $35 it is today, because he was more of a stock trader than a mine maker."

Jack Perry may have been ambivalent at the start, but he became a great supporter of our group as time went on. Ed Thompson recalls him saying later that "Norm Keevil honoured all the promises he made to me," although Jack never said what those promises were. He was a bit leery about our penchant for geophysics though, famously noting that: "Anomalies are like anuses; everybody has one."

The Press Covers the Surprise Acquisition

The deal was announced and the *Toronto Star* headlined "Keevil Group wins over Little L. Lac in Teck-Hughes bid." The story read: "The N.B. Keevil group has won its second battle in a month to take control of a gold mining company," and "It's the second defeat in a month for the Little Long Lac group, which had been seeking to buy enough stock to control Teck-Hughes for some time. Last month the Keevil group outbid Lac and other groups for control of Pickle Crow Gold Mines."

The Mining Journal noted drily:

Geo-Scientific and Goldfields Uranium then stepped out and acquired 17% of Teck-Hughes, giving the companies operating control," but that lacked the drama of the chase and the risks that could only be told by someone on the front lines. It went on to say: "Teck-

Hughes has operated a gold mine in the Kirkland Lake district since 1917, and had paid out dividends totaling $49,000,000 to the end of 1957. But most important is that Teck also owned 81% of Lamaque Gold Mines, which yields over $4,000,000 annually in gold bullion and has operated a 2,000-ton-per-day mill since 1935 in the Bourlamaque district of Quebec.

Teck-Hughes also owned a one sixth interest in Mattagami Lake Mines with its recent multi-million-dollar zinc-copper-silver deposit in Quebec, and a sizeable interest in Consolidated Howey, a holding company with a significant share interest in Geco Mines Ltd., another Noranda affiliate that had made a major copper-zinc discovery in western Ontario. Teck and Lamaque then bought Rio Tinto's holdings in Howey to give the Keevil Group 36 per cent of that company's outstanding stock.

At the same time, the *Financial Post* quoted my father on the philosophy behind the new group: "This money should be back in the mining business. I firmly believe that mine earnings should either go out as dividends or back into scientific search for additional reserves."

Followed by Another Surprise, Canadian Devonian

But that was then, and tomorrow was another day. Norman hadn't reckoned with the other friendly broker, Len Watt.

Some years back, in 1954, a group of Saskatchewan businessmen had discovered oil 200 kilometres southeast of Regina. According to John Leishman, a Regina urologist, he and a local drugstore owner, a lawyer, an insurance salesman, and a candlestick-maker had become intrigued with all the new oil fields being discovered in Alberta and Saskatchewan. They decided to form a little exploration company they named Canadian Devonian Petroleums Ltd, and to seek their fortune in the oil patch.

Naturally, the first thing to do was hire a good consulting geologist to select the right prospective lands from parcels that the Saskatchewan government was about to put out for bids. Their very good geologist picked three parcels, in order of preference Parcels A, B, and C. Devonian bid for Parcel A, with a fallback bid on B should it lose the first, and then on C should it lose A and B.

Devonian was not successful on the bids for Parcels A or B, but was awarded the third prize, Parcel C. This was a 100,000-acre oil lease in south-eastern Saskatchewan. Without funds to explore it themselves, they farmed out the property to Canadian Gulf Oil, assigning it a 50 per cent interest in the property in exchange for drilling a test well. Gulf had had great success exploring for oil in Alberta, and the Devonian syndicate hoped that some of that would rub off on their project.

Sure enough it did. In March 1954 Gulf brought in the Quinn No. 9 well at Frobisher, the first significant oil well in that part of Saskatchewan. It would lead to the Steelman Field, one of Saskatchewan's most prolific oil fields of the day. As it happened, the winners of Parcels A and B were the losers, since wells drilled on them were dry holes. Evidently serendipity applies in oil as well as in mining.

By 1957, Devonian's 50 per cent share of production was almost 600,000 barrels of oil a year that, at the selling price of just over $2 a barrel, gave it a nice gross income of $1,353,055. That was a big number in those days.

Within Devonian, a divergence of opinions as to the future of the company inevitably developed among the eclectic mix of businessmen that had formed it. Its president, Dr Leishman, given his professional background, was naturally inclined to explore further. Vice-president Herb Pinder, the druggist and a fourth-generation Saskatchewan resident, was more inclined to sell.

In twenty-first-century jargon, a process was initiated, and in November 1960, Devonian announced it would consider offers to buy the company or its assets. Five months later, it had received only two offers, both from Gulf's parent company, British American Oil (BA). One was to pay $15 million for Devonian's 50 per cent of the oil field. The second was to make an offer of $4.95 a share for all of Devonian's 3.4 million shares outstanding, which worked out to be some 50 cents a share more than the direct buyout. Both offers were open for acceptance for three weeks.

With Devonian shares trading at $4.50 a share, the board said it expected to be in a position to make a recommendation to shareholders in a week. Dr Leishman, not wanting to sell, or be sold out, approached the Gardiner brokerage firm, and sure enough, the first idea they came up with was to introduce him to the "Keevil Group," by then the most active player on the Toronto acquisition scene. Len Watt brought them together, and there was an immediate bonding.

From John's perspective, here was a group intent on building a company, as opposed to just selling out. From our side, with each of Pickle Crow,

Temagami, and Teck-Hughes having proven ore reserve lives quite a bit shorter than the proven oil reserves at the Steelman Field, it was an opportunity to augment our existing production with a new source of cash flow that would be certain to continue farther into the future. This would give us a better platform from which to continue building a resources company of lasting value.

Besides, it was there.

There were only four problems. First, it was not a mining company, but then oil did come out of the ground and needed the knowledge of geologists as well, so perhaps we could rationalize our interest. Second, we didn't have $15 million available to compete with BA. That of course was a bigger problem. So Watt and my father decided to bid for less than all of the company, offering $5.10 a share for 1.5 million shares. This represented just 45 per cent of the total outstanding shares, but was at a modest premium over BA's bid.

Third, it was decided for some obscure reason to make the offer anonymously through the Guaranty Trust Company "on behalf of one Leonard Watt for an undisclosed client," which undoubtedly seemed a bit mysterious. Finally, the offer was made directly to the shareholders of Devonian rather than to management of the company, which ticked off some of the directors who had already recommended the BA deal.

Nobody said it would be easy.

The Devonian board voted 8 to 1 to recommend the BA offer of $4.95 a share, with John Leishman dissenting on the basis the offer was too low. Nevertheless, BA increased its offer from $4.95 to match our $5.10, again for all the shares, but this time made it conditional on at least 55 per cent of the issued shares being tendered to its offer. It was an interesting ploy, since the process could have resulted in both parties being "successful," but with BA owning 55 per cent and control, and leaving us with the minority 45 per cent.

That's not how these things are supposed to end up.

The deliberations that went on about whether or not we should increase our offer were interesting. Naturally, as one could do then, we had been purchasing some shares on the open market in the course of the game, and we could have deposited them under BA's revised bid and secured a bit of a profit.

However, we were convinced that BA really wanted the deal and concluded that if we increased our own bid one more time, BA would surely top us, and increase our profit. So we raised our bid to $5.25 a share, by this time having disclosed that the offer was from "Dr. N. B. Keevil, on behalf of a mining group that has been seeking a suitable participation in the petroleum industry for some time." In an eerie precursor to what would become the time horizon of many short-term traders' 50 years later, "some time" was actually about 11 days.

Much to our surprise, BA did not up our bid again, but folded its hand, and we were the proud owners of an oil company. John Leishman stayed on as a director of Devonian and would be a valued member of our team for many years after that.

Somewhere, in some alternate universe, BA topped our bid and won the day, and in another Roy Jodrey decided not to sell. Either way, Teck would be much different today, if it still existed, as would all of us who have been a part of it. On such chances the world turns.

Merging and Consolidating, the First "Corporate Simplification" of Many to Come

Meanwhile, efforts had been going on to rationalize the new Keevil Mining Group. As my father had said early that year, even before the Devonian saga began to unfold: "We grew like Topsy. Our group was a complete jumble and now it's being streamlined."

After approvals at various shareholders' meetings, Goldfields had agreed to absorb Geo-Scientific, which had earlier bought control of Goldfields. Teck-Hughes and Lamaque swapped some holdings, with Teck-Hughes buying shares of Howey from its Lamaque subsidiary and Lamaque acquiring shares in Temagami held by Teck-Hughes. When the dust cleared, the result was that Goldfields had become the top company, Teck-Hughes remained the biggest, and Temagami had gone down to the bottom.

Having grown like Topsy, now a few months later the Group had added Canadian Devonian, and further streamlining seemed in order.

This was apparently contagious. George Lonn, in *The Mine Finders*, describes a contemporaneous situation with Thayer Lindsley's Ventures Group that included Falconbridge and QMI, the company that had funded Temagami in its early days. Lonn wrote: "The Ventures complex was indeed a complex, an interwoven network of companies and subsidiaries, and subsidiaries of subsidiaries. The clearing up of Ventures' affairs was as complicated as the situation was complex. The net result was that Falconbridge bought all of Ventures' assets."

Figure 5.1
Teck Corporation executives Sir Michael Butler, Doug Perigoe, Jack Perry,
and Norman Keevil, 1964

In mid-1963, *The Financial Post* carried a headline: "Old names swept away in mine housekeeping," referring to consolidation and merger plans by both Noranda and the Keevil Group. Noranda announced plans to eliminate two holding companies (Mining Corporation of Canada and Anglo-Huronian), to clean up its interests in Quemont Mining Corp., Normetal Mining Corp. and Geco Mines, and to merge with Kerr-Addison Gold Mines.

For our part, we would eliminate Howey Consolidated (a holding company to be wound up), and Teck-Hughes, Lamaque, and Canadian Devonian would merge to create a single, larger new company to be known as Teck Corporation. Interestingly, the ongoing company from a legal viewpoint would be Canadian Devonian, a Dominion-chartered company based in Alberta, with its name changed to reflect the long history of the Teck name in Canadian mining.

After 50 years mining gold, Teck-Hughes had morphed into Teck Corporation, now primarily an oil producer with a dollop of gold, and it was under ambitious new management (figure 5.1).

EPILOGUE, PART ONE

Teck-Hughes already had a long history behind it, back in 1960, but other contemporaneous and even younger Canadian mining companies had outpaced it. After 50 years of mining gold, Teck-Hughes had a market value (the price of its shares multiplied by the number of shares outstanding) of only $14 million. In comparison, McIntyre Mines, founded at about the same time, had grown to $69 million and Noranda Mines, formed following a copper discovery ten years later, was valued at $220 million. The Consolidated Mining and Smelting Company (Cominco) was worth $350 million. The biggest miner in Canada was Inco, at a whopping $847 million. These relative values would change considerably over future years, as fortunes waxed and waned.

Corporate size is not the primary measure of success in the mining business. It ranks well behind other measures such as growth in shareholder value, professionalism, and responsible community practices. However, it helps to be large enough to have the critical mass from which growth is a reasonable aspiration, and not so large as to become slow and unnecessarily bureaucratic. There is said to be a Goldilocks size, not too hot and not too cold, but whatever that was, Teck-Hughes had not yet achieved it.

While Teck-Hughes had paid out an impressive $52 million in dividends over its mine life, its operations had been hampered in its later years by the combination of increasing costs and a price of gold fixed by the United States at $35 an ounce. Its peers that had diversified beyond gold into products traded on the free market had each had their own challenges, but few of these had been as difficult as that cost-price squeeze in gold.

The newly consolidated Teck Corporation was now part of a diversified group producing oil and copper as well as gold, under new geoscientific leadership, and intent on building on that in the years ahead.

PART TWO

INTERMEZZO

Part 2 covers an evolutionary period between the creation of Teck
Corporation in 1963, as just one member of a diverse group of
consulting, exploration, and producing companies known as the
Keevil Mining Group, and the next era beginning in the 1970s when
a change in emphasis and a further series of mergers and acquisitions
helped to establish Teck Corporation as clearly the leading growth
company in the group.

CHAPTER 6

FROM SILVER TO LOBSTERS

We know not through our intellect but through our experience.
Maurice Merleau-Ponty

It has been said we are all the products of our experiences, whether as victims or beneficiaries.

As we entered the 1960s my father had been an exploration consultant for the past 15 years, culminating in his discovery of the Temagami copper mine. He had seen successes by third parties, along with the inevitable misses, but he now had one of his own. He'd seen the recent copper-zinc discovery by the Mattagami Syndicate, and now had a piece of it after successfully acquiring Teck-Hughes. And there had been other regional geophysical successes, notably in the Bathurst area of New Brunswick. There seemed no limit to the potential of the recent geophysical technology and geological insights.

I was fresh out of the University of California doctoral program and a couple of years at the Placer Development organization's Craigmont copper mine, which itself had been a major geophysical discovery. So I was equally enthusiastic about the prospects for further discoveries using the latest modern methods.

Interestingly, the next thing we touched did actually turn to gold or, to be more exact, silver, but geophysics had nothing to do with it.

Silverfields: Discovering a New Mine in the Historic Cobalt Camp

In 1962, around the time of the Canadian Devonian acquisition and merger into Teck Corporation, there was a new mine waiting to be discovered in the historic Cobalt district, where the Northern Ontario mining boom had started back in 1903. The new mine had actually been waiting since 1918, the last time any work had been recorded on the property.

Joe Hirshhorn and my father the consultant had hit it off earlier, so when Joe's associate Steve Kay came across a silver opportunity in Cobalt he brought it our way. Kay was a promoter, in the best sense. Like his mentor Hirshhorn and other successful promoters we will meet later, such as Murray Pezim, Bernie Brynelsen, Bob Falkins, and Robert Friedland, Kay's goal was naturally to make money, but to do so by actually making mines. Sometimes these succeeded and sometimes they failed, but like a rider fallen off a horse, the good promoters tended to pick themselves up, dust themselves off, get back in the saddle, and ride on again. Their contribution to our industry should never be forgotten.

Steve Kay had an innate distaste for the other kind of salesman-promoter, the con artist who was only after a fast buck. I'll never forget running across Steve on the street one day and the subject of one of those other types came up for some reason. I asked about him and Steve said that he was a crook. I responded: "Come on, Steve, how can you say that about someone?" He replied: "Well, he lies, and he cheats, and he steals." It doesn't get much more concise than that.

Kay had picked up an option on some dormant claims in the centre of Cobalt, old claims that had been held in an estate (the Reinhardt Estate) and on which no work seemed to have been done since an exploration shaft had been put down in 1918. However, at one time silver had been mined almost right up to the Reinhardt property, and it was hoped that the vein would continue across the boundary. It looked like a reasonable prospect that needed work, so my father agreed to take it on, and formed a new company to explore it.

My father had taken a fancy to the name Goldfields and would later change the name of Temagami Mining to Copperfields Mining Corporation, so it was only natural that the two would settle on the name Silverfields for the new company. The way in which it was acquired and financed initially was typical of the times.

The Reinhardt Estate received 100,000 of the new Silverfields shares in exchange for assigning the claims to the company. Goldfields and the Hirshhorn interests assigned another group of recently staked claims of no particular pedigree, other than the presence of a moose, to the new company for 400,000 and 300,000 shares respectively. The initial exploration program was financed by Goldfields buying 75 per cent of a 400,000 share underwriting, and receiving options on a further 600,000 shares. Complicated, but it proved very successful for all when it actually turned into a new silver mine – the first in Cobalt in decades.

Drilling results in the first six months were erratic. It seemed that the old silver-bearing vein did not carry on across the property boundary with any strength after all. Initially there were some good silver intersections interspersed with poor ones, but eventually the geological picture began to become clearer. New silver veins were discovered at the other end of the property, and soon a new mine was in the making.

Only 14 months after the acquisition the property had been placed into production, shipping ore to a nearby custom mill owned by Agnico Mines. The next year, the new company built its own 200-ton-per-day mill. Silverfields would produce 18.5 million ounces of silver over an 18-year life before finally closing in 1983 (see colour page 4).

In that era Canada had a three-year tax holiday to encourage the development of new mines. The regulations acknowledged that it usually took a tune-up period of at least a few months to reach what was defined as commercial production, so the three-year holiday did not start officially for several months after production had actually begun. It has been said that Silverfields was so profitable from the start that it had recouped all of its capital expenditures during that tune-up time, before the three-year tax holiday began, and it actually became taxable before entering the tax-free period.

Today one can visit a museum that celebrates the glory days in what is now the small town of Cobalt, and a nearby walking trail named the Keevil Trail. Hughie Moore, one of the key people who kept finding enough silver to keep the mine going for years, is a well-remembered name in the community.

Moving On

With two recent discoveries that had resulted in new mines and with the acquisitions of Teck-Hughes and Pickle Crow, the newly-christened Keevil Mining Group operated five underground mines in Eastern Canada: Teck-Hughes, Lamaque, and Pickle Crow in gold, Temagami in copper, and Silverfields in silver, along with a considerable production of oil from Saskatchewan.

Our mining and main exploration activities to that point had been primarily in Ontario and Quebec. We operated with a small management group, including miners and geologists as well as active directors such as Doug Perigoe and Len Watt, who had been instrumental in some of our formative acquisitions, and Sir Michael Butler, a baronet escapee from the UK. The group would meet regularly, sometimes formally and at other times informally, sometimes in Toronto and at other times at Temagami or one of the other nearby mines. Often it would just be three or four people meeting over lunch to brainstorm the age-old question: "What should we do next"? It was a style that would guide us well, with the players changing over time, for the next 30 years or so.

And once a year we would hold the Annual KMG Curling Bonspiel at one of the mines, generally the one holding the cup from the previous year. As often as not, this would be at the Lamaque mine. They had a neat trick of fielding two curling teams, one of which would join the rest of the mine teams at a cocktail party the night before the bonspiel. In Val-d'Or in those days, cocktail party was not really the most accurate description, and a rusty nail may not even be a legitimate cocktail. In any case, when we all arrived at the rink the next morning the Lamaque drinking team was nowhere to be seen, and four other gentlemen represented the mine. It was generally no contest, which may help to explain why we tended to return to Lamaque year after year. One day we will figure it out.

Five mines may seem like a good base, and it was certainly five more than we had had a few years earlier, but the future was by no means assured. None of the mines had sufficient proven reserves to be sure they would be around for long. We definitely couldn't rest on the ore we had if we wanted to stay in business. We had to keep trying to find more, which is of course the nature of mining. *"Never rest on your ores"* is lesson number one. No successful miner ever forgets it.

Teck-Hughes had been announcing possible closure of its Kirkland Lake gold mine periodically since the early 1950s, but as Silverfields began producing in 1964, the venerable old mine really was nearing the end of its 50-year life. The Pickle Crow mine also had weak reserves and mine exploration was not producing the results we had hoped for. Including Lamaque, all three were suffering from rising costs and the fixed price of gold. Both Silverfields and Temagami were operating well, but they also had limited proven reserve lives, typical of many small underground mines.

Despite our success at Silverfields, the exploration business in Canada had fallen into a bit of a lull after the rash of geophysical discoveries in the late 1950s. It almost seemed as though the low-hanging fruit to be had from airborne geophysics had been picked and, with one notable exception, to come shortly, from the perspective of years later that does appear to have been the case. As Ed Thompson put it in his memoir, *A Boy from Utterson*:

"The mining industry and much of the world was in recession from late 1960 until 1964, when the Texas Gulf discovery at Kidd Creek, near Timmins, galvanized the exploration world. At the Keevil Group we were working with minimum budgets, spending tax dollars for third parties, and farming out our projects to get funding."

Geophysical Engineering and Surveys Ltd (GESL), owned by my father and me, and later with my brother Harold, employed the geologists and managed most of the mining exploration programs for the various Group companies. We operated on a modest cost-plus basis, with the main incentive being a 10 per cent back in right in the event of any discoveries. Our key people, like Joe Frantz, Bill Bergey, Doug Fraser, Terry Patrick, Pinky Robinson, Frank Wank, Wally Boyko, Fred Sharpley, Kevin O'Flaherty, John May, and Ed Thompson, worked for Geophysical. This translated into Geophysique in French, pronounced "Joe Physique," so that was how we were sometimes known to our friends around Val-d'Or.

Geophysique started to look farther afield, and Thompson spent considerable time out West, where there was important new mining action with the development of the Craigmont and Bethlehem open pit mines. Thompson ran an extensive stream geochemical program from a ship along the west coast of Vancouver Island, looking for copper under extremely difficult conditions. Rainfall was over 5 metres a year and the thick vegetation along the streams was some of the most difficult in Canada, so that if one found a sample with anomalous copper and wanted to trace that upstream, it would take a yeoman's effort. It made the hills and forests of the New Brunswick region where I had first experimented with this kind of geochemistry seem like a flatlands golf course.

My brother Harold was on that survey for a time and recounts how the devil's club vegetation, complete with thorns, lent new meaning to the word impenetrable. Once he was working up a stream, ducking under the thorns, and looking up every once in a while to see where he was. He came face to face with a bear. Not waiting to ask it which colour or breed it was, or how hungry, Harold turned and rushed through the nasty, blood-sucking thorns back to the boat, where the rest of the crew was laughing hysterically. Harold says: "I turned back and saw the bear running as fast as it could in the other direction."

The crew completed the program despite the challenges. Ed described the outcome in a way that could apply to many such projects:

Near Tofino, we found Catface Copper, a large copper-molybdenum porphyry-style deposit, but learned it had been staked the previous year by Falconbridge. Our biggest disappointment was that we missed finding what turned out to be a large copper mine for Utah Construction near Port Hardy, built by Utah Construction. A possible explanation was that a beaver dam with lots of organic matter had blocked the migration of copper farther downstream. In summary, the exploration program was an operational success but an economic failure as no mines were found.

Ed came close to finding a mine-to-be at Gibraltar, in central British Columbia, after he negotiated an option for the Keevil Mining Group to acquire two properties called Gibraltar and Pollyanna in 1962. He carried out geophysical exploration and drilling for two years on these prospects, but with copper selling for 30 cents a pound, the copper grade of about 0.4 per cent that he established was far too low to warrant development at the time. As Ed later wrote: "We were always short of funds in the 1960s, so when an option payment came due, the project was dropped."

Cominco and Mitsubishi later acquired the property but soon abandoned it as well. Duval and Placer Development then jointly explored it, before Placer bought out Duval's interest. By the end of the 1960s, strong growth in demand from Japan had sparked a sustained rally in the price of copper and Placer decided to put Gibraltar into production. This may have been motivated by the imminent withdrawal of the federal government's three-year tax holiday for new mines which, as we shall see, encouraged development of the Lornex mine in the Highland Valley of BC at the same time.

Gibraltar continues to be an important copper producer today. Sometimes mining properties go through several owners in that way, before one locates the equivalent of the mother lode, or because economic conditions just change.

I was still with the Placer Group when Ed began working those claims, but I came close to another future new BC mine as well. Craigmont geologist Darryl Drummond and I had gone up to Kamloops one weekend to examine some copper showings in what was known as the Iron Mask Batholith, a smaller granitic body northeast of the copper-bearing Guichon intrusive in the Highland Valley.

One of those copper showings was Ajax, a prospect uneconomic at the time, but now, in 2017, being touted for development by another company. We also walked within a few hundred metres of the buried copper deposit that would later become Teck's Afton mine, but our undeveloped sixth senses failed to recognize it. That property was later explored unsuccessfully by several other professional companies of the highest calibre before Chester Millar discovered an important ore deposit on it in 1972.

At least with Afton, as we shall see later, we would become the last and most successful company to explore and develop the mine, rather than one of the first companies to drop the property.

Sterling S. Tobias Rears His Unusual Head. And We Discover Lobsters

Shortly after I returned to Toronto, I had an experience at the other end of the country with one of those promoters who we in the business run across from time to time. Some of them are respectable; others are distinctly not. I had never forgotten Steve Kay's apt description of one promoter as a crook, and in that particular case I knew the fellow and had to agree with Steve. But there are a lot of mining promoters out there who may have hearts of gold, even if there is none in the ground. As in Ronald Reagan's well-known story, they really do believe that, where there is a hint of evidence, there might be a pony in there.

You had to meet Sterling S. Tobias to appreciate my dilemma. When he came into our office I observed that he was quite portly and wore a jet-black suit, very old-fashioned, but that was okay. He had a very big head and wore a large black hat, of the sort that might typecast one as a nefarious mystery character such as Moriarty. Finally, he had a big, black patch over one eye.

This is just a test, isn't it?

Some of that might have been my first clue, but then I had to consider that Tobias had been introduced to us by my father's best friend, the well-respected Herb Ditchburn. Herb was the straightest-arrow consulting mining engineer we knew. His own father had been the owner of Ditchburn Motor Yachts, maker of some of the finest mahogany lake boats in the 1920s. The company had gone bankrupt in the Depression, but the story about Herb was that he had personally paid off every one of his father's debts over his own career.

That was a pretty good reference, and any friend of Herb's had to be okay, black patches notwithstanding. Moriarty, er Tobias, described an apparently very good, old exploration drill hole on a copper prospect on the island of Grand Manan, off the coast of New Brunswick. We thought it was worth a look, given the excellent credentials of the person introducing him.

Now Grand Manan is known for many things including, according to the Government of New Brunswick website, "attractive lighthouses, beaches, soaring cliffs, colorful fishing boats, wildflowers, whales and seabirds." Nowhere does it mention copper, but that is why we are called explorers. We have a tendency toward hope.

So we sent geologist Terry Patrick out from Temagami to explore this prospect. Terry decided to drill a few holes, none of which encountered any significant amount of copper. He finally drilled one a few feet away from the good hole Tobias had described, and there was even less copper in that one. Terry had been given a $40,000 budget, which was large in those days, and he had enough left over to bring back 40 lobsters. My father, who by this time had conveniently forgotten his glowing referral to me of his old friend Ditchburn, later wrote: "It so happened we were having a directors' meeting at the lodge in Temagami, so these 40 lobsters were crawling over the counter, and we had a great lobster feed at $1,000 each."

Meanwhile, R&D on Geophysical Systems Continues

In those days, Geophysical Engineering and Surveys Ltd was actively carrying out research to find new and better geophysical techniques, while it managed the exploration projects for the Group companies.

Ed Thompson put it well recently when he said: "Looking back I realize that, although we were a small and usually broke Group, we were on the forefront of the new exploration technologies. We were utilizing airborne and ground EM, magnetics, resistivity, SP, the new IP, gravity, soil and water geochemistry and air photo interpretation. Other companies were using some of these advanced methods, but I think we were the most complete."

GESL had made spontaneous polarization (SP) successful at Temagami, had been using airborne magnetometer surveys for years, and since the late 1950s, had been doing R&D to develop an airborne electromagnetic (AEM) system of its own.

Unlike airborne magnetometer surveys, which passively measure the naturally occurring magnetic field of the earth, with AEM an electromagnetic field is generated by running a current through a coil of wire called a transmitter, installed perhaps on one wing of the plane. A second passive coil called a receiver is installed elsewhere, perhaps on the other wing. If the transmitted field is held constant and the two coils are kept a constant distance apart, the secondary field in the receiver will be constant as well. But if there is another conductor somewhere in the vicinity, say a big copper sulphide deposit, it will also have a field generated in it by the transmitter, and this in turn will interfere with what should have been the constant field sensed by the receiver. The difference sensed by the receiver is called an anomaly.

GESL's Dr Roy Clark had been working on installing such a system in a Beaver aircraft for several years. The lower a survey aircraft can fly, the deeper the penetration of the transmitted electromagnetic fields, and the deeper it can explore for those buried conductors. A fixed-wing aircraft such as a Beaver is not as flexible as a helicopter, especially over rugged topography, and generally cannot fly as low, but it is cheaper to operate, and the system is arguably easier to build.

The mines at Heath Steele and Mattagami had been discovered using fixed-wing surveys, but a company called Texas Gulf Sulphur had developed a working helicopter-borne AEM system and in the early 1960s was flying surveys with it in Northern Ontario and Quebec. This would turn out to be highly successful.

We had decided to abandon the Beaver plan and try to build a similar helicopter-borne system under the direction of Doug Fraser, who had just completed his PhD at Berkeley and joined us in Toronto. Doug came up with a bright new concept that would improve the quality of the responses and interpretability, compared with any of the existing airborne systems.

Prior to that time all AEM systems had involved a single transmitter and a single receiving coil, and were really designed to locate conductors of one particular orientation, usually vertically or steeply dipping, and perpendicular to the flight path. A very good ore body oriented differently might elude discovery completely, even with the survey aircraft flying directly over it. Doug came up with a solution to get more and better data. He designed a system with three mutually orthogonal receiving coils, which theoretically should detect a buried conductor in almost any orientation. This way no good ore deposit should be able to elude discovery simply by lying in the wrong direction.

It sounds easy but was ingenious. It was also complicated to design and build, as well as to interpret the results, now coming from three different receiving coils, each responding differently to the anomalous return signals from any conductors below. It would take years to build the first working system, because of technical complexities and because GESL had limited financing available to take it any faster, but in the end, DIGHEM (as Doug christened it) would become arguably the best AEM system available to the industry.

In the meantime, we continued to explore for metals with whatever equipment was available to us, whether geophysical, geochemical, or just plain prospecting. We had started one airborne electromagnetic survey in a region west of Timmins, using a commercially available system that we had under contract. This would soon turn out to be useful after Texas Gulf Sulphur made a remarkable copper-zinc discovery just outside of Timmins. It would prove to be one of the most significant metal discoveries ever made and lead us into one of our most exhilarating, although in the end unsuccessful, exploration programs ever.

CHAPTER 7

THE TEXAS GULF DISCOVERY AT TIMMINS

There are three roads to ruin: women, gambling, and technicians. The most pleasant
is with women, the quickest is with gambling, but the surest is with technicians.
Georges Pompidou

A Major Copper-Zinc Discovery

The Texas Gulf copper-zinc discovery, announced in April 1964, was perhaps
the greatest mineral discovery ever made in Canada and one of the greatest in
the world. Located at Kidd Creek, near Timmins, it led to intrigue, insider
trading, SEC and royal commission investigations, and a host of other shenani-
gans, reported and unreported. Many books have been written about it, perhaps
the most interesting being *The Billion Dollar Windfall* by Morton Shulman,
but a short synopsis of the saga can set the stage for our part of the story.

Texas Gulf Sulphur (TGS) was a well-known American company, having
been the world's largest and lowest-cost producer of sulphur for many
decades, mainly as a byproduct from gas wells in Texas. The market for sulphur would go up and down, as it would for all commodities, and when times
were flush and the need to find more sulphur seemed to be there, TGS would
look for exploration opportunities. When prices went down, these programs
would often be curtailed. Both situations occurred during the course of TGS's
large regional exploration program working out of Timmins.

Sulphur is seldom mined from what we call hard rocks, but usually from
softer sedimentary rocks, either directly or as byproducts from sour gas production. Metallgesellschaft of Germany, which we will encounter later, had
been an exception 100 years ago, mining simple pyrite (iron sulphide, also
known as fool's gold) deposits at Meggen, primarily for the sulphur content.

Canada is host to a large number of important sulphide deposits, such as
Noranda's Horne Mine, Temagami, Flin Flon, Sudbury, and Mattagami, but
these are all mined for their base metals (the copper or zinc or nickel), it

being uneconomic to try to process the rock for its sulphur content as well. In the Shulman book, a Texas Gulf executive is quoted as saying (before the discovery): "I fear that lead, zinc, copper is not a product we want, no matter how big the deposit."

Nevertheless, after a young geologist named Charles Fogarty was appointed vice-president and manager of exploration in 1957, TGS went on a worldwide hunt for economic sulphide deposits, including ones associated with other metals. TGS's exploration program in the Abitibi region of the Canadian Shield had been initiated by geologist Walter Holyk, who was one of the earliest proponents of the then-new volcanogenic theory of the origin of many base metal mines. Holyk had worked in New Brunswick, where some large deposits of that type had been discovered, and had concluded that similar opportunities might occur in the Abitibi region of Ontario and Quebec, stretching from Timmins to Mattagami.

This was contemporaneous with the successes of airborne electromagnetic (AEM) exploration in New Brunswick, Mattagami, and elsewhere, so it was natural to put two and two together and mount an AEM program in the Abitibi, flying out of a convenient base in Timmins. TGS had quietly built its own equipment installed in a helicopter (so a HEM system) rather than in the more commonly used, fixed-wing bush airplanes, and it was ready to start work in March 1959.

A TGS geologist, Leo Miller, had earlier looked at a small rock outcrop in Kidd Township, 20 kilometres north of Timmins, and noted traces of copper and zinc along with pyrite and graphite. As we learned much later, one of our own KMG geologists, Gordon McIntosh, had examined the same outcrop as well while working for another company, but didn't pursue it further. Neither geologist had considered it particularly important.

With the new HEM system ready to fly, Miller tested it over that outcrop with traces of zinc and copper, and sure enough, the mineral showing was just at the tail end of a very strong electromagnetic anomaly. As geologists know well and as we've noted earlier, electromagnetic anomalies can be the result of many things other than economic ore bodies. These include water-filled fault zones, barren or just weakly mineralized pyrite, and barren graphite. In fact, graphite anomalies can be among the strongest of all. Charles Fogarty has been quoted as saying that his company, after testing the most promising anomalies in the Timmins area, had "found enough graphite to fill all the pencils in the world for 100 years."

The lore has it that the Kidd Creek anomaly they used as a test case was so strong that it was thought it must be caused by graphite. For that reason, TGS never tested it by drilling early in the program, even as it was flown over and used to calibrate the survey equipment first thing every morning. And in fact the ore body eventually discovered does contain some graphite, in addition to all of the good copper and zinc stuff. The other story, less interesting but probably more accurate, is that the anomaly occurred on a property owned by the estate of one Murray Hendrie, and that it took four years of off-and-on-again negotiations before TGS was able to gain access to the property, although they could fly over and test it from the air with impunity.

So the helicopter would take off from Timmins, fly over the test anomaly to calibrate its equipment, and continue surveying for hundreds of kilometres to the north and east.

The usual airborne survey procedure is to select a large area underlain by rocks, often volcanic in origin, that are considered to be favourable for economic mineralization. Then the aircraft will fly a grid of parallel straight lines back and forth across the area, operating the survey equipment continuously. When the aircraft flies over a rock formation that is electrically conductive, a "blip" or "squiggle" will appear on the recording paper or tape. The nature of the blip will tell a geophysicist something about what might be buried below.

For the layman, blips and squiggles are quite similar. The distinction is esoteric and beyond the purview of this book.

That is how we come up with anomalies. Each one is different, with some giving stronger electrical responses than others, and some occurring on several of the adjoining survey lines, thus suggesting that whatever lies below might be extensive enough to be important. Some occur in what is considered prospective geology while others are thought to be in the wrong rocks. With all the extraneous things that can cause anomalies, and with their natural abundance, as Jack Perry had pointed out, one can easily drill-test hundreds of anomalies without finding one that represents an economic ore deposit. Good geological interpretation is a must.

So TGS flew off and covered large swaths of Northern Ontario and Quebec that were considered to contain favourable rocks. It continued surveying in this way for almost two years before its helicopter crashed and scuttled the equipment. TGS discovered countless anomalies, which is one of the hidden difficulties of owning one's own airborne geophysical system. The surveyor rapidly comes up with more targets than it can justify testing with ground surveys and drilling, and it is as much of an art as a science to select which ones really ought to be drilled. Finding the anomaly from the air is relatively inexpensive; it is the cost of following up with ground surveys and moving in a diamond drill to test it that eats up the budget.

As it was, in the four years since it began flying the surveys, TGS spent $3 million locating and drilling 65 separate anomalies in Ontario and Quebec, and had discovered nothing of interest. We saw in the last chapter how a $40,000 exploration program was considered expensive in those days of yore, generating not much more than 40 lobsters. The unsuccessful TGS program would have had to generate 3,000 lobsters to be as effective, somewhat difficult in Ontario and northwestern Quebec, far from the coast.

As happens periodically in the mining business, markets were getting weaker, enthusiasm was waning, the helicopter had crashed, and no more flying could be done to find new anomalies to whet the imagination. So TGS's head office decided to shut down the program. Project geologist Ken Darke in Timmins was told to cease and desist from more foolish drilling.

Problem was, Ken had always wanted to drill that first test anomaly to see what was really there under the soil and glacial overburden that obscured most of the rock outcrops in the area. And those protracted negotiations had finally come up with an option agreement with the Hendrie Estate that would allow TGS access to it. So he called his boss, Walter Holyk, who agreed: "Okay, take one last chance; just don't tell anyone." While he undoubtedly meant anyone at head office, the last part would prove prescient.

In November 1963, Darke drilled a hole named Dragon 66, after the year of the dragon and the fact it was the 66th and last anomaly to be drilled before the project really shut down. It encountered 200 metres of high-grade copper and zinc mineralization, running over 1 per cent copper and 7 per cent zinc, and contained significant values in silver as well.

Dragon 66 was the discovery hole in what turned out to be the largest base metal ore body of its type ever found in Canada. TGS tried to keep things quiet while it assembled more land in the area, but diamond drillers and geologists talk. Rumours started flying, all and sundry were buying stock, and there were later accusations of and the odd conviction for insider trading. With the news leaking out, a small staking rush began, and after the discovery was finally confirmed by TGS, all hell broke loose.

Enter Our KMG *Team, Sensing Almost a Sure Thing*

We had been doing AEM surveys in the Ivanhoe area 80 kilometres to the west, using the commercially available Aero Service system mounted on an Otter.* We immediately redeployed it to Timmins and began our own surveys in the townships in and around the discovery. With TGS's helicopter out of service and few if any competitors with recent AEM data, we could locate our own unique set of target anomalies to be followed up by ground surveys and drilling, should we be able to acquire the underlying properties.

With hard proprietary geophysical data in our hands, we had a real technological edge over people who were randomly staking claims just based on proximity to Texas Gulf's property, and it was an exciting time. As our survey plane landed each evening, geologists Ed Thompson, Wally Boyko, Doug McLeod, or whoever was on site at the time would grab the data to see what new anomalies we could pick for follow-up the next day, and then we'd call up our land man, Frank Wank, to get him checking quickly to see if that land might still be available.

Of course, by this time, there had been a huge staking rush, and within days there was no open ground available to be staked, seemingly from Timmins to the moon, just as prospector Jim Hughes had found in Cobalt, 60 years earlier.

However, much of this land was available for dealing, having been staked on speculation by local groups with neither funds for nor the intention to carry out follow-up, scientific work. Whether the land was held by individuals or by promotional companies a deal was possible, albeit expensive. It was a real plus for us to have proprietary geophysical data that would help us decide which claims had anomalies that would make them more attractive to explore than land that was simply somewhere in the general vicinity of TGS. The latter is generally called moose pasture, at least until something is discovered on it, in which case it is not.

Interestingly, the Timmins land situation was unique, with a fair amount of it removed from staking, and that was another key plus for our program. Most of the remote parts of Canada consist of Crown land, open for anyone with a prospector's licence to stake mineral claims and maintain them as long as a certain amount of exploratory work is carried out. This fact of most

---

* For those to whom this sounds strange or even cruel, an Otter is a bush aircraft. However, some animals make good prospectors at times, as in Swedish experiments using trained dogs to sniff out hidden base metal deposits.

nearby land being open and available when a discovery is made is what leads to staking rushes.

In the case of the land around Timmins though, a good part of it had been granted to veterans of the Boer War, while in other parts the mineral rights had been combined with the surface rights and were held by timber companies. The Boer War plots, in particular, were by that time often held in estates or by descendants living all over North America, and tracking them down was not a simple task. This was actually an advantage for us because, being unavailable for staking, many of these properties were still available by the time we had done our survey and determined that there were potentially interesting AEM anomalies on them.

Between the pilots, the geophysicists, and Frank Wank, we ended up with a high proportion of the ground we tried to get, all done more selectively than anyone else other than TGS had been able to do. In the end, we owned rights to over 60 claim groups with electromagnetic anomalies, including about 25 that we considered high-priority targets. After confirming them with further tests on the ground, we were in a position to drill-test those that still looked promising.

The ground testing consisted of further geophysical surveys and geological mapping. With so many properties we were on the lookout for additional ways to filter out the better targets, and Ed Thompson spent a few dark nights doing geochemical tests around the Texas Gulf discovery drill holes to see if mercury or some other geochemical halo might help, but in the end we were left pretty much to geophysical interpretation.

All of our anomalies were close to the discovery, which is considered to be a good thing not only by grizzled prospectors, but also by erudite geologists and geophysicists. Base metal deposits of this type almost always occur in clusters. Noranda, Mattagami, Flin Flon, Red Dog, and Bathurst are all cases in which, where there is one of these volcanogenic mines, there have been others to be discovered.

We geologists call such happy hunting ground "elephant country." Where there is one elephant, chances are there will be more, whether larger or smaller. We had every reason to believe this would be the case in the Timmins rush, and no reason to believe that it wouldn't be. The odds were with us in the kind of exploration project that geologists can only dream about.

We had over 25 good targets to drill, and we tested them all. The results? Nada. We didn't discover a single new mine, nor did anyone else in the area, either during the staking rush or in subsequent years.

It was a finely conceived, opportunistic exploration program, carried out in the air and on the ground by a team of good people, but it seems, surprisingly, that there was nothing new there to be discovered. Peter Laznicka, in the recently published *Giant Metallic Deposits,* notes the common tendency of such deposits to occur in clusters, reporting 254 past or present volcanogenic massive sulphide (VMS) producers in the Abitibi belt of Northern Quebec and Ontario, dozens in the Flin Flon camp of central Canada, and over 100 zinc-lead-copper VMS deposits within a 50 kilometre radius in the Bathurst belt of New Brunswick, 37 of them "ore bodies with a published reserve." Texas Gulf seems to have truly been an anomaly, in more ways than one.

The best laid plans of men and mice gang aft agley, and a little more luck would always help. But there is more to the tale.

The Windfall Fiasco

The absolutely most interesting, strong AEM anomaly that we detected occurred in nearby Wark Township, on land very close to the TGS discovery in the kitty-corner Kidd Township. It was on four claims that had been staked by well-known prospectors John Larche and Don McKinnon of Timmins, both of whom would years later also be involved in the Hemlo gold discovery in western Ontario.

Michael Barnes, in *The Scholarly Prospector,* quotes McKinnon about how he obtained the geophysical report that led him to stake the claims. Apparently, Don had been approached by one of the technicians carrying out an AEM survey for a mining company. This person seemed envious of all the quick riches that the claim-stakers were getting, and he offered to sell Don a copy of his company's anomaly map for $500. Don agreed, but by the time he showed up with the money and saw the map, complete with colour-coded anomalies, the avaricious seller had reneged and raised the price to $1,000.

Don told him to shove it, and watched while the map was placed back in its filing slot and the office was locked for the weekend. When all was quiet, Don hustled the hotel bellman for a key to the office, paying him $100. He took the map, managed to find a way to copy it, and returned the original to its slot, the prospective seller and the company involved being none the wiser. Ken Lefolii quotes McKinnon to the same effect in his book *Claims,* so chances are there was some truth to the story. The technician may not know to this day what happened to his map after he locked up for the weekend.

Whether McKinnon had acquired the claims before getting the map or after is unclear. In any event, he now knew about the strong anomaly on his claims and sought the chance to deal them off for a big win.

Viola MacMillan, famous on the Canadian mining scene as an entrepreneur and for her role in making the Prospectors and Developers Association the biggest gathering of mining people in North America, had determined she was going to negotiate a deal on that ground for her company, Windfall Oils and Mines. Viola locked herself away with Larche and McKinnon until finally getting them signed up in the wee small hours of the morning.

When Viola advised the Toronto Stock Exchange of the deal and of her plans the next day, the Exchange balked at them for technical reasons. She balked back, and a certain amount of bad blood developed. So when she started diamond drilling a few days later and rumours began to spread that Windfall had made a significant base metal discovery, which it had not, Viola refused to comment either way. She was determined to be as stubborn as the Exchange, and the rumours continued to grow.

One real mining company actually believed that Windfall could have made a discovery, since its own data confirmed that the claims contained one of the best AEM anomalies in the vicinity. That company, which some think may have been us, ended up buying a fair amount of Windfall stock and became its largest shareholder for a time. Once again, it was employing the "whatever works" system of exploration.

Chaos ensued in the market and with the regulators when it was eventually determined that there was nothing there. There was no such discovery after all.

A royal commission was formed to review the matter. Viola was exonerated after three turbulent years, although she was convicted of some relatively minor trading offences. Nobody came out a winner, other than the mining company that had picked up the largest block of Windfall – and then only in the sense that the royal commission referred to it namelessly, as a major Canadian mining company. Without admitting a thing, we can say this was the first time that company had been called a major, although it would not be the last.

The Timmins experience was a good lesson about the vagaries of mining exploration. Success is just not easy, even for the best of geologists and the best of plans. We had seen in Temagami that a program based on looking for more of the low-grade nickel-copper pyritic zone might instead discover high-grade copper in quite different rocks. Iconic mining entrepreneur Robert Friedland would have a similar experience years later, when his prospectors, looking for diamonds in Labrador, would instead discover a major nickel deposit. Here though, a program looking for a twin of the first discovery in a new Canadian base metal mining camp would not succeed, primarily because it appears there was no such twin.

The TGS-Leitch Lawsuit

It often amazes us how many of Canada's most important mining discoveries end up in the courts, but perhaps it is not so surprising. With the long odds against success from any given project or drill hole, companies are often inclined to take in joint venture partners to spread the risk. Sometimes these are negotiated by armies of lawyers in hallowed halls in Toronto or like places, but as often as not deals are made by the principals or their employees in the field or in bars after a long day's work. Handshake deals done in the field, with the best of intentions, can come unwound after one side becomes highly successful, seemingly at the cost of the other.

So it was in this case, when in 1963, as its unsuccessful program had been winding down, TGS decided to cut ongoing costs by agreeing to provide a large part of its unexplored AEM data to Leitch Gold Mines Ltd, which was to follow up further with its own exploration. The agreement was that, should Leitch make a discovery on property in the new joint venture area, the two parties would share in it, with TGS holding a 10 per cent interest and Leitch holding 90 per cent. This is a type of agreement common enough in the industry, where one company is looking for data and a place to explore and another is looking to cut its losses. The devil is often in the details.

Karl Springer, the man behind Leitch, was a legend in the Canadian mining scene. He had been successful in silver and gold mining, had been the leading player in establishing the Mattagami Syndicate, and on the side, had helped to found PWA (Pacific Western Airlines), for a time Canada's third-largest airline. He would become one of the early members of the Canadian Mining Hall of Fame.

Morton Shulman described the games around the TGS discovery: "Springer was 65 years old when Texas Gulf announced it had found an ore body of massive proportions in Kidd Township, 14 miles north of Timmins. The revelation was far more interesting to Springer than to most people, because his Leitch Mines had one year before entered into an exploration agreement which gave it rights to lands tantalizingly close to the [discovery] site. In Springer's view the agreement covered the lands that contained the huge ore body. He may very well have been correct."

The agreement in question had been struck at a Toronto's Engineers' Club meeting between David Lowrie of TGS and Charles Pegg of Leitch. Lowrie offered to turn over parts of the TGS data to Pegg for follow up, on the understanding that TGS would receive a 10 per cent share of the profits should Leitch discover a mine as a result. Details were to be worked out between Pegg and Walter Holyk.

This resulted in a written agreement that was signed a year before the discovery. As it turned out, there were serious flaws in the wording. It was possible to conclude, on the one hand, that TGS had purposely excluded the Kidd Creek anomaly area from the agreement, and it was equally possible to conclude, on the other hand, that Kidd Creek was part of the joint venture lands. It didn't help the TGS case that part of the data given to Leitch by its chief geophysicist included the AEM anomaly over the land that would hold the discovery a year later.

It was not clear who would win, as always in such matters, and as Teck would discover first-hand in later years. When lawyers and judges get into the act, it can be a crap-shoot. In a David vs. Goliath battle the odds are usually with Goliath, but gamblers will always be there to take a bet on David. A great many of these bets were taken in the three years the trial consumed, and speculation was rampant. Lawyers and brokers had people in the courtroom every day and were inclined to act on every nuance of testimony as well as the height of the judge's eyebrows during it.

It could not have been an easy decision, and Mr Justice George Gale took seven months to prepare his judgment, in the end concluding in favour of Texas Gulf. His key finding was that, wherever Pegg's recollections and statements differed from Holyk's, the judge chose to accept Holyk's. That opinion is known in law as a "finding of fact," and is almost impossible to overturn on appeal. The principle is that the trial judge can assess first-hand the integrity of the witnesses and decide which side to believe, and appeal court judges must not try to overrule that first assessment.

Nobody will ever know if the judge was right. Both Holyk and Pegg were well-respected in the community, although one was with a major company and another with a smaller one. It was a sad outcome for one of two good men and perhaps, with a nudge toward real justice, even for both.

CHAPTER 8

EARLY PROSPECTING IN CHILE

Nothing is gained by getting ahead of whomever it is you're chasing.
Pete McCarthy

International Telephone and Telegraph Gets a Bright Idea

To this point, we had never ventured far from our Canadian roots. Mc-Clusky had made an abortive attempt to get Cuba, but revolution had intervened. We had explored for copper in a small way in Jamaica and Puerto Rico and were interested in looking for other opportunities outside our home turf, but nothing substantial had materialized until ITT came up with a bright idea.

ITT has been described as the archetypical conglomerate of the era, deriving its growth from hundreds of acquisitions in diversified industries. ITT was led by the famous Harold Geneen, who had perfected the art of keeping ITT's stock price well overvalued, and then using the shares to acquire other companies with a lower price to earnings ratio. Naturally this would result in an increase in ITT's own earnings per share. This would generate a further increase in its stock price, which in turn would facilitate another acquisition, leading to the same result, and so on. It was a precursor of what later became known as financial engineering. It may also have been the 1960s version of a Ponzi scheme, but it can work for a time, as long as there are a sufficient number of attractive smaller fish around to feed the bigger one. The company and Geneen were the darlings of investors in New York.

ITT's subsidiary ITT Chile owned much or all of the Chilean telephone system, and was at the time one of the largest private companies in Chile.

The story begins in New York in 1965, with an internal meeting in the cloistered confines of ITT. The conversation apparently went something like this:

HAROLD GENEEN: We're making a really big profit down there in Chile. What can we do so it looks as though we are putting something back into the country?

RESPONDENT: Well, we use a lot of copper wire in our business. There are a lot of big copper mines in Chile. You can blow a lot of good money exploring for copper. Why don't we start a big copper exploration program?

GENEEN: What if we find something?

RESPONDENT: Don't worry. We probably won't, but we'll look good trying.

GENEEN: Okay. Go for it. Who do we have that can run with this?

RESPONDENT: Well, Frank Harkins isn't too busy, being VP of something or other we just bought. Let's let him do it.

So Harkins, not knowing too much about mining, but that not being a requisite in ITT, calls up Bob Koenig, then the head of Cerro Corporation, a major New York-based mining company active in Peru. Harkins asks Bob who is the best copper exploration guy he knows. Bob, a Harvard Club acquaintance of my father who had provided him an office at Cerro from time to time when he was in New York, who had been an early shareholder in Temagami, and who would soon become a director of Teck, says: "Keevil, he's the best there is. Knows geophysics like the seat of his pants. You have to get him."

So back in Toronto, the phone rings and:

HARKINS: Hi. You don't know me, but I'm Frank Harkins of ITT, and Bob Koenig says I have to get you.

KEEVIL: (pauses curiously): …. Yes?

HARKINS: Ok if I come up there tomorrow morning to get this thing going?

The ITT negotiating position having been established, we meet and propose a deal. Our consulting company, Geophysical Engineering and Surveys Limited, will send its "top international team" down to Chile to look for copper. ITT will put up all of the money, and Geophysical will have a 15 per cent carried interest in anything we discover.

"Okay," Harkins says, "sounds good to me." It sounded pretty good to us too. The mines in Chile were as big as they get. It was the kind of elephant country an explorer could only drool over. We were pretty confident that with our state-of-the-art technology and newfound top international team (a.k.a. Joe Frantz), we could find an elephant, and 15 per cent of that would certainly be a huge step forward for us. We agreed to devise and manage a three-year exploration program for the new joint venture.

Joe Frantz Goes to Chile to Start Looking for Copper

So Joe packed up his bags early in 1966 and, with his family and as much of a team as we could muster, moved to Chile to begin finding copper.

Joe was met in Santiago by Benjamin Holmes, ITT Chile's president and a fine gentleman, who had been the inspiration behind the idea of putting something back into the country beyond telephone wires. (In fact, as we would soon learn, the real problem they had was getting funds out of the country, and they hoped that by producing copper they could somehow convert their local currency profits into hard currency, but that story doesn't have the same socially correct cachet.) Benny proceeded to explain how he thought this had all come about, and he took Joe under his wing. They found a small office in Antofagasta, and the program was ready to get underway.

Interestingly, it was not Joe's first visit to Chile. Bill Brewer, who had been a geologist at Anaconda's huge Chuquicamata copper mine and later a PhD candidate with me at Berkeley, had been consulting for a company called Orengo Mines, owned by a Chilean entrepreneur named Andronico Luksic. Luksic owned a number of interesting copper prospects in northern Chile, including Brujulinas, Centinela, Conchi Viejo, and Chimborazo.

A few years earlier, Bill had written us in Toronto proposing that we visit some of Luksic's properties and consider becoming a partner with him by funding further exploration. One of these properties was Chimborazo, of which Bill wrote in a professional report: "It lies almost exactly in line with and halfway between Chuquicamata and El Salvador," which were two of the most important mines in Chile at the time. It was not a far-fetched observation, since there was copper on the property, and it does seem that there is a periodicity in the location of major mines in Chile. Joe had made a site visit to Chimborazo then, and there had been some additional correspondence between Brewer and us, but nothing developed at the time. Mounting a serious exploration program in Chile was beyond our financial capacity back then, and we were heavily involved in Canada, rationalizing our new interests in Teck-Hughes, Lamaque, Canadian Devonian, Gold-fields, and Silverfields.

But now, early in 1966, we had found a strong financial backer in ITT. Actually they had found us, to be more accurate, but in any event, the grass was looking quite a bit greener on the other side of the equator.

The three largest Chilean mines in operation then were Kennecott Copper's El Teniente, south of Santiago, and Anaconda's El Salvador and Chuquicamata in the northern part of the country. Chuqui was about 150 kilometres northeast of Antofagasta, and ITT had already taken out an exploration option on the well-known and easily accessible Sierra Gorda prospect near the main road between it and the port city. A shallow drilling program was underway, managed by one Sr Bakovic, the property vendor. Joe's time in the early months was taken up largely by monitoring this program, at the same time as getting organized in a new country, hiring local managers, drivers and geologists, and generally getting his feet wet in a very dry country.

The Sierra Gorda program moved on from the shallow drilling started by Bakovic to extensive geological mapping and geophysical techniques, including the relatively new IP, or induced polarization. Arrangements were made to borrow a larger diamond drill from Anaconda, and we completed a few deeper test holes with it as well. However, by mid-year we were growing pessimistic about the prospects for this property and were champing at the bit for newer opportunities. Joe had concluded that the property had low potential for a mineable, secondarily-enriched ore zone and that the underlying hypogene mineralization* was too low grade to be economic. Brewer, who was consulting for us by then, chimed in that it was "a very long shot, as the overall distribution of primary mineralization is spotty, weak and erratic," and, in a mid-year report, "I would strongly suggest that we get out of there and move on to fresher ground," and "my best guess for your next effort ... is the Chimborazo property."

We did abandon Sierra Gorda and began looking for better fish to fry.

---

* In Chile and elsewhere, "hypogene" refers to the original primary copper mineralization occurring in granitic or other rocks, whereas "supergene" or "secondarily-enriched" refers to copper mineralization that has been altered by exposure to surface conditions and is often of higher grade than the underlying hypogene rocks. Many of Chile's copper mines began production on higher-grade secondary mineralization and, in some cases, have gone on to mine the lower-grade primary rocks successfully in later years.

Trying to Educate ITT on Mining Deals

Starting up a new exploration joint venture with a much larger partner who had no experience in the business, although much more knowledge of the country, was never destined to be easy. A full year into the program, and after dropping Sierra Gorda, we were still wrestling with ITT over details such as how to structure deals to acquire potential new prospects. At meetings in New York and Santiago, we were told to try to conclude property acquisition agreements inexpensively, without leaving the vendor with any ongoing interest in his property, despite that being fairly standard practice in the mining business. It was not exactly the best way to get deals on really interesting prospects.

We were also directed to avoid doing joint venture deals with other mining companies, since ITT didn't like partners and wanted to be sure it would dominate any new mines we might eventually build. These were not easy restrictions to have to deal with, and for an exploration man it was like having to work with one hand tied behind his back, if not both.

There Be Otters in Chile

Nevertheless, we kept on looking. We hit upon one intriguing way to gain a lot of regional knowledge in a hurry, and that was to charter a plane and fly the length of the famous porphyry copper belt in its entirety, using the esoteric, high-tech, remote sensing system called "good eyeballs."

Copper minerals generally oxidize to bright colours of green and blue in the arid Chilean environment, and by flying across the country we might see evidence of mineralization that would let us focus in more closely on prospective areas to explore. Perhaps we would see not just direct copper colours, but also red ones indicating associated alteration minerals, or even just the presence of old tunnels that indicated someone had worked there before. It was not the first time this had been done, but it seemed a good start for us.

So, with the help of ITT's contacts, Joe arranged to charter a Twin Otter, a Canadian-built bush plane. Canadians are used to flying to lakes in the north woods in pontoon-equipped Otters or Beavers, whether to fish or to explore for minerals. How an Otter got into the Chilean Air Force was unclear, but it seemed it might be an effective way to reconnoitre the country.

The agreed cost would be only 500 escudos an hour, complete with a full Air Force crew.

In addition to allowing us to look out the windows for evidence of copper in real time, the aircraft was equipped to take aerial photos, with ITT-Geophysical's only extra cost to be the price of the film and processing.

It seemed the Air Force plane's existing setup was for black and white photography only, which wouldn't help much in showing colour anomalies. They claimed to be able to take colour photos and process them as well, but said they were unable to import the film. However, if we could bring in the film they could try to accommodate us. Arguably by now in cahoots with the Chilean Air Force, we were about to try to sneak in a few rolls to see how it worked.

In the end though, it turned out that in order to fly high enough to make the photography useful, and with the weight of a full Air Force crew on board, the Twin Otter would have to be modified, at great expense, so the plan was aborted.

A Multitude of Prospects

There were a lot of well-known copper occurrences available that seemed to deserve further exploration, many of which eventually became producing mines.

Sierra Gorda had been the one we had started on but dropped. It eventually became a producing mine in 2015, owned by the Polish company KGHM and our friends at Sumitomo Metal Mining.

Joe took a fancy to a nearby prospect called Lomas Bayas but wasn't able to negotiate an acceptable exploration option under our ITT guidelines. The property would lie fallow until years later, when Canadian miner Falconbridge acquired it and built a successful mine.

The same applies to El Abra. This was a known prospect of some merit, owned by Anaconda but apparently available had we, with ITT, been able to agree on the kind of deal terms that would be acceptable to us, as well as to the owners. Some years later Codelco, the Chilean national copper company, explored the property extensively, established an important copper resource and held an auction to attract industry partners to develop it. By then Teck was active in Chile itself and would be one of the bidders, although the winner would be Cyprus Amax.

We did drill a few shallow holes at Conchi Viejo, one of Andronico Luksic's properties. Results were interesting, but the copper content was considered too low-grade for the times. Today the Luksic's highly successful mining company, Antofagasta Minerals, is said to have an inventory of more than a billion tonnes of ore with economically mineable grades on the same property.

Another prospect we spent some time trying to acquire from Normines, its New York owners, was Cerro Colorado in the far north of Chile. Once again we could not agree on terms under the ITT guidelines, since the owners apparently wanted to retain an interest in any resulting mining operation. Years later, Cerro Colorado would be developed into a successful mine by a Canadian mining company, Rio Algom.

Los Pelambres was a copper prospect near the Argentina border that had been prospected as early as 1914 by William Braden, who was also responsible for discovering the Braden mine (now El Teniente). However, his work at Los Pelambres was limited to several short tunnels in oxide copper mineralization, and it did not locate the ore deposit that is today one of the world's largest copper mines. Joe Frantz had arranged a helicopter visit to examine Los Pelambres, but the only helicopter capable of taking him to 3,100 metres elevation was unserviceable and, by the time it was back flying, winter snows had set in and Joe never did get to make the examination.

We had another known prospect at high elevation called Quebrada Blanca (QB) on our list of targets, but at over 4,000 metres elevation it was considered too high at the time and we didn't actually visit it. QB would become a Teck mine 30 years later.

It really is amazing how many of today's mines in Chile were known as prospects back then. Some would not have been able to be built successfully, even if their size had been fully known, because at the time their lower copper grades were not economic to mine. Others were known as being in interesting copper-bearing areas but had not then been explored enough to determine whether there was a deposit of sufficient size and grade to be mineable.

In our second year we tried to reach an agreement to explore and develop Andacollo, a copper deposit at low elevation that had been known for years, but where ownership was split among a large group of independent landowners. It was recommended that we make a pact with one of the larger landowners, a Sr Zepeda, and ask him to assemble a reasonable land package for us. I did meet with him in Santiago and he was interested, but with so many separate, small landholdings, some of whose ownership had passed unrecorded through generations and was essentially indeterminate, the task proved insurmountable.

As Brewer wrote: "It is one of the best low-investment copper prospects in Chile but will probably never be developed, due to land title problems and a succession of heirs." That land ownership issue was eventually resolved a few years later with the nationalization of the copper mining industry. Noranda Mines acquired the mining rights from the subsequent government in 1976, as some properties were being denationalized, and explored it for five years before dropping it, due in part to pressure from social activist groups in Canada. Andacollo went through several more ownerships over the years before it was eventually acquired and a mine developed on the near-surface supergene ore by Aur Resources. Andacollo is now a Teck mine following our 2007 acquisition of Aur.

We did come within a few kilometres of what eventually became the Escondida copper mine, one of the world's greatest. At Brewer's urging, Joe Frantz again visited the Chimborazo property in October 1966, and he began a series of meetings with Andronico Luksic, the owner. Finally, an option agreement was actually reached and we were able to start exploring Chimborazo. It proved quite interesting, containing numerous showings of secondary copper minerals that had been moved there and redeposited from a primary source that was probably underneath or somewhere nearby. As it would turn out, Chimborazo is part of the same major, copper-bearing system as Escondida, a world-class copper mine that would be discovered next door some 15 years later.

We also reached an agreement to do some drilling on Sr Luksic's Centinela property, putting down five holes in 1968. Centinela is now a producing mine for Antofagasta Minerals.

We seemed to have been getting quite close in a number of places, although perhaps too early for some of the prospects with lower grades of copper, but the program would begin to wind down quickly for reasons other than geological results.

Epilogue

By this time, ITT was starting to get cold feet. There was political unrest developing, writing on the wall that it could read well, and we were told to start reducing our activities and deal off what properties we could. I wrote to about a dozen other mining companies in early 1968, offering them deals on a list of our joint ITT/Geophysical properties, and received polite expressions of interest but no offers. Chimborazo was not on that list, since we were just starting to drill it.

In mid-1969, with an election about a year away, President Eduardo Frei Montalva apparently sensed there was a mood for change developing in Chile. He announced pre-emptively that the Chilean government would take a 51 per cent interest in Chuquicamata and El Salvador by "negotiated agreement" with Anaconda, the owner. There would be other shoes to drop after that.

With our financing partner backing down, our program, well conceived and in a part of the world that was definitely elephant country due to the large size of its known mines, had to be abandoned. It would be more than 20 years before we would return to explore for gold and copper and to build our first Chilean mine at Quebrada Blanca.

CHAPTER 9

WHEN TECK WAS AN OIL COMPANY

Norman, you have to expose yourself to success.
John Downing

Not many people today are aware that Teck Corporation started as an oil company. When Teck-Hughes, Lamaque Gold, and Canadian Devonian merged in 1963, one of them had to be chosen as the ongoing company, and it was decided that Devonian, a Dominion-chartered company based in Alberta, was the appropriate choice. It was renamed Teck Corporation in light of the long history of the Teck name in Canadian mining.

What had been attractive about Devonian was of course the apparent longevity of its oil reserves and the cash flow from them, compared with the limited proven reserve life of the existing Group mines, Teck-Hughes, Lamaque, Pickle Crow, and Temagami. While we were still most interested in finding new mining opportunities like those in British Columbia, Grand Manan, Timmins, and Chile through various of the associated companies, our biggest single source of cash flow in the Group was oil from Teck's Steelman Field. We were miners first by training and inclination, but since we were producing oil, we felt obliged to explore for it, as well.

We Hire the Best Oil and Gas Team Around

When we acquired Canadian Devonian, we had realized our limitations. Our geological, engineering, and business expertise was all on the mining side and we needed to put professional oil and gas management into the company, so we did what seemed to be the right thing.

Dr Ted Link has been described as Canada's most important petroleum geologist of the first half of the twentieth century. He had discovered the Leduc oil field for Imperial Oil in 1947, starting the modern oil boom in Alberta, and was known as "Mr Oil" in the Calgary oil patch. Link had left Imperial in 1950 to form the consulting firm Link and Nauss, and he later teamed up with John Downing, a good geologist, and John Cooke, a petroleum engineer, to form the consulting firm of Link, Downing, and Cooke. By the early 1960s, when we were looking for talent, it had a well-deserved reputation as one of the premier firms in Calgary.

Ted Link was about to retire, so we hired Downing and Cooke, the balance of the firm, to run our oil business. Downing was to be in charge and responsible for the discovery of new oil fields, and Cooke was to monitor Gulf's operating activities. This was a fairly key job in the early days, because maintaining the Steelman Field's production required injecting water into the reservoir in what was called a water flood to force more of the oil to the surface. Cooke was competent and would do a good job for us on the production side.

And Expose Teck to Success

We were pretty green at the oil game, and Downing became a past master at convincing us of the merits of one exploratory oil play after another. He had that uncanny ability only a few are born with, sometimes described as being able to sell refrigerators to the Inuit. My father and I each had the equally uncanny ability, perhaps common to geologists and prospectors, of seeming to be perpetually in the market to buy those refrigerators. It really is amazing how many can pile up in one's garage before reality sinks in.

This was in the days before PowerPoint presentations, but John would come up with the prettiest slides and maps you could imagine. There would be seismic squiggles showing the virtual certainty of a buried dome under the surface, and for good measure there would be a cartoon oil field drawn in on the slide – just in case we didn't get it the first time.

Many years later, my successor would challenge our mining exploration geologists to "Dare to dream." John was daring us on the oil side, we were natural dreamers, and it seemed pretty easy. The geophysics, in the form of seismic data, rang our bells. It certainly looked a lot simpler than mining exploration, where we knew from experience that the odds were against us. Here we just had to drill down into that big pool of oil John had shown on his slide, and zap, you're rich.

Just to add to the certainty of it all, there would be a nearby pipeline shown on the slide. We would slaver suitably over the prospect and approve an exploratory drill hole, generally quite deep and expensive. Naturally, there would be no oil there. It would end up a dry hole, as they say in the oil patch.

But that wouldn't be the end of it. A few weeks later we'd be shown in another presentation why the oil-water interface had moved slightly west, and the hidden oil field with it. It was therefore obvious that we should drill another hole, with results almost as certain. Well, this still seems pretty easy. Slavering once again, we would drill it, and, you guessed it.

Eventually that first prospect and its succession of wells would be written off as bad luck, but by then we'd have two more slide shows in front of us, and it would start all over again. Some plays would be based on prospective stratigraphic pinch-outs instead of domes, and some on other esoteric rationales.

For a long time, several years, all of them seemed pretty impressive to us oil-inexperienced miners. As has been observed, "insanity is doing the same thing over and over again, and expecting different results." We did discover some additional oil, particularly in the Cullen field in Saskatchewan, but never another Steelman, or as much as we had hoped for.

Downing had a favourite saying about exploration: "Norm, you have to expose yourself to success." Well, we kept on exposing ourselves for quite a few years, until John had acquired the nickname Dry Hole Downing.

John eventually fired Cooke and finally, a year after that and after six years of mostly dry holes, I was sent out to Calgary to fire Downing. I was also asked to present the new oil vice-president to our assembled staff. It was, naturally, my uncle Alan Keevil. Alan, my father's youngest brother, had enjoyed a successful career with a major oil company, Chevron, and had risen to be the most senior exploration geologist in its Canadian operations. He was capable, occasionally like-minded, and, having experienced the inevitable disappointments that afflict all of us in the exploration business, wasn't as inclined to over-sell each prospect he came across. He would be a valued partner and board member until his retirement years later.

To be fair, Downing actually did go on to make some oil discoveries, but they were for his next employer that, ironically, was Lac Minerals. We, in the meantime, would begin looking for ways to exit the oil business as our mining opportunities grew, having finally determined that just because both businesses employed geologists and engineers to bring resources out of the ground, the business models, requisite talents, and experiences were not even remotely the same.

Epilogue

Consistent with what would become a hallmark of our deliberate way of always trying to do the right thing, but at times too slowly, this would take another 15 years, during which we would actually attempt a new takeover in the oil business, to be recounted later. Consistency is not necessarily a virtue, especially in a business that deals so heavily with chance.

I have to say we missed Downing, in part because I still thought there might have been oil buried somewhere in those slides. That guy could really sell.

In fact, ten years after the merger that created Teck Corporation and after a lot of dry exploratory holes, our 4,000 barrels a day of oil from the Steelman Field was still our largest single cash flow source in the Group. That would change with a surge of new mines in the works, but it was that steady income that had helped to keep us going in the meantime. John Leishman's persistence in talking us into joining the bidding for Devonian, and the fact we decided to make that one last bump to BA's bid, not really expecting to win, did pay off.

CHAPTER 10

FEELING THE STONES IN THE 1960S

We will cross the stream by feeling the stones.
Deng Xiaoping

The 1960s were formative years for our new Group, having gone from consultants and geophysical contractors to mine finders and operators, from copper producer to gold and silver as well, and then oil. We'd tried our best to find another mine around the major Kidd Creek discovery and had ventured into Chile for the first time, perhaps a bit early. We were nothing if not eclectic, and our style presaged that described in the aphorism from the future Chinese leader, Deng Xiaoping.

The names in the Group might change, and the pecking order. Having acquired Goldfields Uranium from Joe Hirshhorn, and then teamed up to form Silverfields, it seemed only natural that Temagami Mining Co. should be renamed Copperfields, and it was done. In the process, Temagami, which earlier had gone down to the bottom of the Group ladder, eventually acquired Goldfields and moved back up to the top, complete with its new name.

Wherever it stood in the intercorporate scheme of things, Copperfields' Temagami was our favourite mine, and the lake was where our kids would spend their summers while we chased sirens in Timmins, Chile, and elsewhere.

Copperfields Encounters Canadian Politics

As time passed, the mine proved to be more robust than most people had expected, including my old professor Bill Gross. Despite the small size of each of the high-grade copper ore lenses, Terry Patrick and the rest of the mine staff had been successful in finding additional ones almost on demand. Four new ore zones, numbers 24 through 27, were discovered in 1966 alone. This small mine was proving to be hard to kill.

However, we did have to suspend copper shipments for a while that year due to some bizarre decisions coming out of Ottawa. Copperfields' annual report described it this way:

An event of major importance to the company's future was the change in sale and shipping arrangements for copper concentrates from the Temagami mine, which had previously been sold to Noranda Mines Limited on a term contract basis. Our last contract expired on March 31, 1966. With world prices for copper in the past year substantially above those paid by Canadian domestic smelters (which are influenced by US price-fixing policies) the board of directors decided, after careful consideration and study, to change the marketing arrangements. In February 1966 an agency agreement was executed with Philipp Brothers (Canada) Ltd to sell our product on the world market starting April 1.

On March 1 the federal government announced restrictions on copper exports effective March 20, stating new permits would be granted on the basis of individual consideration, and Copperfields was advised it would be denied an export permit.

It was pretty clear that the new regulation, announced suddenly and out of the blue by Ottawa's mines minister Jean-Luc Pépin, applied to only one mine, Temagami, and benefited only one smelting company, Noranda. This raised "individual consideration" by Ottawa to a new level.

Copperfields refused to be cowed, and instead of shipping more copper concentrate to Noranda, which, as you may recall, didn't want it at all when we started production, we stopped shipments and stockpiled all of Copperfields' output pending a resolution. We said we would shut the mine down indefinitely, if necessary, rather than capitulate.

Six months later, Ottawa did rescind the hastily promulgated regulation, and we were able to resume sales under our new contract with Philipp Brothers. As it turned out, copper prices had dropped significantly by then, and the cost to the mine of this bureaucratic escapade was about $500,000, a huge sum in those times. It was our second unfortunate encounter with smelters, and we were gradually appreciating why it is that independent miners are sometimes a suspicious lot. It would not be our last.

Our end buyer in the new contract we had signed with Philipp Brothers was, coincidentally, Sumitomo Metal Mining of Japan, a company that we would become quite close to over the ensuing years.

A Little Old Lady Buys at the High

While Noranda was evidently better connected in our nation's capital than Copperfields, we were already getting some high-level international exposure, being in the in-boxes of John Diefenbaker, J. Edgar Hoover, Dwight Eisenhower, John F. Kennedy, and Nikita Khrushchev.

Back in Temagami's early days, its share price had climbed rapidly, as is often the case in such situations, and reached a high of $9. Interestingly, one of the few sellers at that price had been Cerro de Pasco's Bob Koenig. One of the few buyers at $9 had been a little old lady from Punkydoodles Corners, near Hamilton, Ontario. She was completely unknown to us, and had been talked into buying the shares by her broker. After the stock price fell from its peak and she had lost much of her investment, she took umbrage with us, writing Hoover and those other esteemed gentlemen. She described both our company and my father in terms best not repeated here, and threatened the worst.

Nothing came of this – each of the illustrious recipients of her letters presumably had bigger fish to fry – but every year she would show up at our Copperfields annual meetings. Given the threats, my father would station two of our best bodyguards, his old lab assistant Frank Wank and a draftsman, Frank Roach, on either side of her. Whenever she reached into her purse to pull out something the two Franks would stiffen up, until it was clear it was just a kerchief and not a gun.

After a few years of this being a non-event, and after I'd reported on some exploration program or other at one of the annual meetings, she came up to me as I was leaving the room and said she couldn't understand how an old reprobate like my father could have such a fine young son. I felt compelled neither to explain nor to argue. So the next year, when I had to chair the annual meeting because my father was away in Australia marrying off one of my sisters, we didn't bother to place the two Franks in their usual spot, thinking nothing would go amiss.

Turns out she had forgotten what a fine young son I was supposed to be, and for the first time she actually made good on her threats. She reached into her purse, took out a rock, and threw it at me. It missed, hitting our new young lawyer Bob Wright instead, which one wag suggested was what lawyers are for. It wasn't even a legitimate rock, but just an old piece of concrete from her backyard, but it seems to have been cathartic. The fine old lady never showed up again. Peace returned to Punkydoodles Corners and the valley.

Alchemy, Turning a Gold Mill into a Copper Mill

Meanwhile, we were continuing to look for exploration success, and one intriguing prospect we came across was Tribag near Sault Ste Marie in Ontario. Drilling by an entrepreneur named Cecil Franklin had come up with a style of copper mineralization that was unique in Canada, a breccia pipe more like the Cananea mine in Mexico than anything we had seen in our country.

Breccia pipes are generally shaped like cylinders or pipes standing on end, extending deep below the surface, appearing on maps to be roughly circular as they intersect the current surface of the earth. They were emplaced long ago as molten magma pushed up from below, and contain fragments of the surrounding rocks that became jumbled up in the pipe along with the remains of the magma as it cooled and solidified. At Tribag, as at Cananea, some of the copper mineralization occurred as little hats on top of the wall-rock fragments within the pipe, as though the cooling magma had pulsed up and down and the copper-bearing solutions had solidified in the gaps left above the fragments as they settled.

That description is probably clear as mud to the lay reader and not quite enough for the specialist, but the deposit was intriguing to us. It didn't hurt that Cananea was one of the major copper mines in Mexico, and a mine like it would be a very attractive target should we be able to prove one up at Tribag.

Since the surface expression of the breccia pipe was circular rather than linear, it had proven difficult to drill with a normal, geometric pattern. Instead of a neat series of parallel drill holes such as we use to test a more conventional, elongated deposit, the layout of the exploration drilling was more like a pin cushion. Holes were drilled from every which way toward the centre, many of them criss-crossing. It was a promoter's delight, because a new hole could be drilled from almost anywhere outside into the known middle and expect to get a good result. To be fair too, there wasn't any other pattern that would have been much better.

To quote Jack McOuat again, we knew how small it was, we just didn't know how big it was. The only way to find out seemed to be to sink a shaft and go underground to explore further from down below. It had worked for us before at Temagami, and it might again here.

Meanwhile, the Pickle Crow mine had turned out to be disappointing. Costs were increasing, the price of gold was still fixed, we didn't find a lot more gold, and it was decided to shut the mine and mill down. The mill was just about the right size for a modest, 500-ton-per-day operation at Tribag, and it could easily be retrofitted to process copper ore, so Teck agreed to purchase some Tribag shares to fund an underground test program, dismantle the gold mill at Pickle Crow, move it 200 kilometres by road and rail to Tribag, and reassemble it as a copper mill.

The rebuild was successful, and the new mine was put into production in 1967, but it would only last for a few years. Unfortunately, after a while we still knew how small it was, but also how big it wasn't. We did manage to locate a second, larger breccia pipe on the property, but it contained a lower grade of copper and was not economic to mine. Tribag is still geologically intriguing, with its similarity to Cananea, but it is fair to say that it was an outlier on our road to success.

R&D on Our DIGHEM AEM System Continued

While we had used an existing commercial airborne electromagnetic system in the Timmins rush, our efforts to build a state-of-the-art system in the Geophysical Engineering consulting unit (GESL) continued in the later 1960s. It was an off-again on-again program, because financing the research and development was always a challenge for a small private company with limited resources. But we did come up with an ingenious scheme to take advantage of special research incentives that were available then through a federal government program under which companies could deduct 150 per cent of R&D expenses against their taxable income. We didn't have much income in GESL, but the key for us was that partners of the taxpayer could waive their own tax deductions and assign these to the innovator.

So we arranged to take in two partners we knew well, and who were interested in the applicability of the research. Neither the Quebec government's Crown mining company, SOQUEM, nor a Japanese company, Dowa Mining, was taxable in Canada, and each was interested in helping to build better exploration tools. Each agreed to fund the R&D pro rata with us, and to assign their tax incentive credits to GESL. As long as we kept the total expenditures within our capacity, our net after-tax cost was low enough that we could keep the project going. It worked, the R&D continued, and Doug Fraser and his team were able to develop the new DIGHEM system that was clearly state of the art.

It turned out to be very successful technically, but we soon learned what Inco and others had learned before. Few companies alone can afford to keep a survey plane in the air, working full time, and follow up the results with the necessary, much more expensive ground search. The alternatives are to park the airborne survey equipment for most of the year; to form exploration syndicates that are able to fly surveys, and, by sharing the costs, follow them up in larger programs than any member could justify on its own; or to make the equipment available to the industry on a contract basis simply for fees, as Inco had done years earlier when it transferred its system to an independent contracting company.

We chose the syndicate route for a while, partnering with SOQUEM, Dowa, Metallgesellschaft, and others in various surveys, one of which would discover an interesting nickel deposit in Montcalm Township, west of Timmins. With reserves of 4.5 million tonnes grading 1.4 per cent nickel and 0.66 per cent copper, it wasn't considered large enough to be economic by the syndicate members at the time, but would later be developed by Falconbridge and is producing today.

That discovery proved the merits of Fraser's DIGHEM breakthrough, with his three mutually orthogonal receiving coils able to detect conductive bodies in three dimensions rather than just two. The Montcalm deposit happened to be parallel to our flight lines and was one of those normally difficult targets. In fact, Inco had flown the same area earlier with a conventional, single receiving coil system, with survey lines in the same direction we had used, and had completely missed detecting that ore body.

Eventually, we reverted to making the system available to the mining industry on a contract basis, and it became a successful independent company under Doug Fraser's direction. He constantly improved the equipment and kept it in the forefront of the airborne geophysical survey business for years. In 2015, Doug was made a lifetime member of the prestigious Society of Exploration Geophysicists for his efforts in this and other work in the field.

Our work with SOQUEM in building the DIGHEM system and in the exploration joint ventures resulted in a lasting personal friendship with its president, Côme Carbonneau, and this association would lead indirectly into an important new joint venture in the 1970s, in which together we would build a new mine near Chicoutimi, Quebec.

Acquiring Control of Area Mines

The syndicate that had discovered the Mattagami mine a few years earlier had consisted of Teck-Hughes, Area Mines, Leitch Gold Mines, Highland-Bell Copper, Iso Mines, and Dome Mines. Its failure to capitalize fully on its major discovery, handing control to Noranda, was a sore spot with us, and we continued to monitor the affairs of the other syndicate partners. All, like Teck, were by then just minority shareholders of the operating company, Noranda subsidiary Mattagami Lake Mines.

Dick Corbet, a well-known mining entrepreneur, had been the force behind Area Mines. He had chosen to begin retiring, and in 1965 agreed to sell his control block in Area to Teck. This, one of the many acquisition chances Ed Thompson had been researching when he wasn't out in the field, would turn out to be the first step in bringing together most of the old syndicate partners, and would help put us in a position to begin a major new mine expansion program of our own in the ensuing decade (figure 10.1).

The main attraction of Area to us had been the liquidity of its significant holding of Mattagami shares, important in those days when capital was hard to come by. In addition, Area had been exploring a copper prospect in the Gaspé Peninsula, a few kilometres from where I had worked with the GSC years earlier. The program had been a joint venture with another small company named Frobex, with each holding equal share interests in Wexford Mines Limited, the property owner. Frobex had a crew on the property, and we had agreed by handshake that it would continue managing the exploration program. Then, if anything interesting were discovered, we would manage the ongoing mine development and operation.

The exploration drilling was not easy, because the eventual ore deposit turned out to be shaped like a buried inclined cigar, and it was easy to miss it by drilling over, under, or beside it, rather than right into it. It would only be after many tens of drill holes that we would get a good handle on its geometry, and in the meantime it was a real case of hit and miss. In the circumstances, where it was never clear after one disappointing drill hole whether the next one might be good or bad, the share prices of Area and Frobex could be rather volatile. Never let it be said that we would play the

Figure 10.1
Norman Keevil, The Right Honourable Roland Michener, and Ed Thompson, 1967

market in those days, especially on inside information, but we wondered why the market sometimes seemed to know more than we did, often by a couple of days. It was quite strange.

By 1968, the drilling had advanced far enough that the outlines of the copper deposit were clear, and as is often the case, once we knew what it looked like, it was easy to look back and wonder why it hadn't been obvious from the start. By this time Frobex had increased its shareholding to slightly more than Area's, and more important, McIntyre Mines, its parent company, had also acquired a significant share position. Between McIntyre and Frobex they held just over 51 per cent of Wexford, and the game was up for the hand-shake agreement naming us as the mine operator.

In the end, McIntyre agreed to provide up to $15 million to finance a 2,500-ton-per-day mining and milling operation, and took control. Renamed the Madeleine mine, it would successfully mine 8 million tons of ore grading 1.08 per cent copper before closing in the early 1980s.

Exploring for Zinc at Restigouche

In the meantime, Teck Corporation had reached an agreement with New Jersey Zinc to continue exploring and, if successful, to place its Restigouche lead-zinc-silver property into production as a joint venture. This was the same property on which our GSC mapping party had discovered base metal sulphides back in the 1950s, and then covered up the evidence. Since then, New Jersey had acquired the property, drilled it, and defined a modest deposit that appeared sufficient to support a 1,000-ton-per-day mining and milling operation. Teck had agreed to undertake metallurgical tests and complete a feasibility study to assess the potential for economic development.

We would spend a fair amount of effort trying to make a go of Restigouche because, while small by today's standards, the deposit was of a size that could have made a difference to an emerging group like ours. Its resource of 3 million tons containing 13.5 per cent combined lead and zinc plus 4 ounces per ton of silver had appeared attractive when we entered into the feasibility study and development agreement.

However, the nature of the mineralization was such that it had been challenging to design a way to make two saleable concentrates, one for lead and the other for zinc (as we now do at the Red Dog mine in Alaska and as do most lead and zinc mines). Instead, it would be necessary to produce a single bulk lead-zinc concentrate, and there were only a few smelters in the world, known as Imperial Smelters, that could treat this kind of combined product.

We had reached the stage at which we understood the deposit well and were beginning to negotiate for the sale of the proposed new mine's eventual concentrate output. This would be our first extensive contact with Metallgesellschaft, which would later become an important shareholder of Teck.

"Metall" had been in the pyrite business for over 100 years and had expanded into lead and zinc refining. Its Toronto sales and purchasing representative, Bruno Petrenko, wanted to help negotiate a smelting and refining contract for the Restigouche concentrate, and we began discussions that would last for a couple of years, start to teach us something more about smelters and refiners, and eventually lead to our fine new lawyer, Bob Wright, showing us how to dance on tables.

Unfortunately, these Imperial Smelters were quite heavy consumers of power, and when oil prices began to skyrocket in 1973, their viability declined dramatically. Their smelting charges had to rise, and this made it less economic for potential concentrate producers such as Restigouche.

More important, we had concerns about potential effects on salmon fishing in the famous Restigouche River downstream from the site. We had received expert advice that, if any copper or zinc metal got into the river, it wouldn't actually kill the salmon, because they were too smart for that. They would simply turn back and return to the sea. However, the net effect, no salmon to be caught in the Restigouche, would have been considered just as bad for the fishermen and their guides, and in any case, it would not have been a good idea to test that expert hypothesis.

We eventually decided to abandon the plan to build a mine. From time to time, other owners have attempted to make a go of it, but it has continued to be a challenge.

EPILOGUE, PART TWO

Part 2 is titled Intermezzo for good reason. It recounts some of the diverse events that occurred as we felt our way between the important discoveries and acquisitions of the preceding years, and the start of the new Teck on a strong growth path in the 1970s, one that would continue for decades.

The seven years after the merger that created Teck Corporation had been an active period in which we participated in three new mines, of which Silverfields was a particular success. Our R&D activities resulted in the DIGHEM geophysical system that would go on to be one of the best of its kind.

We had carried out an exciting, if unsuccessful, exploration program around the major Texas Gulf find at Timmins, thwarted in the end by the discovery that it was, apparently uniquely in Canadian mining, a one-mine "camp." We were part of a Chilean exploration program that was hampered by the fact the mining industry there was about to be nationalized. And we drilled a great many exploratory holes looking for oil that wasn't where we thought it ought to be.

We had a strong team of miners for a small company with a dream of becoming something better. People like Art Foley, who managed the Lamaque gold mine and was on top of every prospector in the region; Max Leavens who ran Temagami; solid geologists like Ed Thompson, Fred Sharpley, Terry Patrick, Gord McIntosh, Doug Fraser, and many others; and financial people who tried to keep us on the straight and narrow. Jim Westell was chief financial cook and bottle washer (we didn't call them chief financial officers back then), and Dave Brown was keeper of the purse.

From a market perspective, we were hampered by the fact we had too many horses to ride, ranging from our private geophysical contracting company and a variety of small exploration and mining companies to oil and gold producer Teck Corporation. As the respected mining analyst Hank

Reimer said: "You never know what they're going to do next," or perhaps who was going to do what, and it was probably fair comment. We didn't always know either. Strangely, sometimes it would even change in midstream, as the stones moved.

Some of the companies such as Silverfields were strong market successes, and others not so strong. Teck Corporation, the flagship and largest company, had paid a moderate dividend throughout, but as 1970 ended, it had a market value of only $32 million, up from the $21 million it had started with eight years earlier. In contrast, our peers had grown substantially, with McIntyre up from $69 million to $411 million, Cominco up from $350 million to $460 million, and Noranda and Inco each tripling in size to $750 million and $3.1 billion, respectively. We could do better.

It was time for a new game plan, refocusing on building up the flagship.

PART THREE

THE NEW TECK TAKES SHAPE

The three key ingredients of any successful mining company are its ore reserves, its people who find, build, and manage the mines, and the financial strength that will enable it to grow. Part 3 will record how all three were upgraded in the 1970s, with Teck taking off in a spurt of new mine-building that would last, with inevitable ups and downs, for several decades.

Our focus will gradually swing to opportunities for large-scale mining in Western Canada, and we will move our head office and most of the management team there. There will be one major acquisition that leads to a lawsuit, but that will work out in the end, and others that lead to unexpected surprises of the right kind. Not wanting to be accused of being too predictable though, we will see a few other forays, friendly or not, with mixed results.

There will be debt crises and solutions, in one of which we find an interesting new partner in Metallgesellschaft.

Politics will rear its ugly head and we will see an unfortunate setback in our new home in British Columbia, a contemporaneous rise of expropriations (a.k.a. "resource nationalism") in some other jurisdictions around the world, a glaring intellectual error in Ottawa that nearly costs us what will become one of our most important new mines, and an intervention by a future prime minister that redeems our faith in governors. The end result of this era will be rampant inflation, apparently out of control despite many who try to lick it, until Paul Volcker manages to stem it. This will lead to a serious recession.

It will be a new and occasionally difficult era in which Teck takes off, sometimes in spite of the political-economic turmoil.

CHAPTER 11

EVOLVING STRATEGY, PEOPLE, AND PROSPECTS

The two most important days in your life are the day you were born,
and the day you find out why.
Mark Twain

As the decade ended, we knew what we had to do. We had to begin combining the main companies in the Keevil Mining Group so that there was a clear number one, making it the growth company of choice for investors. We needed to beef up our ore reserve position substantially with new mines, beef up our operating and engineering strength to help accomplish that, and increase our financial strength to fund it. That is all easy to say, but not necessarily easy to do.

This would be one of those times Andrew Grove would later call a *strategic inflection point.*

The New Engineering Team

In 1968, Andy Anderson, our vice-president for mining operations, chose to leave us to join McIntyre Mines. It was McIntyre that had managed to wrest control of our joint Madeleine mine discovery in the Gaspé, and he would take on the top mine operating role with that larger company. We didn't begrudge Andy going across the street, because it was a step up for him. As well, it gave us an opportunity to replace a good underground mining man with someone having more experience in the larger mines we hoped to build, particularly massive open pit ones such as those being developed in Western Canada.

After the success of Craigmont and Bethlehem in establishing British Columbia's modern open pit mining industry, Noranda had just taken it a step further by announcing plans to develop the Brenda copper-molybdenum deposit as a major, low-grade, open pit mine. This would be the wave of the future.

Naturally, I leaned toward finding someone from Placer Development, which had been seen as arguably the best mining company in Canada when I was working at its Craigmont mine, and which had a stringent engineering discipline that would complement our exploration and entrepreneurial side.

So I approached my old friend Bob Hallbauer, who had been open pit superintendent at Craigmont when I was there, and by this time was mine manager. Bob turned me down politely at first, but I knew his wife, Joan, well and took the opportunity to let her know about this "phenomenal opportunity." To my surprise she agreed it was just that, and was soon able to persuade him to take it. As she put it: "I told Bob that if he was ever going to go far in this business, he'd have to go to Toronto, at least for a while."

Frankly, I knew she was wrong, and that Bob probably would have ended up running Placer Development had he stayed there, but it was a sign of the times in British Columbia in the late 1960s. Toronto was thought to be where the action was, even though some of us in Toronto sensed that was about to change. Regardless, it turned out to be a great move for Bob, and of course for Teck. He would play a major part in building our company in the ensuing years, and I'm sure he enjoyed the rest of his life at Teck more than he would have running Placer. Also, he would actually return to British Columbia shortly, as would our whole company.

So Bob showed up in Toronto, and almost his first words were: "You guys have only got three small underground mines, and they each only have about two years of ore reserves left in them. How the hell do you expect to survive for long, let alone build a major mining company, out of that?"

It was a good question, not exactly lost on us because, of course, we had all been trying to discover more and better mines for a while. However, Bob had a way of stating the obvious that made a person take note. We'd been trying, gosh darn it, but we had to keep trying, harder and better, and, more important, get the job done. It would still take a while and a combination of luck and focus.

And a New Legal Team

Around the same time, another Bob had bobbed up in the person of Bob Wright, who we encountered fending off a rock in the last chapter.

My father had worked with a number of lawyers over the years, one of the earliest being Roland Michener, later The Right Honourable Roland

Michener, Governor General of Canada. "Roly" had incorporated Temagami Mining Company in 1954. Since then my father had dealt with John Aird, the senior partner of Edison Aird and Berlis, and the young Sir Michael Butler of the same firm. Over the years, Sir Michael gradually became the "go to" guy.

Then Michael chose to move west to Victoria, where we weren't yet, and before that had developed the habit of barging into my father's office without knocking. This sort of thing would serve to banish one to non-person status for a time, and Michael had his turn at being "Michael Who?" Having been Norm Who? myself at times, I knew the drill, as did Joe Who? and Bill Who? (a.k.a. Frantz and Bergey.) It was just part of the game, and if nothing else, it did tend to keep people alert.

During one of these episodes it seemed time to take on a new lawyer and George Jennison, one of our directors, recommended his son-in-law, Bob Wright, who was a new partner at the Lang Michener law firm. Bob had been a teacher before studying law and was only a few years into a legal career, but he was intelligent, articulate, exuberant, and only occasionally pedantic. As we learned later he also had a penchant for cutting his colleagues' ties in half as part of any deal-closing ceremony. The rest of us would take to wearing our very worst ties on such occasions.

Bob fit right in, and we will meet him soon at a significant deal closing, when he found an innovative way to get around a broken corporate seal. He would also play a key role in designing our dual class share structure, with multiple as well as single voting shares, as described in chapter 13. He would leave us temporarily for a stint running the Ontario Securities Commission (osc) from 1989 to 1994.

Bob Wright would return to Teck after his time at the osc, becoming vice-chairman and lead director until his retirement in 2007. Michael would resurface as "Michael Again" many times, not the least of which when Bob himself occasionally became Bob Who?

The two Bobs, Hallbauer and Wright, would become key players in helping create the next incarnation of the new Teck.

Adding Financial Strength and New Metal Prospects

Two companies we had been watching for some time were Karl Springer's Leitch Mines and Highland-Bell Resources, each of which had been members of the Mattagami Syndicate with Teck, and still held major share positions in Mattagami Lake Mines Limited. As with Area Mines, they had been high on our list of acquisition targets for a while. However, every time we broached the idea of buying him out, Karl had turned us down, preferring to keep active in the business.

Karl had been a giant in the Canadian mining scene. He had been one of the founding members, in 1932, of the Prospectors and Developers Association, and had been associated with a number of mines including Barymin, one of the largest barite mines in the world, Granduc copper, Leitch gold, Beaverdell silver, Canada Tungsten, and the Mattagami Syndicate he had led.

Leitch had been front and centre in that TGS lawsuit, described in chapter 7, which was finally decided in favour of TGS based partly on some legal principles, but largely on findings of fact and the apparent credibility of witnesses, as seen by the judge. This was a blow to Springer, a straight arrow whom some felt may not have wanted to proceed with the case in any event, but had been forced to by the stock market speculators. Now, rightly or wrongly, his old friend and valued employee had been discredited by the judge.

Karl seemed to lose his enthusiasm and one day in late 1969, as he was about to turn 70, told his sidekick Fred Hall that he was now prepared to sell. Fred was well aware of our long-standing interest and arranged a meeting. Karl came over to my new home on Glen Edyth Drive in Toronto that, ironically, I had recently purchased from Area's Dick Corbet. He enjoyed a lunch of fresh bay shrimp in our backyard, and agreed to sell his control block in both companies to Teck. Perseverance had paid off.

Our interest in these two companies had been to consolidate their blocks of Mattagami shares with those already held by Teck and Area, for a combined 783,000 shares and a market value of $23 million. While small by today's measures, it was important, giving us a much stronger working capital base from which to build. It was part of the third side of the necessary mine-building trio of people, ore reserves, and financial strength.

Sometimes acquisitions turn out to be just what was expected, sometimes better or worse, and sometimes they bring unknown unknowns to light. We will see some of each as the Teck story unfolds, but Leitch and Highland-Bell would be little jewel boxes, and very timely.

Highland-Bell also owned the Beaverdell silver mine south of Kelowna, BC, a mine that, like Teck-Hughes, had started in 1913 and had produced continuously ever since. While it would never be a cornerstone mine for Teck and is long forgotten by most, it was a fascinating small operation that show-cased the talents of its main man, one Bruno Goetting. Bruno was at the same time the mine manager, mine engineer, mine geologist, and mechanical superintendent. That Beaverdell continued producing silver until 1991 was a lasting tribute to this one remarkable miner.

After Bruno passed, his widow, Lily, would send us an old photo of scenes at the mine every year at Christmas. In 2011, I received a poignant card with a general photo, saying she had run out of old photos of Beaverdell. She said she had never wanted to leave Germany and was never comfortable at the mine, but Bruno had been happy.

Leitch also owned a hidden gem, in the form of 63 per cent of a zinc prospect in Newfoundland, with the US mining company Amax Inc. holding the balance. It had been discovered by Springer's prospecting team using our old favourite tool, geochemistry, and had been farmed out to Cominco to finance ongoing exploration several years earlier. Cominco's option was about to expire, and it had asked Leitch to renew this for a further period so it could continue exploring the prospect.

Frankly, we were not particularly interested in zinc at the time, focusing more on gold and copper, not to mention oil, and our initial inclination was to agree to the extension and let Cominco keep exploring it. However, one of our geologists, John May, pored over the maps and took a fancy to the prospect. The drilling to that point had indicated a deposit that was relatively low grade in zinc, but did include a few higher-grade drill holes. John felt there was a chance that we could extend the high-grade part of it with some more work, and he convinced us to turn Cominco down and explore it ourselves after the option expired.

John was right. We resumed drilling and were able to prove up an economic zinc deposit. It would become an important new mine for Teck, the first of a series that would begin to transform the company.

Discovering Niobium, a Joint Venture with SOQUEM

Meanwhile, Ed Thompson had been working on a uranium exploration program in Quebec. Uranium was coming into one of its periodic phases of being in vogue, and a number of companies were using regional geophysical surveys to search for new deposits that might be mined. In our case, we had been flying airborne radiometric surveys and had detected a strong anomaly near the town of St Honoré. However, when we investigated further we found that SOQUEM, the Quebec government's mining exploration company, had staked claims covering the anomaly a week earlier. They had beaten us to it, and that normally would have been the end of it.

SOQUEM had been running a lower budget radiometric survey of its own, simply driving along country roads with a radiometer rather than using an expensively equipped aircraft, as we had. Fortunately for them, the anomaly occurred in rocks beside a road. If not for that, we and not they might have first staked the claims and found the mine.

SOQUEM put down a few drill holes and found that the anomaly reflected a radioactive carbonatite, an unusual type of vertical, pipe-like intrusive rock that often carries exotic metals and minerals. The anomaly was actually due to modest amounts of thorium rather than uranium, but this carbonatite also contained significant amounts of the rare metal columbium.

Columbium was then a metal with a small market but potentially interesting high-tech uses. Some of its alloys are important in the field of superconductivity, in which metals cooled to very low temperatures approaching absolute zero lose all resistance to electricity conduction. This has applications in high-speed superconductive rail transportation, long-distance electrical transmission, and magnetic resonance imaging (MRI) machines used in the health care system, as well as other exotic areas such as in the quantum computers now undergoing research and development.

The element columbium is number 49 in the periodic table. It is in fact the same as the element niobium, with the two having been discovered about the same time by different scientists on different continents. The names were used interchangeably until the middle of the last century, when niobium was made the official name. However, in Quebec it was still being referred to as columbium, largely because of an operating mine near Oka named St Lawrence Columbium.

As Ed Thompson wrote in a memoir:

The mandate of Soquem was to encourage exploration in Quebec and in 1969, just before Christmas, a small ad appeared in *The Northern Miner* soliciting a bid for a joint venture proposal in order to further develop the project. We were pretty broke at the time but it never stopped us from trying. I asked permission to make a bid and Norm approved.

It was the cheapest, low-ball bid I ever made, something along the lines of $100,000 in expenditures in the first year, an optional $500,000 in the second with Soquem to match $1 for our $3, and $1 million in the third year with Soquem matching $1 for our $2, after which we would have earned a 50 per cent interest. Total time spent was probably two hours and I sent it off with no further approvals. The bids were to be in by January 5 or 6.

To my surprise and horror, a notice came back early in January saying that ours was the only bid in on time (although several bids came in later, including one from Quebec miner St Lawrence Columbium, whose president had been in Europe over Christmas).

Our old friend Côme Carbonneau, SOQUEM's president, flew in from Quebec City and met with Ed and me for a brief discussion and lunch. The deal was approved, the lawyers drew up a short agreement, and we had our 50/50 joint venture. I think that in addition to our bid having been the only one to be submitted in time, the fact we had worked together on developing the DIGHEM equipment, and in the joint venture surveys using it, had helped establish a relationship that went a long way toward getting the deal done.

As usual we had limited available funds, but Copperfields still had some cash flow from the Temagami mine, and a need to acquire a new mining operation before that first one ran out of ore. It was decided to put the St Honoré project into it, perhaps confirming analyst Hank Reimer's perennial complaint about not knowing which company would do what next.

We did more drilling, eventually establishing a resource of 40 million tons grading 0.76 per cent columbium oxide. To put this in perspective, the 40 million tons was impressive, over double the size of the important 19 million tons Mattagami deposit, but columbium was a more exotic metal than copper or zinc, with a small and uncertain market. It was a substantial discovery, but one that would take a lot more work to make it economic to develop.

We followed this surface drilling with an underground program to get a look at the ore, along with metallurgical studies. These showed that the project could be economic, provided the current price environment for columbium (a.k.a. niobium) held up. As is often the case in mining, future commodity pricing would be the key risk to assess. We will come back to this in chapter 13.

The Highmont and Schaft Creek Copper Prospects

Also late in 1969, we negotiated two new exploration deals in British Columbia, with Silver Standard Mines Limited and Highmont Resources. Each involved large-tonnage copper-molybdenum deposits that had potential to become new mines.

Silver Standard had operated a silver mine near Hazelton for 11 years beginning in 1947, and since then had been one of the more active junior mining company explorers in the province. Run by Ridgeway "Tugboat Bob" Wilson, it employed a number of highly focused prospectors, geologists, and engineers in a region where we then had a limited presence on the ground.

Ed Thompson had been spending some time in BC but felt we needed a more permanent face in the province and recommended that we make an initial investment in Silver Standard. We agreed to provide $1 million for exploration on its properties over the next two years, earning shares in return.

Silver Standard's prospectors did discover copper on the Red Group prospect in 1971, and two years later this was unitized into the Red Chris claims by combining it with a property held by another company. The property was farmed out to Texas Gulf and others over the ensuing years and now, finally, is being developed as a significant open pit copper mine by Imperial Metals.

Our principal interest in the company and its team was because of a large copper prospect in northwestern British Columbia called Liard Copper. Discovered in 1957 by a syndicate led by Silver Standard, the property had been farmed out to American Smelting and Refining Company (ASARCO), the option had been dropped, and then it was farmed out again to Hecla Mining.

Drilling had indicated a resource of some 500 million tons with interesting grades of copper and molybdenum as well as values in gold and silver. It was remote, complex, and relatively low-grade, but Bob Hallbauer and I had high hopes for expanding it and making a mine there as time went on.

Schaft Creek didn't measure up to our economic tests at the time due to grade and remoteness, but we have continued to monitor and explore it from time to time since, as the average copper ore grades mined around the world have been falling, lower-grade historic deposits can often assume greater importance.

But back then the action in large-tonnage copper prospects was in the more accessible southern part of British Columbia. This was led by Bethle-

Figure 11.1
Joe Frantz and Bill Bergey, key Keevil Group geologists, 1970

hem Copper and the discovery by Cominco of the Valley Copper prospect in the Highland Valley, Brenda Mines developing the first large-scale open pit copper mine in Canada near Kelowna, and Egil Lorntzen's Lornex copper project just south of Valley Copper (see figure 11.1).

A Vancouver entrepreneur named Bob Falkins was exploring another copper prospect to the southeast of Lornex, and in that same eventful year Teck reached an agreement to explore and develop his Highmont property. It would take another decade for us to get it into production, what with other opportunities as well as a new socialist government and a serious recession getting in the way, but it would become the fourth in a sequence of new mines that the new Teck Corporation would begin building in the 1970s.

Epilogue

The year 1969 had been a very good one, presaging what seemed likely to be an exciting future for us. Metal prices had been volatile but generally strong, buoyed by economic growth in Japan and Korea, in an early version of what would later, in the twenty-first century, be called a "super-cycle." We had beefed up our mining engineering side and assembled the seeds of the potential new mines that would begin to change the future of the Keevil/Teck Mining Group, being Newfoundland Zinc, the St Honoré columbium project, the Highmont copper-molybdenum project, and the Schaft Creek prospect. We had also augmented the working capital that would allow us to acquire and develop further discoveries. It was one of those years that comes along occasionally, where a number of good opportunities surface all at the same time.

It was a lesson we would remember for years. In mining, opportunities that will make a real difference, the so-called game changers, are few and far between, and are just not there every year on demand, but when they do occur it can often be in bunches. One must be able to recognize them and be in a position, financially and otherwise, to act when they do occur.

Equally important, the best opportunities are seldom as obvious when first grasped as they may appear to have been years later, with the benefit of hindsight. Of these four, Schaft Creek seemed at the time to be the most exciting, while Newfoundland Zinc and Niobec were smaller and not in any way certain, yet those two became our most important mines for a time. As John Downing said, we have to expose ourselves to success, and hope that there are some winners in the mix.

CHAPTER 12

DIVERTIMENTO: TALES FROM THE WILD WEST

There are strange things done in the midnight sun
By the men who moil for gold.
Robert Service, "The Cremation of Sam McGee"

Although we had just laid the groundwork for three probable new mines and had brought on board one of the best operating people that we knew to help make that happen, three strange, unexpected adventures lay ahead of us when more opportunities came knocking in Western Canada.

One was an offer we made to invest in a target company that, while it was rejected, engaged a number of players that would eventually become part of Teck in different ways. The second involved an almost inadvertent investment that was accepted, began inauspiciously, but in the end brought us an important new mine that would be another game changer for the company. The third saw us take another stab at diversifying into oil which, luckily, didn't pan out.

In each of the first two the situation evolved over the ensuing decade, and we will follow them through in this chapter, even at the expense of having to return later to other events that were occurring while these played out.

Teck Offers to Invest in Bethlehem Copper

A month after we had acquired control of Leitch and Highland-Bell, as well as our deals on St Honoré, Silver Standard, and Highmont, there were rumblings of a chance to expand our interests out West in a bigger way.

Bethlehem Copper had come far since Spud Huestis's discovery. With financing provided by Sumitomo Metal Mining, it had completed construction of a solid new, open pit copper mine in 1962. A second open pit mine had been developed since and milling capacity increased from 3,000 to 15,000 tons per day. It was doing very well.

A short while earlier, Bethlehem had agreed to swap some unexplored claims for a nearby property it needed for waste disposal, with Cominco-controlled Valley Copper Mines being the counterparty. Valley Copper had then drilled the unexplored lands and discovered a major copper deposit underlying them. The grade at 0.4 per cent copper was lower than that being mined at Bethlehem, or anywhere else in the world for that matter, but drilling had shown a resource of close to a billion tons, about 20 per cent of which was on land still retained by Bethlehem. Spud Heustis's prediction that "there's a billion tons up there in the Valley" when we had met him at Craigmont years earlier had turned out to be true, and in fact would eventually prove to be an understatement.

By 1969, Cominco had begun discussions with Japanese interests about the possibility they would provide financing for Valley Copper as well as agree to purchase its copper concentrate production. The group included trading companies Mitsubishi, Mitsui, and Marubeni and represented a consortium of six Japanese smelters that proposed to finance $55 million out of a proposed capital cost of $128 million. The consortium would also commit to purchase 188,000 tons of copper concentrates a year for ten years. This would be similar in structure to the financing and concentrate purchase agreement Sumitomo had given to Bethlehem years earlier.

While we weren't familiar with the status of the latest Japanese discussions, we had been intrigued with Bethlehem for some time. Its original mine was doing well and there was the upside potential of its retained portion of the Valley Copper deposit. We had been exploring more and more in British Columbia, and it seemed a good candidate for us to try to establish a position in an operating mine in the province.

One Friday in November 1969, a month after the Leitch deal and after a large run-up in the Bethlehem share price the previous day, the *Toronto Star* reported that Bethlehem had admitted mysteriously that it was "negotiating with a foreign company to issue a substantial block of treasury shares at $21 a share." It said that its board would meet the next Monday to conclude the deal. It was clear that we should either make our move or forever hold our peace. It was time to fish or cut bait.

We guessed, correctly as it would turn out, that the "substantial block" meant 1 million shares, which would have represented 15 per cent of the company's issued capital following the transaction. This would be the second-largest shareholding in Bethlehem, and, assuming we could work with

Sumitomo, which owned just over 30 per cent as a result of its original spon-sorship of the company, we would be in a position to have considerable in-fluence in helping to build that company for the future.

So on Saturday, I flew out to Vancouver with our lawyer, Sir Michael Butler, while my father and his financial advisors lined up $21.5 million in financing from the Bank of Commerce. We delivered our offer to Bethlehem first thing Monday. It was for 1,000,000 shares at a price of $21.50 a share, which as it turned out was a premium of half a million dollars over the mystery bid. We offered to meet with the Bethlehem board, and explain how anxious we were to join them in the spirit of good fellowship and such things.

Needless to say, it was a shot out of the blue to the Bethlehem directors, who declined our offer to meet, and it seemed to cause considerable con-sternation among them. It was unexpected, and as one Toronto broker who had some interest in the outcome later described it, we had "lobbed it over the transom." Presumably he considered this bad form. That did seem a bit pejorative and was the first I had heard a legitimate offer described that way. In later years, we would have been described as an interloper.

The things people say!

The Bethlehem board meeting dragged on for three days. Reports were that Sumitomo, the principal shareholder, without whose support the com-pany might not even have existed, was unhappy with the proposed transaction that would now dilute its own share position. Sumitomo may have supported the Teck offer, or wanted to match it. Memories differ. Management was nat-urally unhappy with our offer, which upset its carefully laid plans. There was a strange scent of sulphur and brimstone seeping out over the transom.

The meeting was adjourned for a couple of weeks without reaching a decision, before reconvening in Hawaii to settle the matter. In the end the board accepted the original $20 deal, which, it turned out, was with The Grangesberg Co. of Sweden. But this was not before "The War of the Point-ing Fingers," as one participant later put it, threatened to break out be-tween chairman McLallen of Bethlehem and Sumitomo president Kenjiro Kawakami.

Following the issuance of the new shares, Sumitomo was still the largest shareholder but at a reduced level, with Granges now holding 15 per cent. Whether that was the purpose or not, management was suddenly in the catbird seat, sitting pretty between two large shareholders instead of being considered beholden to one. But catbird seats may not always last.

The legendary Kawakami-san, by then president of Sumitomo Metal Mining, had been senior managing director when he negotiated the initial Bethlehem financing in 1960, and I had the opportunity to visit him in Tokyo a few months after our unsuccessful offer. While he was politely circumspect about the extent to which he had supported our bid, his disappointment in the outcome was palpable. His company, and he personally, had considerable pride of authorship about Bethlehem, having financed it so that it could become British Columbia's largest copper mine for a time.

Our meeting led to a close friendship that has evolved between our two companies and their successive leaders, and has survived the test of time for over four decades.

Bethlehem continued to try to look for new opportunities to expand and diversify, with Keith Steeves and Hank Ewanchuck, a good finance and engineering team, leading the charge. While they reviewed a lot of possibilities, it's fair to say that the company was well aware of the fact it could be put in play again at any time, and the preoccupation with self-preservation may have held it back.

Sumitomo eventually decided to end its association with Bethlehem and sold its shareholding to Newmont Mining Corporation two years later, in 1972.

Meanwhile, Cominco had concluded it could not justify building a new mine and dedicated concentrator on its Valley Copper property, and its best hope of capitalizing on its large copper deosit lay in acquiring Bethlehem and its established facilities.

By 1977, Cominco had purchased 37 per cent of Bethlehem in the open market and was clearly chasing full control. Granges by this time was in need of cash and wanted to sell its Bethlehem position. It told Bethlehem management of its decision and the price it wanted, and said it would hold off for a while if Bethlehem thought it could find a white knight, a new shareholder acceptable to management, to buy Granges out. Obviously, if Cominco had been able to buy that large block from Granges, it would have had absolute control, and the catbird seat game started back in 1969 would have been over.

Keith Steeves was carrying the defensive ball and tried to get help from brokers in Toronto, New York, and London to find a buyer. They all told him that Cominco and Canadian Pacific were too important as big potential clients for them to help Bethlehem out.

The Granges offer to give Bethlehem time to find a friendly buyer was to close on a Monday, and six days earlier Keith had cold-called the chief financial officer of Gulf Resources in Houston, Texas to see if it would be interested in buying the Granges shareholding. That led to meetings in Houston between Keith, Hank Ewanchuk, and Gulf officials over the next two days, and on Friday morning Bob Allen, the Gulf chairman, called Keith into his corner office to ask what he had to do to close the deal.

"Just buy the fershlugginer shares!" Keith thought, but instead he phoned the Granges executive in Paris who was in charge of the sale, and it was agreed he would meet Mr Allen on the weekend. So the Gulf corporate jet flew to Paris and the deal was closed on Sunday, just in time. Newmont also declined to submit to Cominco at the time, and Bethlehem survived for another day.

In 1980 though, both Gulf and Newmont sold to Cominco for $37.50 a share and the game was up. Cominco would acquire the balance and swallow up Bethlehem. Keith Steeves, who had been in the Bethlehem boardroom when we tossed our offer in, and who had led the anti-Cominco fight, refused to join Cominco and instead came over to the wild side in Teck. He soon began to enjoy his new life on the other side of that transom, and became one of our key managers and directors for over 20 years, as well as a close friend.

Epilogue

Cominco never did build a mill to develop Valley Copper, but began mining it in a small way and shipping ore up the hill to the Bethlehem mill. The Valley Copper ore body would eventually be combined with other facilities in the area, establishing the current Highland Valley Copper Partnership and the largest metal mine in Canada, as we shall see in chapter 24.

Looking back from the vantage point of the twenty-first century, somewhere, in some alternate universe, the Teck offer was accepted and Sumitomo stayed on as a shareholder. Cominco didn't acquire Bethlehem, perhaps we didn't acquire Cominco, and the current mining world might be quite different.

The Strange Tale of Brameda Resources

Stepping back to when the Bethlehem saga was about to begin, as the 1960s ended the major Valley Copper, Lornex, and Highmont prospects were in the news and the new Brenda mine was in the final stages of construction near Kelowna, British Columbia. Built by Noranda, Brenda was the brainchild of two of its top exploration and development people, Morris Menzies and Bernie Brynelsen. With Brenda under construction, the two left Noranda to strike out on their own, teaming up with lawyer Jacob Austin and an entrepreneur named Merv Davis to form a new company called Brameda Resources (figure 12.1).

The price of copper had been strong for much of the previous few years, peaking twice, in 1966 and 1969, at a level that in constant dollars was almost as high as attained in the recent China-based "super-cycle" years. Fueled by burgeoning Japanese demand, and perhaps pre-saging the later events of 2006, the strong copper price had led to a feeding frenzy by investors in mining.

Brameda was able to raise the then unheard-of sum of $12 million in an initial public share offering at $10 a share in June 1969. It was ironic that it did this on the Toronto Stock Exchange, despite the Exchange seemingly having been trying to avoid speculative new issues since its Windfall fiasco. This may attest to the image Bernie and Morris had at the time, or to the innate inconsistency of brokers, or both.

With the reputation of its illustrious founders and a strong new mining market, Brameda attracted some heavyweight financial managers and engineers who came over from the Placer organization, and an impressive board of directors, including Latham Burns, scion of the Toronto-based Burns brokerage family, and Vernon "Moose" Taylor Jr, a well-known oil man and mining dabbler out of Denver who was also on the Placer board.

In addition to copper, coal was very much in the news during the new western mining boom. Kaiser Resources had started building the Balmer mine in the Elk Valley, and McIntyre's Smoky River and Fording's new mines were in the works. Each of these, as with the copper mines, was designed to feed the booming Japanese market, and was encouraged by Japanese financing.

The plan was that Brameda would capitalize on opportunities in these two hot commodities. But it had great ambitions and went a bit further. It quickly found itself with an eclectic mix of assets, some even involving mining properties.

Figure 12.1
Brameda Resources' Bernie Brynelsen, Jack Croll, Merv Davis, and Jacob Austin

These included the Churchill copper mine under construction near Fort Nelson, a silver property in Arizona, the Casino copper property in Yukon, 14 mineral properties in Mexico, an industrial processing company called Ionarc, a sulphur company called Thermochem, a titanium property in Quebec, oil and gas properties, forest licences, purchase of the established consulting firm Chapman, Wood and Griswold, and some interesting coal properties in northeastern BC. It also owned a floating restaurant on a derelict ship tied up beside the Bayshore Hotel and a golf club manufacturing company, both contributed by Davis.

The new company had started by flying high, much like Icarus. As Keith Steeves later recounted, Bethlehem president Pat Reynolds came into the office one morning to say he was golfing in Palm Desert that day, but would be back that evening. Keith asked how he could manage that, and the reply was: "Merv Davis is flying me down on Brameda's private jet for a game."

Perhaps not too surprisingly, Brameda soon ran into difficulties during the financial meltdown of early 1970. The $12 million financing it had started with had almost disappeared, and the company was burning cash at the rate of a million dollars a month. By then it had loans that were causing consternation at the Toronto-Dominion (TD Bank). The bank's "rainmakers" who had loaned the money had been moved aside, and the "workout people" were in charge.

Eventually, the bank asked Teck to consider putting in $3 million of fresh financing and to take over management of the company. Ed Thompson wisely recommended we take a pass on it, but Bob Hallbauer and I were sent out to Vancouver to size it up, anyway.

Without going into too much sordid detail, after the review our conclusion remained the same. Churchill stunk, the Sukunka coal property contained excellent coking coal but it would have to be mined by underground methods, with which we had no expertise or confidence, the Casino drilling was suspect and the project not likely economic at the time, the golf clubs weren't very good, the finances were even worse than expected, and the floating restaurant was about to sink. And that was the best part of it.

So we call back and tell my father: "Don't do it." "Too late," he says. "I just had lunch with Latham Burns and Moose Taylor and told them we'd do it. It's going to be shared by Area and Highland-Bell."

Oops.

Our new lawyer, Bob Wright, had been in Germany, still trying to negotiate the sale of zinc-lead concentrate from the putative Restigouche mine, but he was called back to do the Brameda agreement and attend the immediate closing. It was amazing how fast that all happened. It was as though, unlike Bethlehem, this time someone out there in BC really wanted our money, *and was determined to get it as soon as possible!*

With the agreements prepared and laid out on Brameda's boardroom table for signing and sealing, a serious problem developed. The handle on the seal was broken and we couldn't close the deal. Hallbauer and I were about to leave without the prized trophy, but as luck would have it nothing would deter Wright. He just jumped up on top of the table, put the lower half of the seal on each signature page in succession, and stomped it with his foot.

So Bob Hallbauer moved back to Vancouver after only two years in Toronto, charged with trying to work his way through this thing.

We closed down the golf club manufacturing plant. We did some more drilling at Casino but couldn't come up with a feasible development plan. We tried to keep Churchill going, but copper prices worsened and we had to close it down the next year. We had to lay off a number of financial people, some of them excellent ones who'd been at Placer earlier, but whom Brameda could no longer afford, and of course we had to terminate its accounting firm and consolidate that work with our own accountants, Coopers and Lybrand. That caused a certain amount of friction in the Vancouver community, with both personal and business repercussions for a couple of years. It was as though the big guns from Toronto had come in to mess up the works, although it would be fair to say that this particular mess had preceded us.

We were able to keep some first-class engineers and a very good young accountant named Bob Shipley, who survived what others may have seen as a purge. Shipley was the only one who knew where the bills were – actually locked away in a drawer in his desk – and he would stay with Teck until his retirement many years later.

Sukunka coal seemed to be the best of the prospects in the Brameda stable. Bob Hallbauer wasn't enthused about taking on an underground coal operation, but with the quality of coal being particularly good, we wanted to give it a chance. Teck agreed to provide some interim funding, and by mid-1971 we had reached an agreement with Brascan under which that company, and an Australian partner with underground coal expertise, could earn a 60 per cent interest in the property by providing further exploration and development funding and arranging financing for a mine capable of producing at least 2 million tons a year of saleable coking coal.

Epilogue

Brascan spent a lot of time and effort trying to make a go of it, but they eventually walked away from the project empty-handed. One other Brameda property, Burnt River Coal, was put into production 25 years later, but is now closed. Looking back now from 45 years onwards, none of Brameda's other properties ever developed into significant operating mines, but there are companies that have been active recently on what was the Casino property, and also once again on Sukunka. Hope springs eternal.

Brameda was one of those stories that seems to occur at the tops of markets from time to time. A bunch of previously successful people get together, led perhaps by a pied piper, and attempt to expand on their prior successes in some new, bigger, and untried fashion. It would happen again 10 years later, when so many previously successful people would be wiped out in the severe 1981 recession. That too would not be the last time.

What became of that group of people who were caught when Icarus flamed out?

Bernie stayed on as chairman of Brameda, and my lasting memory of him is flying back from Toronto to Vancouver one evening on Air Canada flight 149. Bernie had a rock with him, perhaps from Casino, and he spent the whole flight walking up and down the aisles showing it to people. I'm sure we got some new shareholders on that flight. He was later inducted into the Canadian Mining Hall of Fame, deservedly so, for his fathering of the successful Brenda mine and other mines for Noranda.

Morris faded away, a shy man to start with and never a promoter. Davis moved to Los Angeles with the boat, which eventually did sink. Ross Fitzpatrick, who had been the public relations guru for Brameda, went on to found a very successful Kelowna winery and become a senator. Jacob Austin quickly resurfaced in Ottawa and became deputy minister of Mines to Minister Joe Green, then chief of staff to Prime Minister Pierre Trudeau, and eventually a senator as well.

In due course we would discover and build the Bullmoose coal mine on a separate, nearby property, and parlay that into our present status as the biggest coal miner in Canada and second-largest shipper of seaborne steel-making coal in the world. It's fair to assume we never would have explored in that area had we not made the investment in Brameda.

My father liked to say we should always try to turn adversity to advantage. I guess we did, although it took a while, and as a general principle perhaps we should try to eliminate the adversity and keep the advantage.

The Hunt for Home Oil

In early 1972, while we were still producing oil but no longer looking to expand in it, an opportunity cropped up that we couldn't refuse.

Bobby Brown was a well-known businessman from Calgary, who had built Home Oil into one of Canada's largest independent oil companies. Unfortunately, although he was only 58, he was stricken with emphysema and heart problems and wanted to sell Home to set up his estate properly.

He had begun negotiations with Ashland Oil, a large US oil company based in Kentucky, and they were close to a deal under which its subsidiary, Ashland Oil Canada, would buy his company. However, Pierre Trudeau, Canada's new prime minister, had other ideas, and had declared that no foreign company would be allowed to acquire a majority of any significant Canadian natural resource producer. With no Canadian company seemingly ready to step in and help Bobby out, it appeared he would be left hung out to dry.

We saw this happening, and while we had cut way back on oil exploration because we weren't too good at it, we still produced a lot of oil for those days. There was a reasonable argument that by acquiring an existing successful oil and gas company with a strong operating team, we could parlay that experience into a more successful oil business for ourselves.

Besides, it was there.

So we introduced ourselves to Earl Joudrie, the president of Ashland Canada, and between us we developed an ingenious plan to form a joint venture company owned 51 per cent by Teck and 49 per cent by Ashland. It would acquire control of Home Oil from Bobby, with Ashland providing all of the financing through loosely secured project loans to the new joint venture company.

We began negotiations and they progressed fairly quickly. We flew down to Bobby's Palm Desert home on his private jet, met his actor neighbour, Randolph Scott, over lunch on his patio by the ninth green, flew back to Vancouver while I held an oxygen mask to an unconscious Bobby's face, and then on to Calgary and Toronto, all over a few days. Bobby clearly wanted to get it done while he could.

In short order, late one Friday we shook hands on the deal in Bobby's suite in Toronto's Royal York Hotel. Bobby instructed his lawyers and our Michael Butler to meet with Ashland's lawyers in Calgary and draw up a formal agreement over the weekend. We would sign it Sunday and make the announcement first thing Monday. Meanwhile, Bobby said: "I have to go to Ottawa to tell my good friend Joe Green what we've agreed."

It was one of the fastest and more innovative deals we had ever done and seemed to be going as planned, except for one thing. Joe Green was Trudeau's mines and energy minister at the time, and his newly arrived deputy was Jacob Austin, fresh from his aborted Brameda experience.

The lawyers in Calgary were doing their thing, with papers being drawn up and no clangers appearing as the weekend progressed. However, late on Sunday we were informed that a Montreal-listed gas company had shown up, the proverbial interloper, and done a deal with Bobby behind our backs. How that could possibly have happened so fast was beyond us. Our opportunity had been grasped, but lost in the mysterious, unctuous dark of the Ottawa night.

I never begrudged Bobby for taking the new deal that had shown up, because he was dying and trying to look after his estate. It would, though, be interesting to learn some day what actually happened over there between Ottawa and Montreal. Was it Canada's equivalent of "The Bermuda Triangle," where good ships from the outside pass nearby and are swallowed up, never to be seen again?

Regardless, it's probably for the best, and whoever caused us to lose the deal inadvertently did us a favour. Home Oil would have been a great leap forward in scale for us, but I'm sure that we've been better off without it, building more slowly but steadily in the mining business that we know so much better.

CHAPTER 13

CONSOLIDATION

Stability is, in fact, a metastable condition.
Christopher Langton

The Need to Simplify the Group Corporate Structure

The previous chapters covered our efforts to strengthen our management team, particularly in engineering, our improving ore reserves position, and our financial liquidity that was growing with the increased Group holding in Mattagami Mines Limited.

We had not lost sight of the fact that we needed to streamline our corporate structure, transforming a complex situation that included a number of operating, exploration, and investment companies into a simpler one that would be more easily understood and appreciated by investors.

At the time, the main public companies in our Keevil Mining Group were Teck Corporation, Copperfields, Area Mines, Silverfields, Leitch, Highland-Bell, Highmont, Silver Standard, Iso Mines, and Brameda Resources. Not only was the number large and potentially confusing, but in some cases one of the companies held shares of another, and vice versa. It was a corporate version of a cat's cradle.

It was not dissimilar to the structure Thayer Lindsley had put in place in building his Ventures-McIntyre-Falconbridge Group described earlier, or of other mining groups then and before, but there was certainly merit in trying to simplify it, just as Noranda and Lindsley himself had been trying to do from time to time.

The Builder's Dilemma

If we wanted to establish Teck as the clear, principal company in the Group, we would have to roll most or all of the other companies into it through acquisition or merger. This process, and other potential acquisitions in future, would obviously require the issuance of new treasury shares of Teck, at least so long as cash remained in short supply. Quite naturally, we did not want to find control of the company taken out from under us just before our new mine development initiatives bore fruit.

To put our concern into perspective, we had seen that Teck-Hughes and five other companies had discovered the important Mattagami mine, but control had been taken over by Noranda. Similarly, we had been co-discoverers of the Madeleine deposit, but the mine had been taken over and developed by the larger McIntyre Mines. In Canadian mining, it was not unusual to see smaller companies with good new projects being taken out by larger, established companies before they could fully enjoy the results of their discoveries.

Historically, companies with a new prospect or prospects often see their stock prices rise dramatically as investors and speculators get wind of the potential for more and better news. This can last for months. After a while, though, when the drama has subsided and the long slogging work of engineering and financing a production plan begins, followed by the time necessary to actually build a new mine, the pizzazz tends to go out of the market. The shares generally will trade at much less than the real, intrinsic value of that company for a couple of years before recovering to closer or over their underlying asset value.

While the stock market, with its shorter-term focus, will tend to undervalue these companies in that hiatus period, larger, alert mining companies may well not. Most, if they plan to survive, understand the continuing need to add new reserves to their portfolio, and they are often in a position to step in and pick up sitting ducks during that time.

Canadian Mining Hall of Fame member John Bradfield had been an effective CEO of Noranda for many of its growth years, and according to an internal history of that company: "Early on in his executive career he faced a problem all mining operations must eventually face. The great Horne Mine, centrepiece of Noranda, was running out of ore and would be exhausted by the mid-1970s. Bradfield's focus on the development and acquisition of new mines was never lost."

He too might even have said at the time: "Never rest on your ores."

We were aware that, with our portfolio of existing new prospects, we could easily become one of those sitting ducks if we simply merged all of the Group companies into one, putting control "on the street," as they say.

With the package of good mine development prospects we had assembled, we almost certainly would have been taken over, perhaps by Noranda or a similar larger company, well before those new mines could actually be built and bear fruit.

That was not what we were there for.

We could of course have stuck with the safe, complex corporate chain structure that we had, in some cases with interlocking holdings, but if we really wanted to simplify that and retain a measure of control over what we were building, we had to try to find a better way. As John Downing had said about oil exploration: "You have to expose yourself to success." Well, we didn't want to be too exposed, assuming we were going to be successful.

A New Share Structure

We noodled all sorts of ideas, good and bad, along with our two key lawyers, the older Sir Michael Butler and the new, younger Bob Wright, before homing in on one that was innovative and would work.

We would create a new dual class share structure. First, we would convert all of the 4.8 million outstanding and issued Teck common shares into new, multiple-voting shares. All existing Teck shareholders would thus be treated equally, which was the right thing to do. All of those shares remain outstanding today as Class A shares carrying 100 votes per share, and now total 9.6 million Class A shares following a stock split in 2007.

We would also establish a new Class B share that would have a single vote per share to be used for planned amalgamations with some of the rest of the Group companies, and for future acquisitions that might occur.

This would not be the first dual class share structure in Canada, but there were not many for us to compare with at the time. One fallout from that rarity was that we named the multiple-voting shares Class A and the single votes Class B, which seemed sort of logical, without realizing that most if not all of the other, existing dual class situations had done quite the reverse. Well, nobody gets everything right.

In order to establish an initial market for the new Class B shares, Teck, which already held a 26 per cent share interest in Silverfields, made an offer to exchange one new Teck B share for every 2 1/2 Silverfields shares. A majority of the outside shareholders tendered their shares, increasing Teck's interest to 78 per cent.

In 1971, we completed a major merger of Teck with Area Mines, Leitch, Highland-Bell, and Silverfields, offering Class B shares to minority share-holders of each. The merger was approved by a huge majority of the outside shareholders of each company, and from then on it was reasonably clear that Teck Corporation was and would be the major ongoing growth vehicle in what had been the Keevil Mining Group, now the Teck Mining Group.

Two months earlier, we had purchased control of Iso Mines, another member of the Mattagami Syndicate, from J.P. Dolan and Andy Robertson. This had completed the program that saw five of the six original discoverers brought into the Teck Group. Iso would remain separate for a few years, but eventually would merge into Teck, as well. This would bring the number of Mattagami shares held by Teck to 1,058,000, valued at $31 million. It would prove to be important a year later, enabling us to acquire and build the next new mine in our series, one that at that point had not yet been discovered.

Dual Class Share Structures, a Brief Discussion

The merits and demerits of such structures are the subject of ongoing debate, and may be one of those things for which, in the real world, there is no "right answer."

Certainly there have been instances where founders have used them to re-tain a measure of control and have done quite well for their investors. Teck is one, and Google is another that appears to fit this mould. Others have seen rather egregious behaviour. Neither good nor bad governance depends solely on the share structure, and each situation stands on its own merits.

The Teck share structure is what it is, and long-term holders of both classes of shares have done well by it over the years. Teck did not get gobbled up, and has prospered as an independent company. It became the largest, fastest growing diversified mining company in Canada for many years, with important interests in copper, gold, silver, niobium, steelmaking coal, zinc, and oil.

For the Class B shareholder in 1975, when the first of the series of new mines in the new Teck Corporation came into production, an investment of $100 would have grown to $11,000 (with dividends reinvested) in the suc-ceeding 30 years. That represents a compounded annual rate of return of over 16 per cent, a good return by almost anyone's reckoning, and among the high-est of established companies in the world mining industry over that period.

CHAPTER 14

BUILDING TWO MORE NEW MINES

The nation that makes a great distinction between its scholars and its warriors may have its thinking done by cowards and its fighting done by fools.
Thucydides

Adding Engineering Beef

Notwithstanding, and perhaps even explaining somewhat those interesting forays into the Wild West in pursuit of Home Oil, Bethlehem Copper, and Brameda Resources, we had taken Bob Hallbauer's words of wisdom to heart. We knew we needed to move beyond our existing, short-lived underground mining operations, and soon, if we were to build that Great Canadian Mining Company, let alone survive.

With Temagami almost ready to close for good, and with limited proven reserves ahead of us at Silverfields and Lamaque, it was essential to begin developing our new prospects, as fast as we could, and to try to keep adding more.

Bob, with his experience in the Placer Group, where engineering depth had been paramount, began to beef up our capabilities in that area.

Previously, we had tended to use engineering consultants as needed at the head office level, which had worked well when we were dealing with occasional issues at a few small, established mines. We were able to tap into the best professionals suited for particular jobs, rather than having to employ one of each full time. However, Bob knew that, with our clear need to find and begin building a number of new mines, we had to establish a team of professional mine builders in our head office, even before we might have enough new prospects for them to build. In his Placer Development experience, it was far better to have the design and construction management in-house than have to rely largely upon contract engineering firms.

Fortunately, one of the good things the founders of Brameda had done was hire exceptional people, many of them from that same Placer

Development organization we had both worked in earlier. These included key engineers Cory Sibbald and Lee Bilheimer. Bob also recruited ex-Placer hands John Anderson and Mike Lipkewich, who eventually would succeed him, and Charlie Lightall, who had built some of Placer's main mines, as well as Dick Drozd from Texas Gulf's Timmins mine, Jim Thomson, and Stan Siscoe. This would be the nucleus of the engineering team that would help begin to build the new Teck.

For a change, we had more engineers working out of head office than exploration geologists, and both groups shared the same passion, to come up with the chances that could become our next generation of new mines. Unlike consultants, these guys lived and breathed the need to find new mines for us, and it was a pretty exciting period. Everyone, from board members through engineers to geologists, and regardless of particular training, was an explorer at heart, an explorer for opportunities. There were no hangers-on or just watchers. Pride of authorship and silos went out the window.

Newfoundland Zinc Takes Shape

Upon acquiring Leitch, we had declined Cominco's request for an extension of its option period and begun a drilling program of our own. Sure enough, the high-grade zinc core that John May had imagined from a few of the old drill holes proved to be real, and we were soon able to prove up a commercially attractive ore deposit containing 4.4 million tons of 8.8 per cent zinc. That is not large by twenty-first-century mining standards, but believe me, it was important to us at the time.

Unlike with Restigouche, a zinc and lead deposit with metallurgical challenges, tests showed that this ore could be processed easily into an exceptionally pure and high-grade zinc concentrate, one that should attract a premium value from the custom smelters that purchased concentrate from independent miners such as Teck. As well, the ore was reasonably close to surface and could be accessed by an inclined tunnel, rather than requiring us to sink an expensive, deep shaft. Both of these combined to present a potentially low-cost mining and milling operation. Since we were never particularly flush with capital that was a very good thing.

It was also really good timing for us in that the price of zinc, which had been stuck at around 15 cents a pound or less for years through 1972, was about to have one of those step functions upwards that occurs from time to time in the mining business, when old supply sources fall short of new demand. The price climbed to over 30 cents a pound in 1975 when we began production, and never looked back.

We completed a feasibility study and, with our partner Amax, decided to build a mine and mill with a capacity of 1,500 tons per day. Interestingly, illustrating again what a small world the mining industry is, our operating partner on the Amax side was a taciturn, brush-cut engineer named Norm Anderson, whom we would meet again 11 years later in his subsequent role as CEO of Cominco Limited.

The study forecast a capital cost of $18 million to build the mine, or $12 million for Teck's share. Our friends at the TD Bank, headed up by its new president Dick Thomson, agreed in early 1974 to provide the necessary financing despite the fact that the world was enduring a significant recession.

TD had made a strategic decision to become a player in the mine financing business and had set up a team to generate opportunities. Negotiations with both Amax and the bank were led by Warren Seyffert, another lawyer in Roland Michener's old firm, and Warren managed to pull off a solid project financing, despite some strange provincial laws that at the time seemed almost intended to make project financing impossible. It helped that TD was sufficiently gung ho to take a wink from the mines minister in lieu of the kind of security banks normally required.

Seyffert, present at the first of the series of new Teck mines that began in the 1970s, remained close to the company for 40 years, and is vice-chairman and lead director as this book is being written.

Charlie Lightall was responsible for building the plant and a shipping facility at the Hawke's Bay port to the north, working with Jim Thomson and their colleagues in the new engineering group. The workforce was recruited almost exclusively from the immediate area around Daniel's Harbour, including experienced miners who had been away for a while on the mainland in Labrador. The manager was an eclectic Newfoundlander named Jim Hogan, who turned his varied experiences as a mill operator and mortician into a new career as a first-class mine manager.

The mine was completed in 1975, on time and on budget, and was opened officially by Premier Frank Moores and the Right Honourable Roland Michener in front of the 100 or so guests who had made it to the site, surviving the breakdown of a few buses (see colour page 5).

It would produce zinc until its ore reserves ran out in 1990, and while a small mine and not as long-lived as we would have preferred, it would lead us into a new era as the first of a series of successful mines the new Teck would build over the next several decades.

Ironically, given our professional history, geophysics had played no role in the discovery of zinc on the property. The reason is that the zinc sulphide mineral sphalerite, unlike most other sulphides, is not a conductor of electricity. In most zinc deposits it occurs along with pyrite, a barren iron sulphide that is conductive. As a result, zinc deposits like Mattagami and Brunswick can be detected using airborne or ground electromagnetic surveys. It is not widely appreciated, but it is actually the associated barren pyrite, rather than the zinc mineral itself, that causes the electrical anomalies for which we search.

Sphalerite is actually a zinc-iron sulphide, with the proportion of the two metals varying from site to site. At Newfoundland Zinc, it contained very little iron and because of that was an unusual pale yellow colour. For miners and metallurgists this was good, because the zinc concentrate we produced contained an exceptionally high percentage of zinc, one of the highest ever encountered in the mining industry. For the exploration people, though, it meant there was essentially no iron in the system, and thus no associated pyrite (iron sulphide). We couldn't use our favourite geophysical techniques, and the best efforts of geological mapping underground were only moderately successful, so when the deposit was mined out 14 years later, that was it.

I remain convinced to this day that there is more beautiful, iron-free yellow zinc ore buried there somewhere, but unfortunately we were not able to find it.

We Learn about "Free Metal"

While visiting Metallgesellschaft's zinc refinery at Datteln to negotiate sales terms for this high-grade Newfoundland zinc concentrate, we were treated to a thorough presentation on how zinc refining worked. It was so thorough that the technical presenter inadvertently used the expression "free metal" when describing how the refiners added to their more obvious profits. This was followed by a giant sucking-in-of-breath sound by all of the more market-oriented Metall people present.

It seemed that the refiners traditionally paid the miner for part of the contained zinc, recovering most of the rest but keeping that little secret to themselves. Hence the free metal, which was supposed to be a trade secret, judging from the reaction of the presenter's peers. We never saw that particular fellow again.

At that same meeting, Metall also attempted to prove that, because our concentrate was so much higher grade than the usual, we should pay a penalty in the form of a higher refining charge. The argument, perhaps with a small dollop of credibility, was that a large part of the cost of producing a pound of zinc is in the power consumed in electroplating. So, since we had higher-grade concentrate with more zinc than normal, we should pay a penalty compared with what another mine might pay to have lower-grade material processed.

This was a novel concept to us miners, to be told we should pay the refiner more for treating an attractive, high-grade zinc concentrate than we would for an unattractive, low-grade one. We countered by offering to blend our almost pure Newfoundland zinc sphalerite concentrate with some other concentrates that were unsalable or unacceptable to refiners because of their lower grade, such as perhaps the proposed lousy concentrate from Restigouche we had shown them a few years earlier. This might solve their difficult problem of trying to process our really good stuff.

This elicited more sucking sounds, and gasps of: "No, no, no. You can't do that!"

It was our third object lesson about the ongoing tug of war between "the innocent small miner" and the smelters and refiners, the first two having been in connection with our Temagami mine. It would not be our last, although in our later years, after acquiring Cominco, we would on rare occasions actually find ourselves on the side of the refiner.

Q: Why do miners take an instant dislike to smelters and refiners?
A: It saves time.

Building a New Niobium Mine

We saw earlier how Ed Thompson's initiative had earned us a 50 per cent joint venture interest with SOQUEM in the St Honoré columbium (from now on to be known as niobium) prospect. After exploratory diamond drilling and some underground work we had been able to establish an initial resource of 8.5 million tons grading 0.72 per cent niobium oxide, and we began a detailed engineering and marketing study in 1972. It was completed the next year, and showed we could justify building a 1,500-ton-per-day mining and milling facility at an estimated capital cost of $18 million, provided the market price remained stable.

That was a stretch to assume though, because there were only two principal producers of the metal in the world, one being St Lawrence Columbium at Oka, Quebec, and the other being CBMM of Brazil. The underground, high-cost Oka mine appeared to be running short of ore and likely to close soon, but the Brazilian mine was a large open pit operation, with commensurately lower mining costs per ton, and some five times higher grade than ours to boot. It supplied a large majority of the world market and it was clear that CBMM could put St Lawrence and/or our proposed new mine out of business in a heartbeat simply by dropping the price for a while.

At the time, niobium was used mostly as an alloying agent in certain "high strength, low alloy" steels and the market was small, with total world production only about 10,000 tons. However, there were encouraging signs of potential new uses for the metal, particularly taking advantage of the superconducting nature of some niobium alloys at extremely low temperatures.

CBMM had tolerated the existence of the mine at Oka, apparently hoping to encourage consumers to convert to the metal and researchers to continue developing some of those new uses by demonstrating that there was at least one independent producer of the metal outside of Brazil. With Oka declining, our proposed new mine could be that alternative source of supply. At least that is what we hoped, and if we went ahead and built the mine it was what we would have to count on.

Encouraged by what we surmised was an intelligent, market-development attitude by CBMM, we decided to take a chance and put the mine into production, augmented by conventional sales contracts with some European customers.

While the ore at Newfoundland Zinc was shallow and could be accessed by an adit, an inclined tunnel into which haulage trucks could drive directly from surface, development at Niobec would require an expensive shaft to an initial depth of 950 feet. Nevertheless, ore from both would be processed in similar 1,500-ton-per-day milling facilities, and coincidentally, both projects would require the same $18 million investment to reach commercial production.

Our share of the construction costs was expected to be $12 million for Newfoundland Zinc and $9 million for Niobec. The total of $21 million was remarkably low by more recent measures but, being about equal to our total market value at the time, was a challenge. There was also some commodity market risk in that St Lawrence Columbium was still in production in Quebec, and there was no certainty that the Brazilian producers would always be rational about the supposed market-development advantages of having more additional supply from outside of Brazil.

We decided to take the chance and started building Niobec in 1974. Construction was completed and the first commercial shipments were delivered to customers in 1976 (see colour page 5).

It is rare in the mining business, especially for small companies such as we were at the time, to be building two new mines at the same time. This was possible because of the strong team of construction and development engineers we had built up at Bob Hallbauer's initiative. Both of these new mines, and most of those larger ones that followed, were built on time and on budget, and this became both a mantra and a priority for Teck.

And CBMM's wisdom in allowing a second stable source of supply to exist, encouraging customers and researchers to invest in new uses for the metal, appears to have worked well. St Lawrence Columbium did close about the time we started production but, with Niobec establishing that there were still at least two viable producers in different countries, demand for niobium did continue to grow rapidly, and is currently six times larger at over 60,000 tons per year.

Niobec would be a successful mine for Teck for 24 years, arguably showing the best return on investment of any mine we had ever built other than Temagami. Its success was a credit to Ed Thompson's initiative, helped by our solid relationship with SOQUEM's Côme Carbonneau, with whom we had been exploring jointly in the DIGHEM Syndicate, and the work of Bob Hallbauer's new mining and metallurgical engineering team.

Our interest in Niobec was sold to Quebec interests in 2000.*

---

* Teck sold its 50 per cent interest in Niobec to private Quebec interests in 2000 while we were concentrating on building the Antamina mine in Peru and consolidating our interest in Cominco. Niobec was still operating successfully in 2017, 39 years after starting production, and the mine we had built for $18 million was recently purchased for $500 million by a private equity company.

CHAPTER 15

THE SONG OF AFTON

Something wicked this way comes.
Ray Bradbury, after Shakespeare's *Macbeth*

Afton, a New Copper Discovery

Around the time of the Home Oil and Bethlehem sagas, a diamond driller and prospector named Chester Millar began exploring a property next to the Trans-Canada Highway, just west of Kamloops, British Columbia.

The claims had been owned and explored by a series of large and small companies over the years and had seen a fair amount of drilling without success. It appears that most of those explorers concentrated their efforts well away from the highway, finding nothing. I'm reminded of what we, as fishermen in Northern Ontario, often did. After portaging over to a new lake, we were inclined to put our canoe in the water and paddle across to the far side to start fishing. It would be too simple to start by seeing if there were fish right at the end of the portage. The earlier explorers on this property seemed to have had this same instinct.

Chester had a different way. When he wasn't busy working on an outside drilling contract he would take the equipment to his Afton property and drill just off the highway, not at the already heavily drilled far side. It was a good strategy, since he discovered a substantial copper deposit using it.

The mineralization he found was highly unusual, consisting of native copper, or dendritic grains of pure copper, rather than the more common copper sulphide mineral chalcopyrite. In fact, in all of the other large copper properties in the region, Valley Copper, Lornex, Bethlehem, and Craigmont, and in most Canadian mines, the copper occurs only as a sulphide mineral.

When the first drilling results were announced, Afton stock went up from a matter of pennies to almost $10, but a lot of mining people and pundits discounted the news, because nobody had ever found a native copper deposit of significant size in Canada. It was too unusual to be believed. One interesting comment I heard then, from a miner who should have known better, was: "If it's native copper there is no way they can mill it," referring to the milling process used to upgrade low-grade copper ore to a copper concentrate that can be sold to smelters. That was strange, since the very first copper mines in North America were native copper deposits in the Keweenaw Peninsula of Michigan, starting in 1854. Native copper deposits are certainly rare, but not impossible to treat.

The reaction of the Toronto mining and market establishment, still smarting from the memories of its own Windfall saga and perhaps Brameda, was to assume that nothing good could come out of the nascent Vancouver Stock Exchange that had replaced it as the primary source of Canadian venture capital. They missed Afton, and their loss would be our gain.

Bob Hallbauer and I were spending a lot of time back in Vancouver working on Brameda, Highmont, and other projects, and we decided to look at Afton to see if, contrary to that negative conventional wisdom, it should be taken seriously. This started with a visit to the drilling site, and it became clear to both of us that the potential for a significant, mineable copper deposit was real.

We Propose a Development Contract

The more we looked, the more we became convinced that Afton had an excellent chance of making a successful mine, and we met with Chester Millar to try to negotiate a development contract, an option to earn an interest in the property by financing ongoing exploration and development work, and, if warranted, arrange project financing and provide construction management.

Bob and I seemed to hit it off with Chester, who was openly interested in Bob's mining input and perhaps my geophysical or geological thoughts. However, he wasn't interested in doing a development contract at the time, with us or anyone else. "I'm not ready to do the ultimate deal just yet. Why don't you buy some shares out of the market to get a position, and we can talk ultimate deals later?" he said, encouraging us to go into the market and do just that.

By then, Bob and I were confident that Afton would make a mine, and that it would be larger and more profitable than either Newfoundland Zinc or Niobec, both of which we had on the drawing boards and were getting ready to build. The question was, how to get our hands on it?

Taking Chester Millar's Suggestion and Buying Shares

I think it was Bob, while we were taking a break golfing one day, who came up with the novel idea of selling some of our Mattagami shares and using the funds to buy a significant share position in Afton. The idea was that we could then work with Afton to build a new mine, and actively create real value instead of just sitting on a passive holding. It made a lot of sense if we could pull it off, but the trouble was that we had been adding to that Mattagami position for some years, and having increased it recently to over a million shares, Noranda had finally and quite belatedly seen fit to nominate my father to its board of directors. It would not be an easy sell in our own shop. We did raise the idea, but the initial response was negative, just as expected. However, it was an idea that seemed to make sense, and we kept at it.

One day, the renowned mining consultant Bill James happened by our Vancouver office and asked if he could take a look at our numbers on Afton. Turns out my father, perhaps mindful of the Brameda experience a year earlier, had asked Bill for a second opinion, but suggested he should pretend he was in town on other business and was just dropping by for a chat. Bill wasn't too comfortable pretending, and it was fine with Bob and me, anyway. If Bill supported us it could be helpful, and he did just that.

Bob and I returned to Toronto and once again proposed selling enough Mattagami to buy up to 50 per cent of Afton on the market. Even with Bill James' support, it still wasn't easy and the idea continued to fizzle for a while, but one morning my father, Len Watt, Latham Burns, and I had breakfast and tossed it around again. Latham was naturally interested in convincing us because he could see a healthy commission on both the Mattagami sale and the Afton buy side.

At breakfast my father still seemed to be coming around slowly but reluctantly, and I can recall clearly Latham's words: "Norm. Sometimes you just have to bite the bullet." That challenge seemed to tilt the balance, and we agreed to see if we could buy enough Afton shares to get to 50 per cent at a reasonable price.

Once decided, my father was fully onside, and he took charge of the buying strategy, working through one of Latham's traders. We started buying one morning at about $8 a share and kept on for about an hour until it hit $11, at which point we pulled the bid and let the market fall right back, before starting to buy again. Naturally, the next time it shot up on our buying, even just a few hours later, some shareholders who had missed the chance to sell the first or second time showed up as sellers. Then we would pull the bid, wait awhile, and start all over again. It was that kind of fast and frenzied promotional market.

Interestingly, as this was happening we were on a prearranged boat trip for some directors and friends up the BC coast in the *Norsal*, a 135-foot working boat that had once been owned by the Powell River lumber company. It was by then the property of Jack Gibson, a well-known lumber man and chairman of Highmont Mining Corporation, whose copper deposit in the Highland Valley we were exploring, and it was piloted by Highmont president Bob Falkins, one of those mining promoters who had an innate sense of optimism and a heart of gold. There was a piano on board which Bob, an accomplished classical pianist, would occasionally leave the wheel to play.

He and all on board were doubtless wondering why my father was busily on the telephone every few minutes for the whole voyage, occasionally forgetting himself and shouting out: "We just got another 200,000."

It was just a remarkable three days later, after several buying spurts and strategic pauses, that we had bought 50 per cent of the issued shares of Afton. We sold 450,000 shares of Mattagami at the same time to cover the cost, and it was then time to go to the next step and gracefully accept our prize.

Thank you Chester, for a good suggestion that we buy on the market.

Our Next Meeting Doesn't Go Quite as Well

We called up Chester and asked for another meeting. I think he suspected we had been buying because this time he had with him Doug Price, one of his directors, who had a naturally ornery look about him, and a suspiciously familiar lawyer named John Bruk. Once again, there was a strange scent of sulphur and brimstone in the room that made our flesh crawl.

Bob Hallbauer and Sir Michael Butler joined me, and I told Chester we had taken his advice and bought some shares. When he asked how many I made a quick decision to lowball it, rather than appear too pushy, given our earlier friendly meetings, and said we had over 40 per cent. True enough. I also said that we could now offer Afton a better development contract than anyone else, needing to take a smaller equity for arranging financing, since we already were large shareholders. Also true enough.

Chester seemed to accept that, and started musing about wanting to carve out a small piece of land near the lake for a cottage for himself, to which of course we were agreeable. He was, after all, the founder and personally responsible for the discovery. We went back and forth in that vein for a while, talking about where the plant should be sited and how large a milling capacity would be needed, whether we should buy the underlying cattle ranch, and so on. We were not really getting anywhere quickly, but letting the conversation run. Chester seemed completely comfortable with us as the new, largest shareholder, and there was no point in pressing him.

Eventually, Butler could stand it no more and growled: "Come on now. We actually have 50 per cent and want control of the board immediately." Bob and I both kicked him under the table, literally, but the damage had been done. Price growled back that there was no way we could take a majority of the board. They were like two bears ready to attack each other. Bruk started grinning mysteriously. The scent seemed to be getting stronger.

Having held such a successful meeting, we left it that we would meet again in a couple of days, after Chester had returned from a planned trip to the property. We were frustrated with Michael but confident that good sense and governance would prevail. Afton was then, by all normal accounting, ethical, and other business standards, our new subsidiary company. That and a dollar would get you a cup of coffee when dealing with some types.

A strange silence ensued over the next couple of days, with our calls for another meeting not answered. Bruk's mysterious smile assumed more and more Machiavellian connotations. We got wind somehow that Afton might be trying to do a deal with someone else, and suspected it could be Cominco or our old friends across the street at Placer Development. We even stationed our chief engineer, Dick Drozd, outside the Placer office for a while to watch and see if any Prices or Bruks walked out, but not surprisingly, he saw nothing.

Sure enough though, a few days later it was announced that Afton had done a development contract that would give Placer a 30 per cent share interest in Afton on completion of its new mine. This would of course dilute our shareholding down from a majority 50 per cent to just 35 per cent of the company.

This sounded suspiciously like a clone of the Bethlehem deal with Granges two years earlier. Chester, Price, Bruk, and the gang would have two shareholders each at around 30 per cent, rather than one controlling one at 50 per cent. They would sit comfortably in the catbird seat between the two shareholders, just as Bethlehem's management had found a way to do, at least for a while. In the process, they would similarly disenfranchise their largest, majority shareholder, one they had specifically invited in. This time the victim was Teck, rather than Sumitomo.

It seemed to us that, common morality aside, it must also be illegal for directors to issue shares to their friends, especially in order to dilute a 50 per cent shareholder, and in law we had a strong, recent Australian case that supported us. So we sued to have the deal voided. We fully expected to win, both on the law and in principle, but the two are not always coincident. To paraphrase William Shakespeare: "Principals often have lawyers, but lawyers don't always have principles."

The Lawsuit

The case was scheduled to be heard suspiciously quickly, within a few months, and was given to Judge Tom Berger to preside over. Berger, with support from the big labour unions, had run for premier of British Columbia as the leader of the New Democratic Party (NDP) a few years earlier, but had been defeated by W.A.C. "Wacky" Bennett, the long-time leader of a coalition called the Social Credit Party.

Berger's campaign promise had been that he would "institute socialist principles on a non-compromise basis," actually playing into Bennett's usual campaign about defending BC from the "socialist hordes." Bennett had won that election again, his seventh in a row, although it would turn out to be his last. Having lost, Berger decided to take up judging.

As luck would have it, a new election had been called that summer of 1972, after we had bought our Afton position, and after the Bruk/Placer deal, but before the court case was heard. Dave Barrett, who had succeeded Berger as NDP leader, had won, finally defeating W.A.C. Bennett.

The Afton case dragged on for a few weeks, and it was a bit discomfiting to have to hear Placer engineers telling stories that conflicted with those of our own engineers, since we had all been friends for a long time, and many of us had worked for or with them. But as Michael Corleone said in *The Godfather*: "It's not personal, it's strictly business."

At one point in court, Dick Drozd had described our engineering plan to build the milling plant and Tony Triggs, Placer's key engineering witness, tried to make hay out of the fact that Dick had seemingly forgotten to include a sump pump in the conceptual design. Now that is about as inconsequential as it can get in the scheme of things, but witnesses can generate all sorts of confusion in the minds of some judges if they are allowed to.

Judge Berger may not have followed the engineering debate, but he did have a sense of non-technical issues, and there came a time when he asked our lawyer: "Do you mean to say, Mr Giles, that, if the Mafia bought 50 per cent of your company, you should hand them control of the board?" Giles replied: "Precisely, My Lord."

That should have been my first clue as to where it was going.

In December, just in time for Christmas, Judge Berger came down with his opinion. It set a record for major Canadian mining lawsuits, taking only a few months compared with the years that the earlier *Leitch vs. Texas Gulf* had taken.

Berger's conclusion was that Bruk and the others were fully entitled to issue shares to their friends, even after knowing that someone else had bought a majority of the shares in the company. Teck had lost, and Bruk's strange and crafty deal had won.

The Australian case we had relied upon was no longer the latest law of the Commonwealth. The new Afton precedent now held that directors are free to issue shares specifically in order to dilute and defeat some new shareholder that has bought and owns a majority of the company, as long as they "in their hearts" feel it's for the good of the company. Many lawyers may actually agree with that conclusion although, with all due respect to their academic sense of governance, it is pretty loose, and easily subject to abuse. "Well, I sold out the company from under its owners because I woke up in a snit one morning and decided that would be the right thing to do. I truly believe that, My Lord."

If some in the legal community had thought we would lose, we had really thought otherwise, simply based upon what appeared to be right. That said, and to be fair, I have said many times that I'd seen the Placer Development of that era as the best mining company in Canada, and I'm sure many others did, as well. It is arguable that some on the Afton board, perhaps Chester, actually did see Placer in that same way, and saw us as the less experienced interlopers from Eastern Canada. Both views would have an element of truth to them. That would fit with Justice Berger's hypothetical question about what a board should do if it saw an apparently terrible organization acquire a majority interest in "its" company. Obviously, this is a rule seriously subject to abuse, but perhaps having a very small dollop of sense.

A few months after that, Tom McClelland, the new Placer president, invited my father to lunch and offered to sell his recently won development contract to us for $4 million. Tom said that the Afton ore body was upside down, with the best grade at depth rather than near-surface, but I suspect he might also have been motivated to get out of it since the newly elected NDP government was making suspicious noises that were anathema to honest miners. It is even barely possible that he was a bit embarrassed about Placer having participated in what many businessmen would see as a nefarious scheme, despite Judge Berger's conclusion.

In any event, we now had an undisputed position, more than just a majority, and Chester accepted it like the gentleman he was. We took charge of designing and building the new mine.

Chester would go on to form Glamis Gold, a successful gold mining company, and eventually be inducted into the Canadian Mining Hall of Fame, an honour he deserved and we fully supported. Price disappeared from our universe, but Bruk continued to hover around.

Berger would be appointed by Prime Minister Pierre Trudeau to head an inquiry into the proposed Mackenzie Valley Pipeline, which would effectively terminate that project. It happened that I ran across him in Ottawa a year after the trial, and it boggled my mind when he said: "I often wondered if I'd made a mistake in that judgment, but it all worked out well in the end, didn't it?" Thank you very much, Judge.

Actually, it did work out okay. As we'd said to Chester earlier, we were prepared to offer a better development contract for him and the remaining shareholders, since we already owned 50 per cent of the company. We would have had to negotiate a fair additional percentage to be earned, but it could in no way have been as much as the 30 per cent we had inherited from Placer for only $4 million.

Designing the Mine

Now we could get to work doing a proper feasibility and design study.

Stan Siscoe, Cory Sibbald, Dick Drozd, and the rest of Bob Hallbauer's engineering team designed a plant that would handle the native copper ore without difficulty. The solution was unusual for a modern copper mill in that it combined tables, a form of gravity separation that had been used at the historic Keweenaw mines, with froth flotation for the finer material.

The planning was complicated by the need to remove a small amount of mercury that occurred with the native copper. Normally this is done at the smelter level, by one of the custom smelters around the world that buy and treat the copper concentrates produced by independent miners like us. Some of those custom smelters are set up to remove deleterious minor elements like mercury or bismuth in their particular smelting process, while others are not. Naturally, those that can remove it charge even more to treat mercury-bearing concentrates when copper prices go down and concentrates are in surplus, and that is a cross we faced when deciding how to proceed with developing Afton. The proposed smelting and refining terms were pretty hard to bear.

However, our engineers came across a variation of the smelting process, top blown rotary conversion, which had been used by Inco in its copper and nickel processing operations in Sudbury. After a bit of testing, we proved it would work on our native copper concentrate, and that it was a practical alternative to sending it to a custom smelter with its excessive minor element charges, so we decided to build one as part of our processing plant. It would be British Columbia's first copper smelter in the modern era.

Bob Hallbauer and I became television stars for a day in Kamloops, when we did a live show with a town hall meeting to go over our development plans. The Afton property was just outside the town limits, on the Trans-Canada Highway, so there was understandably more interest than had it been kilometres from nowhere. There were vocal opponents, as there generally are for any new idea, but we did get general buy-in from the town, helped by strong support from the local NDP MLA, Nelson Riis, who appeared on TV with us.

Development Delayed by NDP's "Super-Royalty" Proposal

So at this point we had managed to acquire control of the property, design a processing plant including a smelter, and get local buy-in, but we still had to deal with the consequences of a government on the take. Our opportunity to begin building a mine at Afton was further delayed when the Barrett government announced plans for a new super-royalty on copper mines.

The price of copper, which had ranged between 35 cents a pound and 60 cents during the 1960s, had risen to over $1.00 a pound by 1973, based on burgeoning Asian demand. By early 1974, the peak of this strong cycle, copper had reached $1.40 a pound.

We will see in chapter 17 how governments around the world began chasing after the fruits of the resource producers' successes, and the Barrett government was no exception. Its new mines minister was Leo Nimsick, whose only experience remotely related to mining consisted of having been a warehouseman at Cominco's Trail refinery. He was getting advice from Deputy Minister John McMynn and his assistant Hart Horn, neither of whom had much more relevant experience, and the bunch came up with a novel idea on how to rake off some of the results of the mining industry's earlier risk investments.

The plan was to double the normal, historic royalty and impose a new "super-royalty" on copper, in effect grabbing 50 per cent of any copper price that exceeded a base price to be set by the government. This would penalize legitimate investments already made based upon the laws of the day, and in addition would naturally inhibit people considering new investments, such as us with the Afton project.

As Barrett put it to me in one of our meetings: "My advisors tell me that the price of copper will never fall below $1 a pound again, so what are you worrying about?" That assumption, while it would prove to be wildly inaccurate, certainly didn't justify retroactive legislation. As it turned out, the economy went into recession soon after and the price of copper did fall below $1, not to return to that level again until 15 years later, in 1989, and then only temporarily.

These things all conspired to delay a construction decision on Afton. We had faced the Berger decision and the need to reach a settlement with Placer, resolution of the mercury problem, the design of a smelter to handle it, the imposition of the super-royalty, and then the recession of 1974 and collapse in the price of copper.

Fortunately, we had had our two new mining projects in Newfoundland and in Quebec under construction at the same time, a challenge that kept us quite busy.

Finally, in 1975 there was a change in government. The super-royalty idea disappeared, the economy began recovering, and we once again had a government in BC that would encourage responsible development, rather than try to stand in its way. We had nearly completed both the Newfoundland Zinc and Niobec niobium mines successfully by then, and were ready to go ahead with Afton.

We secured the necessary bank financing and started construction of a 7,000-ton-per-day mining, milling, and smelting facility in 1976. These were completed successfully at a cost of $85 million, with the first slab of blister copper poured from the smelter in March 1978. It was the third in a sequence of new mines that would change Teck forever, and the "Third Annual Teck Mine-Opening Golf Tournament" was held at the Kamloops Golf and Country Club (see colour page 6).

Interestingly, Afton also got us into the cattle ranching business for a while. There was an existing ranch near the mine, and we purchased it so we could operate it in conjunction with the mine and provide for the safety of the cattle near the new open pit. Named Sugarloaf, after a local mountain, the ranch at its peak ran almost 700 head of cattle and was a favourite destination for some of our engineers who dreamed of being cowboys. Bob Hallbauer always said he hoped to retire to be the ranch manager. He would never make it, but Max Leavens, retired from managing the Temagami mine, and Bob's successor, Mike Lipkewich, each managed to do it.

CHAPTER 16

DAVE BARRETT AND THE "SOCIALIST HORDES"

It is very easy for chaos to come overnight.
Deng Xiaoping

Meanwhile, as the Afton saga was just getting underway, we had decided to move our head office team from Toronto to Vancouver. I had hoped for years that someday I could move back west, after experiencing the interior country and general beauty of British Columbia while I was at Craigmont. We had hinted at the Highmont annual meeting in May 1972 that we were considering this, and having bought 50 per cent of Afton and with it seemingly now in our camp, it was the right time.

So we announced in June that we would be moving our head office west to Vancouver, just as Cominco had done, entirely coincidentally, a year earlier. It had made sense, given the pace at which mineral development was expanding with large new mines, and potential ones, in British Columbia.

We had no idea an election call was imminent, one that would result in a government of an entirely different stripe.

A Press Conference to Announce Our Move to Vancouver

One of our directors, Canadian Devonian founder Dr John Leishman, had moved to Vancouver already, and he suggested we hold a press conference to publicize the move. We had never had a real, classy press conference before, but it seemed like a good idea, so we agreed. John knew a local public relations specialist named Bill Clancey, who also did double duty as a PR man for Premier W.A.C. Bennett. Clancey set it up for a sunny day in July and this, our first ever press conference, sounded as though it would be fun. We didn't expect too many people, but thought we might get one or two of the business press to attend.

However, between announcing the date and actually holding the press conference two things happened. First, Bennett decided it was a good time to call another election, and did just that. Second, as soon as he called it, he disappeared into the interior of British Columbia, his traditional base, and wouldn't give any of the media his schedule. This apparently infuriated them.

A week passed without the press managing to find him, but unbeknownst to us Clancey had apparently whispered around that Bennett would attend our press conference. So instead of one or two business reporters, we had 40 media types, including all of the big names like Allan Fotheringham, Waldo Blatheringmouth, and Jack Webster. Naturally Bennett didn't show up.

Hallbauer, Leishman, my father, and I sat at this table on a little stage and listened to them all shout at Clancey: "Where is he?" It was an angry mob, with the sense of entitlement that it seems must be taught in Journalism 101. I don't think we got even a single question about Teck. It was not an auspicious start to our move west, and we vowed not to make a practice of press conferences from then on, at least not ones hosted by Bill Clancey.

Where was Wacky? Well, unbelievably, that day he was up in the northeastern part of the province, announcing that his government would be building a railroad into what he called "the northeast coal district," where Brameda's Sukunka project and the nearby, bigger Quintette coal property held by Denison Mines were located.

That sounded good for the northeastern coal projects, and it might have been a logical conclusion by the uninformed listener that we had set this up. In fact, we had never even met W.A.C. Bennett and never would, and were completely unaware of the proposed railroad. Apparently, Steve Roman of Denison had met Bennett earlier in the spring and convinced him it could be good politics or policy to make this commitment. And it was election time.

Bennett did send us a telegram to be read at our press conference, welcoming the company's move to BC. He intoned: "As good corporate citizens of British Columbia, Teck will bring added prosperity and employment to the area. I am sure Teck will play a large part in the glowing future of British Columbia." This was nice, since he had never met us either. I don't recall Fotheringham, Blatheringmouth, or Webster responding appropriately by welcoming us, but they were doubtless preoccupied, haranguing Clancey.

And the NDP *Gets Elected the Next Month*

Bennett had been elected premier in 1952 and had ruled for 20 years, winning election after election by railing that the socialist hordes were at the door. Bob Hallbauer was then our expert on BC politics, and he used to say that nobody he knew would ever admit to voting Social Credit, but when they went into the voting booth they did it, just to keep those dreaded hordes out.

We were pretty confident that sanity would prevail once again but, the night before Election Day, Bob said to me that he had had a clanger. He thought Barrett just might win. It would be a first for the NDP, but it had begun to seem possible.

Bob was not alone in this late-stage revelation. Months later Dave Barrett confided to us: "You know, I never thought we could #x*^## pull it off myself until the night before the vote, when it dawned on me that we just might win." (In all Dave quotes from here on in this story, we will delete his usual accompanying profanities.)

In a recent Barrett biography, *The Art of the Impossible: Dave Barrett and the NDP in Power*, Geoff Meggs and Ron Mickleburgh described the surprise that accompanied his victory. They quoted a column written by the *Vancouver Sun's* Robert Hunter at 2:30 a.m., as the results were announced: "The revolution is all over in British Columbia. The people are in control. The czar has surrendered. Welcome to the Glorious People's Republic of Mainland British Columbia."

According to the book, Barrett called Bob Williams and said:

> "Williams, for Christ's sake. We won!"
> Williams, replying with a strange, metallic voice previously heard only in *2001: A Space Odyssey*, "Yes we did, Dave. I've been doing some thinking about transition."
> "Oh good," said Barrett, who apparently had not.

They met the next morning at a tiny restaurant where Williams pulled out his plan, including making himself a super-minister overseeing five departments, much as Ray Williston had held under Bennett. Dave bought the whole thing.

In the words of Meggs and Mickleburgh, reminiscent of Bob Wright's performance at the Brameda closing a couple of years earlier: "At his first cabinet meeting Dave Barrett takes off his shoes, leaps on the leather-inlaid cabinet table and skids the length of it. 'Are we here for a good time or a long time?' he roars. His answer: 'A good time, a time of change, action, doing what was needed and right, not what was easy and conventional.'"

To my recollection, Bob Wright had kept his shoes on.

"I Want Your Coal"

Presumably because of Wacky's announcement of a railroad to the northeast coal fields and Clancey's role in our press conference, Barrett had assumed we were in cahoots with him – the long-time NDP enemy. It was, perhaps, understandable. The old proverb has it that "the enemy of my enemy is my friend," and of course the opposite might apply as well.

So one of Barrett's earliest moves after he took office was to call Bob Hall-bauer and me over to Victoria and demand that we hand over our coal properties. His first words were: "I want your coal." Well, at least he did call it our coal. That would become questionable as the situation evolved.

We pointed out that we were mine builders, not flippers, and weren't interested in selling. But Dave kept calling us back to Victoria every week or so to insist that we sell him our coal properties. We kept saying no, after which we would have a jovial discussion, and we would all leave it with a smile, until the next time. Dave was a cool kind of guy, and it *was* our coal, even if we were of two minds about building underground coal mines. Well, one mind actually, but we had our principles. In that, we seemed somewhat alone.

At about the seventh such meeting, a very strange thing happened. Barrett had a curtain angled across a corner in his office. We'd never paid much attention to it, but in that seventh meeting the curtain rustled a bit, and a thin, sepulchral, white-haired professorial type jumped out from behind it. It was almost as though he was wearing a superhero cape, or super-villain. I think Dave must have gotten him out of Marvel Comics. Was there a door to another room behind the curtain, or had this strange figure just been hiding behind it, taking it all in? I never did find out.

It turned out this was the patrician Alex Macdonald, Barrett's attorney general and the upholder of law and order – the NDP way. The honourable gentleman said to us: "I want you to understand just one thing. I guarantee that you will never be able to put that coal property into production. All you have is an exploration licence and, if you don't sell to us right now, I'll cancel it tomorrow."

So much for law and order. The sepulchral figure suffered under no such illusions, or sense of decency. He was of course technically correct on the law side, but not the order. Most people, even in most governments, had generally recognized that exploration only makes sense if those who take risks and manage to make the occasional discovery can see a straight path to converting it to a mining lease. It was beginning to be a sign of the times though, as we will see in the next chapter.

Bob Hallbauer and I actually liked Dave Barrett as a person. He probably would have been more fun to have a beer with than Wacky Bennett, had we in fact ever met the latter, but that settled it. From that moment we became the enemy he had thought we were. In our mistaken view, "Thou shalt not steal" ought to apply to those socialist hordes and their attorneys general as well as to the rest of us.

Faced with the unseemly ultimatum from the upholder of justice, we finally capitulated and agreed on a selling price of $20 million. Payment was to be made and the deal to be closed in June 1973, a few months from then.

We went on to other things and were resigned to losing this one, but when June came around, to our surprise the government announced out of the blue that it had "dropped its option" to buy our coal properties. Bob Williams, the super-minister who had orchestrated Dave's cabinet and first 100 days in office, apparently had other plans for his own new office and ministry. He had wondered from the start why Dave had developed such a hang-up about our coal, probably figuring that they'd defeated Wacky already, and it was time to get on with their idea of business.

Dave's offer and our reluctant acceptance had in fact not been an option but a firm deal, however nefariously it had been pressed upon us. It now seemed as though, having made a point, they had lost interest in it, and may have run out of loose cash as well. Certainly they had been spending like drunken sailors on redecorating some of the higher-profile, cabinet ministers' offices.

As to Alex Macdonald, a quote of his survives all of this: "In politics, your opponents are on the other side of the legislature, but your enemies are all around you." With him, I'm not too surprised.

We Continue Exploring the Coal Licences

This was fine with us. We hadn't wanted to sell anyway. We would keep working the property although, as a coal deposit that would have to be mined from underground rather than as an open pit, it presented operating challenges with which we were not experienced and still not all that comfortable about.

Earlier, we had brought in Brascan Ltd, a Toronto-based company whose main assets at the time were in Brazil, as a partner to provide financial support for any development at Sukunka, and they had teamed up with an Australian group with some experience in underground coal mining. They did do a lot of work on the project in the next few years but eventually, in the spring of 1976, Brascan chairman J.H. Moore announced that the company would not exercise its option, would write off its investment in Sukunka, and would return the property to Teck and Brameda. Once again we had it back, wanted or not.

Bob Hallbauer then told the *Globe and Mail* that Teck had two alternatives: proceed to develop the property itself, or take in another partner, preferably one with coal mining experience. He said Teck would continue with plans for a $250,000 exploration program on the adjoining, newly discovered Bullmoose prospect, which had the potential to be developed into an open pit mine.

It was time to regroup once again, finding another partner to take on Sukunka at the same time as we pursued the prospect of developing the Bullmoose discovery ourselves, and we will come back to that in chapter 18.

Barrett Defeated, Bill Bennett Elected

At one of those many "I want your coal" meetings, we were in the government's Cabinet Room, where there was still a picture of Wacky on the wall behind him. Dave had pointed to it and said: "Now that I'm here I'm going to be in power for 20 years, just like him. I'll go out there, pull on my suspenders and roll my big brown eyes at them, and I'll never lose another election."

It's hard to imagine what the fate of BC's mining sector would have been had Dave been right on that. There were in fact no mines built or committed to during his three-year tenure, and there was a six-year hiatus between Lornex in 1972 and Afton in 1978 when there was not a single new mine opened in the province. That despite mining having, historically, been BC's most important or second most important industry.

Barrett did call that snap election in 1975, fully expecting to be able to reverse declining poll numbers by an effective campaign. In this, convinced that he was invincible, he overruled those in his party who had read the poll numbers. They even tried sweet talking to the mining industry in the weeks before the election was called, announcing a new grant of 2 cents a pound of copper for four years for any new copper smelter to be built, but it didn't reverse the mood of the people. Barrett's NDP was defeated by W.A.C.'s son Bill Bennett.

Epilogue

Bill Bennett had never been interested in being in government and was happy with his business in Kelowna, but he had accepted the call when it came. He would be premier for 11 years, culminating in the highly successful Expo 86, after which he would retire from politics. Unlike with Wacky, I did get to know Bill well, and those of us who had the opportunity to share it with him will always remember his triumphant walk down the Expo corridor, complete with brass band and the cheers of thousands lining the route.

With responsible government back in Victoria we could go ahead with building Afton, and two more new mines in British Columbia shortly after that.

Sukunka never did get built, although now, more than 40 years later, companies keep coming back to look at it.

The railroad into northeast coal that Wacky had announced vanished without a trace. Not to be outdone though, in 1975, with an election imminent, the new NDP Minister of Mines, Gary Lauk, announced the NDP's own new new railroad into northeast coal, which at the time still consisted only of the Quintette prospect and the ill-fated Sukunka underground prospect, our Bullmoose mine not yet having been discovered. Not being elected, they didn't build the railroad either.

Five years later, with Bullmoose discovered and ready for development, Quintette ready to be built, and a new government in place, the railroad would finally get a real go-ahead. It was not without interruptions that the universe unfolded as it should, and how that came to pass is the subject of chapter 18.

Despite our differences, we had enjoyed Dave Barrett's sense of fun and humour, which was as attractive as his sense of right and wrong was not. Ironically, he was honoured by being inducted into the Order of British Columbia 40 years later in 2012, the same year that I was. He was unable to attend due to illness and it was tempting for me to offer to accept the award on his behalf, but I refrained.

Bill Bennett would become a director of Teck Corporation for several years after he retired from politics, and proved to be one of our most diligent and productive board members.

CHAPTER 17

THE TURBULENT SEVENTIES

Turning and turning in the widening gyre
The falcon cannot hear the falconer.
Things fall apart; the centre cannot hold;
Mere anarchy is loosed upon the world,
The blood-dimmed tide is loosed, and everywhere
The ceremony of innocence is drowned;
The best lack all conviction, while the worst
Are full of passionate intensity.

...

And what rough beast, its hour come round at last,
Slouches towards Bethlehem to be born?
Willliam Butler Yeats, "The Second Coming"

If the amalgamation of our various KMG interests into a single, focused Teck Corporation had been a strategic inflection point, as Grove later described the concept, the external economy was undergoing an inflection point as well that, while perhaps less strategic, would have major consequences.

A Chaotic Time: War, Socialism, Taxes, and Inflation

The 1970s were the best of times, and the worst of times, as the saying goes. We in Teck actually accomplished a lot, in spite of an external environment that was tending toward entropy, or disorder. We have already seen the impact of the Dave Barrett years, but they seemed in fact symptomatic of the times. When we looked back from the relative calm of the late twentieth century, it was hard to appreciate how chaotic things were back then, although today in the twenty-first century one can sense eerie similarities that, hopefully, represent aberrations rather than a new trend.

Charles R. Morris, in a 2008 book *The Trillion Dollar Meltdown*, put the situation in the US succinctly:

For connoisseurs of misery, the ten years from 1973 through 1982 was a feast of low points. The rate of economic growth was one of the worst for any comparable period since the end of World War II. The country endured one of the worst periods of inflation in American history, and foreign investors fled the dollar as if it were the Mexican peso. Layoffs and short shifts spread through heavy industry. America's once-humming industrial heartland transmuted into the Rust Belt. The OPEC nations increased oil prices tenfold, and an ugly new word, stagflation, entered the political vocabulary.

The chaos had begun a few years earlier, with America's balance of payments affected seriously by the Vietnam War. This had led to a run on the dollar that, in 1971, forced Richard Nixon to abandon the gold standard the US had supported for so many decades. The price of gold was freed from its fixed $35 an ounce and began to be set by the free market. This was good news for the surviving gold miners, after so many lean years, but was a harbinger that dramatic change was ahead.

The inflationary era that had evolved under many western governments of the day held sway. The price of copper that had ranged between 35 and 60 cents a pound during the 1960s had risen temporarily to over $1.00 a pound by 1973, encouraging the Barrett government's abortive attempt to impose its super-royalty.

Governments around the world looked at this "new era," often with greedy eyes. The United Nations trotted around advising governments like Panama on how they should change their mining tax policies to take better advantage of their resources. Of course, there were no mines in Panama then, only potential ones, and partly as a result of such free advice, this remained the case for another 40 years.

The Blakeney government in Saskatchewan found a novel way to expropriate without compensation, or at least by minimizing it. His government increased royalties on potash mining substantially, thus reducing the value of the private sector mines involved. Then he nationalized some of them, ostensibly at "fair market value," but only after having arbitrarily reduced that value with his prior, royalty bump. The combination was, de facto, expropriation. A nice trick if you can get away with it, like taking candy from a baby.

Self-styled "resource economists" like Mason Gaffney, an earlier Berkeley graduate like me but of somewhat different persuasion, began to satisfy his sense of envy with his own novel ways of justifying expropriation, ways that would inhibit the ability of miners and others to do useful, creative things such as discover and build new wealth.

Newfoundland created a royal commission on resource taxation and appointed Gaffney to head it up. His report concluded with one strange recommendation: that in future anybody should be allowed to explore for minerals in the province, but if one of them happened to discover something of value they would then have to negotiate the terms of development with the government. This would ensure that the discoverer would earn no more than the lowest possible return he could be squeezed down to, leaving little or no reward for the risk taken.

That, of course, is an odd way to try to encourage high-risk exploration. For the most part people who explore for minerals, whether grizzled prospectors or geoscientists, do so in the hope of discovering "The Mother Lode." If the chance of a large reward for success is taken away, there is really very little motivation to risk the time and effort, against long odds, of exploring in the first place.

In a meeting after Premier Frank Moores received the report he asked for my comments, and I compared it with how successful risk-takers are rewarded in Las Vegas. There, the business model is to encourage people to take similar risky bets, as in exploration. When someone occasionally wins big at the slots or another game, the house rings bells to draw attention to the win, thus encouraging more players to come and try their hand. The house doesn't invite the winner into the back room to negotiate his or her payoff. Moores understood this instinctively, and literally threw the thick Gaffney report into his wastebasket, right in front of us. Not all jurisdictions were as wise.

Elsewhere in the world, Chile's first step toward nationalizing the copper industry had begun in 1969 with the forced sale of Anaconda's key mines at Chuquicamata and El Salvador, presaging full expropriation in 1971. That same year Mexico nationalized Anaconda's Cananea copper mine as well, and within a few years that proud company, considered an icon in the world mining industry for years and the sponsor of industry-leading scientists like Reno Sales and Chuck Meyer, had disappeared entirely.

The macroeconomic climate, always uncertain at the best of times, seemed to be getting even more so. And that was only in the first couple of years of the decade.

Adding More Beef to the Muscle

If the world seemed to be becoming more chaotic, we were at the stage where we were trying our best, some would have said against our basic instincts, to become more orderly. We had begun consolidating the various KMG companies into a single lead vehicle, Teck Corporation. We had acquired the prospects in Newfoundland and Quebec that would become the first of our next generation of new mines, as well as the Afton copper deposit that would follow them. And we had moved the head office team to Vancouver, although with interesting timing just before the election of Dave Barrett.

On the people side, we had added engineering and operating muscle, beginning with Bob Hallbauer and the strong group he had helped assemble. It was time to beef up the financial side as well.

When we had moved our headquarters to Vancouver, Jim Westell, who had been treasurer and our key financial person for years, chose to stay in Toronto where he had deep roots. Jim had been solid as a rock, but had been afraid to take a vacation for the previous three years since, as he put it, every time he went out of town the Keevils would find some deal to do. I think getting us out of town, and his hair, might have been a relief for him, and in any case he was getting close to the time to retire quietly.

So we let out word that we were on the lookout for someone, and we decided that we should join the elite group of larger companies and, for a change, designate Jim's successor as chief financial officer. One of the Vancouver people Bob Hallbauer and I had become close to since Latham Burns had handed us Brameda was his local point man, Joe Murphy. Joe was a hard-living, cigar-smoking character out of a Damon Runyon novel, and he offered to solve our problem by introducing us to Don Hiebert.

Don had been in Cominco's finance group in Montreal and, as a rising star, had been sent to Harvard Business School in order to groom him for greater things. He had just graduated from there when Joe convinced him to jump ship and join Teck. Ian Sinclair, then the head of Cominco's parent company, Canadian Pacific, was apoplectic, and never forgave us for poaching him. We were, of course, dutifully crestfallen, genuflected, and then got on with it.

Don would be with us for six years and did yeoman's work in helping get Newfoundland Zinc, Niobec, and Afton financed, which required some effort since in all cases the construction cost would be close to or higher than our company's entire market value at the time. It would also be in an era of the first oil shock, extreme inflation, and interventionist governments, all of which would test the mettle of the best of us in the natural resources business.

The Yom Kippur War, the Oil Shock, and Federal-Provincial Wars

On 6 October 1973, the holy day of Yom Kippur, Syrian and Egyptian forces invaded Israel, with support from some other Arab nations. Israel was caught unaware but not unprepared, as it turned out. Initially seeming to have been overwhelmed, within days it had gained the upper hand, and, less than three weeks later, a ceasefire was worked out with UN help.

The fallout from this was an Arab oil embargo, put in place by the Organization of Arab Petroleum Exporting Countries (OAPEC) against the western countries seen to have supported Israel in the conflict. This included the US, the UK, and Canada, among others. By the time the embargo was formally lifted six months later after negotiations at the Washington Oil Summit, the price of oil had risen from $3 a barrel to almost $12. This led to a severe recession and gasoline rationing, particularly in the United States. It had a serious impact on the mining industry as well. Demand evaporated and the price of copper fell like a rock to less than 60 cents a pound, despite Hart Horn's advice to our friend Barrett a few months earlier that it would never again go below a dollar.

US miners cried foul and began to lobby for the imposition of a tenfold increase in import quotas on copper and zinc. Ross Duthie, then the president of Placer, said: "The proposed U.S. tariff would ruin the Canadian copper industry. You can only stockpile copper, as with any other product, for so long before you go out of business." Gerry Hobbs, president of Cominco, railed against all of the "government-owned copper mines in Chile, Zambia, Peru and Zaire that produce flat out, creating excess supply and low prices." This mantra became the conventional wisdom of the times.

Undaunted, Canada tried to follow suit by attacking its own producers. Prime Minister Pierre Trudeau began what some interpreted as a war against the provinces when, seeing provincial governments reaping income from their resource taxes and royalties, which had long been tax-deductible, his government decided to make them non-deductible and grab a piece of the pie itself. This was often reported as "federal-provincial squabbling" over resource taxation, but whoever was actually the squabblee and who the squabblor, we producers were caught in the middle.

In Saskatchewan, for example, the royalty on Teck's oil production increased tenfold between 1972 and 1976, from 35 cents a barrel to $3.50. With the Trudeau government's declaration of non-deductibility, we would pay the full royalty to Saskatchewan, and also pay taxes to Ottawa on that same amount as though we had been able to keep it, even though we hadn't, in effect being taxed twice on the same income. As a result, in the last quarter of 1976, for example, Teck reported $1.8 million in petroleum earnings before taxes and royalties. After the dust of the two squabblers cleared, we the producer were left with 15 per cent of that. The two feuding levels of government took 85 per cent.

This was described by one wag as being a resource tax system "that would do Lewis Carroll justice." Even Lewis Carroll couldn't possibly have imagined this era among civilized people, although Bonnie and Clyde might have.

They were difficult times, but we had to keep trying to manage our business and do creative things. Times would actually get worse as the decade ended, with inflation soaring out of hand and no end in sight.

Rationalizing Our Oil Interests

Regardless of our concerns about taxation, by 1976 our oil holdings were increasingly an anomaly in what was a growing mining company. To illustrate the relative values, back in 1971 oil production had been quite important, contributing $3.6 million to Teck's operating profits compared with only $433,000 directly from mining. By 1976 though, we had Newfoundland Zinc and Niobec in production, Afton starting construction, and two more potential new mines in the works. Mining profits were due to increase dramatically, and we could consider weaning ourselves from oil as a source of cash flow.

Our experience to that time had been that we produced oil, sold it, and then poured much of the proceeds back into the ground based on pretty slide presentations, generating a giant sucking sound. Oil production was still a decent business, although it was increasingly being tapped by government taxation. It was oil exploration that we had realized was not part of our core expertise.

It seemed to us we had three options to rationalize that anomaly: sell the oil holdings outright, stop exploring and retain the holdings primarily to fund new mining projects, or deal them into an operating oil company with good management, of a size where our production might enhance its value, and in which we might retain a measure of control and participation in its growth.

That third option was in our minds in 1976 when we purchased 25 per cent of North Canadian Oils Ltd (NCO), a Calgary company, from its founder Frank Rubin. His son Bob was by then president and we agreed he could stay on in that role, since he seemed to understand the oil business reasonably well, certainly better than we did. Our expectation had been that we would later arrange to roll our oil properties into NCO for additional shares, ending up with a substantial shareholding in a well-managed, separate oil company as our new mines came on stream and began contributing more significantly to our profits. We could then stay with our new oil vehicle or sell it as a good, going concern, depending upon how the world unfolded. It seemed like a good idea.

Reality often gets in the way of a good plan, and as we came to the second part of it and were looking at rolling our Steelman oil field and other interests into NCO, we had difficulty agreeing on values with Bob Rubin. That is understandable, but when Bob said at one point: "I represent all of the shareholders, not just Teck," it not only rankled a bit, but we could see that things weren't likely going to work out. The point was fair enough and as it should be, but not the attitude.

Fortunately, we had come to know the iconic Jimmy Connacher of Gordon Securities quite well. Always alert to doing a possible deal, he put us in touch with Jimmy Kay, a Toronto clothing magnate who, for reasons that are as obscure to me as they are unimportant, wanted to get into the oil business. Kay controlled a company called Dylex, and with Connacher's assistance, we quickly worked out a deal to sell our 25 per cent shareholding in North Canadian to him.

I telephoned Bob Rubin's Calgary office to see if I could meet him in Toronto "to introduce him to someone." It turned out that he was in Halifax and could meet me the next day, so I flew to Toronto in the morning and met Bob at the King Edward Hotel. We went upstairs to Kay's room, and Jimmy was there with his lawyer Trevor Eyton. I said to Bob: "I'd like to introduce you to your new owners." We chatted for a few minutes and I left them, flying back to Vancouver the same day. We made a $2.5 million profit on the whole transaction, which wasn't bad for five months of work and a plane trip.

Unfortunately, NCO was also listed on the New York Stock Exchange, and we weren't aware of US tax regulations related to short-term profits, those made on investments held for less than six months. We got a letter from the SEC demanding payment of US excess taxes, and I'll never forget the reaction of our chairman, the Right Honourable Roland Michener. He was apoplectic, raging about "extraterritorial intrusions into our country" or some such. Apoplexy aside, we needed to do something, and it was settled for a relatively modest sum of a few hundred thousand dollars.

One should never say die, and we started in with a similar rationalization plan again a few years later. Oil prices had moderated after the excitement of the 1973 Oil Shock had abated, but surged again with the extreme inflation of the late 1970s. In December 1979, Teck purchased a 25 per cent interest in Coseka Resources, a well-run oil and gas company operating out of Calgary, for $36 million.

This time the relationship was more constructive. Coseka's president Peter Kutney actually wanted to add our oil production to his own oil and gas holdings. He welcomed our chief financial officer, Don Hiebert, to his board of directors, and we planned to negotiate the ultimate transfer of properties in an orderly fashion.

However, this sound idea was overcome by the events of the next year as "the great inflation" seemed increasingly likely to lead to "the great correction," and 17 months later we sold that same shareholding for $77 million. It was, as we shall see, just in time.

It is a bit out of sequence, but to complete the story of our exit from conventional oil production, we would finally manage to accomplish it in stages from 1983 through 1990 by selling our petroleum assets to Trilogy Resources for shares, and then selling Trilogy.

Our share of oil reserves in the Steelman Field had peaked at 20 million barrels, and its contribution of some 4,000 barrels a day of production had been important to us for many years as we assembled and built our package of new mines, but it had become redundant. Teck was finally out of the business of exploring for and producing oil and gas, some 30 years after acquiring Devonian.

Times change, and 15 years later, in 2005, Teck would again become exposed to oil as we took a 15 per cent interest in the Fort Hills Partnership, formed to develop the Fort Hills oil sands property north of Fort McMurray in Alberta. In this case though, it would be based upon Teck bringing our mine operating expertise to the venture, which would combine open pit mining of the oil sands with conventional petroleum industry expertise to be contributed by an oil industry partner.

The partners would change with time but ended up being Suncor and Total Canada. Teck's partnership interest in the venture is now 20 per cent, and as of early 2017, construction of a $17 billion mine is well advanced. Teck's share of proved plus probable bitumen reserves in the Fort Hills oil sands property alone stood at 570 million barrels at the end of 2016, and our share of the 190,000 barrels a day of planned bitumen production capacity is expected to be 38,000 barrels per day, each dwarfing the reserves and output that were so important to us back in those earlier days. The world works in mysterious ways.

Encountering Debt Problems, and Resolving Them

Returning to the mid-1970s, one of the fallouts of a turbulent era is that optimistic or entrepreneurial people can run afoul of the debt devil, and both my father and I encountered that creature at different times in the period. It was certainly a learning experience, and one that most entrepreneurs will encounter at some point. In fact, any who have yet to do that are almost bound to in their future.

In my case, it happened in the early 1970s after we had put together the properties that would be the building blocks for our future. I was so certain about them that I borrowed heavily to buy Teck shares, in anticipation of that fabulous day ahead. I didn't count on any of Dave Barrett, Alex Macdonald, or the Yom Kippur War and consequent recession, and my debts were soon at least twice my net worth. Fortunately, that net worth was low, the loans were small and at three different banks and none of them noticed me. I managed to skate through, but it was nerve-wracking. It is an experience one doesn't forget.

By 1977, when we already had the first two of those new mines in production and a third under construction, things should have been looking very good for us. However, the downturn, low metal prices, and tax indecencies all combined to leave my father with a similar but larger debt to assets problem. He was, by his own description, a gunslinger or riverboat gambler, and his solution was naturally more innovative than just hunkering down and hoping to escape notice, not to mention the fact that the bank had already noticed.

Faced with a difficult level of personal debt, his ingenious solution was to borrow *more* money and use it to buy additional Class A Teck shares in the market, over and above his previous core holding. It will be recalled that, on creation of the dual share structure, all 4.8 million of the previously issued common shares were converted to Class A shares, so there were a reasonable number held by the public that could be purchased. His plan was to sell these extra shares at a premium to a compatible buyer who would support what we were doing and, hopefully, be fairly passive. The story of how that unfolded is interesting, and would have some important indirect impacts on Teck as well.

Initially, my father kept his situation to himself and one of his long-time financial advisors, Len Watt, who put him in touch with the American conglomerate, Union Carbide, as a potential partner. That large industrial company was not widely known in the mining industry, but actually did operate several US mines producing tungsten, uranium, and vanadium, and seemed interested in doing a deal to help him out.

However, time passed and negotiations soon began to break down. Carbide had this strange idea that, if they solved his financial problem, they should have some kind of real hold on my father and the rest of his shareholding. They referred to it as "needing a clear path to control." It seemed that passive was not a word in Carbide's corporate vocabulary, and this initiative was not going well.

By now the cat was out of the bag and Bob Wright and I were in on the plan. We were asked who we might know as a possible passive buyer. Bob suggested Associated Metals, New York metal traders that he had met. I suggested our long-time friends at Metallgesellschaft, and someone came up with Messina Transvaal, a South African company that Roland Michener's geologist brother, Charlie, had consulted for after retiring from Inco.

We asked my father how many extra shares he had for the partner and what price he wanted. He replied that it was 675,000 Class A shares and that he wanted $8 a share. I think they were trading at $6 or less at the time. Bob Wright and I said we'd go to work. We decided we'd start by asking for $10 a share, and see where it went from there. So Bob went off to New York, I called on Metallgesellschaft. and Charlie arranged for us to meet David Thompson, co-chief executive officer of Messina. In each case we said the price would be $10, and in each case they replied: "Okay, sounds good."

This was probably the easiest negotiation we'd ever had. Maybe we had priced it too low?

Our job now, price not being an issue, was to decide which of the three we'd prefer as partners, and we fairly quickly decided it was between Metagesellschaft and Messina, each an international mining company that might bring new partnership opportunities to Teck. So we started negotiating with the two of them.

First, we took David Thompson on a fishing trip to Stuart Island, off the coast of British Columbia. David actually caught the largest salmon and told anecdotes about geranium farming for perfume and about his mentor, "The Commander." These were stories that I can't remember now but we all thought were hilarious, and we got along well. This guy is a lot of fun, I thought.

However, when we returned to Vancouver and got down to the hard bargaining, David tried to tie us up in knots, even more so than it appeared Union Carbide had been trying. He was pleasant enough in this, but there were no ifs, ands, or buts about it. He wanted to be sure Messina had a clear and unequivocal path to control, even if it would be delayed, and anyway not for long!

We also met with Metallgesellschaft, whose people took a longer-range view. As its president Karl Gustaf Ratjen said: "We've been in business for over 100 years, and we have the patience to wait until you're ready." As well, we knew Metall from many concentrate and joint venture negotiations in the past, and several of its people had become good friends. We were also aware that Messina was subject to South African exchange controls, and would have difficulty getting funds out of the country to join us in future joint ventures, whereas Metall suffered from no such restrictions.

It actually was a simple choice to pick Metall, but I thought at the time that if I ever got the chance to have David on my side of the bargaining table, I'd take it. I knew David wanted an opportunity to move with his family to Canada, and as it happened, that chance would come for both of us within two years.

So Metall bought the shares for $10 each, to hold 14 per cent of the outstanding Class A shares. Karl Gustaf Ratjen and Heinz Schimmelbusch joined the Teck board and Ratjen became a very supportive board member. The press reported him as saying a few months later: "Teck is an investment and it also generates projects. The best partners are those who are active, hungry and competent." He flew back to Frankfurt "with a briefcase full of mine development proposals from Teck."

The working relationship was good from the start. In addition to Karl Gustaf and Schimmelbusch, Klaus Zeitler also joined the Teck board, and he would remain one of our closest friends for many years to come, long after Metall lost its shareholding. All made good directors: they were compatible, knowledgeable internationally, and brought good ideas. Metall would join us as partners in some projects, bringing marketing knowhow as well as risk financing.

Initially, Metall owned the new block of Teck A shares directly, but as time went on it seemed a good idea to meld the two blocks, Metall's and some of my father's, into a joint voting block. The lawyers spent a lot of time looking at ways that might work for both, but in the end it was my brother Harold who came up with a simple solution: to meld them into a jointly-held new holding company aptly named Temagami Mining Company Ltd. It became known as "the Pamper box solution" because the idea occurred to him while riding on Lake Temagami in his motor skiff and that was the only paper available to write it down on (figure 17.1).

So, some time after the initial purchase, Metall and my father formed a new Temagami Mining Company, this time a private holding company. Metall rolled its A shares into Temagami and my father rolled a slightly larger amount in as well, so that he would own 51 per cent and Metall 49 per cent of the new vehicle. Combined, Temagami would hold the largest voting position in Teck, and this has continued ever since.

Interestingly, back at Berkeley one of the minor requirements for a PhD had been the ability to read in two other languages, in addition to one's primary language. Naturally I had enough French to cover one off, but the second one had become a choice between German and Russian, both of which would have to be learned. I had debated with myself and eventually chose Russian, on the premise that most scientific publications in German would quickly find themselves into an English translation, whereas that was less likely to happen in Russian. Academic that I was trying to be at the time, I decided I'd teach myself Russian so I could keep up with publications in both languages.

Imagine my surprise a few years later, when it became evident that most Russian geological publications were also being translated into English fairly quickly. If only I'd taken German instead. Then, when our new friends from Metallgesellschaft, like Schimmelbusch, would break into German in

Figure 17.1
Harold Keevil as he came up with the "Pamper Box solution" while on Lake Temagami

a taxi or in a meeting, all the while casting sidelong glances at me to see if I understood, I could have. It might have been especially interesting if I'd understood, but I was able to pretend I didn't.

Dr Werner Busch and the Temple of Gold

In 1979, a year after that investment by Metallgesellschaft, Bob Hallbauer, my father, and I were asked to visit them in Austria to speak about our company. This was at a seminar Metall had organized that included speakers from two of its other recent international investments as well. En route to Vienna we were being guided through the historic monastery of St Florian by Karl Gustaf Ratjen, Schimmelbusch, Zeitler, and Metall's financial vice-president, Dr Werner Busch, from whom we would seek words of wisdom beyond the scope of our limited knowledge.

Our Lamaque mine, and the gold industry at large, had received a new lease on life after President Nixon took the US off the gold standard in 1971, finally freeing up the price of gold. By 1979 gold had soared to US$400 an ounce.* However, inflation was rampant, costs at Lamaque had gone up dramatically as well, and we weren't sure what the future might hold.

So in that august setting of an important old monastery, with its stained glass windows and ethereal music, and in the presence of the most impressive Werner Busch, who we were sure would understand such matters better than us, we asked what Metall thought would happen to the price of gold. Busch replied immediately that it had gone too high and was sure to come down.

Perhaps forgetting what had been done to the scribes and pharisees in a temple almost 2,000 years earlier, we took this as a message from on high, not to mention from Werner Busch.

My father asked if he could use the abbot's study to make an important telephone call. Leaving the rest of us to listen to the music played on the famous Bruckner organ in the basilica, he went inside, closed the door, and sat down at the abbot's desk. With a giant crystal crucifix hanging just over his head, my father called his broker and sold the next two years' worth of Lamaque's gold production forward at US$400 an ounce.

Within six months, gold had soared to over US$800 an ounce and we had a huge loss. So much for inside information from such exalted sources.

Acquiring Yukon Consolidated, and an Interest in the Lornex Mine

Some of our other financial transactions in the period had better results.

Yukon Consolidated Gold Corporation, the brainchild of famed UK promoter Newton Treadgold, had been incorporated in 1924 to consolidate gold dredging activities in the Klondike region of Yukon Territory. The stories about its financing, promotion, and operations could fill a book, and have, in fact, in Lewis Green's fascinating *The Gold Hustlers*.

---

* Prior to 1970, the Lamaque labour union had negotiated a price participation clause for its members. If the price of gold, and/or the EGMA (Emergency Gold Mines Assistance) payments went up, they would get a piece of the action. It had never paid off, so in 1970 the union leaders insisted this incentive be removed in favour of higher wages. The next year President Nixon freed up the price and it took off, never to look very far back. It is not known what happened to the union leaders.

Years later, with the Klondike gold rush a distant memory, Yukon would provide some early funding to prospector Egil Lorntzen to help him explore a copper prospect in what would become British Columbia's Highland Valley Copper district. Not far from Bethlehem Copper's mine, Lornex would turn out to become the first large-scale open pit copper mine in the region, with an initial daily mine and mill throughput of 38,000 tons. This was, in the mid-1970s, the largest metal mine in Canada, dwarfing Bethlehem, Craigmont, Brenda, and the undeveloped Valley Copper deposit we saw earlier

The controlling shareholder in Lornex Mines was Toronto's Rio Algom, with a 68 per cent shareholding. Yukon held 22 per cent, with the remaining 10 per cent being held by Egil and public shareholders. Lornex was considered by most, and not the least by Rio Algom, to be an appendage of that company.

Yukon was itself by that time controlled by Atlantic Assets Trust, a fund managed by Ivory and Sime of Edinburgh, Scotland. In addition to its holding in Lornex, Yukon had about $20 million in cash and marketable securities. With us still having more ideas than cash at all times, we were always interested in friendly acquisitions of other companies that were flush with cash, particularly if they held good mines or prospects as well. It had worked for us before.

When Yukon came into our sights in 1978, we were trying to decide how to approach them to see if it was for sale. Don Hiebert said that he knew its president, Neil Ivory, who was resident in Montreal where Don had lived in an earlier time when he had been with Cominco. It was agreed that Don would call Neil Ivory, which he did. The answer was short and sweet. There was no way Ivory and Sime would sell.

That should have ended it, but Norm Rudden, our treasurer and a person who didn't understand why we should take no for the final answer, asked why we wouldn't call Scotland directly, just to be sure? Well, why not?

None of us knew anyone at its Scotland headquarters, so I said I'd try the call, not really expecting it to pay off. I saw that an Ian Rushbrooke from Edinburgh was on the Lornex board, so made a cold call to him to see if the shares would be for sale.

Ian turned out to be quite friendly, almost eager for a taciturn Scot. He said they most certainly were interested in selling, and that in fact he would be in Vancouver in two days and we could try to work something out then.

So we met for lunch at my house. Ian, whom I'd never heard of, let alone met, became "my new best friend," as they say, and we did a deal. We bought their 54 per cent interest in Yukon for $8 million and 444,000 Teck B shares, and Ian agreed to sit on our board of directors.

Thank you Norm Rudden. This was a good illustration of why the adage "nothing ventured, nothing gained" should never be forgotten.

We called a board meeting by telephone that afternoon to approve the deal. All of our directors were agreeable, although Karl Gustaf grumbled a bit about our style of doing quick, opportunistic deals by telephone rather than following the usual, deliberate, Germanic ways to which he was accustomed. It was, to be fair, his first ever Teck board meeting, and in due course Karl Gustaf got somewhat used to us. Metall, on the contrary, would get less deliberate as time went on, much to its chagrin, but that is for another story.

The Yukon deal would have been a reasonable one in any case, but as with some earlier acquisitions, there was a jewel box hidden in there, this time a large one. It turned out that George Albino, the CEO of Rio Algom, had been planning to announce a doubling of capacity to 80,000 tons per day at the Lornex mine. This of course would result in a huge increase in value for the shareholders, which now included us. Whether Ian had been aware of the plan or not is unclear, but I think Albino never forgave us for scooping Yukon out from under him.

Through our new Yukon holding, we were entitled to two members on Lornex's board, and Bob Hallbauer and I filled those. With Rio Algom holding the hammer with 68 per cent of the shares, the Lornex meetings tended to be a bit of a governance travesty. No information was provided beforehand to the independent directors like us. A few rudimentary slides might be shown at the brief meetings, but no paper was handed out for the record. We were even discouraged from taking notes. During one meeting Bob brought out a camera and tried to take pictures of the slides, but was roundly criticized for inappropriate behaviour.

I began to realize why Ian had been so quick to agree to sell. They, and now we, were definitely the minority shareholder, and were treated accordingly.

In any event, the expansion was announced and construction began shortly after we bought our shares. The purchase proved to be one of the better ones we had made to that date. We would complete a merger with Yukon later that same year, bringing the cash and valued Lornex interest directly inside Teck.

Starting to Build a New Mine at Highmont

We had acquired an option to build the Highmont mine back in 1969, the same year that we acquired what would become the Newfoundland Zinc and Niobec mines, as well as the Schaft Creek copper deposit. However, with two new mines to be built in Newfoundland and Quebec and our subsequent acquisition of Afton, the low-grade Highmont copper prospect had been relegated to fourth in line.

The Highmont property actually contained part of the whole Highland Valley copper deposit, which stretched from Bethlehem and Valley Copper at the north end, through the Lornex mine in the middle, and then the Highmont property uphill and to the southeast. The copper and molybdenum grades varied over the large system, with Highmont having relatively more molybdenum than the other parts. In all cases the copper grades were low by historic mining standards.

We had continued working on the feasibility study while we built those first three new mines, including driving a tunnel underground and excavating vertical shafts up from it to get bulk samples from places where we had previously drilled holes with good ore grades. The purpose was to test a hypothesis that some of the friable molybdenum mineralization may have been washed away during the drilling process, and that actual mineable values could be slightly higher than those shown by assaying the drill cores.

The underground work had tended to bear out that hypothesis, although it wasn't conclusive, but the fact that we had to try to prove it at all illustrates the risks inherent in mining extremely low-grade deposits like these. Unlike a high-grade mine such as Temagami, Craigmont, or Kidd Creek, every fraction of a percentage point in assay results can count in a low-grade deposit.

Eventually, after Afton had been completed in 1978, we announced a production decision on Highmont. With the delay, the capital cost estimate had risen from the $65 million we had announced tentatively in 1971, and now amounted to $150 million for the planned 25,000 tons per day operation. Construction began in 1979 and was scheduled for completion in mid-1981, a two-year span in which economic conditions would become even more volatile.

CHAPTER 18

BULLMOOSE COAL, SAVING ORDER FROM CHAOS

It is the highest impertinence and presumption, in kings and ministers, to pretend to watch over the economy of private people.
Adam Smith

As this is being written in 2017, Teck Resources is now the second-largest producer of seaborne steelmaking coal in the world, after the BHP-Mitsubishi Alliance in Australia, but how we got there was not particularly easy.

It had started with an investment in Brameda Resources that didn't work out at first but, with good geological work and a bit of luck, one thing led to another, and we found a new and much better coal deposit than the one first on display. It would almost be lost through government fiat and mismanagement as well as a severe recession but with perseverance these tribulations were overcome, and we were able to build a successful new coal mine at Bullmoose Mountain in northern British Columbia. This is the story of how Teck began in the coal business.

The Madness of Crowds

When we left our activities in the northeast coal region in chapter 16, we had managed to regain our Sukunka coal licences after Dave Barrett's Minister of Everything had tired of them. But we would find later that Brascan, which was to finance development of the deposit, had decided to abandon the project. We now had it back and had to decide what to do about it.

This was a time when many of the major oil companies had decided the grass looked greener on the other side of the fence, particularly in copper and coal mining, and seemed intent on chasing deals. In one classic example, British Petroleum (BP) had bought the Kennecott Corporation, just before copper and molybdenum prices cratered. Industry analysts were routinely describing BP's move into minerals as an unmitigated disaster. Less than eight years later, B P would turn around and sell its B P Minerals division to mining giant Rio Tinto, just before metal prices and Kennecott's fortunes were about to turn back upwards.

In 1977, the oil giant Atlantic Richfield Company (ARCO) bought Anaconda Copper, which had seen its major copper mines in Chile and Mexico expropriated early in the 1970s. The price of copper promptly fell, and ARCO was forced to suspend operations at the miner's remaining Butte mine in Montana. Anaconda had also held large coal operations in Wyoming, and ARCO's plan had been to diversify its energy business into coal. Six years later its founder, Robert Anderson, said he had hoped Anaconda's resources and expertise would help him launch a major shale oil venture, but that the world oil glut and the declining price of petroleum made shale oil moot.

And this was in 1977!

Earlier, Shell Oil had acquired Billiton and operated it as Shell's mining arm for a while before eventually getting out, selling it to Gencor Limited.

It seems that some large companies are distantly related to lemmings. One will make a move in some direction, and its competitors will feel the urge to follow. Sometimes the path may lead to greater glory, and other times to a cliff. The lemmings back in the pack are often the last to know.

Sukunka was one of the best coal projects available in terms of coal quality, and Shell, Gulf Oil, and B P were all willing to take a hard look at a purchase or joint venture. For our part, we still had little interest in pursuing the underground resource. It was a matter of finding a way to feed their appetite on the Sukunka part, while somehow retaining the upside potential of our new open pit coal prospect at Bullmoose.

Understanding the Geology

To understand what happened next, it's helpful to step back and review briefly the coal geology of the area.

Coal occurs in sedimentary rock formations, having been laid down as flat layers of organic material in swamps and wet lowlands many millions of years ago. In northern British Columbia, the beds that have now become coal seams were laid down in the Lower Cretaceous geological period in which dinosaurs flourished, about 100 million years ago. Dinosaur footprints can be found today in some of the nearby sedimentary rocks.

These organic layers alternated with other, economically uninteresting sedimentary rocks like shale or sandstone, and this whole sequence of inter-bedded rocks became buried deep in the earth below other, later rocks.

It is the pressure and temperature from that deep burial that converts the organic material to coal. Depending upon the degree of metamorphism, the coal as it occurs today may be suitable for use in making steel (coking or metallurgical coal), for simply burning to generate power (thermal coal), or for nothing much at all. Most coal produced in the world today is suitable simply for power generation, but a small proportion has the right combina-tion of low impurities, heat content, and sufficient coking strength (ability to support the load of iron ore above it in a blast furnace) to be used in steel-making. Of that, a small proportion is of exceptional quality and is known as high-quality coking coal.

Eventually, erosion of the later, near-surface rocks may expose the older, once-buried sedimentary formations that now contain coal, and make them accessible to be mined.

In mountainous country such as we find in British Columbia, some of these deeply buried sediments have since been uplifted and become exposed at surface by the forces that formed our mountains. These are often no longer horizontal but may be inclined, folded, or faulted, which of course, com-pared with simple, flat-lying sediments, can complicate mine planning.

Complicating it further, mines in British Columbia produce coal from rock formations that contain several distinct coal seams that are inter-bedded with barren sediments. The coal must be separated from the inter-bedded waste rock either by mining it selectively or in a coal washing plant, which is equivalent to a mill, or concentrator, in metal mining.

In the northeast coal region where we were exploring, the most impor-tant coal beds occur in one of two quite separate rock units, the deeper Geth-ing Formation, which contains the Sukunka coal seams, and the younger Gates Formation, laid down as carboniferous sediments some three million years later. The Gates Formation currently lies about 300 metres strati-graphically above the Sukunka coal seams.

The Sukunka coal that had been the focus of the exploration by Brameda, Teck, and Brascan is exceptionally high-quality coking coal. The fairly flat coal seams as they are now exposed outcrop on the side of a steep mountain and extend deeply into it. They can be sampled at the surface outcrops or by driving tunnels into the mountainside along the coal seams, and that plus di-amond drilling is how we obtained samples that proved the quality.

Unfortunately, that geometry also means that the coal would have to be mined by underground methods, as opposed to the kind of large-scale open pit mining that is used by most modern coal and metal mines in Western Canada. Underground coal mining can be dangerous, because the coal often contains methane gas that can explode in confined tunnels. It also involves mining techniques with which few Canadian miners are familiar, and which are generally more expensive than open pit mining. All of those are reasons why we had brought in financial or experienced underground coal operating partners previously, and were inclined to do so again.

Meanwhile, very little work had been done exploring for coal in the Gates Formation in the vicinity of Sukunka. It was known to contain significant coal seams elsewhere in the area, notably on Denison's Quintette property to the south, but little attention had been paid to its potential in the area that Brameda had staked out.

Bill Bergey Discovers the Bullmoose Coal Deposit

In 1976, Bill Bergey, who had been a major player in the Temagami discovery, designed a program to look for areas in which the Gates Formation occurred close to the surface. He was looking specifically for places where the slope of the present mountainside was dipping at the same inclination as the underlying Gates rocks, so that there was a chance of finding coal close enough to surface that it could be mined economically by open pit methods, without having to mine too much waste rock to get at it. His rule of thumb was that the coal should be buried no deeper than beneath 30 metres of overlying waste rock, and that the seams be approximately parallel to the surface.

Bill is one of those geologists with an eclectic mix of talents from geology through geophysics to geomorphology, another example of reasoning that "whatever works" is good enough. In this case, he used the regional geological maps that showed generally where the Gates coal seam occurred, and air photographs that could be interpreted to identify dip slopes.

Once possible dip slopes were identified, they could be tested by diamond drilling to confirm or reject the possibility of quality, accessible coal. Bill's drilling in 1976 indicated some 60 million tonnes of apparently good-quality coking coal on what we named the Bullmoose property. More work would have to be done to confirm coal quality and marketability, but first impressions were that this smaller but near-surface resource stood a much better chance of being economically mineable than the well-known Sukunka coal seams far below it.

The Negotiations with Oil Companies

Returning to our plans for Sukunka, we were offering to sell it outright to one of the international oil companies lusting after it. We also wanted to retain the Bullmoose part of the large property, in case further exploration would result in a commercially viable coal deposit there.

Of the suitors, BP was very interested in Sukunka because of the exceptional coking coal quality, and seemed most likely to ignore the potential of the coal seams in the Bullmoose area. This made for a reasonably simple negotiation, and in early 1977 an agreement was reached to sell them 100 per cent of the deep Sukunka portion of the property while we would keep 100 per cent of the near-surface Bullmoose portion. BP would pay $25 million on closing and a further $5 million upon the proposed rail access being completed. This was an important deal for us, because we needed some of that $25 million to put back into the Bullmoose property, so we could determine how much coal was actually there, and whether or not it could in fact be mineable economically.

There was one complication. Coal and other exploration licences are defined by surveys on the surface of the earth, and extend downwards with vertical boundaries. While part of the Bullmoose coal seams was on adjoining and separate properties, part was in the Sukunka licences, although well above and separate from the Sukunka coal seams.

So we had agreed with BP that we would divide the property, not by vertical lease boundaries alone, but in such a way that BP purchased rights to the deep Gething coal and we kept the upper Gates part, even where one coal seam lay vertically above the other. It is a method used often in the oil business, where one company might earn rights, say, below the Devonian formations, and leave the rights above that with the selling party. It is not that difficult to understand or to explain, apparently other than to some oil company lawyers and bureaucrats.

"We're the Government; We're Here to Help"

These are said to be the seven most frightening words in the English language.

The Pierre Trudeau government was still hanging its hat on its nationalistic decree that no foreign investor could acquire a majority interest in any Canadian resource property. BP would have to overcome this restriction when it sought approval from the Foreign Investment Review Agency (FIRA). So we advised BP and its lawyers to point out that they were purchasing only the underground half of the coal property, and that we were keeping the potential open pit half. They were buying 100 per cent of half of the coal and 0 per cent of the other half, which, using simple arithmetic, could be argued as buying 50 per cent of the coal prospects, not 100 per cent. Initially we thought they understood the concept and would run with it, but perhaps because their chief geologist was blinded by Sukunka and never saw the value of the Gates coal showings at all, they didn't. How they expected to get it past FIRA otherwise is still unclear to us.

We tried to keep our eyes and ears on how it was going, but it was not easy. Eventually, one day we heard a solid rumour that it was not going at all well in Ottawa, and that our deal was likely to be rejected. I called the FIRA official who had the file, one Konrad von Finckenstein, and said I'd like to explain our position. His response when refusing to even meet with or listen to us, unbelievable as it may sound, was: "The seller has no status with FIRA."

That was one of the most obtuse comments I've ever heard, even coming from Ottawa. It doesn't take more than a moment's thought to realize that, in an open marketplace, it's reasonable to assume that perhaps half of the proposed deals negotiated by intelligent Canadians and presented to FIRA might actually be better for the Canadian seller than for the foreign buyer, or at least be advantageous to Canada as well. It would have seemed useful for FIRA to have been willing to listen to the seller's viewpoint as well. That is not rocket science.

Jean Chrétien Saves the Day

The rumour mill out of Ottawa began to get hotter, and one Friday we learned that FIRA planned to turn down our deal with BP at its regular meeting the very next Wednesday. It was our last chance to try to do something about it.

The minister in charge of FIRA at the time was Jean Chrétien, the future prime minister, who none of us other than our lawyer Bob Wright, a well-established Liberal functionary, had ever met. Bob arranged for us to meet Chrétien the next Monday afternoon.

Wright, Hallbauer, and I arrived in Ottawa Sunday night, and first thing Monday morning we went to see two of the other ministers that represented British Columbia, while we waited for our date with Jean Chrétien. Neither of those BC ministers had the slightest interest in our problem. One spent the whole time powdering her nose haughtily. The other was no more helpful. This didn't seem to augur well for our upcoming meeting with the minister who actually did have the file, but we went in to see Chrétien with our heads high, although our optimism diminished.

By this time our argument was well rehearsed, if fallen previously on deaf ears, and we started in to describe it to minister Chrétien. We pointed out that we were hoping to sell 100 per cent of the uneconomic, bad half of a coal property so we could keep 100 per cent of the other, good half. Surely this would be better than selling the permitted 50 per cent of both the economic and uneconomic parts? It would be good for both Teck and Canada, and probably not so good for BP.

Chrétien listened for about two minutes and then said: "Either BP is very stupid, or BP has very stupid lawyers. Hold on a minute." He picked up the phone, called the head of FIRA and told him not to deal with the BP submission that coming Wednesday. He wanted to meet with him first.

A little more than a week later, our deal was approved by FIRA after all. We now had the whole Bullmoose property, plus the funds from BP to keep on exploring it. Within a few years we were able to build a successful, major mine there. BP had Sukunka, which they too would eventually realize was not worth trying to develop, and abandon.

I've had an admiration for Jean Chrétien ever since. He had an uncanny ability to get to the core of an issue quickly and accurately, and the willingness to deal with it.

Convincing the Japanese Steel Mills

Securing the Bullmoose property and raising the funds to continue exploring it was just part of the battle. Once we had established our coal reserves, we needed to convince the Japanese steel industry of the quality of the coal and arrange for long-term purchase contracts with them, this at a time when that whole steel industry was in recession and already trying to renegotiate its existing, prior purchase contracts with the southern BC producers.

We needed to arrange for extensive investment, whether by government or privately, in new rail and port infrastructure to get the coal to the coast and on board ships to Japan or elsewhere. And we would need to coordinate that with the much larger and better-known Quintette project that Denison Mines had been promoting for some years.

We also had to overcome the fact that Teck had never mined coal, although for that matter neither had Denison, and that the established coal miners in southeastern British Columbia were, to put it at its kindest, not exactly our biggest supporters in Japan. They were not averse to denigrating our relative inexperience in coal mining to the Japanese, in hope of maintaining their secure position as the only steelmaking coal suppliers from Canada.

In fact, some reports had them almost convincing the Japanese steel mills, which operated as a buying consortium, that our relatively small mining company, experienced primarily in metal mining, was just interested in promoting the property, and then selling and running. After all, it was pointed out by nefarious persons-unknown, but perhaps from southeastern BC, that we had just sold Sukunka for a good price.

Nobody said it would be easy.

That was the stage when Bob Hallbauer led a delegation to Japan to present the new Bullmoose project in early 1978. There had been brief, earlier presentations to the two coordinating mills that handled negotiations with Canadian producers, but this was the first one in which all six major steel mills were present.

Our newly-christened "chief coal engineer," Dick Drozd, set up the presentation. The steel mill experts were gathered around both sides of a long narrow table, and Dick had put up a series of maps on the walls, starting on the long wall on one side, proceeding along it to the end, and across to and down the other side wall. Each map or drawing showed some key part of the planned mine, in a nice, orderly sequence.

The meeting, which would take all day, began with Dick at the start of the first wall, eloquently describing the drawing in front of him and explaining its finer points. Then he proceeded to the next drawing, and went through its important features in some detail as well. This continued up that wall, across the head of the table, and back down the other side, consuming a good part of the morning.

At the end, Bob realized that some of the steel mill representatives were still looking ahead at the first wall, many with their eyes shut, and some emanating polite noises which sounded suspiciously like snores, while Dick was busy finishing his presentation behind them, to their backs.

It was not the most auspicious start, and things may have seemed to be accelerating downhill when one of the steel mill's experts asked Dick: "How deep were the trenches you put down to test the surface oxidation of the coal?" Naturally this was the one thing Dick hadn't checked, and, when he couldn't answer, the Japanese person turned and said: "Mr Hallbauer, next time please bring someone who can answer all of the questions."

However, by the end of the day the mood had turned. Bob and Dick had done a fine job and the steel mill representatives had begun to realize that this was a serious project that could be worth continued interest on their part.

But the lack of infrastructure remained a problem. Bullmoose theoretically could truck a limited amount of coal, perhaps up to 500,000 tonnes a year, 100 kilometres to the nearest railroad operated by BC Rail, but there was no coal loading port at the end of its north-south rail line. There was talk of building a small port near Squamish, in Howe Sound, or of using the Neptune facility in North Vancouver, but doing something at the Pacific port of Prince Rupert seemed more logical.

We kept working on the engineering and feasibility study in the months that followed, but with only lukewarm support from Japan, which still thought they were paying the existing southeastern miners too much. Nissho-Iwai, our designated trading company for the property, continued to work diligently to keep us in front of the steel mills as an option, should they eventually want to encourage a new coal producer.

By 1980 the situation began to change, with the steel mills emerging from a long slow period, and planning to convert some of their oil-injection blast furnaces to coal as the price of oil continued to rise. This would require an increase in coal purchases from the two main suppliers, Australia and Canada, and Australian production had been hampered recently by a series of labour disputes at the mines, railways, and ports.

Canada was beginning to look relatively attractive again, and the level of Japanese interest turned from trying to find ways to secure small incremental tonnages from existing producers to trying to encourage as much as 5 million new tonnes in one fell swoop. If this could be done, and at the same time arrangements made to establish a major new coal port at Prince Rupert, that would add capacity and alternatives to balance off the constraints of the main existing rail and port systems in southern BC

Finally, instead of politely hearing us talk of possibilities, the steel mills became active supporters of the plan to develop what would once again become known as the northeast coal project. Bob Hallbauer was invited back to Japan to negotiate with NKK, the main coordinating mill for Canadian coal purchases, in June 1980. The meeting was hosted by NKK's managing director Nemoto-san, indicating that the talks were to be serious.

Bob proposed a sales contract for 1.7 million tonnes of clean coal a year at a price of $75 a tonne, based upon estimated capital costs as of June 1980. Our proposal was that the actual price would be adjusted to cover escalation in capital costs between then and 1983, when the proposed mine, rail, and port could be completed and ready to ship coal. This was at a time when the price for coal from the southeastern producers was $63 a ton, and the difference would be the incentive pricing required to encourage construction of the new mines, the rail links, and a new port at Prince Rupert.

It should be recalled that this was at a time when inflation in North America was rampant, and Bob was concerned that Teck not take all of the risk. Nemoto-san asked what the additional price component would be at the time of first shipment and Bob said he didn't know, but that $10 a tonne might be enough to cover inflation until then. The $75 base price itself appeared to be generally acceptable, but the uncertain escalation part was not well received on the Japanese end. However, Nemoto-san asked his people to continue to negotiate.

Denison was in Japan at the same time to negotiate for the nearby, larger Quintette project, since it was understood by all parties that it would be necessary to have both new mines built in order to gain financial support for the proposed new infrastructure. Its talks followed a similar pattern except that Cliff Frame, Quintette's chief negotiator, indicated he would accept a fixed price of $80 with no escalation if that would get the deal done.

While negotiations on price dragged on, Nemoto-san led a delegation to Ottawa to encourage support for northeast coal, and received a reasonably warm reception from the federal government and CN Rail. They met in Toronto with Denison, who by then appeared ready to sign off on a price just under $80 for Quintette.

Nissho-Iwai, doing its best to facilitate matters, agreed with Bob's suggestion that Nissho take a 10 per cent joint venture participation in the mine to show support, and they quickly agreed on a price of $8 million for this, plus of course an obligation to fund its $30 million share of what was expected to be a $300 million project.

The Nemoto mission met with Hallbauer in Vancouver on its way back, and Bob promised to come to Tokyo shortly with a final offer. Interestingly, although we didn't know it at the time, BP, which still held the Sukunka prospect, had also met with the Mission in Vancouver to try to have Sukunka reconsidered, but without success. The Japanese mills were no more interested than we had been in that potential underground mine, and BP soon abandoned all work on its project.

During our Christmas holiday we received an urgent call to return to Tokyo for "secret" negotiations during the Japanese New Year holiday. Teck had been holding out for a higher price than Quintette, including the variable portion, and in private meetings with Bob Hallbauer, the NKK managers indicated that this might be acceptable after all.

Parallel Negotiations with Governments

If the interplay between buyer and seller was complicated, the need to find a way to finance the infrastructure was even more so. It would require a new rail link from the existing BC Rail and CN lines at or near Prince George to the new town of Tumbler Ridge, where the proposed rail loading facility would be located. It would require shipping arrangements to be agreed with CN Rail from Prince George to the port, and construction of a new coal loading facility at Prince Rupert, likely at Ridley Island.

In Ottawa, Prime Minister Pierre Trudeau had been defeated in June 1979, and a new minority Progressive Conservative government had been elected. It was unclear what if any policies might change with respect to the northeast coal project that, while not progressing quickly in the previous few years, had at last become an active file. One of the ministers most supportive of it had been Robert (Bob) Andras, who had been Minister of State for Economic Development under Trudeau.

Then, in the spring of 1980, the minority Conservative government was defeated, and a new election was in sight. It was being actively and even emotionally debated in Ottawa whether Pierre Trudeau should or would run again, or stand aside for new blood.

A number of strong ministers from Trudeau's previous government paid him nocturnal visits as he pondered the choice, some encouraging him to stay and others to stand aside. Bob Andras was one of the latter. Trudeau took what became a famous "walk in the snow" one evening, and returned to declare he would run again. Bob Andras saw the writing on the wall, and announced he would not.

We had been impressed by Bob's enthusiastic support of the northeast coal project, and strong sense that what we proposed would be good for Canada, so we asked him to come west to join Teck as a vice-president. Bob knew whom to talk to back East, and he took on the task of managing our negotiations with Ottawa. He was extremely effective, and so dedicated to completing what he started that, when he was diagnosed with cancer shortly after joining us, he insisted on carrying on with the plan. I recall plane trips back East with him while he was in obvious pain, but he kept at it.

Bob Andras passed away in November 1982, before the mine was completed, but by that time he knew it would be, and that he'd been a key part of making it happen. I was honoured to have been a pallbearer at his funeral, along with Liberal luminaries including Donald MacDonald and John Turner. Bob was a great guy, extremely effective on a tough file and, as with Jean Chrétien, without him northeast coal might never have gotten off the ground.

The Complications Continue

Getting this whole thing negotiated and assembled was a bit of a chicken and egg situation, in that the Japanese steel industry would not have contracted to buy the coal under firm, long-term contracts unless the infrastructure commitments were in place, but neither the provincial nor federal governments would have committed to the infrastructure investments without those long-term marketing arrangements being agreed on. All of the diverse parties had to come to a positive conclusion at more or less the same time. It was, as one participant described it, a bit like trying to herd cats.

Government plans were complicated by political noise. In BC, the NDP opposition was highly critical of anything proposed by the Bill Bennett government, just as a matter of principle. Minister of Economic Development Don Phillips, known as "the mouth that roared," was a strong proponent, so they weren't.

The provincial government was willing to help BC Rail build a spur line extending 120 kilometres from its existing north-south line through to Tumbler Ridge, and to share with the mines some of the costs of establishing the new townsite. It was also prepared to help both Ottawa and the miners where appropriate with the cost of building a new coal-loading port at Ridley Island, near Prince Rupert.

Support federally was less clear. CN Rail, at that time still a government-owned Crown corporation, would need to upgrade its existing east-west line with stronger steel rails, the older 100-pound rails being unable to handle unit coal trains. This in some ways was a no-brainer, because CN would quickly earn back its upgrading investment from the new coal shipping charges.

It was the Ridley Island port question that caused some of the most contentious delays in getting the final agreements assembled. To get it resolved Denison and Teck offered to finance and build the entire port themselves, and also to make it available on commercial terms to any other new coal shippers that would come along later to use it. We wanted to be able to control our own destiny for at least that part of the overall infrastructure costs, rather than be beholden to some other company, whether a Crown corporation or not. When Ottawa persisted in keeping control of the process, we seriously considered switching locations and building our own port elsewhere, perhaps at Kitimat.

Finally, in October 1981, Teck, Denison, and Canada signed an agreement to allow for the shipping of coal out of Ridley Island. The port would be built at a cost of $275 million by the National Harbours Board and owned, perhaps not surprisingly, by an old Montreal company named Fednav. Later, in 1991, the federal government would buy Fednav's share of Ridley Island.

The northeast coal project was finally ready to go. Quintette and Bullmoose would put up $1.3 billion and $300 million respectively, which were our construction costs to build the two mines. Ottawa would hand the $275 million port to Fednav, and CN would upgrade its rail line on a commercial basis. BC Rail would finance the spur line to connect Tumbler Ridge with its own existing line, which in turn would connect with CN's.

The total costs are generally rounded off when describing this as a "$2.5 billion mega-project." It sounds easy when you say it this way, although it was the most complicated, and seemingly neverending, set of negotiations we'd ever experienced.

Building the Mine

The project was budgeted at $300 million, more than three times what our Afton mine and smelter had cost, and double that of our planned Highmont copper mine. It would be our biggest undertaking yet.

Finally, Bob Hallbauer and his team were able to begin actually building the mine, 12 years after we got into the coal exploration business through Brameda and its aborted Sukunka prospect. It was five years after Bill Bergey and Ruben Verzosa had discovered a better mousetrap at Bullmoose, on an adjoining property.

Mike Lipkewich, another of our numerous Placer Development alumni, had been general manager at the Afton mine, and Bob gave him the option of moving to Tumbler Ridge to oversee construction and operation at Bullmoose, or accepting a promotion to Vancouver as general manager of Teck's Metals Division. Afton was by that time operating smoothly, and Mike chose Bullmoose, taking eight members of his Afton team with him to get the new coal project underway.

Mike and his team pulled it off again, completing final engineering and building the mine and plant within two years from the deal signing. The first trainload of coal left the loading station near Tumbler Ridge on 1 November 1983, just 18 months after construction began, and one month ahead of schedule. The whole thing had been completed for $273 million, $27 million under budget. This was an impressive feat, considering that the nearby Quintette mine, built at the same time as our mine, suffered an over-run of 10 per cent (see colour page 7).

It had taken only seven years from discovery to completion of mine construction, despite the seemingly insurmountable odds against it and the delays that kept cropping up. It was a credit to an exceptional team of close to a dozen people, each of whom made major contributions along the way.

Interestingly, with shipments from the mine to the port beginning ahead of schedule, an inventory of our coal started to build up there. The port was in danger of getting plugged, with no ships on the way. It turned out that the Japanese steel mills had assumed we would take several months to achieve full production, which was apparently considered normal, but in fact it had been achieved in a matter of days. Bob Hallbauer told them that he might have to call a press conference to draw attention to our problem, but the JSI managed to juggle its ship destinations and the problem was resolved.

Teck celebrated its Fifth Annual Mine-Opening Golf Tournament at Prince Rupert a few months later, following a special train trip all the way from Tumbler Ridge. Guests on the trip included Nemoto-san and dozens of his Japanese compatriots; a host of bankers, consultants, investors, and suppliers; and of course the whole engineering team that had made it happen.

Despite difficult economic times, the honey pot provided by suppliers and bankers, and for which the golfers competed, reached a record high amount. David Thompson, by then our new chief financial officer, who doesn't play golf but takes a strange enjoyment in raising money, played a key role in this. He wrote as follows:

> The CN Railway provided a special passenger train to take all of the Opening Day guests from the mine to Prince Rupert. It was a tradition that when Teck opened a new mine it held a golf tournament where prizes were awarded, paid for by donations from the company's suppliers and, particularly, the banks.
>
> Dick Drozd and I were given the task of raising the donations whilst we were on the train. We started in the first carriage at the front of the train and obtained numerous contributions from our suppliers as we walked through the first few carriages.
>
> We began to notice the absence of the Japanese banks and were told that they were retreating toward the last carriage, in the hopes that we would not find them. When we reached the last one they started to explain apologetically that they did not have any authority from Tokyo to make any donations. However, we were able to explain that this train had an international phone service so they could phone their offices in Tokyo, which were by then open. There would of course be no charge for the telephone call. In the end, all the Japanese banks contributed and the prize fund reached a record of $70,000. The ceremonies and the golf tournament were a great success. As usual, Bob Hallbauer and Norm Keevil won numerous prizes as a result of their competitive spirit.

Some have suggested that David, seeing the potential profitability of this, went out and surreptitiously began taking golf lessons ahead of the next mine-opening tournament. If so, it has not been recorded how long it took before he abandoned the quest, not realizing what all golfers have long since learned, which is, as the well-known mine-finder Robert Friedland once observed: "The situation is hopeless, but it's not serious."

Epilogue: The End Game

Bullmoose had given us a successful launch in the coal mining business. It would lead eventually to Teck being asked by the banks to revitalize the Balmer coal mine in southeastern BC, built years earlier by Kaiser Resources, which had gone into receivership. Renamed Elkview, it would be the linchpin that would lead to all of Canada's major steelmaking coal mines being consolidated into a single entity under Teck's control, creating the Elk Valley Partnership that is now the world's second-largest seaborne shipper of coal to the steel industry.

Without Teck having been in the vicinity working on Sukunka, the ingenuity of Bill Bergey, the quick mind of Jean Chrétien, the support of the provincial government and the Japanese steel industry, the hard work of Bob Andras, and the performance of our mine-building team under Bob Hallbauer, Dick Drozd, and Mike Lipkewich, it would never have happened.

Jean Chrétien left government for a while but returned later and became a very effective prime minister. The FIRA functionary remained in government roles of ever-increasing responsibility for another 30 years. Only in Ottawa.

CHAPTER 19

CHINA, A GIANT STIRRING

China is a sleeping giant. Let her sleep, for when she wakes she will move the world.
Napoleon Bonaparte

China Emerges from an Interlude

At the same time that rapid changes were occurring in Canada and elsewhere in the western world in the late 1970s, important events that would eventually affect us all were underway in China. I had the privilege of visiting that great country several times in the early days as that was unfolding.

There are extensive books with Western insight on the most recent evolution that was occurring, including the recent *On China* by Henry Kissinger and *Deng Xiaoping and the Transformation of China* by Ezra F. Vogel. These go into great detail about a period of change that may, in hindsight, seem to have inferred some sort of grand plan or destiny.

Far be it for me to try to describe even a small part of what went on in China over the last century, but a few brief words on the country's path leading up to our visits may be in order, given the changes that were underway then, and how important they have become to us in the decades since.

China had enjoyed one of the oldest and often strongest civilizations in the world for much of the last 4,000 years. From around 1270 until 1911, it had been ruled in succession by three long-lived dynasties, beginning with the Mongol Kublai Khan, the grandson of the conqueror Genghis Khan. It was Kublai Khan who, in 1265, ordered the construction of a major palace in Beijing that was the precursor of the Forbidden City. It would become the capital of the country for much of the succeeding three dynastic regimes, his Yuan, the Ming, and finally the Qing.

A war in 1368 drove the Yuan Mongols from power and established a new dynasty, the Ming, which would rule for almost 300 years until 1644. It was followed by the Qing Dynasty, which would also rule for nearly 300 years until it too collapsed, beset by incursions from an expanding western world on its borders.

According to the International Monetary Fund, as reported in *The Economist*, China had been the largest or second-largest economy in the world, in terms of purchasing power parity, for most of the time since the birth of Christ and, as recently as 1820, produced a third of global output.

For much of its history China had been isolationist, like the United States more recently, but for different reasons. China's emperors and their coteries had enjoyed the sense of occupying the highest level of civilization for centuries, and it was as though the sun rose and set on their great country. The world was made up of Chinese and the other, lesser people from nearby countries whose main purpose was to be supplicants to the Empire. Perhaps in retrospect the reasons were not so different.

But times changed as the nineteenth century drew to a close. External forces were impinging on the periphery, militarily and economically. Their small island neighbour, Japan, gave China a shocking defeat in the sea battles of 1885. As Vogel wrote: "Along the coast and even along some of the land borders, the Chinese military could not stop the advance of foreigners, and civilian leaders could not halt the expanded commercial activities," and "as the challenges to the system grew more severe, it remained difficult to convince the rulers in Beijing that their system, which had survived for almost two millennia, was under serious threat."

By the time Deng Xiaoping was born in 1904, China's last dynasty, the Qing, had been irreparably weakened by its inability to deal with both interior rebellions and the intrusions of foreign powers along the coast. That dynasty finally collapsed in 1911 and the country entered into a period of warring states. A Chinese Republic under Sun Yat-sen was established after the fall, but was short-lived and was followed by a similarly short-lived military regime. Power then devolved into the hands of regional governors and military commanders.

Kissinger quotes from a fourteenth-century Chinese epic, *The Romance of the Three Kingdoms*: "The Empire, long divided, must unite; long united, it must divide." It would be almost 40 years before it would begin to be united again.

The new Chinese Communist Party was formed in the countryside in 1921. By that time the Nationalist Party, started by Sun Yat-sen and then led by Chiang Kai-shek, had gradually achieved a measure of control over parts of what had been the Qing Empire, but the efforts of both sides were affected by invasions from Japan during the 1930s. With the end of the Second World War Japan was gone and the country was left divided, with both the Communists and Nationalists aspiring to central authority.

In 1949, the Communists under Mao Zedong finally defeated the Nationalists, who retreated to the island of Taiwan. China was, for the most part, once again unified.

Deng Xiaoping was a military commander under Mao, self-trained, as were most of the leaders of the internal war. After the Communists won, Mao was clearly in charge, but for the next 25 years Deng was never far away from his side. Both would be leaders in the fateful "Great Leap Forward" of 1958 to 1961, designed to transform the country from an agrarian economy to an industrialized communist society. It would end in "The Great Chinese Famine," resulting in tens of millions of Chinese deaths. In the aftermath, Mao's star faded for a time and Deng's, the pragmatist looking for solutions rather than drama, may have risen, although it seems that was not necessarily seen as a career-enhancing move.

Sure enough, in 1966, shortly after the failure of the Great Leap Forward, Mao and his wife, Jiang Qing, unleashed the "Cultural Revolution." The influence of the Red Guards, a student initiative at one university, spread across the country and was co-opted by Mao to eradicate the "four olds:" old customs, old culture, old habits, and old ideas. Old books and art were destroyed at random, and museums were sacked.

The movement soon descended into attacks on people rather than objects. Intellectuals, "capitalist roaders," and other old leaders were attacked and forced to indulge in public self-criticism, often before being sent into the countryside to work as simple labourers and learn appropriate humility. Many of them suffered physical as well as psychological attacks, and Deng's oldest son was hurt so badly he became a cripple for life. Deng himself was relegated to menial tasks for several years before being reinstated.

According to Henry Kissinger: "Mao's China was, by design, a country in permanent crisis; from the earliest days of Communist governance, Mao unleashed wave after wave of struggle." He quotes from a letter Mao had sent to Jiang Qing in 1966: "The situation changes from a great upheaval to a great peace once every seven or eight years. Ghosts and monsters jump out by themselves. Our current task is to sweep out the Rightists in all the Party and throughout the country. We shall launch another movement for sweeping up the ghosts and monsters after seven or eight years, and will launch more of this movement later."

One of the few older leaders who appeared to have survived most of the various traumatic episodes intact was Zhou Enlai, well-known and admired in the West as a cool foreign minister under Mao. Zhou, ever the pragmatist, was once asked what he thought of the French Revolution. His response: "It's too early to tell." Nevertheless, in 1973, as Deng was being brought back into the leadership fold, he was asked to attend Politburo meetings to lead the criticism of his old friend Zhou.

Nothing lasted forever then, and by the end of 1975 Deng was back in Mao's bad books once again. Like Michael Who and Bob Who, whom we saw in chapter 12, he would from time to time become Xiaoping Who, and he was instructed to resume his own self-criticism. It may have been around then that he coined another of his famous aphorisms: "It is very easy for chaos to come overnight."

The great upheaval Mao had promised every seven or eight years seemed to have become perpetual, but his time was due to end at some point, and a key question would be who and what would succeed it. In January 1976 Zhou passed away, followed in September by Mao's own demise. An era had ended, and a new one would evolve, albeit slowly at first. Before leaving, Mao had once again removed Deng Xiaoping from all official positions and elevated Hua Guofeng to be acting premier.

Soon after Mao died, it became clear that his widow, Jiang Qing, was planning to lead a group of comrades in a putsch to seize power. Interestingly, it was actually Mao himself who, realizing something might be up, had derisively named the conspirators "The Gang of Four" some months earlier. Hua and his confidantes, sensing the plot, went about arresting the gang members in the dead of night, and the threat was eliminated. Then Hua, as the anointed leader in charge, could begin to consolidate his power. To help in this, he announced that, in addition to criticizing the Gang of Four, the Party would continue its criticism of Deng Xiaoping.

For some people, it can be said that nothing comes easily. However, there is another old Chinese saying: "If you wait by the banks of the river long enough, you'll see the bodies of your enemies float by." Deng had a lot of support from others in the Party, and it soon became evident he should once again be brought back into the fold. The problem was that, while he and Hua had worked together many times, they didn't see eye to eye philosophically.

Hua's claim to fame was to have been chosen by Mao, and his banner was that Party policy should be based on the "two whatevers." This was to say that "whatever policies Mao supported, and whatever instructions Mao gave, should still be followed," according to an editorial in *The People's Daily*. Deng was the pragmatist who was to coin the aphorism about it not mattering if the cat was black or white, as long as it caught the mouse. He was a proponent of "the four modernizations:" science, technology, agriculture, and national defence, and of the need to open up to western experience to achieve these.

Notwithstanding their apparent differences, Hua saw the need for Deng's talents, as well as the upswelling of support for him in some quarters, and indicated that there would be a time for him. Not to be out-aphorismed, Hua said: "When the rain falls, a channel for transporting the water is formed automatically," and, in case that wasn't fully understood: "When the gourd is ripe, it falls off the vine."

Sure enough, Deng was soon given back most of his official roles, including vice-premier, vice-chairman of the Party, and a member of the Standing Committee of the Politiburo. In his acceptance speech, he supported Mao's legacy and Hua profusely, although admitting that errors could have been made at times. He said: "If after my death people will say that what I did was 70 per cent correct, that would be quite good." He tried to create room for flexibility, and said: "We must revive and carry forward the practice of seeking the true path from facts, the fine tradition and style which Chairman Mao fostered."

That is just a small sampling of the evolving situation when I began a series of visits to that great but recently isolated country, at the time largely unfamiliar as far as the West was concerned. Historians and others have written countless thousands of pages on the subject, some even contradictory. I pretend no claim to either accuracy or depth, and this is only to remind the reader that the China we know today in the twenty-first century was a much different place back then. It was about to embark on a major growth trajectory, one that would remain largely unnoticed in the western world for some time.

The 1979 BC Trade Mission to China

I was fortunate to have had the opportunity to visit China in those changing times, first participating in a provincial trade mission in 1979.

Bill Bennett had succeeded Dave Barrett as premier of British Columbia, and was one of the first Canadian leaders to recognize both the changes occurring in China and the potentially rising importance of Asia and the Pacific Rim as an economic partner. The 1979 trade mission was prescient, as one of the earliest contacts between Chinese and Canadians in the modern era. It presaged the eventual establishment of British Columbia as Canada's gateway to Asia, and was an example of Bennett's farsightedness. The mission included a diverse group of businessmen and entrepreneurs led by Bennett's Minister of Economic Development, Don Phillips.

On arrival at the Peking airport, we were driven downtown in three government limousines. During the whole trip into town these were the only three cars we saw. Driving down the main street, we passed through some 10 or 15 unmarked lanes of bicycles going each way, all ridden by Chinese wearing almost identical blue Mao suits and Mao hats. Without any sounds from the limos and with the riders apparently not looking back the bicycles would magically part to allow us to pass and then just as quietly return to their previous positions. It was a fascinating start to a 14-day trip, and now, 37 years later, is a surreal memory when we visit exactly the same street in Beijing and see six lanes of cars moving rapidly in both directions, and the new hotels and shops lining the sides of the road.

We toured the important historic sites in and around Peking such as the Forbidden City, the Summer Palace, the Ming Tombs, and The Great Wall. We visited glass factories where dozens of girls worked at long tables assembling toys and, at the other extreme, small steel mills where I have a vivid memory of a young lady standing atop a furnace doing something with a ladle lowered into a raging fire just below her. In all cases there were banners outside the premises reading "Warm Welcome to Visitors from British Columbia."

I had been interested in tungsten at the time, and in the fact that China seemed to have endless tungsten resources that would appear periodically on the market, creating a surplus and driving prices down. The few producers in the West, particularly in Canada and California, where we had just visited Union Carbide's Bishop mine, had often complained that Chinese production statistics were unavailable or unreliable, and that this made it difficult for them to forecast future supply and prices.

On the way to The Great Wall I asked our young tour guide, who seemed quite well-informed, about China's future output of tungsten. Her reply, with a twinkle in her eyes, was that it would be much lower because "a lot of our mining and geology maps were destroyed during the Cultural Revolution, and besides, we're running out of ore." The fact that these were probably related was not lost on either of us.

We met formally in a huge room with the Minister of Defence and his deputy minister from another part of the vast country, and it was fascinating to see them relying upon an interpreter in conversation between the two of them. Precisely why we were at that ministry was not altogether clear, since at the time British Columbia's fleet of military vessels was slightly smaller than the one Peter Sellers had commanded in *The Mouse that Roared*.

I noticed that the interpreter spoke English with a perfect Brooklyn accent, complete with the street slang one would expect. I asked him when he had lived in the US, and he said he had never been outside of China. He'd learned his English from a missionary, who must have been a New Yorker.

We went on to Shanghai, where we stayed at a government guesthouse that had once been the French embassy. This was a completely different setting than Peking, with more motor vehicles, many historic European-style buildings in good repair, and a bustling flow of ships on the Yangtze River. Interestingly, there were signs of colour in the clothing which had not been evident in Peking, often simply a scarf, but clearly a difference. As I returned to Peking several times in the next two years, the same Mao suits and hats would be prevalent, but each time I would notice more colour than on the previous visit. It was evident that a sense of encouraging individual self-expression was returning, and that change was in the air.

The same applies to visits now, many years later. The most common observation one hears from frequent visitors, Teck people, and others, is marvel at how much change there has been since the last trip, even just a short time earlier. The pace, then and now, continues to amaze most travellers.

In Shanghai and later Canton, we visited more plants and factories before leaving by train for Hong Kong. It had been a tiring 14 days in one sense, but as an introduction to a country that was on the verge of reassuming its major position on the international stage, it was important and unforgettable.

Unlike most federal or provincial trade missions, where it is expected that participants will sign contracts or letters of intent that have been agreed in advance, this one was intended as an introduction only. It would be up to the individual participants to follow up as each saw fit. Some did, and others didn't.

Our Return Visits over the Next Two Years

I had come away impressed with the people we met. They were friendly and open compared with the prevalent Western preconception of a fearful, closed society. It was a vast country, which some mission participants saw as a potentially huge market with a population of a billion potential smokers or Coca Cola buyers. Given our business as mine developers, I saw the other side: a large country with interesting geology, relatively unexplored, a place where we might go to discover and build new mines using the new geophysical technology and geological insights of recent decades.

It has to be understood that this was during the era in which the conventional, Malthusian wisdom among those who chatter was that the world was in danger of running out of resources. We in Teck had just built three new mines in Canada and had two more on the drawing boards, but as befits any good miner, we were ever on the lookout for the next ones after that. The exploration and development potential of that vast country, China, looked very tempting. The question was how to follow up that idea?

Rong Yiren, "The Red Capitalist"

As luck would have it, Henry Yung, one of my neighbours in Vancouver, was a nephew of Rong Yiren, an important Chinese whom Barron's magazine once headlined as "The Red Capitalist," a name reportedly given him by Deng himself. Rong Yiren had been one of the three Rong brothers who had run the largest textile operation in China, with 35,000 employees, in the years leading up to Mao's 1949 victory. Two of the brothers had then left China, one ending up in Australia and the other, Henry's father, in Brazil. Rong Yiren had stayed behind.

Mao had seen the need for Rong's talents, and he became part of the country's government, eventually rising to be head of light industry for all of China. He was purged and relegated to street sweeper during the Cultural Revolution, and members of his family were attacked savagely, but Deng had rehabilitated him after it was over.

Rong was, at the time of our visits, chairman of China International Trade and Investment Corporation (CITIC), a government investment company he and Deng had founded in 1978. CITIC's initial aim was "to attract and utilize foreign capital, introduce advanced technologies, and adopt advanced and scientific international practice in operation and management." The company they founded has grown into the biggest conglomerate in China today, with over 44 subsidiaries operating in many sectors across the Chinese economy. Rong would later also hold the roles of vice-chairman of the Bank of China and vice-president of the People's Republic of China.

Henry Yung went with me on my second, private visit to China to arrange introductions as well as to advise and interpret for us. He arranged for us to visit CITIC and to meet Rong Yiren several times in 1980. The second of these private visits included a small dinner with the Rong family at his home in Peking. His personal chef had previously been head chef at the Hawaiian Hilton, and dinner was appropriately exotic, including turtle soup, which consisted in fact of a removable turtle shell on top, hiding the insides of a cooked whole turtle beneath it.

Rong's home was not at all ostentatious from the gated front, but in the backyard he had planted a rose garden that he said was the best in Peking. In each later visit, we would make a point of taking him a new, exotic rose. For CITIC, short on computing power in those early days, we would bring the latest in what passed for portable computers.

Rong would later visit us in Vancouver, and we took him north to Savary Island on Jack Gibson's motor vessel the *Norsal*, the same boat from which we had managed the buying program that had won us the Afton copper mine. We fished for salmon with him while his wife jigged for cod. We rode bicycles, Peking style, along the beachfront dirt road, and finished with a lobster roast on the beach, with lobsters flown in from our zinc mine in Newfoundland (see colour page 8).

Meeting the Ministry of Metallurgy

Rong introduced us to the Ministry of Metallurgy, where we were told that decisions on mining exploration and development were made at the time. Our reception was good, and we were invited to return with a team to look at possibilities to work together.

We returned with a couple of our key engineers on our third visit, and sat across the table from the vice-minister of Metallurgy and a few members of his team. We told them we were interested in finding joint opportunities to explore for minerals using the new geophysical and geological techniques we employed in Canada, and that this could be in either established mineralized districts or in new grassroots exploration.

The first thing the vice-minister did after the opening pleasantries was, literally, reach under the table and bring up a set of maps of a nickel mine then in production. Jinchuan was the largest nickel operation in China, and one the government hoped to expand, perhaps with our help. This was intriguing, but we weren't in the nickel business, it was not really the kind of exploration-based play we had in mind, and the scale was a bit beyond our then still relatively small company. Jinchuan is now the fourth-largest nickel producer in the world.

So, while we were hemming and hawing, he reached under the table and came up with a copper project, Jiangxi, again quite large and of more interest. It was a major copper deposit in production that they hoped could be expanded, and of course in the years since it has been. Jiangxi Copper is now China's largest refined copper producer. In hindsight, we probably should have grasped whatever opportunity it presented, but it was a producing operation and not the kind of exploration project we had set our minds to look for at the time.

It has been said, generally unfairly, of some of us geologists that we would rather look than find.

As we pondered this, he reached under the table again and came up with maps of a zinc project they had in production in a modest way, and that perhaps could be expanded. I think there was one other prospect, but the bottom line is there was serious interest in doing something with us, and we agreed to send over some specialists to look at each possible project on site. That we did in the ensuing months.

The vice-minister entertained us at dinner the evening before we left after those first meetings, and I was introduced to a then-popular Chinese drink called Maotai. It comes in a bottle looking suspiciously like a can of WD-40, but does seem to taste somewhat better, especially in such social circumstances. He and I shared a number of toasts to our imminent success, and it is not recorded which one ended up under the table first.

On the plane back to Tokyo on the way home, I sat beside a gentleman who said he was with Anglo American, a larger mining company from South Africa. He had also been hoping to find mine development opportunities in China, and had arranged to be the guest of the Ministry of Geology, seemingly a logical place to start discussions. The problem was that this ministry had absolutely nothing to do with actual mining exploration and development at the time. But by the time my seatmate had realized this and tried to visit the Ministry of Metallurgy instead, he was told that was impossible because he was the guest of Geology, and besides Metallurgy was busy with other guests.

I didn't have the heart to tell him where we had been, and that we were the other guests. I never did find out if he came back or not.

Finding Ways to Make a Chinese Joint Venture Work

Of course there is a long way between wanting to do something together and the details, and in subsequent meetings in Peking, we started to focus on how we might be able to make a joint venture work.

We had a lot of experience with joint ventures in Canada, but reaching agreement at home was usually pretty straightforward. There were the usual questions such as: which side was contributing what asset, which would put up what proportion of the capital, which would operate any resulting mine, and what would be the relative sharing in the profits.

Each deal would be different in detail, but in Canadian projects we had the advantage that both sides worked with and understood pretty well the same accounting and business principles, so in a broad sense, a joint venture negotiation was not much more than filling in the blanks. Lawyers might have us believe differently and will cringe at the thought, but that was it in a nutshell.

In China at the time, it was not nearly that simple. While we weren't too familiar with "generally accepted accounting principles" as they might have been in China in those days, it seemed reasonable to assume they would differ materially from those we normally dealt with.

Without digging down into more detail than is necessary, there seemed little commonality of experience between us in how to account for labour costs, capital costs, transportation charges, and product pricing or sales, just for starters. A modest mine we might operate with 500 people could be the sole source of employment and revenue for a town of 20,000 people, supporting the hospital, school, government, and everything else in the area. This is a degree of multiplier effect with which we were not familiar. It was a situation that, back in those early days, seemed difficult to resolve with simple accounting for profits and losses according to Canadian practice, so it would have to be done some other way. A fairly obvious answer was some form of barter, and we focused on that in our ongoing negotiations.

Some of the ideas put forward for a theoretical 50/50 joint venture were along these lines. Teck might supply and import at its cost all of the heavy equipment (large trucks, mills, etc.) that weren't then available in China, and also provide overall engineering, construction, and operating management. China might supply, in addition to the prospect, the building materials, concrete, bricks, and mortar that were available locally as well as manpower for both construction and ongoing operations. China could also provide transportation by road or rail to deliver 50 per cent of the mine's product to the coast and on board ships for Teck's ownership and disposition. China would retain the other 50 per cent of the production for its own use or sale.

In other words, there would be no financial accounting needs and no concerns about manpower levels from either side's viewpoint. The trick would be simply to determine what proportion each side's contribution might be worth in terms of a joint venture percentage, make sure transportation was actually available, and then get on with it. Obviously this would be easier said than done, and the devil as always would be in the details.

But Negotiations Were Curtailed When the 1981 Recession Hit

There was mutual interest and we were making some progress when the western world went into the 1981 recession, considered at the time to be the worst since the Great Depression. The Club of Rome's fears about resource scarcity became a distant memory. The world didn't seem to need more new mines, nor would it for many years. In Teck, we went from being expansionist to pulling in some of our more extraneous horns, selling off pieces of assets outright or taking in partners to be sure of surviving the deluge.

With little imminent need for new mines it put paid to our initial attempts to do exploration and development in China. In retrospect, it was too early in any case and may never have been doable in a way that would stand up. Perhaps we were a bit ahead of our time, as in Chile a decade before.

Epilogue

Looking back from the perspective of 2015, our plans then may seem a bit ludicrous, but they did make some sense at the time.

It's ironic that, as time passed, China became fully competitive with many of the old established heavy equipment manufacturers in the West. China now builds trucks, mills, and world-class steel plants as well as anyone, and better than some, and has become the main buyer of a huge percentage of the world's mining products. Today, one might easily wonder why we would have expected anything else?

One also wonders whether Deng himself could have anticipated the magnitude and timing of the changes as they stand today? He did say in 1980 that his objective was to quadruple China's gross national product by the year 2000. When asked how this would be accomplished, he is reported to have said: "Hu knows?" In fact, his associate Hu Yaobang did know, and informed him that this would require a compounded annual growth rate of 7.2 per cent.

I guess we know now he really could have anticipated it, or at least hoped for it, and in fact China did do it, quietly and consistently. For many of us in the West, it took longer than it should have to notice and act upon that.

We would return to China more than 20 years later, and I was in Beijing in October 2005 when Rong Yiren passed away. China had changed much, as had we, each by feeling the stones as we crossed the stream, but first we would have to deal with the entrails of the deceased Club of Rome, and all the spirits, ghosts, and monsters from the 1970s.

EPILOGUE, PART THREE

The 1970s was a watershed decade in the history of Teck.

Despite sometimes chaotic economic times, with low economic growth, rampant inflation, and interventionist governments of various stripes, Teck was able to assemble the people, prospects, and financial capacity to build or acquire interests in four significant new mines, with two more on the drawing boards. While some of these were larger than others, it was a record pace seldom equalled in the mining industry's history and unlikely to be in the future, given the longer lead times that seem to be accepted to get things done in the twenty-first century.

Key to this was a series of mergers that saw most of the various companies that had been part of the diverse Keevil Mining Group, and the prospects they held, consolidated into one corporate vehicle, Teck Corporation. In a series of moves, affiliated companies Leitch, Highland-Bell, Silverfields, Area Mines, Iso Mines, Brameda, and Yukon Consolidated were all amalgamated into the new Teck. It would become the clear flagship for what had been a group of interrelated and at times competing companies.

Interestingly, our people had assembled the prospects that could become these new mines in a variety of ways. The zinc prospect that became the first new mine in the merged Teck Corporation had been an unheralded part of Leitch Mines when we acquired it. The Niobec deposit had been discovered by the Quebec government's exploration company SOQUEM, our old DIGHEM partner, and acquired by KMG when it was offered for development in an auction. The Highmont copper-molybdenum prospect was obtained through a negotiated development contract, while the Bullmoose coal prospect was a discovery by our geologists after working on a different, uneconomic coal prospect nearby. We acquired the Afton copper deposit after buying 50 per cent of the shares of the discovering company on the open market, and had the good fortune to buy 22 per cent of the large Lornex mine just before its operator announced a doubling of its capacity. "Whatever works" continued to be a useful exploration tool, augmented by all the science we could muster.

We have said many times: "A mining company without ore reserves is an oxymoron," and "The three key elements of a successful resources company are its ore reserves, the right people to develop and operate them, and the financial strength to pull it off." It can never be said too often.

We made important strides with the second element, operating people, beginning with Bob Hallbauer joining Teck from Placer Development, which in those days still had a reputation as one of the best-operated mining companies anywhere. Under Bob we were able to build up an engineering capacity that rivaled that of the old Placer.

There was one more thing, the ability to last long enough to actually build those mines, without being swallowed up by an interloper.*

With established, larger mining companies generally on the lookout for opportunities to acquire mines or ore deposits, and often able to recognize underlying value well ahead of most stock market investors, simply combining our group of companies into one would have put us "in play." Almost certainly, one of the existing larger companies would have swallowed Teck up before we could implement even a portion of that new mine development program. We even had a good idea which of them would have pounced.

Our solution was to establish a dual share structure, reclassifying all the existing, issued Teck common shares as a new Class A share, carrying 100 votes per share, and creating a new, single voting Class B share to be offered to minority shareholders of the Group companies being amalgamated, as well as used in any future underwritings, mergers, or acquisitions. It did work, and as we will see, Teck has been able to grow into a great, independent Canadian mining company, surpassing many of its potential predators.

At the ends of Parts 1 and 2, we compared the value of Teck with several of the other Canadian companies that had begun more or less contemporaneously with us.

In the following 10 years to 1980, both Inco and McIntyre had declined in size, losing a significant part of their earlier market value. Cominco and

---

* Interloper: A term to be invented by some notorious acquisitor in the aggressive 1990s, used to describe some other acquisitor who tries to interfere with the first one's prey, a.k.a.: raider, black knight, or "that darned other guy."

Noranda had continued to grow significantly, with Cominco tripling and Noranda being up by five times to $3.7 billion. Despite turbulent times, those were good years for both of them.

Teck had actually grown the most dramatically in size, up almost 17 times from $32 million to $546 million in the decade. More important, Teck had created significant value for its shareholders: $100 invested in Class B shares as the first of the new mines started production in 1975 had grown over 14 times to $1,480 by 1980.

Dr Norman Keevil, consulting geophysicist and explorer, on the cover of *The Northern Miner* newsmagazine, 1953

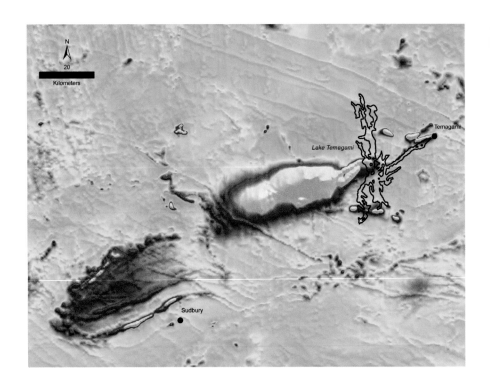

The Emerald lake magnetic anomaly, still not fully explained, and the major Sudbury nickel-copper mines to the southwest

Artist's depiction of the diamond drill hole that discovered the Temagami mine, 1954 (Painting by Frank Halliday, part of Teck and Keevil family archives)

Frank Halliday's depiction of the two near-surface Temagami copper lenses, separated
by a barren diabase dyke

The mine on Temagami Island. Surrounded by pristine lake country

Head frame over underground shaft at Silverfields mine

The author underground with one of the many deeper high-grade copper zones discovered at the Temagami mine, 1966

The Right Honourable Roland Michener at the opening of the Newfoundland Zinc mine, 1975. Access to the mine was through an inclined tunnel

The Niobec niobium mine near St Honoré, Quebec

The author, Chester Millar, and Norman Keevil Sr examining drill core at Afton prospect, Highmount's Bob Falkins behind, 1974

The Afton copper mine and smelter in ranching country near Kamloops, BC, 1981

Tony Yoshida, Mike Lipkewich, Takashi Fuse, Keith Steeves, Bob Hallbauer, Dick Drozd, David Thompson, and Lorne Hunter at the Bullmoose mine, Tumbler Ridge, BC

The first trainload of coal leaving Bullmoose in 1983

Teck's chief engineer Dick Drozd serving Newfoundland lobster,
with Rong Yiren and wife at Savary Island, BC

The David Bell gold mine at Hemlo, Ontario, with Noranda's Goliath
head frame and the Williams mine in the background

All three Hemlo mines produced ore from the same gold deposit. As the
mine opening in the photograph illustrates, the deposit dips down and
crosses onto the Goliath property at depth and to the north.

The Highmont copper-molybdenum mine as it began production in 1981, with the Lornex mine in the background

The Highland Valley Copper site in 2016. With a milling capacity of 140,000 tonnes per day it is the largest metal mine in Canada, and one of the largest in the world.

One of 13 seven-story high modules fabricated in the Philippines for Cominco's Red Dog mine in Alaska, opened in 1989. These modules were shipped to Alaska and transported by road 85 kilometres to the mine site where they were assembled into an operating mill.

The Red Dog plant site, 2014

Loading a coal train at the Elkview mine, Sparwood, BC

Author Norman Keevil and his wife Joan underground at Sumitomo Metal Mining's Hishikari gold mine, 1997

Ore sorting at the Hishikari gold mine

Robert Friedland, the author, and Raymond Boulle as they stand on Voisey's Bay
nickel discovery outcrop in 1995

Sumitomo's Imamura-san, Aoyagi-san, Shinozaki-san, and the author at a Canada-Japan Businessmen's Conference at Lake Louise, Alberta, 1993

The large Antamina deposit lay in part under a shallow lake, with the first excavation beginning on a high mountain top to right, 1999

Official opening of Quebrada Blanca mine, 1995. Solvent extraction and electrowinning plants at right, with mine trucks. Insets top to bottom: George Tikkanen, Gaston Fernandez of partner ENAMI with Joan Keevil and author, and Robert Wright, Teck chair

Mill construction at Quebrada Blanca 2 in 2022. Top: Alex Christopher, Teck President Harold "Red" Conger, retired CEO Don Lindsay, and Amparo Cornejo. Bottom: Teck CEO Jonathan Price with construction team

Wisdom, painting by David Lee, with three messages: Everyone could use a wise old owl looking over his or her shoulder; even a wise old owl goes out on a limb sometimes; but if the limb breaks, a wise old owl has wings to let it fly away safely

PART FOUR

A SEA CHANGE IN THE WORLD

*Political cycles turn after an extended period of either conservative or liberal
hegemony brings the baser, more self-seeking, or barmiest elements to the fore
... in a kind of Gresham's law of incumbency.*
Charles R. Morris, after Arthur Schlesinger, Sr

If the 1970s had been an era of sulphur and brimstone, of devilish
government and inflation running amok, the 1980s would begin
much differently.

Paul Volcker had been appointed chairman of the US Federal
Reserve Bank by Jimmy Carter, and was charged to "lick inflation to
the ground." Unlike so many others who had said this before, he
would actually succeed, increasing interest rates progressively until
they reached an unheard-of 20 per cent or more. As one might expect, this would be at great cost to those who had been riding the
inflation wave. Many entrepreneurs who had been successful for a
while by flying high on a debt binge would, like Icarus, plummet into
receivership, or at least into an abyss. The great inflation era would
end with a bang.

It seems a truism, which unfortunately has to be learned again
and again, that riders of waves should beware the aftermath of
the crests.

The western world, thought previously to have been in danger of
running out of resources, would find that it had plenty, perhaps even
too much for a while. It would not be the last time this would happen.
This would lead us into a new era that would later become known as
"the 20 years of declining resource prices, in real terms," although
as that era started none of us were aware how persistent it would be.

There would be a sea change in western world politics, from the
flower-children era of intervention and expropriation to Thatcher-
Reaganism. This would not necessarily make building things easier,

except that the challenges to be faced would tend to be cyclical, real-world economic events rather than those introduced by government fiat.

Teck would survive this meltdown through good fiscal management, thanks in large part to a new chief financial officer in the person of David Thompson, who we had first encountered in a fishing boat in Desolation Sound when he was hoping to acquire Teck for his then employer, Messina Mining. With a few timely sales and partial divestments, it would be possible to keep growing and adding value despite the imminent, and worst, financial downturn since the Great Depression.

CHAPTER 20

HEADY DAYS AS AN ERA NEARS ITS END

Don't gamble. Take all your savings and buy some good stock and hold it until it goes up. Then sell it. If it don't go up, don't buy it.
Will Rogers

There were storm clouds ahead as the 1980s started, but we weren't immune to considering things we shouldn't. This is a characteristic that seems to apply to a lot of entrepreneurs toward the end of any boom time, eventually leading to the financial demise of some. Fortunately, we passed on most of it, and what we did do turned out not to be too damaging. As well, 1980 saw David Thompson come on board from South Africa, and he would play a key role in keeping our ship heading in the right direction.

Chasing "the Great Inflation Hedge"

Inflation had become worse and worse, showing no signs of abating despite various dear leaders in various countries vowing to lick inflation to the ground. The price of oil, which had stabilized six months after the Yom Kippur Oil Shock, jumped once again. Metal prices were on the uptrend, led by gold. The Club of Rome, the most recent incarnation of the myths of Malthus, predicted that the world would soon run out of resources, and we were said to be entering "a new era of resource scarcity." Hard assets, such as metals and oil in the ground, or real estate and buildings, or even steel plants, were deemed to be the best inflation hedge, since every year it would cost more to replace them, and people began chasing after these.

Our three new mines were doing well, and we had two more on the drawing boards, plus the Lornex expansion. We too were on the lookout for more opportunities to buy or build assets. As we have seen, the grass had been looking particularly green across the ocean in China, with its supposedly vast, untapped mineral potential beckoning.

With inflation rampant and hard assets growing in value by the day, many entrepreneurs were prepared to go on a buying binge, loading up on debt that would in the end be paid off in debased dollars. It was eerily similar to a later new era in 2007 when people at large were chasing yield, this time in a low inflation and extremely low interest rate environment rather than high, but with a similar outcome as the world financial system eventually imploded. In both cases many people kept gambling right up to the end, for, as the head of one of the major US investment banks famously said in 2007: "As long as the music is playing, you've got to get up and dance. We're still dancing."

In 1980, people in the brokerage community were continuing to bring us new ideas, as they always do. Some of these we looked at seem rather strange in hindsight, but perhaps we are all dancers.

Brokers Try to Sell Us Steel Companies

One of these ideas, promoted by Jimmy Connacher's Gordon Securities, was that we take over Stelco, a large steel company with operations in Hamilton and elsewhere in Ontario. We had a lot of time in those days for Jimmy and his high-flying brokerage firm. It was the forerunner of investment banking in Canada, armed with backing where necessary from the rising Brascan Group, later renamed Brookfield. The genius behind Brascan was Jack Cockwell, and one of Jimmy's best mining analysts was a young Chris Thompson, who would later go on to become chairman of Goldfields of South Africa. With the small mining world in which we live, both Jack and Chris would years later become valued directors of Teck.

We would generally give anything Jimmy's team brought over a good hard look. But when his top steel analyst visited with an exciting report on Stelco, proceeding to tell us what a steal it was and that we should buy the whole company, we decided to pass. It proved to be the right decision for a lot of reasons, not the least of which were our lack of knowledge of the business, high interest rates, and concerns about an impending, severe recession.

But one tale from the times about another steel company is worth telling, if only to illustrate the general silliness of it all. As the market euphoria neared its peak, the brokerage firm Thomson Kernaghan approached us with a pitch to buy control of a company named Slater Steel. Slater had an operating steel plant near Hamilton, Ontario, and happened to have a fair amount of cash in the till. The latter was still somewhat attractive to us and, since hard assets were all the rage with investors, getting a steel plant into our mix, either to operate or to sell onward, wasn't totally out of the question if we could keep the cash on the way through.

But, before we leapt at this new opportunity, it occurred to us that it might be a good idea to actually see this steel plant. This was notwithstanding our faith in the broker, and in our old friend Len Watt, who had brought us Canadian Devonian and Union Carbide earlier and was now promoting the Slater idea. I was nominated to do the visit, armed as I was with absolutely no knowledge whatsoever of the steel business, but in good company on that score.

However, we were advised to keep our interest secret, so what to do? Len came up with the ingenious idea of getting me fitted out with a toupée, so that I could go in incognito, masquerading as an analyst with Thomson Kernaghan. We went to a professional wig-fitter he knew, presumably from previous devious affairs, and I was properly measured. The next morning, with the toupée ready to be picked up, I went with the broker to the wig shop and put it on over my "boney Toni." I guess they stuck the toupée on with something, because it seemed secure enough, albeit a bit odd. It wasn't completely clear to me that it would stay in place throughout the visit, but we geologists, while we may know nothing of steel, are used to dealing with risk.

We arrived at the plant and were ushered in to see the plant manager. I guess the meeting was going okay, because he didn't recognize me, and if my questions and answers were as dumb as I sensed, he probably just took that as being typical of steel analysts. Then he said: "I suppose you'd like to see the plant," to which I agreed, naturally. What happened next was one of the more unforgettable experiences of my secret agent career. The manager handed me a hard hat.

Now this should not have been entirely unexpected, but you have to appreciate that I already had a wig stuck on my head that felt as though it might fall off with the least nod, and to have to put a hard hat on top of that was like trying to wear two big, ill-fitting hats, one on top of the other. I walked around the plant like a zombie, stiffly moving my head as little as possible. The plant manager must have thought I was even more of an idiot than when I was asking questions in his office.

Fortunately, no one recognized me, so the tale has not been widely spread until now. Luckily, we turned down the golden opportunity to buy Slater. It was one of many things promoted to us at the time that we actually did not do, although for some of them the reasons have been long forgotten.

TDC: *Technology Development Corporation*

Naturally, in times such as these, the eclectic mind is able to see opportunity lurking around every corner. True to Downing's instructions, we were tempted to expose ourselves to success from time to time, and in 1980 we had formed a company to pursue non-mining things, calling it TDC: Technology Development Corporation.

I wasn't going to tell you about the oysters, but why not?

Tap Pryor was an entrepreneur from Hawaii my father had run across socially. He had been the force behind Sea Life Park, a popular tourist attraction for interacting with dolphins. It was, apparently, a commercial success and is still operating today. He was also a director of the small commuter airline Royal Hawaiian Air, and I remember flying with him one day as he told me that it had made better financial results the last year than United Airlines. I almost bit, until I realized United had lost a bundle, and it was just that Royal Hawaiian had only lost about half as much. Tap could really sell. So, naturally, one day he convinced us to invest in his new, on-land oyster ranching operation.

Now, most oysters prefer living and growing in salt water somewhere in the oceans, and generally in colder waters than occur in Hawaii, but Tap had a better idea, and actually managed to patent it. He leased some flat land with an abandoned airstrip in northeastern Oahu, and built 32 shallow ponds, each about 0.25 acre in size, on the old strip. Filling these with a few feet of brackish water, he began to raise phytoplankton, which grew like gangbusters under the prolific sunshine on that part of the island. This was to be the food source, because it seems phytoplankton is considered a delicacy by oysters, should any happen by.

The water supply was important, since it had to be clean and a bit salty, and by drilling a deep hole into a reservoir a few hundred feet down he found a suitable source, brackish water with just the right flavour for oysters.

Then he built a series of inclined trays with riffles in them in which he could place small oyster fry, gradually run the phytoplankton-laden water over them and watch the little ones grow. It was said that in cold northern waters it would take up to three years for oysters to reach commercial size, but that with his process they would achieve the perfect size in nine months.

It seemed to work, and when I first visited the site I was able to sample a few of the grown oysters, pronouncing them among the best I'd ever tasted.

Tap then regaled us with his next plan, which was based on the assumption that the favourite food of abalone, another even more valuable crustacean, was oyster waste. How he had determined that remained a mystery, but we took it at face value. Tap planned to install the abalone trays downstream from the oyster ones, and we could sample them as well the next time we were there.

A year later, I again visited the operation. On the drive over from Honolulu, I'd asked Tap how the abalone were doing and he said: "Just fine." After the usual site tour, we stopped for a couple of beers and a few oysters, and I actually ate 23 of them, a new record for me. They really were good, and sales were booming, largely to Japan. I asked the site manager where the abalone were, since I must have missed seeing them. He told me they'd all died six months ago.

I guess that should have been another of those first clues that I sometimes miss.

I haven't mentioned what was done with the water after it had passed over the oysters and the missing abalone. Under the usual regulations, it couldn't just be disposed of into the ocean, so Tap's team had drilled a second well into another deep reservoir. They were pumping the waste water down into it, and that seemed to be working out.

Things were going along okay, with growing sales in Japan, and Tap was anxious to expand upon this elsewhere in the Pacific. He had the idea that the rather poor island of Ponape, near Guam, would be a natural place for Oyster Farm 2, and that it could be financed amply with United Nations funds. So he arranged a visit to see the governor and, naturally, my father and I went along.

It was a fascinating trip. It took us an hour by jeep on rough roads to get from the small airstrip to the inn only a mile away where we were to meet him. We walked around a bit, among half-naked girls, little pigs rooting around, and mangoes and other trees with abundant fruit. A poor island maybe, but a bit idyllic, and of another time as well. The governor was quite interested, especially in the part about UN funds, and Tap left convinced we could pull off a real deal.

With the future bright, and with Tap talking it up to who knows whom, we were approached indirectly by an Indonesian investor who dearly wanted to own a piece of Tap's oyster business. In one of those strokes of genius, or just blind luck, we decided to sell out to him.

That is how we got into and out of the oyster business. Some months later, it was discovered that many of the oysters had acquired a parasite that, while purportedly not harmful to humans, made the oysters a bit unsightly. The Japanese market dried up, and things were tough. It turned out that the reservoir into which the wastewater was being pumped had breached into the earlier reservoir from which we drew the clean, fresh water, and somehow had created conditions under which the parasites, unlike the abalone, were growing and prospering. The operation went into receivership in 1982.

Perhaps we'll leave the desalination and lithium-molybdenum battery research projects for another time, along with how Teck got involved in drilling for oil and PIP Grants in the Beaufort Sea under Marc Lalonde's National Energy Program. "What's a nice young company like you doing in a place like this?"

Success Generates Mining Analyst Support

Despite such eclectic forays into the great unknown, our mining adventures had gone extremely well, even normally. With the success of three new mines and others in the pipeline, some of those analysts who, like Hank Reimer, who had been worse than ambivalent before, turned to full support.

In mid-1979, Gordon Securities' Chris Thompson put out a glowing Research Report on Teck Corporation, saying among other things:

Teck is a mining company with a long ancestry and which has developed a new image under the stewardship of the Keevil family. Teck's most notable achievements have been the decisions, taken during a period of a major recession and poor metal prices, to introduce three new mines at a time when few if any major mining companies could afford, let alone dare, to do the same. Subsequently Teck's engineering and project teams brought the mines on stream cheaply and quickly; again something few mining companies managed to do during the 1974–1978 inflationary period. All these mines are now flourishing in this embryo boom in commodity prices.

In addition to the success of the new mines, Teck has been active in obtaining new ore deposits which should provide it with scope for further growth," and it goes on to refer to Highmont, and "others of lesser importance such as the small Montcalm nickel deposit, the Bullmoose coking coal project, an expansion in their columbium mine, and beyond them, the large Schaft Creek copper-molybdenum deposit in northern BC, which in due course could become a major mine.

The future did look rosy, as often happens even when there are whispers of alarm bells out on the horizon. As it would turn out, this boom was not to last.

A Major Addition to Our Financial Team, at the Right Time

We saw earlier how Metallgesellschaft and Messina had faced off over the chance to acquire a shareholding in Teck, with Metall having come out on top. Messina's David Thompson had actually won the congeniality contest during our negotiations, but had been more than a wee bit on the too tough side when it came to negotiating details. Metall had been more relaxed, relying upon what its people saw as its own inevitability. We had said back then that we'd like to have David on our side of the table someday if the opportunity arose, and in early 1980 it did.

One afternoon, four months after we had bought our 25 per cent shareholding in Coseka Resources, Don Hiebert and I were seated together on a flight to Toronto for a Teck board meeting. Since we'd left Vancouver we had been talking about various odds and ends, but as we were on our final approach Don said to me: "Norm, I'm having trouble at home and I have to get out of Vancouver. Peter Kutney's offered me a job at Coseka, and I'd like to move to Calgary and take it."

"Don, that would leave a big hole for us to fill," I replied. "Let me sleep on it."

My first thought was that this could be the opportunity we'd been looking for to get David Thompson into our camp, and at the same time accommodate Don's wishes. So, the first call I made when I got to my hotel was to the Thompson home in Johannesburg, South Africa. It might have been Gail, David's wife, who answered and said that he was actually in Toronto on business, staying down the street at the Royal York Hotel. She asked what was up, and I told her we were going to see if David would come over to us in Canada. I think she said something like that would be peachy, and when could she come?

I called David, and we arranged to meet him for breakfast the next day. He was enthusiastic about taking on the job and we agreed on some numbers, but he said he'd have to talk to Gail. I had a pretty good feeling what she'd say. It was clear they both wanted to move to Canada.

When I got to the office, and just as the board meeting was about to begin, Don came over to say he was having trouble agreeing to terms with Peter Kutney and might not be able to move over to Coseka after all. I said: "That's too bad Don, but we've already hired your successor."

I wasn't intending it to sound cruel, although it may read that way, but from that point on my job was to try to help resolve the impasse between Don and Peter, and I'm glad to say that it worked out. Don went over to Coseka and did well there, becoming its vice-president as well as president of Coseka Resources (USA), and we finally had David on our side of the table.

This proved to be as timely an arrival as Bob Hallbauer's had been 12 years earlier, bringing in an entirely different kind of new blood.

When Bob had come on board we were facing some tough questions about our longevity-challenged ore reserve position. We had addressed these in the ensuing years, and with our new mines and projects, we were in a much stronger position on that count. When David arrived, we had the engineering and reserves part covered pretty well for the time being, and the tough questions were more on the financial side. We had funded the first three of our current series of new mines with bank project debt, and they were in good shape, but the next two larger ones would require a capital investment of about $450 million.

Our market capitalization at the time had grown from $20 million five years earlier to about $500 million, but with the planned cost of our two new mines being about 90 per cent of Teck's total net worth once again, and with interest rates skyrocketing, we were ready for a different kind of reality check, this time financially instead of on ore reserves.

It was time to stop dancing and grab a chair before the music stopped.

CHAPTER 21

MANAGING THROUGH AN UNPRECEDENTED RECESSION

What we are witnessing now is the greatest redistribution of wealth
we will see in our lifetimes.
Morton Shulman, 1981

When David Thompson started with us in March 1980, the Bank of Canada interest rate was an unheard-of 14 per cent. By the following January this had increased to 17 per cent, and by August it was almost 22 per cent. Obviously something was going to break. David's number one priority, and that of all of us, was to ensure that it wasn't going to be us (figure 21.1).

Storm Clouds on the Horizon and Blowing Our Way

By that time, we had committed to build the Highmont mine at a projected capital cost of $150 million, which was already higher than the total combined cost of our three previous new mines. We also had the Bullmoose project on the drawing boards at an estimated further $300 million, and had spent a lot of time and effort getting into a position to do both.

We were doing well at existing operations, with ordinary earnings having increased from $1.8 million five years earlier to $32 million. Operating profits were up tenfold from $9.4 million to $100 million. Long-term debt was only $179 million, of which $ 138 million was project debt and only $41 million corporate debt, although these would rise substantially with the two new mines on the drawing boards. The numbers will seem small to those used to talking of billions in the twenty-first century, but I can assure you that they were at least as significant to us builders then as the much larger numbers common in today's world are.

The Club of Rome myth was still in full swing. Inflation was running in double digits, the price of oil was once again soaring after the revolution in Iran, and hard assets were widely thought to be the great inflation hedge.

Figure 21.1
David Thompson finally landing his big salmon, 1980

The value of a mine or steel plant that was already in production could seemingly be measured more easily than that of a new project that still had to be built, with its uncertain construction costs in a period of rampant inflation, and as we saw, many previously sound businessmen began to chase as-built hard assets at almost any cost. This, it seems, may be part of the eternal cycle.

The full spectrum of government leaders had tried to dampen the inflation flames over the 1970s. Both Richard Nixon and Pierre Trudeau had tried wage and price controls. These hadn't worked. Rampant inflation began to seem the new norm, and unbeatable. Finally, Paul Volcker, the Fed chairman appointed by Jimmy Carter and supported strongly by Ronald Reagan, killed the golden goose when he allowed interest rates to climb to well over 20 per cent in 1981. This was a level previously unheard of, and one that plunged the world into The Great Recession.

Teck's earnings fell from a record $32 million to $12 million in 1981. The price of copper fell to its lowest level in constant (inflation-adjusted) dollars since 1946, just as construction at our new Highmont mine and the Lornex expansion were nearing completion. In 1982, Teck would suffer its first loss in over 60 years of mining.

The Recession began officially in July 1981 and ended in December 1982. US unemployment reached 10.8 per cent, the highest since the Depression, and a level not even reached in the later, equally severe 2008 recession, although the recent one is fresher in our memories. In Canada, unemployment peaked at 13 per cent. Much of the economy ground to a halt. Long-time-producing companies were failing at a record rate, as were many banks, whose customers could no longer service their loans.

A lot of over-leveraged people in the US and Canada were hurt, some even wiped out, when the music stopped playing. In Canada this included previously quite successful land developers, some that would later rise from the ashes to new successes, and some of whom went under for good. They were generally doing what had worked well, and then suddenly it didn't. Few people escaped the impact.

I happened to be on the board of a periodical called *The Money Letter* at the time, along with Trevor Eyton and Jimmy Connacher. It could have been a case of the blind leading the blind, except that the leader was a respected physician, coroner, and financial guru named Dr Morton Shulman.

I recall one day, as we walked down the street after a board dinner, Mortie turned to us and said: "What we are witnessing now is the greatest redistribution of wealth we will see in our lifetimes." He was only half right, because he passed away in 2000, but the rest of that group have seen another equally serious recession since. Which was most severe is debatable, depending upon whether one was there and how leveraged for one or the other, and is in any case academic. Both were very damaging to a large number of people and corporations, and in both cases the worst outcomes were avoidable.

Fortunately, Teck, with a strong nudge from David Thompson, managed a course correction in time.

Early Asset Sales Control Debt and Keep Teck Healthy

Bringing in new blood from time to time can help reinvigorate a company, even if it's only by enunciating the obvious, especially if by doing that it helps change direction in the right way. It also helps if the old blood will listen to the new, and vice versa.

With David on board, we stopped studying every steel, oyster, or forestry acquisition idea, such as MacMillan Bloedel, that some broker brought by. I gradually reduced my trips to China, despite a continuing fascination for the country and where it might be headed. David didn't even have to say much, as he seldom does anyway. We all just became more conscious that we should not chase ideas that were obviously high risk and non-essential in that new, financial bubble era.

As the Canadian bank rate hit 17 per cent in January 1981 and copper prices continued to fall it was becoming ever clearer that we had to start reducing the risk of debt putting us under serious stress. Fortunately, Metallgesellschaft, which had arranged the molybdenum sales contracts, had been anxious to get an ownership piece of the Highmont mine ever since we began construction. We were in a mood to oblige, so in February 1981 we completed a deal to sell them a 20 per cent partnership interest for $22 million. Metall of course also assumed responsibility for its 20 per cent share of the project financing, or another $30 million. As a result, our exposure on the project was reduced by over a third, from the planned $150 million to $98 million, and we still retained 80 per cent ownership.

At the same time, we converted our indirect 73 per cent share interest in the Afton public company to a direct 73 per cent joint venture interest in the mine. We didn't want to buy out the minority ourselves, as the share price had risen to over $50 since the mine achieved production. But Metall was interested in owning a piece of this mine as well, so it agreed to put up the funds to buy out the minority shareholders' 27 per cent. Once we owned it all between us we were able to convert Afton into a 73 per cent/27 per cent joint venture held by the two of us. While not specifically a debt-reduction transaction, this did give Teck access to our 73 per cent share of the mine's cash flow directly, rather than having it sequestered in a subsidiary company, and it was achieved without our having to use our own funds to complete the expensive rationalization.

It was our first use of what we might call The Afton Gambit. We were faced with the practical necessity to remove a minority partner, but in a market where the price was out of line with our concept of reality.

Interestingly, we would try to pull off a similar manoeuvre with another minority interest almost 20 years later, as we will see, but the proposed partner changed CEOs and backed out. That time we would bite the bullet and pay up to buy out the minority, but The Afton Gambit is worth keeping in mind for future use. It is precisely in frothy, overpriced markets that partners anxious to pay up can often be found waiting at the door.

In May 1981, we sold our Coseka shares for $77 million. This represented a $41 million pre-tax profit over the 16 months we had held them but, more important, a further debt reduction. It was a touch and go negotiation between Teck and Bramalea, the buyer, and almost foundered in the final bargaining fisticuffs over the half-point cost of a bank guarantee for a deferred part of Bramalea's purchase price. That guarantee would prove crucial as Bramalea itself got into financial trouble in the ensuing recession, and fortunately Warren Seyffert and David Thompson did find a way to get agreement on it. Warren has always had a highly effective way of listening quietly, and then finding a practical solution that actually allows an important deal to get done.

That same month, we reached the agreement with nine Japanese steel mills to sell them 1.7 million tonnes a year of steelmaking coal from the Bullmoose mine, beginning with its planned completion at the end of 1983. However, with an expected construction cost of $300 million we would still be exposed to the risk of cost overruns or continued weak economic conditions, so we decided to sell off minority interests in the mine to reduce those risks.

We had already sold 10 per cent to our coal trading company Nissho-Iwai of Japan during the coal negotiations, and in early 1982 sold another 39 per cent interest to Lornex Mining Corporation. This left us with a direct, controlling position of 51 per cent in the mine as well as an additional 8 per cent indirect interest through our shareholding in Lornex.

The combined impact of the divestments to that point totalled $284 million in savings, including cash from the sales and the reduction in our construction commitments. This was already well over 50 per cent of our total market capitalization, and there was more to come.

There was one final step in the plan, and that was to bring in another partner for a further 30 per cent interest in Highmont. Negotiations had been ongoing throughout the spring of 1982 for the sale of this interest to the Kuwait Investment Office (KIO), a London-based sovereign wealth fund. By mid-year the terms had been agreed, with KIO to pay us $50 million for a 30 per cent interest in the Highmont project. This represented simply 30 per cent of the construction cost, with no payment for the equity interest, reflecting the fact the recession was well underway by that time. Our negotiating position had become somewhat more precarious, to put it mildly.

As it turned out, it took months to complete the agreement, and we were sweating bullets as time went on, but the agreement did close in November 1982. Once again David's messianic qualities had proven successful, despite his occasional imitations of Doubting Thomas.

The combination of all of these transactions amounted to a pre-tax saving of $334 million, compared with where we would have been had they not worked out. Interestingly, the combined savings were just about twice the amount that our total long-term debt had been prior to the program being started. It was, proportionately, an unprecedented debt reduction program, achieved just in time. Without these moves we could actually have gone under, as so many others had in those difficult years.

It was a lesson well learned. A strong balance sheet can be crucial to survival when times get tough, and a weak one disastrous. It is a truism worth repeating endlessly, something of which I am, too often, accused.

We were not only able to keep control of the two new mines and keep construction going as planned, but at the same time be in a financial position to acquire a distressed sale interest in another, widely sought after new project. This was the Hemlo discovery that would result in two important new gold mines for us in the ensuing years.

This was another lesson relearned and worth repeating, because it is hardly surprising that the best opportunities will often occur to those in a position of financial strength, when others are weakened.

CHAPTER 22

THE HIGHMONT MINE AND METAL PRICES

The herd instinct among forecasters makes sheep look like independent thinkers.
Edgar Fiedler

The Highmont Mine Completed, but in Difficult Times

Our engineers managed to complete the Highmont project on time and on budget in 1981, continuing a perfect record in that respect. However, it turned out to be a difficult start-up during the severe recession, with both copper and molybdenum prices collapsing. It was another learning experience, as we found that the anticipated safety valve of floor price contracts is not necessarily perfect. I will come back to that.

The official opening of the Highmont mine was held in June 1981, presided over by the Right Honourable Roland Michener in his last duty before retiring as chairman. Sadly, Bob Falkins, the entrepreneur who had been the forceful promoter of the project for more than a decade, would pass away in early 1982, but he had lived to see his dream become a reality.

By year-end this project had been completed, construction at Bullmoose was underway, our finances were in great shape, and we had an exciting new project in the works at Hemlo. My father moved on to be chairman and I was appointed president and CEO of Teck.

There was a further augmenting of the guard that occurred about the same time, as another person who would become a key player in Teck's future came across from one end of the Highland Valley to the other or, more literally, from Bethlehem, across the street in Vancouver, to Teck.

Keith Steeves Joins a Winning Team

Keith Steeves had been the senior financial executive at Bethlehem, and in fact had been in its boardroom when we tossed our offer over the transom a decade earlier. He'd been there when Sumitomo later sold its shares to Newmont, had helped Granges to sell its shares to Gulf Resources in a friendly deal a while later, and when Cominco had made its first, unsuccessful bid for Bethlehem. But, after Cominco finally was successful in acquiring all of Bethlehem in 1980, Keith decided it was time to move on.

Keith wanted to stay in Vancouver and in mining, and Teck was in need of an executive to manage the sale of our growing mix of products, now including copper, zinc, coal, niobium, and molybdenum as well as gold. Bob Hallbauer and I knew Keith and his talents, including his legendary golf handicap, so it was a natural for us to get together, and he agreed to come on board.

As he was about to start work, Bob called him up and told him he was needed at Highmont's official mine-opening the next day, and to bring his golf clubs. So Keith showed up at the mine, just south of Bethlehem where he had worked for years, toured the brand new plant, the most modern in BC at the time, and attended the obligatory mine-opening blast and speeches to celebrate the occasion.

The ceremonies dispensed with, Bob took him aside and said that we were now going to Kamloops to play some golf, and Keith was introduced to our Fourth Annual Mine-Opening Golf Tournament. Now, opening a new mine every year isn't actually very practical in the real world, but since it was our fourth one in six years we allowed ourselves a little poetic licence.

As usual, we called on the various banks, equipment suppliers, and other third parties that had worked on the project to contribute something to the prize money for the tournament. This reached something like $20,000 for our fourth such event, a record that would last until the next one, two years later, at Bullmoose. This formed the nucleus of the reward available to the winning golf teams, but would be augmented by an auction at dinner the night before the tournament, as participants vied to buy the rights to their own team.

It was the first Teck Mine-Opening Golf Tournament for Keith. The teams were drawn, and Keith found himself teamed with Dr John Leishman, the Regina physician who had delivered Canadian Devonian to us years earlier. John actually didn't play much golf, but nobody was going to ruin Keith's fun. They also had Rusty Goepel, a Vancouver investment banker with a knack of winning.

The bidding started, and we egged Keith on to bid for his team. It didn't take much egging because, as a long-time accountant, he could see the leverage in bidding after the kitty already had all that free supplier cash in it to split among the winning bidders. In fact, if you bought all of the teams, you were guaranteed a profit of $20,000, the initial pot put up by the suppliers.

The result: Keith's team won despite all odds, and he took home "gigadollars" in hot cash. He described the day to his wife, Norma, and said: "I like this company." She replied: "That's it. We're never moving on again." They never did.

Experience Trading in Copper Futures

Our other bets were not always as successful.

Paul Volcker's massive increase in interest rates had finally licked inflation to the ground. Copper had been one casualty of the recession, falling to its lowest price in 35 years. However, world stockpiles of refined copper were still at relatively low levels, and because of this, it seemed to some of us that the price of copper should soon recover.

There was a historical basis for this. Low inventories usually lead to better prices, unless for some reason demand dries up and the inventories start to rise. There was of course an equally historical basis for that correction taking much longer to occur than most people anticipated, but we were all young and relatively inexperienced in such matters in those days.

Bob, Keith, and I were convinced of this potential recovery, influenced as well by our assumption that Ronald Reagan had a mid-term election coming up in 1982 and wouldn't let Volcker continue to keep up the severe, unprecedented pressure on interest rates. So, we started buying copper futures personally. David, bless his soul, declined. That should have been our first clue. Why do I always miss these things?

Futures markets for metals, oil, hogs, and other commodities are well traded on recognized exchanges. These markets are useful for producers and consumers, allowing them to lock in prices for future deliveries or sales of metals or other goods. In this way they can avoid unexpected losses should market prices change abruptly against them.

These markets are also used by speculators, like the three of us, although possibly most speculators are more sophisticated than we were. We miners, of course, actually produced the copper and had a good idea of the costs of doing so. We knew prices had become too low to stay there forever, considering what it cost most of us to produce a pound of it. However, that is a classic case of a little knowledge being a dangerous thing.

Without going into all of the sordid details, the people who run such programs are glad to lend to us speculators on margin, in which we put up 10 cents or so on a dollar of commitment, and only have to put up the rest when we close out the deal and collect our winnings. Except that if things go the wrong way and there seems to be increasing potential for losses, instead of delivering the winnings, the financier will make a margin call and require us to put up more cash. There is, as well, a creature of indeterminate genealogy in the game known as a contango. It has been suggested I try to describe it, but the better advice for most people would just be to stay away from speculating, and in that way avoid the darned animal.

Unfortunately, the copper price was not moving up as we had expected. Keith, who was responsible for managing the company's copper sales, and was expected to know everything about the price at all times, said: "It got so that I was hating to listen to the copper price as I was driving to work, because of the expected margin calls." Eventually we were "eaten up by the contango," as they say in the business, closed out our positions at a loss, and vowed never to do it again.

The story illustrates how we as a company could also have been optimistic that a resumption of good times might be right around the corner. Copper prices were indeed historically low and refined metal inventories were low as well, which is unusual and generally metastable. The high interest rates were unheard of and, like the inflation they actually were licking, should have been metastable too. In fact, the rates really would begin to come down, but as has turned out to be common after such financially induced recessions, recovery can take many years.

Experience with Floor Prices

Operationally, the Highmont mine was a reasonable success from the start. John Anderson, another of the engineers who had joined us from Placer, Dick Drozd, Cory Sibbald, Lee Bilheimer, Mike Allan, and the whole engineering team had combined to bring it on stream on budget and on schedule. The mill was state of the art, but our financial timing wasn't as good as Keith's had been at the mine-opening golf tournament. The prices of both copper and molybdenum were low and weakening fast.

We had never assumed that the historically high molybdenum price of over $20 a pound would last for long, and for that reason had negotiated a floor price of US$7.50 a pound as a protection for our senior bank financing commitments. This, if you said it quickly, was supposed to mean that we would still be paid that minimum even if the market dropped below it. We had also negotiated a floor price of 80 (US) cents a pound for copper.

We would be paid all right, but the devil was in the details. In each case the customer would send us the difference between the actual market and the floor price as a non-recourse project loan to the mine. But while these would not be the direct responsibility of Teck and partners as owners, any such loans would have to be repaid by the mine out of future profits when the prices recovered, and after all of the senior bank debt had been paid off.

The feasibility study had shown that, provided we could build the plant on budget, which we did, we would be easily cash positive at those negotiated price levels, which we were. Given the uncertain times, that appeared to be a good insurance policy. However, there was a flaw in that simple solution. When the market soon did fall below our floor prices, the customers were dutifully paying that $7.50 and 80 cents a pound for molybdenum and copper. But for accounting purposes we naturally had to treat the difference paid by the customers as a loan to the project, which it was, rather than as sales revenue. We couldn't include it as income in our earnings statements, where the mine was showing a loss.

In one way it was working as planned, with the mine receiving the necessary floor prices and being cash positive, so it could service the banks. However, the subordinated customer loans on its books were increasing with each shipment of copper and molybdenum. For every pound we produced the Highmont mine was diminishing the future prospects for its owners further and further as the floor price loans grew. If that continued for long, sooner or later the mine would be valuable only to its creditors. We also had to listen to whining from those customer-creditors, many of which were German consumers that Metall had introduced to us. They were honouring their contracts, but reluctantly.

So in 1984, we agreed to take a payment of $5 million in exchange for releasing them from their purchase commitments. Highmont was released from its built-up customer loans, and suspended production. Each of the three Highmont partners, Teck, Metall, and KIO, took responsibility for its share of the remaining bank construction loans onto its books directly. The plant would be kept on care and maintenance until it could be put back into production three years later, but in a completely different way.

Was negotiating the floor price contracts a mistake? Certainly they had been a safety valve that was worth having as protection in the event of a temporary fall in prices. However, structured as they were with the price difference becoming loans to the project, rather than an actual purchase of metal at those floor prices, it was unsustainable if prices stayed lower for longer. The contracts probably couldn't have been structured much differently, and having them in place did allow us to operate normally for a couple of years to see if prices might recover, but as often happens, it took a lot longer than expected for that to occur.

Morenci, a Missed Opportunity

Those early 1980s were difficult times for copper producers everywhere. Phelps Dodge, one of the major US copper producers, had operated a number of mines in Arizona for years, but in 1983 it experienced a strike that shut down its copper mines for almost three years. This included its Morenci mine that had started production way back in 1872.

By 1986, the mine was starting back into production, but Phelps Dodge, still smarting from its experience, invited Japan's Sumitomo Metal Mining to buy a 15 per cent interest in it for $75 million. After Sumitomo agreed, Phelps also offered a similar 15 per cent interest to Teck, and Bob Hallbauer and I visited the mine to size it up. We turned down the opportunity, but it was a fascinating experience, seeing something like 30 small-ball mills lined up to process what one or two large autogenous mills might do today. It was like the old Bethlehem milling complex, but much larger.

One of the most intriguing things about the Morenci visit was seeing the first significant solvent extraction-electrowinning (SX-EW) operation for copper in the world. Morenci had extensive dumps of mine waste containing copper minerals that had not been recovered in earlier mining and milling, and were obvious from the green oxide copper minerals that marked the dumps.

A team including Tim Snider, a young chemical engineer, had developed a method of leaching these dumps in situ and then passing the copper-bearing solutions through tanks in which the copper would be plated out onto cathodes, hence "electrowinning." It was a new technique then but would become widely used in the world industry, including at Quebrada Blanca, a mine we would develop in the 1990s.

Tim Snider would go on to build and operate other Phelps Dodge mines, eventually becoming president of the company. Years later, in 2015, after

Phelps Dodge had been absorbed by Freeport McMoran, Tim would become a key member of the Teck board of directors. It is, as we have seen so many times, a small world we miners occupy.

Epilogue

As it turned out, metal prices would not recover meaningfully for a long time, and we were at the start of what has become widely known as the "twenty years of declining commodity prices in real terms," or "the barren years." It became a difficult period for the mining industry, during which supply exceeded demand for much of the time. The surpluses were generally not enormous in any given production year, but their persistence led to a buildup of metal and mineral inventories, low prices, and tough times for the industry.

It would be an interregnum in which many of the weaker players in the business disappeared, and a few stronger ones survived. Without the change in direction and balance sheet medication David Thompson had fought for and started even before the severe recession officially began, we could well have been one of those weaker ones.

Keith Steeves' arrival rounded out the "five amigos." This was the team of my father, who had started the whole thing, Hallbauer the miner, Thompson the numbers man, and me, who were, along with our corps of engineers and geologists, taking the venerable Teck Corporation to a new level.

Two or more of us would meet informally for lunch several times every week, unscheduled and just whoever was around, brainstorming about operating and other issues. These sessions always ended with a "What do we do next?" conversation, with nobody afraid to toss out a wild idea, and nobody else afraid to shoot it down.

It worked. All five of us were on the board of directors, along with other non-management people. What it meant was that by the time ideas were ready to be presented for action they had been thoroughly argued out. Presentations were by well-versed directors to other well-versed directors. The results were by no means a fait accompli, but were generally without benefit of sales jobs.

It was certainly not your garden-variety twenty-first-century corporate governance style, and perhaps easier in a small, growing company, but in my view it was one of the things that helped make Teck the company it became.

CHAPTER 23

HEMLO AND THE GOLD HUSTLERS

Gold is where you find it.
Prospector's truism

In the spring of 1981, David Bell and Corona Resources, financed by Murray Pezim, had made a significant gold discovery near the town of Hemlo, Ontario. As the financial chaos of the Volcker Recession accelerated late in the year, Pezim and Corona needed help, and Teck, with its financial affairs by then in good shape, was in position to negotiate an attractive development contract. Hemlo would prove to be another major stepping stone in the development of our company.

Gold Really Is Where You Find It

The first recorded discovery of a gold occurrence in the area was back in 1929, as reported by J.E. Thomson of the Ontario Geological Survey in 1931. Around the end of the Second World War, Peter Moses from Hemlo located another gold occurrence in the area, and a group of mining claims was staked. A Dr Williams acquired an interest in these claims and did some exploratory diamond drilling in 1947. He did enough work to patent the claims, or secure title almost indefinitely, and they stayed dormant in the Williams family for years after that. These would become known as "the Williams property" in a 1980s lawsuit.

In 1948, Lake Superior Mining Corporation acquired 41 claims just east of the Williams property and did some drilling, with sporadic gold results. In 1951, Teck-Hughes Gold Mines optioned the property from Lake Superior and did some drilling of its own. The results were not sufficiently interesting for Teck-Hughes to pursue them further, particularly with the price of gold still fixed at US$35 an ounce, and the option was dropped. There was little interest in the area for many years thereafter.

The rediscovery of potentially economic gold in the Hemlo area occurred in early 1981, two years after the price of gold had peaked for a time and just as soaring interest rates were setting the stage for the ensuing recession. The discovery would result in newsworthy diamond drilling results, a staking rush, corporate manoeuverings, a lawsuit, and eventually in three new gold mines. Other than the fact there were three mines to be discovered rather than one, it was not unlike the Timmins base metals rush of 15 years earlier, and some of the same players were involved.

David Bell's Discovery

In December 1979, prospectors John Larche and Don McKinnon, whom we met earlier in Timmins after that earlier Texas Gulf discovery, staked some claims on ground in western Ontario that had just become open, or available for staking. They then tried to interest various senior mining companies in optioning the property and carrying out exploration, but without any success. They were turned down by all of the big name companies, including Esso Minerals, Noranda, Placer Dome, Mattagami, Northgate Exploration, Amax, and ASARCO.

Eventually, McKinnon enlisted the help of a young geologist named David Bell, who introduced him to promoter Steven Snelgrove. Snelgrove took an option on the claims and flew to Vancouver to see if he could find someone to fund some work on them.

Nell Dragovan of Vancouver was managing Corona Resources, a newly-formed exploration company promoted by Murray Pezim that was looking for properties to explore. Corona acquired the claims from Snelgrove and hired David Bell to look after a drilling program. They started drilling in the same area Teck-Hughes and others had back in the 1950s, and the early, near-surface results were similar, narrow and not particularly high grade in gold. However, Pezim had the faith, as always, and kept raising funds for a few more drill holes.

By the spring of 1981, Corona had drilled an extraordinary 75 exploratory holes on the property, and Pezim had arranged several tiers of financing amounting to $2.5 million to support this, still not encountering much success. There definitely was gold there, but just as with Teck-Hughes in the 1950s, Corona had only found narrow zones that didn't appear to be economic to mine.

Ken Lefolii in his book *Claims* quotes Rocco Schiralli, part of the Snelgrove syndicate that sold the claims to Corona: "You know, it's lucky for everybody that a guy like Murray had those claims. If I'd had them, I'd have quit after seven or eight holes. I go for results, and most guys are like me." But as Pezim said: "The risk-taking public can never forgive a quitter, and the Pez group of companies will never quit trying."

Sometimes in exploration, perseverance pays off, and as with Ken Darke's 66th drill hole at Timmins years earlier, the 76th drill hole put down by David Bell hit pay dirt. That was in May of 1981, and the hole was one of the deepest then drilled on the property. More follow-up deep drilling continued to come up with good gold values, and it appeared that the surface mineralization that had been tested in earlier times was only a hint of the better ore that lay below it. The Pez had pulled it off, along with Dragovan and Bell.

Teck and Lac Visit the Site

In those days, the Toronto press tended to scoff at promotional stories coming from Vancouver Stock Exchange-listed companies and this was no exception. But at least two senior mining companies took the results seriously. Geologists for Lac Minerals and Teck visited the property to look at the results and inquire about the possibility of some form of joint exploration agreement.

John May of Teck met with David Bell and Dragovan to try to option the property, but was told that Corona wasn't yet ready to do what Chester Millar of Afton had earlier called the ultimate deal. They were having too much fun exploring, but each side agreed to keep in touch.

Likewise, Dennis Sheehan of Lac visited Bell that spring and was shown the drill core. Bell explained his hypothesis about the gold deposit being strata-bound, or confined to a particular metamorphosed volcanic rock bed. He thought it might be volcanogenic, genetically related to the original volcanic activity that laid down the rocks in which it occurred, although this is still the subject of debate in the geological community.

Regardless, Bell noted that the same volcanic rocks extended west across the boundary between Corona's claims and the Williams ones, and said that the gold-bearing rocks appeared to extend onto the Williams property. He said that Corona was attempting to acquire the Williams property through the services of Don McKinnon. Sheehan reportedly commented that this would be a good idea.

It certainly was. As it turned out with subsequent exploration, the gold deposit discovered by Corona extended both west onto the Williams property and north, at depth, onto a third property.

It took McKinnon some time to track down the right Williams family, by then living in the US, but by June he had done so and made an offer to Dr Williams' widow to purchase that property. He soon suspected that there might be competition from another company, and in July, on his advice, Corona sent a further offer directly to Mrs Williams. However, it turned out that Lac had also approached Mrs Williams for its own account, and in late July she agreed to sell the property to Lac.

Pezim was apoplectic. Corona immediately sued Lac, claiming that it should disgorge the Williams property and assign it to Corona. Once again, Lefolii quotes him: "I'll settle with those bastards the day they give me back what they stole from me."

The trial would go on for years and become one of the most watched scenes in Canadian mining circles in the early 1980s.

Teck Becomes Corona's Operating Partner

The recession had begun officially in July 1981, and as the year wore on the repercussions of extreme interest rates and a collapsing equity market began to impact more and more people. Murray Pezim was one of them. We had kept in touch with him, but he had been reluctant to part with the discovery he was calling his baby.

However, by November Murray was sweating bullets himself. He tried to deal the property to Placer, which by then had changed from the diversified mining company that Bob Hallbauer and I had worked for and was now interested primarily in gold. Apparently Placer considered the prospect too small to be of interest, and declined his proposal.

One day I got a call out of the blue from Murray, who opened by saying: "Norm, I have to do a deal, right now." I asked him if he'd like me to come over to his place and he said no, he would come over to our Vancouver office instead. He did that almost immediately, and within less than five minutes we'd agreed on the outline of a deal. Teck would buy 200,000 shares of Corona from him at $5 a share, for a risk investment of $1 million. We would take over management of the property and spend additional funds as necessary on further exploration, engineering, and a feasibility study, earning additional shares at $5 a share. If the work turned out to be positive, we would have the right to arrange financing to develop a new mine, and earn a 55 per cent share interest in Corona Resources as a result.

Now this formula for a development contract was the standard one, in which the senior company earns shares in the junior company and eventually holds a majority of it upon building the mine. It was a formula Murray had seen many times and understood, and it was how we arrived at the percentages. However, we had found that one of the problems with the senior company holding its interest through shares of the junior discoverer is that the profits eventually accrue downstairs in the junior company, and can only be accessed by the senior company through dividends. This can be inefficient for tax and other reasons, including the negative investor perceptions of companies who hold too many assets downstairs and are seen as holding companies.

We had seen this while owning shares in Afton Mines Ltd. The mine had become quite profitable, but Afton would have had to pay out full corporate taxes before sending dividends upstairs where, as we were busy developing other new mines, we had ample tax shelter. We had resolved this earlier in the year by buying out the minority shareholders of Afton, following which the mine had become a joint venture between Teck and Metallgesellschaft, rather than being held in that separately taxed subsidiary company.

So, with that in mind, after Murray had agreed in five minutes to the familiar 55:45 split in the ultimate share ownership between Teck and the existing Corona shareholders, we took another two minutes to propose improving the arrangement with a small modification. Instead of Teck having the right to earn a 55 per cent shareholding in Corona, we agreed to change it to our right to earn a 55 per cent joint venture interest in the property itself, rather than shares, upon having arranged financing and placing it into production. We would share in Corona's Williams property in the same way, should the lawsuit be successful.

This would be better for Teck, and Murray understood that it could be better for him and his shareholders as well, since Corona would remain an independent company that could continue to do interesting things itself, rather than have to face the future as a controlled subsidiary. It could, if the Hemlo project proved successful, try to go on to build the next Teck, as we had done after Temagami, or for any other independent purpose they might have in mind.

Murray Pezim was an out-and-out promoter, as loud and boisterous as it gets in his high moments. Not all of the many projects he promoted proved successful, and in fact – as it goes in his business – most were not. He had an engaging way of describing it when a stock he'd promoted went sour: "I can always tell you when to buy, but I never tell anyone when to sell." Fair enough, but he did have some remarkable successes to boast about, including the large Eskay Creek gold mine in British Columbia. He was a character, in some ways larger than life. In my experience, if you shook hands on a deal with Murray, you could count on it being honoured.

The Corona Gold Deposit Does Extend onto Adjoining Properties

Over the next few months, Teck carried out extensive, additional drilling to explore the property, with 23 of the first 24 drill holes encountering ore-grade values in gold. Within six months, or only a year after the discovery, Teck had calculated a geological reserve of 1.3 million tons of 0.3 ounces of gold per ton.

Whatever the origin of the gold deposit, strata-bound in the conventional geological sense or not, the steeply inclined tabular rock formation in which it occurred was tilted at an angle so that, as it got deeper to the north, it crossed onto claims held by Goliath Gold, a company headed by two well-known mining men, Dick Hughes and Frank Lang. That would limit how deep our mine could go before the ore zone crossed the boundary onto the Goliath property. Of course, the formation also trended west toward the Williams property, and the constraints of the two property boundaries would limit how much tonnage of ore we could expect on the Corona claims alone (see colour page 9).

We had assigned a young geologist named Bob Quartermain to work on the Corona option, and he kept a close eye on the results as Hughes and Lang began to drill on Goliath. In late 1982, Bob and Bruce Durham, another geologist who had worked on our Corona project but who was by then working for Hughes and Lang, visited the Goliath property together to look at the core from Hole #2, one of its early drill holes. Interestingly, just as with Temagami years earlier, the first hole had been drilled down a barren diabase dyke, but unlike Anaconda, Hughes and Lang had drilled a second one, and it turned out to be the discovery hole.

Bob and Bruce visited the core shed, and saw box after box of mineralized core that looked identical to the ore we were finding next door at Corona. It was pretty clearly an extension of our mineralized deposit, being even thicker on their property. After opening nine boxes still in mineralization, it was obvious that this could represent a major discovery. Bob went to the payphone at his hotel and called our Toronto office to give his report. He estimated the mineralized zone to be about 90 feet thick and that it could grade an impressive 0.25 ounces of gold per ton, based upon his experience with our own drilling results. He suggested the possibility of a resource of at least 2 million ounces of gold. If so, it would be as much or more as we thought we had on the Corona property.

Geologists from our Toronto office contacted Hughes and Lang, but they proved to be equally enthused about their prospects, leading to somewhat of an impasse on values. Noranda was said to be interested in the property as well, although Quartermain had heard that it was trimming its exploration budget by some $8 million and might not be too competitive. Still, we would have to pay up if we wanted to get a deal.

It seemed time for an innovative way to break the log jam, and someone came up with the idea of letting our good friends at Metallgesellschaft buy into the property, as they had done before with Afton, giving us the right to back in at some future time. David Thompson, who has always had an innate capacity for hoarding cash whenever possible, thought this was a great idea, and raised it with Metall while on a trip to Germany for other reasons.

This time it didn't work out. Metall passed on the opportunity, and so did we. Noranda did get the Goliath property for the princely sum of $8 million, which in hindsight may well explain why it was cutting the rest of its exploration budget by that amount, as rumoured. As it turned out, there was more gold there than even Quartermain had projected, or Hughes and Lang had imagined, and it was a very good deal for Noranda, which built a mine on it named Golden Giant. I still have regrets that, knowing what we knew then, we didn't act upon it more aggressively.

Teck's Decision to Build the First Mine at Hemlo

Meanwhile, Lac Minerals was drilling on the disputed Williams property to the west, and some months later announced a geological resource of 1.8 million tons of rock containing 0.175 ounces of gold per ton, thus confirming that the gold-bearing horizon did indeed extend across the western claim boundary, as David Bell had told Dennis Sheehan.

The gold zone on the original Corona side of the boundary had turned out to be rather narrow. It was confined to that rock strata noted earlier, and the best drill intersections continued to be quite deep. The rocks that contained the gold did extend west onto the Williams property as expected, but unless the courts would support our contention that it should be returned to Corona, which could take years to determine, we would be limited in the scale of any mine we could build.

We concluded that the largest mining and milling operation the Corona claims alone could support would be about 1,000 tons of ore per day, so we proceeded to start the detailed engineering for a feasibility study based upon this capacity. This confirmed that we could develop a profitable mine at a capital cost of $90 million, accessed by a shaft to a depth of 1,100 feet, and we decided to go ahead with building the first Hemlo gold mine. We named it the David Bell mine in recognition of his role in managing the drilling program that discovered the important gold deposit.

A Historic Mine Financing

All that remained was to secure bank financing, exercise our development contract, and get on with building the mine. Given the unusually high grade of the ore, as well as our construction commitments elsewhere at Bullmoose, we were determined to achieve a healthy proportion of this construction cost as a non-recourse project loan from one of the major banks.

With such project loans, in those days the banks would generally fund something in the order of 50 per cent to 60 per cent of construction costs, standing first in line for repayment out of initial cash flow from the mine. Once the mine was up and running, their only recourse in the event of non-repayment was to take over the property itself. We, as the senior operating company, would normally put up the balance of the construction cost as a subordinated loan, either using our cash reserves or by borrowing those additional funds corporately and then advancing them to the project. Usually, the banks required a completion guarantee from the senior, managing company but, once construction had been completed on target, that company was off the hook for the bank's project loan.

We wanted to ask for the maximum possible in project financing, and had the wild idea that we might set a Canadian mining record and get much more than the conventional 50 per cent or 60 per cent, perhaps even close to 100 per cent, through a non-recourse project loan.

Our lead bank in those days was the Bank of Montreal, which had led the Bullmoose financing. Of the other large banks, the Bank of Nova Scotia was strong in gold, and CIBC considered itself the main mining bank in Canada. The TD Bank had been helpful in building our Newfoundland Zinc mine and our Toronto office was in its building, so we saw them fairly often.

I had a chance to talk to TD's CEO, Dick Thomson, and said that we would be looking for a full 100 per cent project financing. Dick was a young CEO, not much older than I was, and was and is a perfect gentleman. He had led the bank's move to finance Newfoundland Zinc for us, but said that TD was not particularly keen on financing gold mines at the time, because of the extreme volatility of the price in recent years. He very politely advised us to look elsewhere. He also tried to discourage us from seeking even close to 100 per cent project financing, because that just had never been done.

Undaunted, David Thompson went out for financing bids from several of the other banks.

As the deadline for bids neared, we were told by the Bank of Montreal (BMO) that, despite it then being our lead bank, both corporately and on the Bullmoose project, and despite the fact that the bank's mining department was keen to participate, its chairman, Bill Mulholland, had just decreed that he wanted nothing to do with gold financing either. David was worried about the possible impact on the other banks if our lead banker was not seen as an interested bidder, so he asked BMO for a letter indicating that they thought it would be a very good project for Teck, even if not for them. They agreed and supplied one.

With the offers in a few days later, CIBC was ahead, although still not where we had hoped it would be. But one of its executives, Peter Cole, came over to see David and ask how CIBC was doing. He seemed worried that they might not be able to beat BMO. David replied that CIBC's bid was pretty good, "but we have a very strong letter in from BMO." David neglected to say that while there actually was a letter, it was not an offer at all.

The worried Cole asked that we give him a little time, and a day later came over with an improved bid which – much to everyone's surprise – gave us the 100 per cent non-recourse project financing we had wanted, although never fully expected. It was even better than that. The 100 per cent included a recoupment of all our prior expenses on the project and had no completion guarantee. But if we did complete construction within our $90 million target, the bank would lend Teck and Corona an additional 30 per cent for general corporate purposes.

It was an unheard of 130 per cent project financing. Needless to say, we accepted it. This was easily the best project financing ever for a significant new mine. Given today's changed banking environment, it is doubtful it will ever be repeated.

We did build the mine and mill on schedule and, at $80 million, well under budget. It started up in 1985, and marked the return of Teck to our historic status as a gold miner, the old Lamaque mine finally having closed after a long convalescence the year before.

Bob Quartermain continued working on the David Bell mine for a time, but eventually he would be assigned to manage Silver Standard Mines Limited, in which we had bought shares 15 years earlier as part of our initial ventures into British Columbia. Bob Wilson, its founder, had passed away and Quartermain would take over management for us. We would later carve out the Schaft Creek property as well as two others, Minto in Yukon and Red Chris in BC, and then sell our remaining shareholding in Silver Standard, which Bob would go on to build into a major player in the silver exploration world. Bob would also be instrumental in acquiring a prospect for us in Mexico, which would become a significant copper-zinc resource called San Nicolas. After he left Silver Standard, he would found a new company, Pretium Resources, which is now building a high-grade gold mine in British Columbia. He, like Bill Bergey, is one of those rare birds known in the industry as a mine-finder.

In the Courts, the Williams Lawsuit

While the David Bell mine was being built, Lac Minerals was also proceeding with construction of a mine and mill on the Williams property, notwithstanding the ownership dispute and the pending trial. The mineralization on that side of the boundary contained a lower gold grade than at David Bell, but there was a larger resource in terms of total tonnage, and it would support a larger mining and milling operation. Lac decided to place the property into production at a rate of 6,000 tonnes per day. They would take their chances on the trial.

One of the first orders of business in a major court case, after selecting the lawyers, is what is known as examination for discovery. In this, lawyers for each side interview officers for the other side, privately but under oath. The purpose is to discover the "facts," or at least what each might say were facts when the case gets to court. If a witness chooses to say one thing in discovery and another in court, it can create a bit of confusion, often not to the benefit of the witness. It helps the trial lawyers, who tend to operate under a well-known adage: "Never ask a question in court unless you already know the answer." This process took several months, with discovery of Murray Pezim, David Bell, and Nell Dragovan on the Corona side, and Peter Allen and Dennis Sheehan on the Lac side, among others. The lead lawyer for Corona was Alan Lenczner, assisted by Ron Slaght and Larry Page.

There was a lot of interest in this case by the public and the investment community. Just as with the earlier *Leitch vs. Texas Gulf*, there was an element of David against Goliath, with success offering bigger relative investment gains for Corona, the smaller company, than a loss would for Lac Minerals, the Goliath. Investors and speculators alike played the game, sometimes with exotic gambits, including betting on one side while hedging on the other, but as often just trying to guess the winner. Other than those few who could be in court daily, or hire someone to be there, these investors tended to rely on the daily newspaper reports as to who was getting ahead.

During any trial there are days when one side presents its case and, if managed reasonably competently by the lawyers, it will tend to come across as quite compelling. Another day there will be cross-examination of witnesses, and the other side may suddenly appear to have made a compelling case of its own. The lawyers will benefit from knowing what had been testified in discovery, and be able to formulate their evidence or attacks on the other side appropriately. They thus have a head start and either side can often be seen to be winning on any given day. The judge, meanwhile, is sitting there trying to figure out what actually did happen.

The salvos back and forth can be quite impressive, with guns blaring and trumpets ascendant. It can be like "The Charge of the Light Brigade," except that instead of a steady fall into the valley of death, the charge can go back and forth for days. In the common parlance, each side will "have its day in court" as the trial goes on. It can be confusing at times, especially for reporters.

In order for the observer, or those speculators, to reach any kind of conclusion as to how the case is going, it is necessary to be in attendance for each side's days in court, rather than just one or the other's. Either that, or depend upon a neutral observer who is there or read all of the transcripts as they are issued, usually with a lag of a few days.

The case was important to us, and we had a young lawyer from Lang Michener attend in court most days and report back. I attended some days when there was a key witness to be assessed, and read every transcript as it came out, as did Bob Wright, also from Lang Michener. The young lawyer and I both came to the conclusion that, contrary to what appeared to be the popular consensus, Corona was winning more of the skirmishes than it was losing, and that it just might win the whole thing.

However, that was not the sense of the general investing public, many of whom may have recalled a similar situation back when Leitch sued the much larger Texas Gulf, and lost in the end. It certainly would not have been the sense of anyone just reading the Toronto newspapers, which, not surprisingly, included some in our own shop. Having had the experience of losing the earlier Afton case that we had been told was in the bag until the judge started asking pointed questions, we were naturally skeptical, and aware of those who argued we should try to settle it.

Efforts to Settle Out of Court

I'll never forget one meeting at the King Edward Hotel in Toronto, when Lac's president Peter Allen came over for a one-on-one visit. I was ready to offer a settlement, with Corona's approval, under which both sides might end up with their heads high, but Peter seemed uncomfortable in the extreme. He sat on the edge of his chair, without even taking off his winter overcoat. He was polite, but I've never seen anyone so nervous.

It could have been because his father, Jack Allen, was still around, and was thought to have been bested a couple of times by my father 20 years earlier, including in the Teck-Hughes takeover. It could have been something else, but it seemed strange that Peter would be there ostensibly to talk settlement, and yet not be prepared to say anything. Later on, we planned another meeting, arranged for breakfast in the same hotel, this time with Corona's new chairman Ned Goodman as well, but Peter simply didn't show up at all. Nothing came of these attempts from our side to broach a settlement, fortunately for us as it turned out.

So as the trial wound down, most people on the street, reading the Toronto press, expected Lac to win. The only person I can recall being convinced we would win was the young Lang Michener lawyer who had sat in on the whole trial for us. Possibly his boss, Bob Wright, might have been starting to believe as well that we had a chance.

David Thompson, tending to be neither a believer nor a disbeliever in most things, but being the ultimate pragmatist, had quietly arranged, by buying stock in the open market, that we would own 4.9 per cent of Lac before the Judgment came down.

The Judgment Is Announced

On 3 February 1986, almost five years after the events in question, we were advised suddenly that the decision of Mr Justice Holland would be handed down that afternoon, after the close of markets.

Bob Hallbauer and I were out of the country, but when it came time to find out the results, we telephoned in to our Vancouver office to listen live. We must have missed the news by a few seconds, because when David Thompson answered the phone it was with a high-pitched scream of "We won!!!!" You had to be there and know David to appreciate the moment. He of all people had been the most skeptical about our chances.

David had been in a meeting with a very important investment banker when the phone rang, and David went out to take it. He then went into our boardroom to field some calls, including the one from Hallbauer and me, and to celebrate with our staff. David doesn't drink much, but he determined that the occasion called for champagne, so he sent Dick Drozd out to buy a bottle. Dick of course came back with a case, and the proceedings carried on.

Then someone said we should be represented over at the Corona shop as well, so David decided that, as the senior Teck person in town, he'd better go over there. He found Murray Pezim in a large party, surrounded by what seemed to be every broker in town as well as a bevy of attractive young ladies. David was in the process of congratulating Murray when one of the young ladies approached and said there was an angry contractor out there demanding payment for some Pezim home renovations he'd been working on. Murray said: "Send him in" and told him that, with the win, he was now about to get paid.

David returned to the celebration at Teck and completely forgot about the very important investment banker who had been cooling his heels somewhere in our office. History does not record how long the banker stayed there or, for that matter, who he was.

Winning this landmark case was one of those key events that occur rarely in a company's history, but it would not be over for another three years until

Lac exhausted its appeals. Six more judges at the Ontario Court of Appeal unanimously upheld Mr Justice Holland's decision later that year. However, in the final appeals stage with the Supreme Court of Canada in 1989, it was only upheld by a narrow, split decision, much to my surprise and to that of Ned Goodman and Peter Steen, who by then had taken over Corona, and who were sitting with me in the Ottawa courtroom.

In each appeal, David had his hedge in place, and we owned 4.9 per cent of Lac before the decision came down. Interestingly, in all three cases, the price of Lac shares dropped after the decision, we held on for a time, and in the end the price recovered enough to give us a small profit. Hedges are not always supposed to work that way, but these did.

The Judgment

It was a long trial, and the judgments of Mr Justice Holland, the Ontario Court of Appeals, and the Supreme Court of Canada take up hundreds of pages.

This is not the place to review the findings, other than to say that the trial judge found that Lac had improperly acquired the property after having begun trying to negotiate for a joint venture and, in the course of this, being advised that Corona itself planned to acquire the property and was working on it.

There was testimony from expert witnesses as to what the practice in the industry might be, or should be. This included a who's who of renowned miners and consultants, including Jack McOuat, Paul Kavanagh, Jim Gill, David Robertson, and Duncan Derry. The views were not all consistent. Some testified one way, some another, and some in between.

Perhaps the most telling testimony on the subject came from Lac president Peter Allen himself. On the matter of whether beginning negotiations for a possible deal on a mining property created an obligation not to act to the detriment of the other party, Peter answered as follows:

> If one geologist goes to another geologist and says, are you interested in making some sort of a deal and between the two of them, they agree that they should consider seriously the possibility of making a deal, I think for a short period of time, while they are exploring that, that

any transference of data would be … I would hope the geologists would be competent enough to identify the difference between published, unpublished, confidential and so on but in the case that they weren't, there was just some exchange of conversation or physical data, then I would say that while both of them were seriously and honestly engaged in preparing a deal, that Lac and the other party would both have a duty toward each other not to hurt each other as the result of any information that was exchanged.

And to the follow-up question:

Q. Does the obligation not to harm each other that you referred to, et cetera, flow from the fact that they were in negotiation or discussion about a possible deal itself so long as it's a serious matter as you said? [Mr Allen]. Yes.

It was an important answer, referred to in the trial judge's conclusion as well as the Supreme Court's. It was also an honest answer, and I have always admired Peter's integrity in giving it.

Epilogue

This was a case about which every exploration geologist should have at least a modest understanding, so as hopefully to avoid getting himself, herself, or their company into trouble. Perhaps the simplest advice would be: "If it doesn't feel right, then don't do it."

CHAPTER 24

HOW HIGHLAND VALLEY COPPER EVOLVED

He lacks an appreciation of the finer points of bad behaviour.
Davos Seaworth, *Game of Thrones*

While we were building the David Bell mine, we were hoping to rationalize our interests in the Highland Valley, where we had our suspended Highmont mine and mill and owned a piece of the large Lornex mine. These would both eventually become part of Highland Valley Copper, or HVC.

HVC today is one of the largest copper mining and milling operations in the world, processing 140,000 tonnes of ore per day through its huge mill. How this came to be is an interesting tale involving two prospectors with dreams, innovative engineers, financiers, and a small dollop of infamy. The story of how it was bootstrapped up from several raw prospects could fill a book of its own, with more colour than can be included here. Someone should write that book, but here is a small part of the story, some of which I touched upon earlier.

Spud Huestis and Bethlehem

The presence of copper-bearing rocks in the area had been known for a long time, as far back as 1919, but the father of mining in the Highland Valley was New Brunswick-born prospector Herman "Spud" Huestis.

Spud got his first taste of prospecting in the historic Mesabi mineral district in Minnesota. He began prospecting in British Columbia in 1926 in, among other places, the Highland Valley area, where he found signs of copper mineralization. He prospected all over in the intervening years, but in 1954, Spud returned to the Valley and convinced two Vancouver businessmen, Pat Reynolds and Jack McLallen, to back him in further prospecting around those old copper showings. After evaluating these and other new copper occurrences, Spud staked about 100 claims, and in 1955, the trio formed Bethlehem Copper Corporation, with McLallen arranging the initial financial support to begin drilling some of the new showings.

They soon established three zones of copper mineralization: the Jersey, East Jersey, and Iona, which held an inferred tonnage of 68 million tons of potentially economic copper mineralization, grading about 0.7 per cent copper. This was small and low grade in comparison with the large porphyry copper deposits being mined in the US and elsewhere, but Spud and the geologists that the trio had retained thought they could turn it into a good little mine, and that there was a chance of expanding that tonnage significantly. They were certainly prophetic.

The only problem was that they had limited funds to finance building a mine, and the whole thing could have ended there. Development of small, very low-grade ore deposits like this had not often been tried anywhere, and certainly not yet in BC. The likelihood of obtaining bank or investor interest to back them seemed slim to less than slim.

But by chance, a group of Japanese businessmen, including some from the Sumitomo Group, happened to arrive in Vancouver in the summer of 1959. Sumitomo Metal Mining, whose historic Besshi mine was close to shutting down after mining for an amazing 250 years, was looking for new sources of copper concentrate for its nearby Toyo smelter at Niihama. It was a timely visit, and later in the year McLallen visited Tokyo for 10 days and presented an imaginative and far-seeing feasibility study, prepared by Wright Engineers of Vancouver. It recommended that Bethlehem build an open pit mining and milling complex on the property.

Despite the price of copper being only around 30 cents a pound, Sumitomo Metal Mining's senior managing director, Kenjiro Kawakami, liked what he saw. He agreed to help in the financing and to purchase all of Bethlehem's copper concentrate for a 10-year period. SMM put up the princely sum of US$5.5 million to acquire a 30 per cent shareholding in Bethlehem. This would be enough of a start that the company could secure the rest of the financing needed to get the mine into production.

The numbers were definitely different in those days. So was the speed at which decisions were made and mines built. Construction began in 1960, and by 1962 Bethlehem Copper was in production at a mining and milling rate of 3,000 tons per day. This was within a few months of the start-up of the new Craigmont mine, not far to the south, where I was then working.

Spud was on a roll, and I remember him coming by Craigmont one day to regale us with how much copper there was up there, a few kilometres to the north. "There's a billion tons up there in The Valley," he would tell anyone who would listen. "Sure Spud," we thought, "but at what grade?" We at Craigmont were spoiled by our grades of around 2 per cent copper, and I had even seen 28 per cent copper at Temagami. These low-grade things at well under 1 per cent seemed a bit scary.

It turned out Spud was not only right, he was conservative. As this is being written in 2017, 5 million tonnes of copper have already been produced from The Valley, from over a billion tonnes of ore mined. And there is much more to come. Meanwhile, Craigmont has come and gone, as mines will do.

The Discovery of Valley Copper

By the time Bethlehem was up and running, a lot of prospectors and junior companies had acquired mineral claims in the vicinity, most of them downhill from Bethlehem and in the bottom of what was known as the Highland Valley.

Bethlehem president Pat Reynolds held personal interests in some of these claims, and, realizing that a lot of small properties in diverse hands had little chance of being developed individually, he convinced the various owners to pool their holdings into a single company called Valley Copper. At the same time, he arranged for Cominco to be brought in with the right to explore and develop any discovery. It was the first consolidation of mining properties in the Highland Valley, although it would not be the last.

Meanwhile, Bethlehem was finding itself restricted at its mine up on the hill at the northeast end of the Valley. Needing land upon which to dump mill tailings and waste rock from its operation, it offered to buy six adjacent claims from the Valley Copper pool. Cominco's response was that it never sold exploration claims but that it would exchange six claims with Bethlehem, and each would retain a royalty on the other's claims if anything was discovered and developed on them.

Bethlehem agreed and asked which claims Cominco wanted. They were in the bottom of the valley, well away from Bethlehem's property. The Bethlehem board and Spud Huestis asked their mine manager if some drilling should be done on those lower claims before relinquishing them. His reply was not to bother, because there was nothing there.

The first drilling on those claims by Cominco resulted in the discovery of low-grade copper mineralization that, with ongoing drilling, eventually grew into the huge Valley Copper ore deposit. Keith Steeves insists to this day that

Cominco must have done enough earlier exploration in the vicinity to know that those claims were vital. In any case, as it turned out, the copper-bearing rocks also crossed over onto some claims Bethlehem had retained. In the end it appeared that Cominco had about 80 per cent of the new ore deposit and Bethlehem about 20 per cent.

As noted in chapter 12, Cominco had begun preliminary negotiations with Japanese smelting companies to arrange financing and concentrate sales contracts, at just about the time we were approaching Bethlehem with our own offer to purchase Bethlehem shares. As it turned out, with the grade at Valley Copper being very low by standards of the day and with copper prices worsening, those negotiations in Japan were suspended. Cominco declined to build a mill on the Valley Copper property at the time, and in fact never would.

Egil Lorntzen and Lornex

Another prospector had been active in The Valley at around the same time as Spud and, later, Cominco.

Egil Lorntzen, a dour but affable Norwegian, located copper-bearing rocks to the southwest of Bethlehem in 1964. He staked some claims and formed Lornex Mining Corporation to begin exploring these further, with the new company obtaining financing from two established mining firms, Rio Algom Mines Limited and Yukon Consolidated Gold Corporation. YCGC was the company that had years earlier been one of the main players in the famous Klondike gold rush in Yukon Territory, but by the mid-1960s it was primarily a mining investment company.

In the next three years, Lornex carried out extensive drill testing of what turned out to be a large, if low-grade, copper deposit. It went underground to obtain a bulk sample of the mineralized rock and subjected that to milling tests using a small 100-ton-per-day pilot plant. This program, completed in 1968, indicated a resource of 293 million tons averaging 0.427 per cent copper and 0.014 per cent molybdenum.

This grade might be considered interesting now, in 2017, but back then it was decidedly scary. In fact, it was unheard of. When one has to assay to three decimal points to estimate grades, the decision to start building a mine is not a slam dunk. There is little margin for error. In this respect, it was similar to our own later experience at Highmont, where we had to try to prove the possibility of a molybdenum upgrade factor to justify going ahead.

Lornex and its two major shareholders, Yukon Consolidated and Rio Algom, then made a courageous decision. They completed a feasibility study, arranged financing, and in 1970 committed to build a new mine and mill with a designed capacity of 38,000 tons of ore per day. It was completed and commercial production achieved late in 1972, shortly after the NDP's Dave Barrett was elected.

There is a story, possibly apocryphal, that it was the Carter Royal Commission on Taxation's recommendation to phase out Canada's three-year tax holiday for new mines that prompted the construction decision. That could have encouraged Lornex to make the decision to go into production then, rather than delay, so that they could receive a part of the remaining incentive during that phase-out period. If so, perhaps perversely, this program that had been put in place years earlier to encourage new mine development would have had its finest hour when it was being phased out.

Lornex's timing turned out to be propitious. Although it had to encounter the problems of a Barrett NDP government just after starting production, it also had the benefit of a couple of good copper price years early on, and that helped it to pay back much of its initial capital costs reasonably quickly.

Six years after starting production, Lornex announced a doubling of its ore reserves as well as a doubling of mining and milling capacity to 80,000 tons per day. That would make it clearly the largest metal mine in Canada and one of the world's largest. As we saw, Teck had acquired an interest in the mine through Yukon Consolidated, just before the expansion announcement.

Japanese Smelters Had Proven to Be Good Partners

The Japanese smelting industry had been instrumental in helping Bethlehem and Lornex get the necessary financing through their long-term sales contracts, and had attempted to do the same for Valley Copper. It was a complementary relationship, since Japan had few natural resources and was beginning to rely on manufacturing exports for its growth. BC had prospects for copper mine development but needed markets for the copper concentrate, as well as financing.

When the Bethlehem agreement was inked in 1960, the price of copper was about 30 cents a pound, and the agreement included a price participation clause. These are not uncommon in the business, and give the smelting or refining purchaser a part of the upside potential should prices increase in future years. In this case, Sumitomo would get 60 per cent and Bethlehem would retain 40 per cent above a certain higher price level. It was, in some ways, the reverse of our Highmont floor price arrangement, and it proved equally able to get offside.

Sure enough, that participation level was soon reached as copper prices rose beyond the strike point, but with inflation increasing, the mine's production costs were rising as well. Bethlehem was starting to get squeezed. The price of copper was much higher than envisaged when it had entered into the financing agreement, but Sumitomo was getting most of the increase.

Keith Steeves had joined Bethlehem by this time and recalls its president, Pat Reynolds, insisting to him that the agreement had to be renegotiated. Keith's response was: "There's no way. A contract is a contract. We signed it, and we have to live with it."

Pat was undaunted, and the two of them took off to Tokyo to see what could be done. The conversation went something like this:

REYNOLDS: The price of copper is going up but so are our costs. You're getting most of the benefit and we need to change the terms.
SUMITOMO: Polite silence.
REYNOLDS: This wasn't the spirit of the agreement. We're struggling and need help.
SUMITOMO: What do you think would be fair?
REYNOLDS: Change it to read Sumitomo gets 25 per cent of the price participation, instead of 60 per cent, and we keep 75 per cent.
SUMITOMO: Okay. That seems fair.

And as Keith recalls it, they shook hands and went off to have a good dinner.

The Japanese had a reputation for sometimes taking a long time to make decisions, often because they neeeded buy-in from a great many participants, but in this case it was a simple, straightforward, and surprisingly quick "yes."

This was Keith's first experience in dealing with Japanese companies, and he never forgot it. In Japan, business was done based upon friendships, handshakes, and a few pieces of paper to record the intent, rather than hanging the other guy out to dry. Some years later Keith had a chance to reciprocate. By this time, copper concentrates were in surplus, thanks in part to Japan's success in encouraging new production. While this was presumably the objective, in fact it had been more successful than expected and had led to difficulties for the Japanese smelting industry, which had agreed to buy more than it could then use. So a high-powered delegation led by Nippon, and including Sumitomo, came to Vancouver to try to get a solution. The request was that all of the Canadian concentrate shippers agree to cut back their contracted tonnage by 20 per cent.

First the delegation had gone to Placer Development, which refused them outright.

Meanwhile, Keith Steeves had gotten wind of the mission's goal and had gone to the mine to see what the impact would be. Tom Liss, the mine manager, pointed out that Bethlehem would have to go through a planned low-grade cycle in the pit some time soon anyway, and it would be easy to advance that by a year or so. So when the delegation came to Bethlehem's office and asked for a 20 per cent cut, Keith was ready. He asked them to give him a few minutes and left the room. After 15 minutes, to imply he'd actually been deep in contemplation and doing something, he returned and said: "Okay. I've talked to the mine. It's done. We'll reduce our production by 20 per cent for the next year." The favour had been returned, face was saved, and it was at no great cost.

The Valley, as the 1980s Began

There were various corporate manoeuverings in The Valley as the 1970s drew to a close and the 1980s began. Teck had acquired control of Yukon Consolidated and merged with it, giving us a direct interest in Lornex Mining Corporation. Lornex had announced the doubling of capacity shortly afterwards, and was in the midst of that construction program.

Cominco had kept its eyes very much on Bethlehem. As described earlier, although its first takeover bid had failed, a second one in 1980 would succeed, and Cominco by then owned the Bethlehem mining and milling facilities. For a time after mining stopped at the original Bethlehem mine two years later, Cominco would truck Valley Copper ore up the hill to the old mill to process it into saleable copper concentrate. It was not, in a perfectly engineered world, the most efficient way to develop Valley Copper, but at the time, given low metal prices, it seemed the most practical way.

Teck had completed construction at its Afton copper mine, only a few kilometres northeast of the Valley but in a different geological environment, and was finally beginning construction of the Highmont mine to the southeast of Lornex. It would be completed in 1981, but the mine would close three years later as post-recession copper and molybdenum prices remained low.

The Start of Consolidation

By 1985, the price of copper had fallen from the dollar a pound level reached at the end of the previous boom to around 65 cents a pound, and all of the mines developed on the premise of higher prices were struggling. The situation in The Valley was ready to be rationalized, if agreements could be reached to combine the various mine and mill ownerships into a more efficient package.

Lornex had the largest operating mill in The Valley, with its expanded 80,000-ton-per-day mine being part of the same large copper deposit that included Valley Copper and Highmont. The major shareholders in Lornex were Rio Algom, with a 68 per cent interest, and Teck Corporation, with its 22 per cent interest. Teck and its partners, Metallgesellschaft and the Kuwait Investment Office, had Highmont, with the second-largest and most modern mill but with operations suspended.

Cominco had the largest part of the copper deposit, but production was constrained by the limited size and location of the Bethlehem mill. Cominco couldn't afford to build a modern new mill of its own, and obviously was interested in joining forces with either or both of Lornex and Highmont to gain access to a debt-free and larger, more modern milling facility than it had at Bethlehem.

There was ample room for a deal that would benefit all three parties. Teck had an ownership position in both Highmont and Lornex and we were already partners with Lornex in the Bullmoose mine. The logical approach was for us to join forces to negotiate a deal with Cominco.

We suggested that to George Albino, but it met with an adamant refusal. In his humble opinion, Lornex did not need Teck. There was only one party for Cominco to deal with, and that was Lornex. That seemed consistent with what we knew as George's rather commanding style, as seen earlier while describing our subordinate role as directors of his company.

Interestingly, I had come to know Sir Alistair Frame, the CEO of Rio Tinto (Rio Algom's majority shareholder) quite well and would visit him in London regularly. Each time for the past few years he would ask me: "How are you getting on with George?" and I'd tell him. He would say each time that he would have to do something about that, but nothing had actually happened.

Anyway, on being rebuffed by Albino, we decided to open direct discussions between Highmont and Cominco. We each understood that to consolidate The Valley most efficiently Lornex would need to be included, but by first doing a deal between us, Cominco's and our negotiating position could be improved. The addition of Lornex would be very valuable, but not at any cost.

A "Gentleman's Agreement"

Eventually Albino's ears began burning and he became concerned that Cominco would play Highmont and Lornex off against each other in an attempt to negotiate a better deal with one or the other. The bounders!

So, after Bob Hallbauer and I had attended an early 1986 board meeting at the Lornex mine site, Albino approached me with a proposition, just like the one he had rejected earlier. "Norm," he said, "Let's make a deal. Let's agree that neither Lornex nor Teck will do a deal with Cominco alone, without the other's agreement. We should negotiate jointly and find a way to put all three facilities together."

That still made as much sense as ever and I agreed immediately. We had an interest in both Lornex and Highmont, and a common objective of finding a way to combine all of the Highland Valley operations into a single, more efficient package. So I accepted George's offer, and we shook hands on it.

Then, a couple of months later, in July 1986, Lornex and Cominco announced a unilateral agreement to merge their interests in The Valley on the basis of 55 per cent to Cominco and 45 per cent to Lornex. Highmont was completely excluded. Albino had gone behind our backs despite our agreement, which he himself had proposed.

At an ensuing Lornex board meeting called to approve the Cominco agreement, Hallbauer accused Albino of welching on a deal. He shouted back: "Where's the paper?" and said that it was only a "gentleman's agreement." It seems he was prepared to acknowledge that it didn't apply to him.

I've said earlier that my father and I each had a tendency to trust people and handshake agreements, and I still do. It seems to work out most of the time, just not always.

The Guard Changes

Three months later, in October 1986, Teck and two partners, Metallgesellschaft and MIM of Australia, a large company with lead and zinc mining operations, bought control of Cominco from Canadian Pacific Limited (CP). The purpose was not to achieve anything in particular regarding further consolidating the Highland Valley, but was primarily so we could participate in the development of Cominco's massive Red Dog zinc deposit in Alaska, but I suppose it could have occurred to us to say: "Here we are, George."

A month later we learned that, following a lunch break in a Rio Algom board meeting in Toronto, George Albino had returned to the boardroom to find that he had been removed from office. Sir Alistair Frame had finally done it, although I'm sure for reasons of his own.

Rio Algom appointed Ray Balmer, its chief operating officer, as the new CEO, and relations between us took a 180-degree turn for the better. It was understood that some accommodation between the Lornex/Cominco partnership and Highmont was appropriate and would happen. In addition, we developed a plan to have Rio Algom and Teck jointly acquire the small outside shareholdings in Lornex and wind that company up, operating the mine as a joint venture, and allocating Lornex's interest in Bullmoose between us.

Highland Valley Copper, the Consolidation Completed

The following year Teck, Cominco, and Lornex reached an understanding to combine the three operations into one, Highland Valley Copper, with the Highmont share being a 5 per cent joint venture interest and Cominco and Lornex sharing the balance in their originally-agreed 55:45 proportion. Highmont's share, representing that of its partners Teck, Metall, and KIO, was certainly less than it would have been if the promise to bring all three together at the start had been followed, but it was a good thing that the consolidation was finally done. Highland Valley Copper has been one of Canada's most important mining and milling operations ever since.

In one of the more impressive mobile engineering feats seen in Canada, the Highmont mill was disassembled into four main units and trucked down the hillside to a new foundation next to the original Lornex mills, where it was reassembled and became a key part of the new joint operation.

The components moved included a large autogenous mill weighing 680 tonnes, flotation modules weighing up to 1,500 tonnes, and the pebble crusher building, intact, at 12 metres by 18 metres by 20 metres high. The various pieces of equipment were transported down a specially built road 38 metres wide and 10 kilometres long winding down the hill. The vehicle carrying the parts of the mill, one large component at a time, was a 224-wheeled complex of trailers provided by Premay of Vancouver and known in the business as a shirley, for reasons that are best left unsaid. One major mining journal headlined the move: "Highmont mill moves downhill ... on purpose."

The disassembly, move, and reassembly cost $70 million, but was an investment well made by the new partnership. As a result, the combined mining and processing capacity of HVC increased from 90,000 to 120,000 tonnes per day (see colour page 10).

Epilogue: HVC, *a Major Mine, Created by Bootstrapping*

HVC is one of the largest mining and milling complexes in the world, one that was never designed as such from the start. Given the ore grade of around 0.4 per cent copper, it would never have been built as a stand-alone mine at the time. If it were to be built today, it would involve a construction cost well over $6 billion.

In the end, today's HVC had been brought into production by the efforts of four different mining companies before being optimized by the agreements combining the operations. By 1987, it was finally one mine, a joint venture owned by Cominco, Lornex, and the Highmont partners, Teck, Metall, and KIO.

In the first 40 years since Lornex began operations in 1972, the mines had produced over 11 billion pounds of copper and 200 million pounds of molybdenum, making the combination the largest copper producer ever in Canada, and one of the largest in the world. In 2014, HVC completed a major mill optimization program, at a cost of $500 million, that will extend its life through 2026 at least. Additional copper resources in The Valley could prolong this further, although they remain to be defined and will require further capital investment if they are to be developed.

It has been a historic Canadian mining story that started small, going back to Spud's discovery half a century earlier, and ended with a major mine that had been "built up by the bootstraps," as miners will sometimes say.

CHAPTER 25

ACQUIRING COMINCO, THE FIRST STAGE

Thinking outside the box is much easier with help from people who were never in that particular box in the first place.
Alastair Dryburgh

There are some years when a few eventful new things happen, and others in between when nothing much does. In Teck's long history, it has seemed that things that turned out to make a real difference have tended to occur two or three years apart, on average, although sometimes they were bunched together and at other times were further apart. When exceptional opportunities do occur, they need to be grasped or they will just be watched as they pass by. Conversely, as in fishing, there are times to throw the little one back and wait patiently for the good ones.

In some respects, 1986 was another one of those bunched years. It was the first full year of production at our new David Bell gold mine at Hemlo. It was when the Supreme Court of Ontario came down with its judgment awarding the adjoining Williams gold mine to the Teck/Corona joint venture. And it saw the formation of Highland Valley Copper, initially combining just the Lornex and Cominco operations.

I had been Teck's president for several years and my father was still chairman of the board. My brother Harold had become part of Peter Brown's Canaccord empire, and our younger brother Brian had finally succumbed to our blandishments, left the Lang Michener law firm, and joined us as vice-president, legal affairs.

And it was the year we bought control of Cominco.

Teck and Cominco, Before the Deal

Teck and Cominco had been two of the oldest operating mining companies in Canada for over half a century before the deal that brought them together in late 1986. Teck had begun in Kirkland Lake with the discovery of gold in

1912 by James Hughes and Sandy McIntyre. Cominco's history went back even further, with a series of entrepreneurial and promotional escapades in the late 1800s. These had culminated in the Canadian Pacific Railway colossus acquiring miscellaneous properties that would eventually be combined into the Consolidated Mining and Smelting Limited, later shortened to Cominco Limited.

The two companies' paths had been parallel and as such had never come close to crossing. Teck had been primarily a gold producer for its first half century, and Cominco was a lead-zinc company. As a gold producer, Teck-Hughes sold the output from its gold mills directly to the Canadian mint or like buyers, selling at the published market price. As a base metal company, Cominco was also involved in smelting and refining, and in marketing its main lead and zinc output as well as byproducts such as fertilizers to a variety of customers. Aside from the technology involved in actual mining and milling, the business models were not similar at all.

Cominco had entered the 1980s with an environmentally important but costly program to modernize its old Trail smelting and refining complex. It had lost money in three of the preceding four years and, according to one hand who had been there at the time, in 1984 survived only with the help of an infusion of funds from CP Limited, its major shareholder.

As part of Cominco's debt management program, CP had just helped itself to Cominco's 40 per cent share of a jointly-held company known as Fording Coal. As a railroad company that transported all of that coal to the coast at a substantial profit, CP had been very much interested in the coal mining side, but less so in the rest of the mining and smelting business.

Recently, Cominco had discovered the large Red Dog zinc deposit in Alaska, but CP had its own debt problems and had no interest in investing more in any mining ventures other than coal. Its interest in Cominco was quietly offered for sale, and Cominco management had been trolling selected industry partners that might be willing and compatible. One that apparently had expressed serious interest in buying the control position was Anglo American of South Africa.

If our two companies had substantially different, parallel histories, there were a few budding signs of convergence. In 1971, Cominco had moved its head office to Vancouver from Montreal and, entirely coincidentally, the following year Teck had moved from Toronto to Vancouver. By the mid-1980s the two had head offices just down the street from each other. Both by then had their sights on diversifying, particularly into copper and the Highland

Valley. Each had made an attempt to take over Bethlehem Copper and had failed at first. Cominco had finally succeeded in 1980 after two false starts.

Cominco had held an option on the Newfoundland Zinc property when Teck had acquired control of Leitch, but that option had expired soon after, and Teck carried on to discover and build the mine itself. Norm Anderson, by now Cominco's CEO in 1986, had at the time been head of Amax Canada, Leitch's partner in Newfoundland Zinc, but that was just another coincidence in a small mining world.

Canadian Pacific Makes Us an Offer We Didn't Refuse

In late 1985, my father and Bill Stinson, the new president of CP, were attending a dinner. Afterwards Bill approached him and asked if we would be interested in buying CP's 53 per cent shareholding in Cominco. At the market price at the time, this would have cost some $500 million. Our own company had a total market value of only $670 million, and taking on a new debt of $500 million to buy Bill's already debt-heavy Cominco was out of the question. Stinson didn't receive a lot of encouragement.

A few months later, in early 1986, Dominion Securities approached David Thompson with a similar proposal. Since they knew him well enough to know that he was seldom one to be caught in a weak moment, it's hard to see why they would have taken the time, except that is what investment bankers do. Throw it against the wall and see what sticks.

As David tells it: "Our first reaction was still unfavourable. Cominco was five times larger than Teck in both revenues and the number of employees. It had lost money in three of the last four years, and was losing again in 1986. Cominco had been trying to modernize its smelting and refining assets since 1980, most of which was still to be completed, and as a result it had more than $1 billion in debt at the end of 1985."

With modernization projects at its Trail refinery ongoing, this debt had the potential to keep growing, and construction of the Red Dog mine, Cominco's biggest and potentially most important new asset, had not even been started. It was reasonably clear why CP would want to sell, but it continued to be less so why we would want to buy.

The asking price for CP's 53 per cent shareholding was still at least $500 million, well beyond what we would or could pay. The economy was still weak after the 1981 recession, and we had been through a serious but successful debt restructuring, following which we were quite comfortable. However, two of Cominco's mining properties were world-class: Red Dog, the largest undeveloped zinc ore body in the world, and the newly-formed Highland Valley Partnership, which would be the largest copper mine in Canada. So we decided to sign a confidentiality agreement and proceed to do some limited due diligence. Who knew what interesting avenues might evolve?

Structuring a Deal

To avoid market rumours, the review team was kept small and there were to be no site visits. On Cominco's side it was CEO Norm Anderson and its controller. On our side, the mining team consisted of Bob Hallbauer and Mike Lipkewich, and on the financial and commercial team David Thompson and his number two man, John Taylor.

A "no site visit due diligence study" is probably the ultimate oxymoron. However, David's plan was to somehow structure something that would, with a relatively small investment, give us management control and sufficient time to determine whether we had a sow's ear or a silk purse in our hands. If the latter, we could go further. If not, we could somehow regroup and go on to the next big thing. Our limited due diligence showed enough potential value to support this approach, and we decided to go on to the next step.

The plan was also to assemble minority partners with whom we were compatible. Metallgesellschaft was one logical company. It was already a shareholder in Teck and a joint venture partner in the Highmont mine. It had a large trading position in lead and zinc, Cominco's main products, and operated zinc refineries as well. Heinz Schimmelbusch, who was a director of Teck and ran Metall's Mining and Smelting Division, quickly bought into the plan. The next step was to find a suitable third player.

Metall had several joint ventures with MIM, and David knew Bruce Watson, its new CEO, quite well from their days in a Harvard Advanced Management Program some years earlier. So David and Heinz flew to Brisbane to meet Bruce, and they reached agreement on a proposal for CP.

Teck would hold 50 per cent and Metall and MIM 25 per cent each in a new vehicle, Nunachiaq Inc., which would offer to acquire a 30 per cent shareholding in Cominco from CP. CP would be asked to dispose of its remaining

23 per cent through a secondary offering to institutional investors. The total cost to Nunachiaq would be about $300 million, of which Teck's share would be $150 million.

The net effect of the plan was that we would have effective control for $150 million, rather than spending $500 odd million. Like the old miners who would sink a shaft to go underground and have a look at the ore, this would give us a chance to peek into the entrails and see what we could do with them. Quite ingenious, if we did it right.

So a negotiating meeting was arranged in the Teck office with Bill Stinson, accompanied by his investment bankers, lawyers, and financial officers. David Thompson, Klaus Zeitler of Metall, and a senior lawyer represented our side.

Stinson had been trying to sell CP's holding for at least six months, without success. He had over $6 billion in debt upstairs in CP, and his number one priority was to begin reducing that. Anglo American had seemed like a possible buyer for a time, but nothing had come of it. Our proposal would let him take 30 per cent of the debt off his books immediately, including CP's reported share of Cominco's debt. He was a willing player, despite protests from his team as David began to set out his usual stable of conditions.

These included immediate placement of eight of our nominees as directors, which would require replacing some independents as well as CP nominees. David also asked for a five-year loan from CP to Nunachiaq, which meant that CP would be lending us money to help us pay them for the company.

I was beginning to appreciate again our own wisdom, when David had failed to get the deal to buy those Teck A shares that Metall had won back in 1977. We had concluded then that if we could ever have David on our side of the table, we would be ahead of the game. We had done just that when he joined us two years later, and here again was proof of that pudding.

David and Stinson were in constant touch by phone as the details were worked out, and a schedule was developed to complete our purchase and have the CP secondary share sale take place in October.

At the last minute, a major problem arose regarding the proposed financing of the Red Dog Mine, which was supposed to have been committed already by the banks and was crucial to our numbers. We had been assured by CP that the banks had agreed to a long-term US$150 million letter of credit (LC) payable to the Alaskan government, which it would use to build an access road and port north of the Bering Strait. In fact, the financing was not in place at all, and the banks had just refused to issue the LC. This had been a key part of the financing plan for Red Dog; it was almost a third of the planned US$415 million capital cost.

The deal was in tatters, but after hours of bargaining, David and Bill Stinson rescued it with an agreement that had CP guarantee half of the LC indefinitely and the Nunachiaq partners the other half, both on behalf of Cominco. Finally, after another week of long hours and late nights, the formal agreements were in place and the deal could be announced as planned, on 13 October 1986.

David had pulled off a miracle, with a structure that fitted all four parties, but there was more to come. On the announcement of the deal, and with Teck now the sponsoring shareholder in place of CP, those same banks that had refused to issue the LC called David back and told him they had changed their position. They would now issue the LC as originally contemplated, with no parent company guarantees necessary. They were evidently also anxious to get a piece of the balance of the Red Dog financing.

A few days later, David and I flew off for Europe to outline the partners' plans to investors in London, Frankfurt, and Paris, and to raise money by selling Teck shares. With the help of Jimmy Connacher's Gordon Securities and Credit Suisse First Boston, the deal sold out and we had raised $62 million. In the end, the total purchase price of the CP deal had been $280 million, of which CP loaned back $75 million for five years, so the net cash outlay was $205 million, with Teck's share $102.5 million. We had already had surplus cash of over $50 million and had raised $62 million from the European trip.

As David later described it:

Teck had gained control of $2 billion of assets and had not needed to use any bank borrowings to do so. One afternoon, a few weeks later I was called to the Teck boardroom. There was a small number of staff there drinking coffee and eating cakes. The Keevils gave short speeches thanking me and my staff for the successful completion of the purchase and announced that the company would give some small gifts. The largest parcel contained a casual leather jacket. The second a white scarf and goggles, and the smallest parcel contained the keys to a new white Mercedes SL 560 convertible that was already waiting in the car park of the office. It was a total surprise and typical of the Keevils' spontaneous generosity.

A few days later, during one of our periodic extraterrestrial experiences, also known as a Lornex board meeting, George Albino asked what discount factor we had used to evaluate the Cominco investment. I responded that it was a secret. He then said: "I didn't think Teck used discount factors." We usually do, as had been drummed into me in my days at Placer Development, but then there are unusual circumstances from time to time. In fact, with a deal structured like this, the real worth may be in what is often called option value – what you can make of it in time.

In that respect we would take a longer time than perhaps we should have to reach the end point, but that is for later, as the story evolves.

What Have We Done?

At this point, we had acquired effective control of Cominco without stretching our financial resources. The question was what to do with it. Obviously, we should try to get its debt down and Red Dog into production, and we should put our best operating man in to try to manage it and make it better if we could. It was now, as is said in some other country, Cosa Nostra, or "our thing."

This was unlike any acquisition we had made before. Cominco had diverse operations from the old Trail zinc refining and lead smelting facilities, fertilizer plants that had begun as by-products or offshoots of those facilities, and several zinc and copper mines. It also had a huge head office, seemingly overstaffed compared with Teck's.

In comparison, when we acquired Teck-Hughes, it only had two mines, with almost all its staff situated at the producing operations and just a rudimentary head office. Canadian Devonian's main asset had been oil production operated by BA, with a skeleton staff to look after it. Leitch had been a simple, friendly matter of buying out the founder, managing its passive Mattagami share position, and recognizing the hidden values in its jewel box. Yukon Consolidated had been similar.

None of these acquisitions had involved more than a few employees, let alone hundreds. In all cases, we had walked in and taken complete charge, without any complications of note. Furthermore, Teck-Hughes, Devonian, and Leitch were essentially debt-free, and were good cash cows that could be farmed. In contrast, Cominco had over a billion dollars in debt, very large in those days, and had been losing money for the last four years. This one would hardly be as easy.

As The Borg was known to say in a later era: "You can be assimilated." In this case, it was not as clear which of us would be the assimilator and which the assimilatee.

The Globe and Mail headlined that we had acquired control of a company "four times our size." This may have been true a decade earlier, but by 1986 it was not nearly accurate in terms of relative values, earnings, or in the number and scale of mining operations, where Teck was already larger. But it seemed to be true in head count, which for many corporate and other organizations tends inevitably to grow larger with time, almost inversely proportional to its nimbleness or growth prospects.

Our First Taste of Cominco

Our eight nominees were elected and eight previous directors resigned. Bob Hallbauer went over to our new affiliate and became president and CEO of Cominco. David and others from the Teck-Nunachiaq side went onto the board, including Metall's Heinz Schimmelbusch and Klaus Zeitler and MIM's Colin Kaiser, and I was elected chairman.

Norm Anderson was an old industry friend from our Newfoundland Zinc project, and I told him we'd be pleased to have him stay on the board. He knew the inner entrails of the company, had been a colleague of ours earlier, and could provide continuity. Norm did what he saw as the right thing. He had never felt he was really the CEO of Cominco until the previous one, Fred Burnett, had left the board, and said he would not put Bob Hallbauer in the same position.

Norm, who we understood had been trying to get Anglo American to buy those CP shares instead, said he was glad Teck had bought them, because it would be "better for Cominco to be controlled by a mining company than by a railroad." He was, as always, a class act.

It soon became even clearer that Cominco was a different kind of company from those with which we were accustomed. One of the early events we attended was the official opening of a new ammonia plant, owned jointly with an Alberta Crown corporation, at Joffre, in Alberta. Now, we hadn't bought Cominco for its ammonia, and weren't entirely sure why it needed this plant anyway, but we were determined to show the flag and attend in force. What struck me most of all, other than its finely engineered workings, was that every senior Cominco representative was wearing exactly the same outfit, a dark blue blazer and grey trousers. It was eerie, as though they had all bought their clothes at the company store.

When it came time for our first board meeting to do actual business, Norm Anderson's previous assistant/bodyguard called me up to ask when I would like to go through the five-hour dry run that was expected. Apparently this was a custom at Cominco, designed to vet everything management might say at the real meeting. It would ensure that nothing unexpected might come up in front of the CP owners. We had never heard of such a thing, so I said we should skip the dry run and script, and have an unrehearsed, wide-open meeting, our way.

Epilogue

As we closed the Cominco deal, Heinz Schimmelbusch, whose Metallgesellschaft had been mining zinc for over 100 years, made the comment: "The trouble with the zinc business is that there's only one good year in ten." He would prove to be prescient. Some on our side may have come to wish he had said that earlier in the process.

Heinz would shortly flip his 25 per cent to MIM, which also mined zinc. However, MIM had only been doing it for 50 years or so, and thus may not yet have had enough time to figure it out. They too would eventually sell to us. It seemed they each decided upon and executed a choice on the option value quickly, while we retained the responsibility of being the largest, but less than majority, shareholder for a long time.

As if to show again what a small world we miners live in, Norm Anderson and Keith Steeves happened to be next-door neighbours in Vancouver's Point Grey area. In 1981, as Cominco completed the acquisition of Bethlehem, Norm had called up Keith and said it's time to come over and have a drink. They talked about everything but the takeover, and shortly after that Keith joined Teck for his eventful first day at the Highmont mine-opening golf tournament.

Now, in 1986, as we acquired control of Cominco, Keith called up Norm, who came next door to Keith and Norma Steeves' home for a drink. Again there was no discussion of the deal.

Jimmy Connacher's favourite admonition to his people about fair dealing had been "What goes around, comes around." Dealing well with people in a small world is a wise life choice, since you never know whom you'll meet again on the way up, or down, or sideways. There was this time when Hallbauer and I came around a corner in the Winnipeg airport only, to our surprise, to run across ... Well, maybe I'll tell you that one later.

CHAPTER 26

NEW MINES AT RED DOG
AND LOUVICOURT

It's better to do a few things slowly, than a lot of things fast.
Pete McCarthy

The Red Dog Decision

The main item of new business at that first Cominco meeting was Red Dog. Should we commit to putting it into production or not? This decision had been held in abeyance while CP fretted, although most of Cominco's management below the very top had been unaware of its plan to sell. Their biggest concern had been that this great new mine was not supported by CP and might never get on the rails, so to speak.

A solid engineer named Hank Giegerich was in charge of the project and made the presentation, along with Jim Gowans. The two of them had combined to build the successful Polaris zinc mine on Little Cornwallis Island in the Arctic. Having completed it successfully in 1981, they were the experts on building mines up there where the summer days of the midnight sun alternated seasons with the winter days of no sun at all, and the polar bears became nearly invisible, although they remained quite hungry.

Hank was clearly nervous, unsure of what these new Teck people might have in mind. He actually needn't have been, because for our part, the primary reason for buying into Cominco had actually been to help develop Red Dog, but I guess we hadn't made that clear yet.

Anyway, Hank went through his long presentation, and Jim Gowans asked David Thompson what he thought of the chances of financing it, given that CP hadn't been particularly enthusiastic about helping with any commitments. It was a legitimate concern, given that the budgeted capital cost was 50 per cent higher than any mine we'd built before. Jim still recalls David's response: "If it's the biggest mine of anything, we can get the financing."

David didn't let on he had just heard from those banks that earlier had refused to issue the key letter of credit without a parent company guarantee, but had now capitulated, which explains why he was so uncharacteristically ebullient.

I asked Jim if he thought they could build it faster, cutting a year off the schedule. He said they could try, but it wasn't really a fair question, given the need to schedule every delivery to the site, as well as the actual construction tasks, around severe winter conditions that included months of near pitch darkness. The schedule at hand had been well thought out to accommodate this.

Bob Hallbauer had a few other questions that he wanted to ask, to be sure all the cards were on the table, but soon it was time for the response. I thanked Hank and asked: "Is there anyone here who thinks we should *not* put Red Dog into production?" There was not, or at least nobody said so, and the vote to approve it was unanimous. The sense of relief in the engineers and other Cominco hands who were present was palpable.

Bob Hallbauer Takes Charge at Cominco

Bob Hallbauer had been involved in the Cominco evaluation and negotiations, and was by far and away our most senior qualified mining person to take on management of the company. It needed someone who could manage its existing operations, both mining and refining, and get Red Dog built successfully.

Bob also had a long family history with the Trail region, having been born and raised near Nelson in southeastern British Columbia. He had grown up "in the shadow of the smelter," as is often said in the mining business. His father had been a master mechanic in gold mines near Nelson, and Bob had worked in some of Cominco's mines as a student. If he had been raised elsewhere, he might never have considered a career in mining.

To Bob, and to most people who followed mining in BC, Cominco and its decades-old Sullivan mine and Trail smelting and refining operation had been icons in the mining business long before any of them had heard of Teck. So he instinctively wanted to fix Cominco, its debt, and perhaps some of its population, but not to change what had made it an icon. It was not an easy challenge for him.

Completing the HVC Consolidation

Although it was not the main reason for making the acquisition, it was important to all of us to tidy up things in the Highland Valley. As we saw earlier, Lornex had broken ranks and dealt with Cominco alone, leaving a small but important asset, the modern Highmont milling plant, out in left field. It would make sense to complete the process, adding it to the combined joint venture in some way. It was evident that this would best include taking the plant apart and reassembling it down the hill at the Lornex mill location, adding once again to its capacity.

Bob Hallbauer recused himself because of the inherent conflict of interest and asked Ted Fletcher and Bill Robertson, two of Cominco's top engineering executives, to work with Teck's engineers and come up with a plan that would be fair to all parties in the circumstances. This was done, and the move of the whole plant downhill to the Lornex site completed the following year, as described earlier.

Lowering Cominco's Exploration Costs

In early 1987, as part of the necessary debt reduction program, Bob and the board decided to spin out Cominco's international exploration projects to a new subsidiary company called Cominco Resources International (CRIL). Initially, these were to be primarily gold projects, and Cominco's Buckhorn Gold Mine in Nevada was included in the package, along with a virtual United Nations of other gold properties around the world.

The prospectus read in part that CRIL "will acquire from Cominco an interest in a large gold property in Chile that will be ready for a 1987 production decision, and partially delineated gold deposits in the United States, Mexico, Chile, Peru, Brazil, France and Italy awaiting drilling of identified mineralization."

It almost sounded like Murray Pezim. Did Bob and I actually sign that?

The Chilean property was Marte, a gold prospect in the Maricunga area that was held in a joint venture with Joe Oppenheimer's Anglo American. The new company also had a copper prospect in Mexico and beryllium properties in the United States. It was the kind of potpourri that arises from a good, perhaps a bit unfocused, international exploration program.

With a broad property evaluation from Wright Engineers, the offering of one common share and one warrant of CRIL raised $37 million for Cominco, and put some $30 million in planned exploration expenses for 1987 and 1988 downstairs into the new subsidiary, for a total balance sheet improvement of $67 million over two years. It was not a lot compared with where the debt had been, but every little bit counted, especially with more capital needing to be invested in Red Dog.

CRIL would be an interesting exercise. Its formation would save immediate cash for the parent company and allow work to be continued on a number of prospective properties, as planned. One of Cominco's key geologists, George Tikkanen, took a team downstairs and did some excellent work there. Its continued activity in Chile would lead to acquisition of the Quebrada Blanca copper deposit, which would become an important mine for Cominco and Teck.

In the end, though, CRIL became a distraction within a larger, operating mining company. As a junior public company, its exploration focus had to be largely what the market wanted from day to day, which in those days was gold. As well, major company exploration is theoretically more efficient when carried out deliberately and scientifically, rather than at the ephemeral response of the junior stock market. The solid scientists assigned to it had to develop a Jekyll and Hyde persona, the promoter part of which just didn't come naturally.

In 1995, eight years after it had been formed, Cominco Limited reacquired the 44 per cent of CRIL held by the public, in exchange for 5 million Cominco shares. This was described as a transaction that "provided a simpler, more efficient ownership structure and enhanced the ability to fund the development of the mineral projects of Cominco Resources."

It is not recorded just who actually wrote that one.

Red Dog, the Discovery

Completing the HVC consolidation and working to fix Cominco's cash drain aside, our most important task was helping to get Red Dog built properly, but first it's interesting to track how Cominco became involved. It had taken alertness, patience, and negotiating ingenuity, each of which in one way or another seems to be a part of most exploration successes.

The discovery of zinc in the area has been attributed to a bush pilot and prospector named Bob Baker, who in 1968 spotted a large area of rusty stain in a creek in northern Alaska. He had a red dog, an Irish terrier named O'Malley, and ever since the property has been known as Red Dog. Baker mentioned the rusty stain to a geologist working for the US Geological Survey, and its 1970 report noted the presence of zinc and lead mineralization in the area. Nothing much happened immediately, with zinc selling around 13 cents a pound and the region being remote. Then, in 1971, much of the area was withdrawn from exploration as a result of the Alaska Native Claims Settlement Act.

By the mid-1970s, zinc had almost doubled in value, as we had experienced to our benefit at Newfoundland Zinc. The US Bureau of Mines (USBM) contracted Watts, Griffiths, and McOuat (WGM) to review the mineral showings in the region, and assess whether some of the known mineralized areas should be reopened for mining development. WGM discovered boulders and outcrops containing high-grade lead and zinc, and the USBM dutifully reported this in a press release.

As George Koehler and George Tikkanen reported in a retrospective paper in *Economic Geology* years later, Cominco geologists exploring elsewhere in Alaska heard of this report and within a few days were on site to examine the showings themselves. Although the actual land where the boulders occurred was still withdrawn from exploration, there was open land nearby and they immediately staked claims to cover this.

The next year the Northwest Arctic Native Association Regional Corporation (later NANA), representing native Alaskans from the region, applied for ownership of the withdrawn lands under the Native Claims Settlement Act. Meanwhile Cominco, operating under legal advice that the area might now be open for staking, pegged claims over what turned out to be the main zinc deposit and began drilling. The first hole encountered 46 feet of 45 per cent zinc and 10 per cent lead, a grade almost as unusual as the discovery hole at Temagami years earlier. Cominco completed eight holes, not all of which were in ore, before the US Bureau of Land Management filed an injunction to stop the drilling.

With title not at all clear, but the zinc deposit potentially exceptional, CEO Norm Anderson took personal charge of the project and, with geologist George Tikkanen, began discussions with NANA representatives. After suits and countersuits to protect each other's positions, the parties reached an agreement in 1982 that would allow the property to be developed. NANA was acknowledged as owner of the land. Cominco would develop and operate a new mine on the prospect, with NANA to receive payments of $1 million a year plus a 4.5 per cent net smelter return royalty until Cominco had recovered its investment. Thereafter, NANA would receive 25 per cent of net profits, increasing by 5 per cent every five years until it reached 50 per cent.

It was a good deal for both sides, and a credit to Anderson, Tikkanen, and the Cominco team that had seen and grasped the opportunity. It was also a credit to the forward-looking leadership and shareholders of NANA, who saw the potential of the new mine to help create a stronger future for the people and communities of the Northwest Arctic.

Exploration resumed, and by 1986, reserves at Red Dog had been shown to be 85 million tonnes grading 17 per cent zinc and 5 per cent lead, with significant byproduct credits in silver. It was possibly the second-largest zinc deposit ever discovered, after Broken Hill in Australia. Parsons Engineering of San Francisco had completed a feasibility study for a 6,000-ton-per-day mining and milling operation. Including infrastructure to get the output to the coast and on board ships, the capital cost was projected to be US$415 million.

Ironically, it was too much of a good thing for CP. The last thing it wanted was to run up more debt to build more zinc production. So the success of Anderson and Tikkanen, doing what they were supposed to do, had resulted in CP putting them up for sale. That had been the situation when CP approached us, and we acquired management control of Cominco.

Building Red Dog

One of the things that concerned Bob Hallbauer was that, while Cominco did operate eight mines, the same as Teck, it had actually only built one significant new one, Polaris, in the previous decade. And in that case the whole plant had been built adjacent to the St Lawrence River in Quebec and barged 5,600 kilometres up to the plant site on an island in the Arctic Ocean. Both Giegerich and Gowans had been part of the team that built Polaris successfully, and could bring that experience to bear at Red Dog.

However, during that same 10 years Teck had built six new mines successfully, and had a corps of engineers that were right up to speed on managing mine construction. This was, and is, an art best learned and kept current through experience. Bob was determined that one of his Teck people be part of the construction program as well, and he asked Teck to second Lee Bilheimer to Cominco to do just that.

Lee was a hard-rock miner from the Missouri mining country. Another Placer Development alumnus, he had done the feasibility study for Newfoundland Zinc and worked on the engineering and construction as it was being built. He had then moved on to coordinate the programs at Niobec, Afton, and Highmont. He had been construction manager for the large Bullmoose coal project that, as with all the others, had been completed on time and within budget.

Bob arranged for Lee to be appointed vice-president, Cominco Alaska, and he was assigned responsibility for managing the engineering, procurement, and construction of both the mine and port facilities, working with Jim Gowans as manager of engineering and Hank Giegerich as general manager of Red Dog. It was a complicated arrangement, but with what would be our biggest new mine investment yet, Bob needed to feel as comfortable as possible with it.

As Lee put it in an unpublished memoir:

Initially I had to move to Pasadena, California where I stayed for eight months working on engineering and procurement with Parsons Engineering Co. and Cominco people. Parsons had been chosen because of its experience designing oil-drilling platforms for Alaska's North Slope. These gigantic platforms had been fabricated abroad, floated through the Bering Sea in summertime, and moved onshore by specially designed centipede-like transporters from Holland.

We were to do the same thing with Red Dog, the first time it had ever been done in the mining industry. Thirteen mill-plant modules, each the size of a seven-story building, were fabricated in the Philippines. We then put them aboard two ships and transferred them to barges in the Aleutian Islands in Alaska. The barges were then towed to our Red Dog port, and the modules taken 85 kilometres up the slope to the plant location, using two 70-foot long self-propelled transporters, each with 76 tires.

The huge modules being moved at about 2 kilometres an hour over the barren tundra was an awesome sight. After they reached the mine site, they were set in place and hooked up like a giant LEGO game to make one of the largest pre-assembled mills ever (see colour page 11).

Construction was completed in a little more than two years, on schedule despite a few sleepless nights for Lee, Hank, Jim, and the rest of the team, and at a total cost of US$487 million, $72 million over budget. The official opening was held in July 1989, with ceremonies at the mine site and in the village of Kivalina. It was a big success all around.

This was my father's last mine-opening before he left us four months later. He had been battling multiple myeloma for a year and was bone tired, but managed to find the energy to dance at the Kivalina ceremony.

Louvicourt: A New Copper-Zinc Discovery in Quebec

That same year, two companies jointly discovered an impressive copper-zinc deposit in Louvicourt Township, not far from where our old Lamaque gold mine had been. One, Novicourt Inc., was a Noranda affiliate, and the other, Aur Resources, an independent exploration company run by Dr Jim Gill. Jim, who had been an expert witness on the losing side of the Lac/Corona lawsuit, was an excellent geologist and was the leader behind the discovery.

We had become reasonably close to Jim over the years after the lawsuit, and approached him to offer help in engineering and financing the potential new mine. Jim was also related to Owen Owens, Cominco's vice-president, exploration, so we visited the property jointly.

We liked what we saw, and negotiated an agreement that saw Cominco and Teck jointly purchase 3.3 million treasury shares of Aur for $35.5 million, as well as buying 600,000 shares from certain shareholders of Aur. This gave Teck and Cominco together a 19 per cent share interest in the company. The funds would enable Aur to do more drilling to delineate the mineral deposit and begin a feasibility study. Teck and Cominco were also given rights to participate up to 40 per cent in any future share issuances by Aur.

The Louvicourt deposit would turn out to become a good medium-size copper mine that Teck and Noranda would help to build in the early 1990s. It would be the first of a number of deals between Teck, Noranda, Cominco, and Aur that would have an impact on each company in future years.

1989 – A Good Year Before the Tide Began to Turn

For the most part, 1989 was another one of those periodic good years.

Teck and Corona had won the lawsuit over the Williams gold mine at Hemlo in 1986, the same year we acquired control of Cominco, but it was still subject to appeal. In 1989, the Supreme Court of Canada finally ruled on the case, and it had come down in our favour, albeit by the skin of its teeth.

And we completed construction at Red Dog, once again our biggest new mine yet in terms of capital cost, if not in tonnes mined per day. Both of these had kept us busy. We had set the stage for what would become our next new mine at Louvicourt in Quebec with the investment in Aur Resources.

Also in 1989, the smaller of the two government-owned Chilean mining companies, Enami, put Quebrada Blanca, a potentially economic, heap-leaching copper prospect at high elevation near the Bolivian border, up for bids. Cominco and its 61 per cent-owned CRIL were the successful bidders, jointly earning a 90 per cent interest if they arranged financing and committed to bring the project into production within 18 months of the signing. It was an ambitious timetable, but one that helped us to win the auction. This project would soon become the Quebrada Blanca mine, to be developed by Cominco and Teck, as we returned to Chile a much different company than when we had been there more than 20 years earlier.

Epilogue: The Sad Passing of a Founder

Sadly though, it was the year my father, Dr Norman Keevil Sr, passed away at age 79. He was young almost to the end, after an inspiring career as an eclectic researcher, professor, exploration consultant, mine-finder, and company-builder. He left a company still on the rise, and would have been proud of what it became as more years went on. Before he passed away, I was able to let him know that he was to be inducted into the Canadian Mining Hall of Fame the following January. His response: "Harumph, another award," but he did appreciate it.

Not long after that, and only a few years after joining Teck, my youngest brother, Brian, passed away from non-Hodgkin's lymphoma, far too soon, at age 40. But the apple doesn't fall too far from the tree, and Halley, one of Brian's daughters, with her own love of geology and mining, attended Cambridge in the UK, and is currently taking her PhD in geology at the Colorado School of Mines.

EPILOGUE, PART FOUR

The 1980s had again proven to be a reasonably good decade for Teck.

We had been quite successful growing the company by acquiring prospects and building new mines in the 1970s, but the external environment had become chaotic, culminating in the extreme Volcker interest rates and major 1981 recession.

That recession, naturally, had a serious impact on many companies that had ridden the debt binge carelessly. Fortunately, we had adjusted course ahead of the recession, selling some assets and bringing in partners on other new projects as part of a major debt reduction program. This had actually put us in a position to invest in the future when times looked their worst, acquiring the David Bell gold project at Hemlo in the midst of the turmoil.

By the end of the 1980s, we had followed up our three earlier new mines and the timely Yukon/Lornex acquisition with a new copper-molybdenum mine in the Highland Valley, which became a part of Highland Valley Copper; two new gold mines in Ontario; the Bullmoose coal mine in BC; the acquisition of management control of Cominco; and through Cominco the new Red Dog zinc mine in Alaska. We had also acquired an interest in Aur Resources' Louvicourt base metal discovery, and Cominco had acquired the Quebrada Blanca copper prospect in northern Chile.

The net effect was that we had acquired and/or built nine new mines in 15 years, and had two more on the drawing boards. This had led directly to a 32-fold appreciation in value for our long-term Class B shareholders: assuming dividends had been reinvested, $100 invested in 1975 would have grown to $3,200 in 1990.

PART FIVE

THE 1990S, A SLOW ERA FOR MINING

The 1990s would continue to be a period of slower growth for most companies in the mining industry. The secular decline in commodity prices that had begun in the mid-1970s had been interrupted briefly by several bounces (as the following chart for copper, a bellwether commodity, shows), but as we now know, it would continue until five years into the twenty-first century.

Of course, information for the last 10 years of this chart was not available to us as we began the 1990s. We were somewhat optimistic since we had just seen a couple of years of recovery through 1989, but the ensuing three or four years of declining prices would be real and be felt by the entire industry.

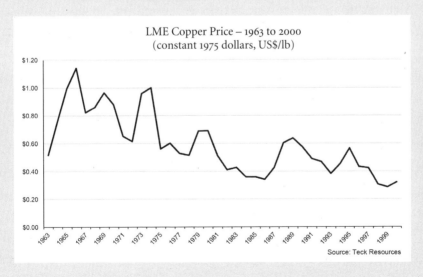

LME Copper Price – 1963 to 2000
(constant 1975 dollars, US$/lb)

Source: Teck Resources

A long secular decline in the price of copper was evident for 25 years following the strong years of the late 1960s and early '70s

It would be a new era for us in Teck in different ways as well. The deaths of my father and my brother Brian had been disheartening. As well, after 15 years of strong growth through mine development, the acquisition of control of Cominco in late 1986 had been a deviation from what had made the company. The mine opening at Red Dog seemed for a time to be carrying on the trend. But then, with copper and zinc prices declining, Cominco would experience significant losses from 1991 through 1993, which in turn Teck would have to take into its books as well.

And we had changed in subtler ways. Instead of continuing to forge ahead in our own way, during this time we were trying to sail two ships, with perhaps neither making the progress it might have. Most important, Bob Hallbauer had been diverted from his passion and strength, which was mine-building, to having to administer at the same time a rather large debt-ridden affiliate not of our own making.

Between us we still had the nucleus of the team that had done well in the preceding 15 years, but with its attention at times on two horses, rather than the old single-minded focus. We would participate in two more new mines and would add an important second coal mine at Elkview in the first half of the 1990s, but our growth rate in adding shareholder value would slow. It would not resume until after two ad-ventures involving important mineral discoveries later in the decade, and then only after several years in the investment community's penalty box while we built a major new mine in Peru.

CHAPTER 27

RETURNING TO CHILE WITH QUEBRADA BLANCA

Trust arrives on foot, but leaves on horseback.
Johan Thorbecke

We returned to Chile in 1989 after 20 years away, following Cominco's agreement to explore and develop the Quebrada Blanca prospect in the Andes Mountains inland from the port of Iquique.

A lot had happened in the Chilean copper scene since our earlier exploration program under Geophysical Engineering and Surveys had been suspended in 1969. Nationalization of part or all of the industry by then had seemed increasingly inevitable, and it did in fact occur in two phases, beginning with President Eduardo Frei Montalva that summer, and completed by his successor, Salvador Allende, the next year. Most of the major copper mines and prospects ended up owned by the new national copper company, Codelco, with smaller prospects eventually in the hands of Enami, a second national copper company.

That government soon fell and was replaced by a "temporary" military government, one that would set a new benchmark for the word. Three years after taking power, it announced that it would not return the expropriated copper mines to their former owners, but wanted to encourage new copper investment by international mining companies. Notwithstanding a certain inconsistency in that position, some companies did take up the opportunity.

Noranda Mines Acquires the Rights to the Andacollo Prospect

One of the first international companies to accept the challenge to bid on newly denationalized mining properties was Canada's Noranda Mines, which in 1976 negotiated the right to explore and develop a copper mine at Andacollo, near La Serena.

We had looked at Andacollo back in the 1960s. It was attractive then because of its extensive, known copper mineralization and location at relatively low elevation, close to the coast. However, that copper occurred under a large number of properties, large and small, with ownership that was in many cases poorly recorded and indeterminate. We had met with one of the larger landowners in the hope of getting his help in assembling a workable land package, but it seemed a hopeless task and in any event time ran out as our program was suspended.

By 1976, the land issues had been resolved, if a bit arbitrarily through nationalization, and the mineral rights lay with the government copper companies. Noranda was able to negotiate an option to earn a 49 per cent interest in Andacollo if, after further work, they agreed to develop it. The proposed investment was estimated to be $240 million, a large sum for those days, well over what Lornex had invested to build its contemporary BC mine, and close to what we were anticipating for our Bullmoose mine.

By 1980, the projected costs had escalated to $400 million, and at the same time Noranda was under attack from NGOs of the day for considering any such investment in Chile. The Task Force of Canadian Churches had attended five consecutive Noranda annual meetings to protest against it. Finally, the company announced it was abandoning the project for business reasons.

Placer Development held an option on Andacollo for a short time after Noranda, but also dropped it after concluding that the original primary, or hypogene, resource was too low grade to be economic at the time. Heap-leach technology for supergene copper ores, such as we would use later at the Quebrada Blanca SX-EW mine, was then in its infancy.

Teck looked at the prospect carefully again in 1990, with our erstwhile evaluator of new business opportunities, Gary Jones, recommending that we make an offer to Enami to develop it. We didn't, moving on instead to Quebrada Blanca. Aur Resources eventually acquired the key properties and put a heap-leach copper mine into production in 1996.

Developments on Other Prospects from the 1960s Program

It's interesting that a number of the copper prospects that Joe Frantz had identified in that earlier exploration project have since become producing mines. These include our original Sierra Gorda property as well as Lomas Bayas and Cerro Colorado.

Two that Joe had flagged but hadn't been able to visit were Los Pelambres, a prospect acquired and developed years later by Andronico Luksic and now the world's sixth biggest copper mine, and Quebrada Blanca. QB was located in the High Andes near the Bolivian border and had seemed too remote to be of interest back in the 1960s.

On the one hand, we appear to have come close to what became a number of good mines but, on the other, none were obviously economic enough to develop in those days, even if we had somehow been able to hang on to them through the era of nationalization.

The Chimborazo prospect never did make a mine on its own, but it did continue to lead explorers into the area, and eventually to the 1981 discovery of Escondida by a team that included the famed geologist David Lowell. Now owned by BHP and Rio Tinto, it is one of the world's greatest copper mines, but it was not immediately clear when and if it could be developed economically.

I recall talking with Sir Alistair Frame, Rio's highly respected CEO, about Escondida during a London visit in 1984. The price of copper was hovering around 63 cents a pound, and Sir Alistair was worried that it might never become economic in his lifetime. He felt it needed at least 85 cents a pound in then-current dollars to justify construction, and that this could be years away. As it turned out, copper prices climbed temporarily to over a dollar a pound by 1988, and Rio and BHP bit the bullet and decided to build Escondida.

Similarly, Los Pelambres was not obviously economic in the early days, and it went through several owners before it could be developed. Codelco put it up for auction in 1978, and Teck looked, but declined to bid. Atlantic Richfield won the auction and drilled off a resource, before giving up and selling it to Andronico Luksic in 1986.

After Andronico acquired the property, it would still be years before it could be financed into production. He began by trying to find ways to start with a smaller mine, based on high-grade sections of the deposit, but with copper prices in continued decline through much of the 1990s, it was not easy. Finally, in 1999 a partnership was arranged with Japanese companies that took a 40 per cent interest in the project, committing to purchase the copper concentrate output and assist in the financing. It was the Bethlehem story all over again, 40 years later. After years of hard work, Andronico's Antofagasta Minerals was able to put Los Pelambres into production.

If I may repeat what bears repeating often, nobody said it would be easy.

It was not always easy for us, nor for Sir Alistair Frame and Rio Tinto, and certainly not for Andronico Luksic. Success in the mining business, wherever one is, seems to require some combination of good fortune, perseverance, and timing.

With QB, we were fortunate that the new Cominco Resources (CRIL) was in Chile in the late 1980s, and came across an opportunity to bid on the Quebrada Blanca copper prospect when Enami put it up for sale. Being short of funds and supposed to be exploring for gold, it brought in Cominco Limited, and later Teck, as the majority partners.

Discovery at Quebrada Blanca

The presence of copper at QB had been noted as far back as the 1800s, not surprisingly, since there was little vegetation at that altitude in the Atacama altoplano and the ample rock exposures contained green and blue exotic copper minerals that could be seen by anyone walking by.

Of course, not many people did walk by at 4,200 metres above sea level, but some had. There were old prospecting pits and shallow shafts on the QB property itself to prove it. And the nearby Collahuasi property to the east had supported a small mining town in the early 1900s. Saline ponds on the property were visited occasionally by flocks of pink flamingos, identical to those one is used to seeing on idyllic islands at sea level. And from time to time, the land was overrun by one or two llamas, also known as vicunas. With llamas, two may be considered a herd.

Anaconda Copper, at the time the owner of the large Chuquicamata mine north of Antofagasta, had staked some claims on QB in the 1950s, after noting anomalous coloured rocks in what may have been Chile's first regional airborne colour photographic survey. Its geologists mapped the property, noting the possible existence of a secondary enrichment blanket of copper.

Primary copper mineralization in Chile occurs mostly as chalcopyrite, a copper sulphide, just as it does in the US and Canada. However, with the deep weathering conditions in parts of the country, surface copper sulphide mineralization is often leached away and the copper is redeposited somewhere nearby as secondary copper minerals, such as chalcocite and covellite. Often this results in deposits that are richer in copper than the original primary deposit from which they came. These supergene, or secondary enrichment blankets, occur in the vicinity of the original deposits, but can be displaced and are not always immediately on top of the primary ones.

Anaconda's initial reports in 1959 had suggested that such a blanket might well be found with further exploration at Quebrada Blanca, but there is no record of the company having done any more work, probably because of the high, remote location and the existence of other prospects located more conveniently. We had made a similar decision, site unseen, in 1968.

The claims became part of Codelco's portfolio following the 1971 nationalization, and Codelco drilled one exploration hole in 1975, intersecting 12 metres of 1.39 per cent copper, all as secondary enrichment. Superior Oil and Falconbridge optioned the property from Codelco in 1977 and did extensive mapping, drilling, and metallurgical testing over the next five years. Getting to the property was not a simple task, using unpaved roads a distance of 260 kilometres from the port of Iquique, and in 1979 they built a 2.5 kilometre unpaved airstrip to facilitate access.

Falconbridge's work in the early 1980s indicated a supergene resource of over 50 million tonnes of good-grade copper that was close enough to the surface to be mineable by open pit methods. However, when it came time to exercise its option and make a production commitment in 1982, copper prices were weak, the world economy was in deep recession, and the option was dropped. By that time the property had been transferred from Codelco to Enami, the smaller of the two national copper companies.

Enami Puts QB *up for Bids*

QB lay dormant for seven more years until 1989, when CRIL geologists in Chile learned that Enami was seeking partners to develop it. It was too big for CRIL alone, which had been concentrating on smaller gold prospects since being taken public, but Cominco Limited agreed to bid with it as a joint venture, and the two were successful in acquiring an option to develop the property.

The key to making QB into a good mine at that time lay in using relatively new technology known as solvent extraction–electrowinning (SX-EW). Acid-soluble copper is leached from dumps or waste piles of copper-bearing minerals, and the copper-rich solutions are then treated in a solvent extraction and electrowinning facility, with copper metal plated out onto solid copper cathodes.

Phelps Dodge had demonstrated the process successfully at its Morenci mine in Arizona, and Sociedad Minera Pudahuel (SMP), a small Chilean company, had come up with a patented bio-leaching variation at its Lo Aguirre

Mine near Santiago. It showed promise as a way to speed up the leaching part of it, and Cominco decided to invite SMP into the venture in exchange for the use of its new technology.

So, initially, Cominco and CRIL each held a 38.25 per cent interest in QB, and Enami and SMP held carried 10 per cent and 5 per cent interests (with no financing requirements). As well, SMP was granted an option to acquire an additional 8.5 per cent interest that, along with the Cominco and CRIL interests, would be proportionately responsible for financing. It may sound complicated, but it was typical of mining industry joint ventures, where there is often a vending company, one or more financing and operating companies, and other interests granted for providing technology or services. This is in fact the norm, something ITT had had difficulty coming to grips with in our 1960s program.

The bid included an aggressive requirement to make a production commitment within 18 months, or return the property to Enami.

Developing Quebrada Blanca

After the Cominco group acquired an option on the property, it began the necessary test drilling to confirm the Falconbridge work and acquire enough data to support a full feasibility study. This established ore reserves of 78 million tonnes assaying 1.4 per cent copper, all in the supergene zone, and within a designed open pit.

Additional secondary mineralization occurred outside of the pit walls and beneath the planned pit, and it appeared that in this case the original hypogene sulphide mineralization lay directly below the supergene deposit. Assaying about 0.5 per cent copper, it was considered too low grade to develop at the time. This would become important later.

Metallurgical testing showed that the supergene mineralization was in fact amenable to the SMP bio-leaching process, and within just over a year Cominco had completed a feasibility study confirming the economic viability of the project. The plan was to mine the deposit using conventional truck and shovel open pit methods. The mined material would be placed on flat ground in heaps and irrigated with water and sulphuric acid. SMP's acid-loving bacteria would be introduced to the system, speeding up the natural leaching process. The copper-bearing solutions would be collected at the base of the heaps and delivered to an SX-EW plant, where the copper would be electroplated into large slabs of essentially pure copper, known as cathode copper.

The proposed mine would place 17,000 tonnes of copper-bearing material a day onto the heaps. At the other end of the process, annual output from the SX-EW plant would be 75,000 tonnes a year of copper. Building it would take about 34 months and cost an estimated US$300 million.

It soon became evident that its share of the project was still too big for CRIL, and arrangements were made to bring Teck in as a partner, covering CRIL's financing obligations and leaving it with a 10 per cent carried interest. At that point the ownership interests had become Cominco 38.25 per cent, Teck 28.25 per cent, SMP 13.5 per cent, CRIL 10 per cent, and ENAMI 10 per cent, with Cominco designated as operator.

About this time, I visited the QB property along with Cominco's Bob Hutchinson. There were sample piles scattered around from the earlier Falconbridge work, and the odd vicuna and pink flamingo. There was little vegetation at that altitude, and an eerie sense of calm, aided by the fact that it seemed wise to walk around very slowly, rather than run and risk passing out from oxygen deprivation.

We had flown in by light aircraft, landing on the old Falconbridge airstrip at QB. On the way back to Antofagasta we touched down at the recently built Escondida Copper Mine, soon to become one of the world's most important. Ken Pickering, who had cut his engineering teeth at Utah Construction's Island Copper Mine on Vancouver Island, was the mine manager and gave us an extensive tour. In our small mining world, he would join Teck as a board member years later, in 2015.

Construction began in 1992, starting with mining waste rock to expose the ore body, and building the processing facilities. The project progressed fairly well, considering that at that time none of the owners nor the independent engineering contractors had ever built a project of any size or kind at an altitude of 4,200 metres in the High Andes. In fact, to our knowledge no significant project of any kind had ever been brought into production on time and on budget by anyone at that elevation, and this proved to be no exception. There were delays in assembling some components as parts failed to arrive on demand, leading at times to excess costs. However, the plant was completed successfully, with the first cathode copper produced in December 1994 (see colour page 12).

Some delay and cost overruns were not surprising in the circumstances.

But the lessons learned by us, and by others in high-altitude construction programs elsewhere, would stand us in good stead later, when Teck would help build another, larger High Andes mine in Peru, this time on budget and on schedule.

The Annual Mine-Opening Golf Tournament was held on the golf course of the El Teniente mine, south of Santiago.

Meanwhile, Teck Bids for Part of the Nearby Collahuasi Property

The Collahuasi copper deposits occur just east of QB, and in fact in the early days both Collahuasi and QB used the same rudimentary airstrip on our property to reach the prospects.

It was an inclined, east-west gravel airstrip, following the slope of the mountaintop until, at its downhill west end, what had been a gradual slope steepened up considerably. Given the high altitude and extremely thin air, the amount of lift under the aircraft wings was much less than at sea level, and landing and takeoff were tricky. Generally, whatever the wind direction, we would land going uphill. And whatever the wind, we would take off to the west, downhill, to build up a good head of speed. As we came to the end of the runway and went over the cliff, it was always in the back of one's mind that maybe this time we weren't going fast enough to keep flying, but it generally seemed to work out.

Later, as we built the mine, we replaced that airstrip with something flatter, eliminating a certain amount of excitement. We also made it more difficult to drive a golf ball over 600 yards, which even I could do at that altitude, downhill.

The first Collahuasi copper deposits of the modern era had been delineated in the late 1980s by a consortium of Shell Billiton, Chevron, and Falconbridge, and by 1991 the property was said to have a reserve of 1.2 billion tonnes grading just over 1 per cent copper. Chevron, having been another of those major oil companies chasing after mines, had decided that it was now high time for it to exit the mining business, and put its one-third interest up for sale.

Teck, with our new interest in the adjoining QB property, decided to bid, and we put in an offer. It was designed by the indomitable David Thompson and was supposed to look like US$80 million. However, given David's innate distaste for giving away cash, and perhaps for keeping things simple, the purported $80 million was made up of a convoluted collection of optional bells and whistles, complete with a few dollars in actual cash. I can't recall exactly how it was supposed to work, and in any case it is academic now. What I do know is that I couldn't come up easily with the $80 million number, so it's not clear that Chevron could either.

It didn't really matter. Even at face value, our magical US$80 million turned out to be the third-highest bid. The second-highest bid was US$120 million in cash from Rio Tinto. And the highest was US$180 million from Joe Oppenheimer's Minorco, a South American unit of South Africa's Anglo American. Joe, incidentally, was completely unrelated to the Oppenheimer family that had founded and controlled Anglo, but he claimed that by remaining silent on the subject, it was amazing how many doors it opened for him.

We were close to him at the time, having been involved in a joint venture on CRIL's ill-fated Lobo-Marte gold prospect in Chile. I remember Joe complaining to me over lunch one day that he'd "left $60 million on the table," that being how much higher his bid had been than the second place one. My response was: "Joe, you just bought a great property, and in five years nobody will ever remember what you paid for it." I'm sure that turned out to be true. We had occasion to evaluate Collahuasi again when we considered acquiring Falconbridge/Noranda a few years ago, and it's fair to say that the interest Joe had bought was eventually worth many billions of dollars to his company.

One important thing we have learned about good, long-life mineral properties is that it's not so much what you pay for them, within reasonable limits; it's how you pay for them. The trick is always to avoid excessive financial leverage, so that the debt devil can't destroy you before it's possible to pay it off. If you can avoid going under in the early days, then the eventual value of a long-life mine will generally prove to be worth much more than the acquisition cost.

Bidding for a Development Contract on El Abra

Another Chilean copper deposit we attempted to acquire around that time was El Abra, a property 70 kilometres north of Calama that Joe Frantz had highlighted. It had been an Anaconda prospect back then, but by the 1990s it was owned by Codelco, the Chilean state copper company that had acquired Anaconda's assets. Codelco had done considerable drilling and established a substantial copper resource, following which it had invited development bids from international companies. It was offering to sell a 51 per cent joint venture interest in exchange for cash and a commitment to finance a mine into production. We decided that this time we would make the bid through Cominco. Bob Hallbauer wanted to keep it simple, using such easily measured currency as cold hard cash, rather than smoke and mirrors.

Meanwhile, others were preparing bids, among them the legendary mining entrepreneur Milt Ward, through his newly merged Cyprus Amax. Working on the valuation team was an ex-Navy Seal and by then PhD in metallurgy named Ed Dowling, who has been a valued director of Teck since 2013. He described the process by which Cyprus came up with its offer.

Cyprus had produced a thorough conceptual plan to produce 225,000 tonnes of copper a year. After analyzing the probable construction cost and projected copper prices, the team concluded that Cyprus could justify a purchase price in the mid- to upper US$300 million range. A long internal discussion took place, with the initial offer under consideration being $350 million. It grew to $400 million, but someone suggested they should bid $401 million, just in case someone else had the same number. Then, in case others might think the same way, they ultimately arrived at a bid of $404 million.

So, Ed Dowling and the team arrived at Codelco headquarters in Santiago to present their case. They were led to an anteroom in which others from the industry were gathered around their own little stacks of bid documents. These included Phelps Dodge (which had just commissioned the Candelaria mine), Anglo American, BHP, and Bob Hallbauer and me from Cominco, in the process of building QB.

As Ed recalls it:

All the other groups were staring intently at Cyprus Amax, as they were each carrying light, spiral-bound bid documents about 2 centimetres thick. We were lugging in our bid documents, as well as complete development study plans composed of multi-volume books that in total were about 60 centimetres thick. There was some small chat between the parties, but a nervous atmosphere prevailed. Ultimately, each team was called in to present its bid and how it would be financed. Then each was summarily dismissed with little fanfare, and the waiting began.

Our bid was $185 million, part of a cluster of bids between $100 million and 200 million, which is to be expected when all parties are working off similar discounted cash flow (DCF) models. Gary Jones' recollection is that the Phelps Dodge bid was quite a bit higher, between ours and that of Cyprus, with both companies apparently prepared to stretch beyond simple DCF calculations for strategic reasons.

Soon Cyprus was informed that its $404 million had won the bidding. It had certainly trumped our offer handily. Fortunately for Cyprus, it had included a provision that it could conduct a limited amount of check drilling to confirm the resource model. This was begun almost immediately, and the new twinned holes drilled by Cyprus encountered copper grades significantly lower than those from the adjacent Codelco holes.

Ed Dowling recalls: "After much work, constructive engagement and more than a little embarrassment, it was proven that Codelco's exploration drilling work had been solid, but that bias had inadvertently been introduced during the sampling and assay lab work. A renegotiation of the acquisition price downwards to $330 million was eventually agreed."

Epilogue

El Abra was built and achieved commercial production at a construction cost of $1 billion in 1996, a year after Quebrada Blanca. This was followed closely by an expansion at Escondida, led by Ken Pickering, and the commissioning of Collahuasi, all just a few years before Los Pelambres would come into production. It was a lot of copper to bring on stream in a short period, and as the last part of the "20 years of declining prices in real terms" was still unfolding. When copper prices fell again in 1998, El Abra was barely covering its financing costs, and the mine was sold to Phelps Dodge. Good times would come again, but as is often the case in the business, it would take a few years.

Our interests in the Quebrada Blanca mine would be sold to Aur Resources in 1999, as part of several steps leading to a merger of Teck and Cominco. Aur would operate it successfully for several years, and expand in

Chile by starting another mine on the old Andacollo prospect. Teck would then reacquire QB as well as Andacollo, when it bought Aur in 2007.

We had drilled five deeper holes into the hypogene copper zone beneath the QB open pit back in the early 1990s. By 2007, it appeared that the copper values that had seemed too low to be economic back then were now more attractive, and worth exploring further. Subsequent drilling was successful in establishing a major copper resource and Teck is now, in 2022, developing the deeper hypogene copper ore beneath the original supergene deposit, and this is expected to extend the life of the Quebrada Blanca mine for several decades to come.

CHAPTER 28

FINANCIAL PROBLEMS IN COMINCO

Never mis-underestimate the importance of liquidity.
After George W. Bush

Meanwhile, Cominco's financial difficulties were requiring a lot of attention from Teck's management. The combination of too much debt and zinc prices that had fallen too low led to significant losses from 1991 through 1993. In addition, Teck had to report these indirect losses in its own financial statements under what is known as the "equity accounting" rule. In the circumstances, we had to continue trying to find innovative ways to shore up Cominco's finances.

Selling a Potash Mine

One of Cominco's better, somewhat unsung, mines was the Vanscoy potash operation in Saskatchewan. Built in 1969 and one of 10 potash mines operating in the province at the time, it had survived the 1975 partial nationalization by the Saskatchewan government. Cominco had held tough, retained ownership, and was still running the mine when we came on the scene in 1986.

Vanscoy was part of Cominco's fertilizer division, which also included the new Joffre nitrogen plant in Alberta, a number of facilities in Trail that processed byproducts from its lead and zinc refining operations, and a major distribution centre for its Elephant Brand fertilizers in Spokane, Washington.

John Anderson, a capable American gentleman, managed the fertilizer division, and for several years after our acquisition John would regale us with stories about why the last year had been unusually bad for fertilizers, but good times lay just ahead. It went something like: "Last year we were hit by a drought in Kansas, so few farmers were able to buy fertilizers." Or the next time we learned that: "This year it rained so hard that nobody wanted to buy potash." And then: "The future is going to be rosy, if only we can tap that

Chinese market; it really needs us, but the Canpotex marketing cartel that sells our potash needs to do a better job convincing the Chinese of this."

And so on for several years. It began to sound a lot like Dry Hole Downing's perennial optimism, although in fact I think Anderson was quite credible and would eventually prove to be accurate. It was just that the good times we expected, or hoped for, always seemed a bit far off. In addition, Cominco was still struggling with more debt than it should have had. So when David Thompson came up with the idea of spinning the division off, as a prelude to selling it completely and reducing debt, the idea did not fall on deaf ears. Bob Hallbauer was reluctant, because he recognized that Vanscoy in particular was a good operation, and real miners never want to sell good mines, but he went along with it.

In 1993, Cominco sold 40 per cent of the fertilizer division to the public as Cominco Fertilizers in an initial public offering, raising $72 million. Bob Hallbauer was appointed chairman and Grant "Woody" MacLaren, an independent Vancouver businessman, joined the board of directors.

Then, in 1994, Cominco sold the balance of its interest for a further $210 million. Bob resigned and Woody took on the position of chairman, a role in which he excelled. The company changed its name to Agrium and, managed independently since then, has expanded into a very substantial, successful enterprise.

Combined, the sales did help reduce Cominco's debt significantly. Was it the right thing to do? Hindsight is easy. Agrium has done very well, having grown into a profitable $15 billion company. Bob Hallbauer's instinct may well have been right, but in some alternate universe, still held as a secondary division in what was primarily a zinc-lead and copper company, the fertilizer division would never have had the freedom to acquire and grow that Agrium had gained as an independent company.

Discipline in the Zinc Mining Business

In addition to our day jobs of finding, financing, building, and operating mines, in the 1990s we were learning a lot about the impact of discipline, or the lack thereof, in the zinc business.

On the mining side, this is simply because the barriers to entry are low, and entrepreneurs naturally will rush in any time they sense a vacuum, or a looming shortage of the metal. The total world market for zinc is much smaller than that for copper, and the grades of zinc deposits are often as much as 15 times higher. As well, size matters, in reverse; attractive high-grade zinc deposits are smaller than most lower-grade copper deposits, so the time and capital it takes to locate and build a new zinc mine, and begin contributing to the next surplus, is often less.

There are usually enough smallish, known, high-grade zinc deposits that can be built or reopened to quickly fill any budding shortage of the metal.

The Faro zinc-lead deposit in Yukon is one case in point. Discovered in 1964 by Al Kulan, Aaro Aho, and Gordon Davis of Dynasty Explorations, and later financed by Cyprus Mines of Los Angeles, Cyprus Anvil Mining Corporation began producing zinc and lead in 1969. The mine had good years and bad, and eventually closed in 1982 when metal prices plummeted. Faro was reopened in 1986, but by 1993 it had again been decimated by low prices, went into receivership, and closed once more. Not to be outdone, another company acquired the property and put it back into production in 1994. The mine was again closed in 1998, this time for good, with most of the heavy mining and milling equipment being sold and shipped elsewhere.

We are not immune to the tendency to reopen old mines or prospects when prices increase. Years later, in 2006, Teck Cominco and Noranda would decide to put the small Pillara zinc deposit in Australia's historic Lennard Shelf district into production as the price of zinc took one of its spikes upwards. Naturally, we would be forced to close it two years later as market conditions once again worsened.

In 2014, we responded to the expectation of higher prices, since some important large zinc mines around the world were closing, and began redeveloping the old Pend O'Reille mine in Washington State. This is a small deposit of limited extent, but with a high content of germanium as a byproduct. We can recover germanium profitably at the Trail smelting and refining complex, which is a leading world producer of the metal. There are always reasons, often even good ones, but the impact is inevitable. As a result of these and many other similar decisions, periods of high zinc prices have, in the past, tended not to last for long.

The same, of course, applies to many other commodities. Periods of high prices inevitably lead to the building of new productive capacity and, eventually, surplus supply and low prices. The cycle goes on, and on.

Just as the barrier to entry for new zinc producers tends to be low, for most mines and in most commodities there are also barriers to exit. When prices fall in the face of surplus supply, most miners will try to keep producing rather than cut back or shut down, hoping that other, higher-cost producers will go out of business first. That seldom happens quickly enough, and the cyclical lows tend to be unnecessarily prolonged.

Discipline on the Zinc Refining Side

On the refining side, there are common tendencies that can lead to over-supply as well.

The zinc production chain includes a number of custom refineries, many of them in Europe that, unlike Trail, do not have captive mines owned by the same entity. They rely upon purchase of concentrates from independent, often small miners scattered all over the world. The refiners charge a processing fee of so many cents per pound of zinc in the concentrate, often with a price participation kicker should prices climb above a floor level. As such, one would think they would have the same interest in higher prices as the miners, and thus perhaps an inclination to be disciplined, cutting back production a bit when demand softens, as it occasionally and inevitably does.

After all, that's what car manufacturers and other producers of such things generally do when demand falters, rather than see cars, soap, and whatever pile up in their lots.

Not so with custom zinc refiners. Many of them appear to be motivated instead by the observation that: "The last pound of zinc I produce is the cheapest." True enough, perhaps, but the ironic outcome is that when demand and prices fall, the refiners' instinct is to increase production rather than hold it back, exacerbating the problem. Since all the excess zinc that is produced can end up somewhat out of sight in a warehouse, such as those of the London Metal Exchange, this just means inventories build up, and build up, and prices stay lower for longer. Perhaps, if they were stored more visibly in an open-air car lot, people in that part of the business would act differently.

When Bob Hallbauer took ill and needed some time away, I took on the interim CEO position at Cominco for a couple of months. Now, administration is not one of my talents, and I've never pretended it was. With a bit of luck, I might do exploring or building, but I don't do managing. However, one thing that sometimes works for me is to look around corners, and perhaps find a little different way to do things. Why do things the same old way, eh?

The outlook for zinc had been reasonably good when Red Dog began production. Prices had increased to around 50 cents a pound and stayed there for a while. However, zinc inventories soon began climbing again and the price fell, costs had gone up, and Red Dog was starting to feel the pain.

So we sat around Cominco's boardroom table, fretting about how our new mine was suffering from low zinc prices and how it was "all the fault of those custom refineries that kept producing flat out and flooding the market with zinc." Heinz Schimmelbusch suggested it might be different this time. While he couldn't speak for those European custom refiners, he pointed out that most of them had young new managers (like him), and we might expect them to act more intelligently.

Hmmmmm, I mused. Was it time for Cominco to show leadership and shut down Trail for a time?

Ted Fletcher, then Cominco's main man on that side, gave me his baleful stare. Ted was one of the greatest Italian chefs of any mining company, and he knew pasta like nobody else. He also knew smelters and refiners. He pointed out that a two-month shutdown at Trail would not be enough, just removing 60,000 tonnes from the market. That would only be effective if others went along, but of course we weren't permitted to talk to anyone else, probably not even to hope. Ted said that Noranda had cut back one time in the past, but nobody else had followed.

Schimmelbusch couldn't restrain himself and began chuckling mysteriously.

Nevertheless, Ted said he'd look at the costs and impacts on our workforce. Two weeks later, in mid-January, Ted, his sidekick Bill Robertson, CFO Bob Stone, and marketing guru Roger Brain met me and recommended two shutdowns, one in April and one in August. We needed to supply special zinc shapes to certain customers, and we could make enough up to April to cover that shutdown month, and similarly from May until August. We could also sell surplus power from Trail's dams in August at a good profit, and it's a good vacation month for employees. Ted proposed we make an announcement later that week.

We did announce. Once again, nobody followed, presumably realizing that we had planned to shut down for part of the time for normal maintenance, anyway. I think Ted knew exactly what would happen, or wouldn't.

Whether it was because of the miners, the refiners, or just a law of nature zinc supply was generally in surplus and the price low for another 11 years.

Epilogue

The commodity price cycle persists for most metals and minerals today. Every time there is a shortage, entrepreneurs rush in, create new production, and eventually a surplus. Prices then fall, and miners fail to respond as proactively on the other side, by reducing production and working off the surplus quickly.

We don't always act logically. From the mine manager to the CEO, there is a tendency to operate flat out, actually increasing production in the face of low prices, just like that custom zinc refiner. It takes an exceptional mine manager to take pride in announcing that his or her production was down this year, perhaps by purposely switching to a lower-grade part of their ore deposit.

I sometimes think of Walt Kelly's cartoon character, Pogo, who said: "We have seen the enemy, and he is us."

CHAPTER 29

THE MORE THINGS CHANGE ...

If you gaze long into an abyss the abyss will gaze back into you.
Friedrich Nietzsche

The more they remain the same. Every time a mine closes, it seems to be déjà vu, all over again. And we try to offset it by building new ones, or finding a way to bring old ones back.

It is the nature of the business that mines are built, begin depleting their ore reserves as soon as they start production, may add reserves as they go along, but eventually run out of ore. Sometimes that is a long time away, as much as 50 years in the case of mines like Teck-Hughes and Niobec, but more often it is a lot shorter, as in 10 to 15 years.

Depletion of reserves is inevitable, and a company that "rests on its ores" is destined, eventually, to decline. One that replaces the ore it mines with extensions, new discoveries, or rational acquisitions can arrest and even overcome this. Such a company may actually be sustainable, in the old way of the word.

The industry as a whole, and the consuming world, requires periodic discoveries and the building of new mines to offset that inevitable depletion of ore reserves. Real sustainability as a company, or an industry, cannot occur without that, unless of course the world miraculously discovers a way to live without mined products.

The first half of the 1990s saw the closure of three of our earlier mines, in zinc, silver, and gold, as ore reserves were exhausted; the addition of a small new zinc interest in the Arctic islands; the start-up of a new copper-zinc mine in Quebec; and the acquisition of two new coal mining interests that would lead eventually to Teck becoming one of the world's major suppliers of steelmaking coal.

In 1990, our Newfoundland Zinc mine was finally closed permanently, 15 years after it began production. It had been the first of a sequence that eventually became 10 new mines in 20 years and it was a disappointment to see it end, but that happens in mining.

Interestingly, we had suspended production for a short time in 1986, as the price of zinc had dropped significantly. Sixteen months later we were encouraged to put the mine back in production, aided by an interest-free loan from the Newfoundland government. We did restart the mine successfully, the price of zinc recovered, and we paid off the loan in about 12 months. I can still remember the look on the face of the Mines Minister when we delivered the repayment. His words were something along the lines of: "This is not supposed to happen in Newfoundland; nobody ever repays government loans."

That same year, Teck added a modest amount of new zinc production when our Nunachiaq joint venture bought the minority 22.5 per cent share interest in Pine Point Mines. This was part of a program, jointly with majority owner Cominco, to privatize the company and turn it into a more tax-efficient operating joint venture, much as we had done with Metallgesllschaft and Afton years earlier. Pine Point had built the Polaris zinc mine on Little Cornwallis Island in 1982, and it would continue producing until its reserves were exhausted in 2002.

An interesting feature of Polaris was that the galena (lead sulphide) mineralization in some parts of the ore deposit occurred in crystals that were exceptionally low in radioactivity, compared with normal galena from other mines, or from the main part of the Polaris mine. These unique lead zones could be sorted at the mine, and the lead shipped to the Trail smelting and refining facility separately from the mine's normal production. This special lead was then repackaged and sold for Trail's account as "low-alpha lead" to Intel, the large semiconductor producer, at a price that was orders of magnitude higher than that of the normal run-of-mine lead.

There they go again. What was it I said earlier about miners vs. smelters?

Our little Beaverdell mine south of Kelowna finally expired after producing silver for 78 years. This truly had been a one-man show, kept alive and well for years by Bruno Gœtting, whom we met in chapter 11. But the end was nigh at last, and Bruno rode off into the sunset, a remarkable example of one of those great old-time miners most of us can only read about.

As the 1990s began, Rio Tinto had tired of its investment in Rio Algom and sold its majority shareholding to the public. Rio Algom had then decided to privatize its subsidiary Lornex Mining Corporation and, as a result, ended up with 75 per cent of the Lornex assets directly, with Teck holding the remaining 25 per cent. This increased Teck's direct interest in Highland Valley Copper to 14 per cent. Cominco retained its 53 per cent interest in HVC, and Teck of course continued to hold an additional indirect interest through its shareholding in Cominco.

Our Afton copper mine suspended operations in 1991 due to weak metal prices. Like Newfoundland Zinc, it reopened in 1994 and produced for another three years before the open pit resource ran out and the mine was closed for good in 1997. Years later, with copper prices much stronger, an independent company, New Gold, would acquire the property and develop an underground copper mine beneath the original open pit we had mined.

And development was underway on the supergene copper mine at Quebrada Blanca.

With the help of the investment in Aur made by Teck and Cominco in 1989, Jim Gill was able to complete a drilling program and define a significant copper and zinc deposit on his Louvicourt Township property in Quebec. The announced resource of 36 million tons grading 3.1 per cent copper and 1.34 per cent zinc, and with silver and gold values as well, was considered by many to be the most significant discovery in Eastern Canada since Texas Gulf's, and Dr Gill was named *The Northern Miner's* Mining Man of the Year in 1989.

In early 1992, Teck and Aur agreed to a development contract under which Teck would finance Aur's 50 per cent share of construction financing on a debt basis, earning a 25 per cent interest in the property. Noranda provided financing for the balance owned by its Novicourt affiliate. Cominco passed on the opportunity to participate, given its commitments in Chile and its financial position.

This was, like the David Bell mine interest we had acquired a decade earlier from Corona Resources, an example of earning a joint venture interest in a new mine by providing construction and operating management and arranging project financing. In our experience, *earning* an interest in a new mine in exchange for providing construction management and arranging financing tends to beat paying cold hard cash to buy it.

Teck's mine development team, including Mike Lipkewich and Lee Bilheimer, fresh from his work helping to build Red Dog, took charge of the development, with input from Aur, and worked hand in hand with engineers seconded from Noranda. The mine began production successfully in 1995, the same year as Quebrada Blanca.

It's interesting that Teck was participating in two new mines at the same time in the mid-1990s, just as it had done earlier at Newfoundland Zinc and Niobec, and then at Highmont and Bullmoose.

CHAPTER 30

EXPANDING IN METALLURGICAL COAL

Sooner or later, something fundamental in your business world will change.
Andrew Grove

While the QB and Louvicourt mines and other stories were unfolding in the early 1990s, two things were happening that would lead to Teck having a much stronger presence in coal. In each case, urged on by some of the creditor banks, we acquired another coal mine that had been placed into receivership. These would set the stage for strategic moves in later years that would take Teck to a new plateau as a leader in the world's metallurgical coal business.

Teck Acquires Management of the Quintette Coal Mine

Denison's Quintette mine had been an essential part of the northeast coal mega-project, along with our Bullmoose mine. However, building it and getting it into production had not gone nearly as smoothly.

There had been serious design and construction problems at Quintette, and the final capital cost was well over the projected $1 billion, unlike the nearby Bullmoose mine that we had built under budget. As well, the ash content (impurity) of the Quintette coal was over the contract specifications, and operating costs were higher than anticipated. In 1985, one year after the ceremonial mine opening, Denison, the largest shareholder, the mine operator, and the original promoter of northeast coal, wrote off its entire investment of $240 million.

Teck and Denison had each negotiated firm prices for their production with the Japanese steel industry, but with subtle differences. Bob Hallbauer had insisted that the Bullmoose contract price be firm for at least five years, so we could be confident we could repay the bank loans. Denison, on the other hand, was optimistic that prices might go even higher, and had insisted on a price review clause three years into the contract. As karma would have it, world coal prices did not go up, but fell instead, perhaps helped by the excess supply that both our arrangements with the Japanese steel mills had helped bring about. Quintette, in addition to its higher than expected production costs, was facing possible revenue problems at price review time.

It was a lesson we never forgot. Again, it's not so much what you pay for something; it's how you pay for it. With a long-life asset, the main objective has to be to ensure that one can pay back the financiers. After that, the owner can benefit from a paid-off operation for a long time. Taking chances to optimize profits in the early years before payback can prove to be penny-wise and pound-foolish.

In Denison's case, the JSI took the renegotiation to arbitration, and the end result was a lower price for Denison's Quintette mine, which just compounded its problems. Cliff Frame, who had spearheaded the Japanese negotiations for the company, was terminated, and Denison sought court protection from its creditors in 1990, six years after starting production.

By then, the 44 banks that had financed Quintette and the JSI all wanted to get rid of Denison as manager of the mine, and Teck was approached to take it on by the Bank of Montreal and CIBC, which were leading the negotiations on behalf of the large banking syndicate. One problem was that Denison held a life-of-mine management contract and received fees net of expenses of $8 million a year for the service, despite having written off its own investment.

David Thompson was leading the negotiations for Teck and recalls the situation.

Bill James had recently been appointed CEO of Denison. Norman Keevil knew him well, as 15 years earlier Bill had been on the Teck Board, before going on to become CEO of Falconbridge. I had a series of meetings with Bill in the Denison head office in Toronto. They were decorated in the style of Louis XIV, with Napoleonic paintings of Steve Roman, the founder, in the reception and most meeting rooms. Bill took me on a tour of the offices, which were sparsely populated with staff because Bill had already cut the overhead. As we walked Bill would explain that everything is for sale. As it turned out, that would apply to everything but a beautifully lit globe of the world in his corner office.

Bill, always a colourful character, was partially deaf due to a mining accident. He used his impediment as a negotiating tool, often not hearing any points that didn't suit him. He realized that Denison and

Quintette were near the end of the road, yet he managed to extract $15 million from us to transfer the contract.

We took on the management contract and agreed with the banks to reduce the basic fee to half, at $4 million a year, but offset that with a deal that Teck would receive 25 per cent of any cost reductions once Quintette was removed from bankruptcy.

Further price negotiations with the JSI were necessary and generally went well, but a plethora of tomfoolery occurred over the ensuing months. A single creditor bank out of the whole 44 tried to scuttle some of the key agreements. A bureaucratic misunderstanding with an Ottawa creditor also threatened to derail things, and a key minister in the NDP government in British Columbia appeared to prefer to see Quintette go bankrupt and close rather than play ball. In the end, all of these side issues were resolved, and Quintette was able to stay open for a few more years.

With Mike Lipkewich taking charge, we were able to reduce the unit costs at Quintette substantially. We lowered the production rate and, with the agreement of the JSI and the banks, Bullmoose increased its own production and paid a royalty to the banks for permitting us to take over that tonnage. In the first year, the banks received $60 million and Teck $20 million through our contractual participation in the cost savings.

However, in the long run it was not possible to operate Quintette successfully at the world market price of coal. The mine was closed when the second round of the JSI sales contracts expired in 1998. The washing plant, storage, and rail sidings were kept in place in case it proved possible to reopen the mine in the future. As the mine closed, we negotiated a final deal to take out the banks, and all of Quintette's trucks and shovels were transported to other Teck mines where they could be put to good use.

Meanwhile, our Bullmoose mine continued operating profitably until its coal reserves were exhausted in 2003.

The CJBC and Competition Between Canadian Coal Mines

Ever since the northeast coal project had been raised as a possibility, the southeastern producers, mainly the Cominco/CP Fording operation and Kaiser Resources, with its Balmer mine, had lobbied behind the scenes to try to prevent the new northeast project from going ahead. Their concern had been that there could be too much Canadian coal on the market, preventing any of the existing producers from being able to negotiate the strong prices they wanted. The JSI, in agreeing to premium prices for the new northeast coal mines, may have had much the same in mind. It is, after all, a commercial world out there.

After northeast coal was a done deal and the mines were being built, the game would still continue, one of its venues being the annual Canada-Japan Businessmen's Conference (CJBC). Meeting in May every year, alternately in Japan and Canada, this conference had been started in 1976 under the impetus of David Culver of Alcan, Jean Chrétien, and Hisao Makita, chairman of Japanese steel company Nippon Kokan. It had become the main gathering and, through side meetings, negotiating forum for much of the metals and minerals business between the two nations.

The Canadian side was represented mainly by CEOs of the major mining and other companies, and, similarly, the Japanese side included attendees from the highest levels. I had the pleasure of co-chairing the Metals Subcommittee for a number of years, and there was a degree of camaraderie on both sides, because we were all more or less like-minded producers just doing our best for our companies. In the case of the metals group, our prices were for the most part set in world markets, and both the Japanese and Canadian members had a similar interest in sharing data in the interests of better knowledge.

After he joined us in 1981, Keith Steeves generally attended the Coal Subcommittee, which tended to be dominated by Fording representatives, but which Keith was permitted to chair occasionally. In coal, there was no set world market, and it was a meeting directly between buyers and sellers, with coincidental private negotiations that would set the price. The Japanese side spoke as one voice, through the JSI, but the Canadian side was balkanized between a number of competing companies, and was the furthest thing from a cartel that one could imagine.

Those who hold that cartels are an evil thing should be pleased, although it could be argued from Canada's perspective that we might have benefited from playing the same game as our buyers. It may well have been that both sides would have been better off if we had combined forces and knowledge in the same way the JSI did. In a more perfect world, that might help to level out the highs and lows that otherwise tend to creep in. I have occasionally suggested the same thing for other cyclical commodities, but to no avail.

However, that perfect world was not the case, and the games went on. At the CJBC Coal Subcommittee, the parties would exchange views, as was expected of them, and then some time later the real negotiations would be carried out in private. A typical case might have the JSI convincing one coal producer, perhaps Fording, to agree to a low price the JSI wanted and an agreed contract tonnage, perhaps 1.5 million tonnes. This would then be widely reported and held out as the new contract price for the coming year. The other producers, perhaps Kaiser's Balmer mine or Greenhills, would be expected to capitulate. Since there was only one large buyer, the JSI, that would become the price for all for the ensuing year.

Unsaid, and never reported officially, would be a side deal, under which the JSI, which always arranged the shipping, would send over a few mysterious additional ships to pick up some secret, extra tonnage from that deal-leading producer. These became known on our side as "black ships." Which company would be the beneficiary in any given year might change, although from our vantage point up north, we always suspected Fording took the foremost, with smaller producers getting the hindmost.

That said, we were doing very well with Bullmoose, and now had a foot on Quintette, which had extensive reserves that might someday become more valuable. Coal was one of our products but had been of lesser moment than gold, copper, or zinc. Then a new opportunity raised its head.

Teck's New Elkview Coal Mine

David Thompson's newfound interest in coal and the banks' problems continued, and as David wrote in an unpublished memoir:

> Three weeks after the judge approved the creditors' compromise for the Quintette mine, the Balmer coal mine in the Elk Valley of southeastern BC locked out its 1,300 employees. World coal demand had been affected by the recession of 1990 to 1992, and as a result the annually negotiated price with the JSI had fallen. The problems of Quintette and the possibility it might close had raised hopes of the other Canadian competitors but, once the settlement had been reached, the two largest coal mines in B.C., Fording and Balmer, demanded concessions from their unions. Balmer's union was led by Ezra Deanna,

an aggressive and very left-wing individual who had no interest in compromising, and as a result the lockout looked likely to continue indefinitely.

The Balmer mine had been developed by Kaiser Resources some 20 years earlier, at about the same time Fording Coal started up under CP and Cominco. Run by Edgar Kaiser Jr in 1970, Balmer had been the first Canadian coal mine to sign a long-term sales contract with the JSI. In 1981, Kaiser, with impeccable timing, sold its coal and energy interests to BC Resources Investment Corporation (BCRIC), a Crown corporation, at a very high price, just as the 1981 recession was about to swamp the resources and other BC businesses.

BCRIC had been an idea of the BC government to promote resources development, and it had gone public in 1979 with every adult BC resident being given a few free shares, and encouraged to buy more at $6 a share. As it happened, with the ensuing recession it turned out BCRIC had paid too much for the assets it had purchased, and as David went on to note: "A few years later most of BCRIC was virtually bankrupt, and the only surviving entity was its Westar Mining unit, which owned the Balmer and Greenhills mines. Westar had a reputation for weak management, and the Mine Workers' Union had forced them into a series of concessions leading to over-manning and low productivity. Westar did not have the financial strength to fight such a militant union and in mid-1992 it entered receivership."

The receiver determined that all of Westar's assets should be sold, including the Balmer and Greenhills mines.

The Balmer mine had great appeal to Teck. Its major customer had always been the JSI, with which Teck was on excellent terms. The mine had long-life, high-quality reserves and, until recently, had been highly profitable. Greenhills was situated farther north in the Elk Valley, almost adjacent to the Fording mine. It had been developed for the Korean market, and Posco of South Korea had a 20 per cent interest.

As we analyzed the creditors of Westar it became clear that there was a divergence between the security positions of the various major creditors. Balmer's largest creditor was the Bank of Montreal, Teck's principal bank, which sent a senior analyst out to Vancouver to work with us. We also made contact with the JSI's Mr Naruse, who had helped us with Quintette. He responded that the JSI would have to remain neutral but would work closely with Teck if we were able to purchase Balmer.

Three other companies submitted bids for either Balmer, Greenhills, or both. Teck decided to bid only for the Balmer mine and we offered $85 million. A month later, the NDP government of BC announced that the receiver had made his decision and Luscar Mining of Alberta had been awarded both mines.

However, David was not to be outdone, perhaps remembering Norm Rudden's cogent advice back when we were turned down initially in our quest to buy Yukon Consolidated and its Lornex interest. Rudden had convinced us then not to take no for an answer, and David did the same thing here. He saw from the details of the winning bid that, while it might have given more to the creditors at large, it would return less to BMO than ours did. BMO's loans ranked second to CP Rail's, which had loans of $75 million to both mines. Ingeniously, David had Teck offer to guarantee repayment of that $75 million if BMO purchased the loans from CP, which of course, in the circumstances, CP was happy to go along with.

When the receiver's decision came to court for approval, BMO announced that it was now the primary creditor and would not approve the sale to Luscar. The judge ruled that Teck would get the Balmer mine, and there would be a new round of bidding for Greenhills. There were threats of actual lawsuits, but none prevailed, and it was over. David's ingenuity and close relationships with Michael Rayfield and Neil MacMillan of the bank had sealed the deal, and the Balmer mine was ours.

Teck soon reopened Balmer as the new Elkview mine, initially at half the production rate Westar had been operating. All prior employees had to reapply and were carefully selected for their ability and dedication to working. The Mine Workers' Union was shut out. The mine reopened as non-union, but we encouraged the Steelworkers' Union to come in, and that was approved by a free vote of the workforce.

Balmer had been badly over-mined, and waste removal, or stripping, had fallen badly behind. The new mine plan that Teck developed gradually expanded production as the waste rock to coal ratio could be brought into line, and the mine again reached its full capacity of 6 million tonnes per year at the end of the 1990s.

The Elkview mine was profitable from the start, and it benefited materially from the transfer of new mining equipment from the closed Quintette mine. In 2003, Elkview would become the key chip in the consolidation of the Canadian steelmaking coal industry.

David Thompson had played a lead role in expanding our coal interests and had moved well beyond your typical chief financial officer. He would soon take on a new role as CEO of our Cominco affiliate, following the untimely passing of Bob Hallbauer.

CHAPTER 31

PROSPECTS COME AND GO

Organized people are just too lazy to go looking for what they want.
Albert Einstein

Unlike with King Midas, not everything in the evolution of an entrepreneurial mining company turns to gold.

Sometimes we try for a deal that, like a Greek siren, looks too attractive to resist. Occasionally, as with Home Oil, we lose it, but that one turned out to be very much for the better. Often, we start out on prospects with enthusiasm, but for various reasons they just don't turn out as planned. There were a few of these in the 1990s. Hope springs eternal, but success is elusive.

Seeking Gold in Kazakhstan

Although we had diversified into copper, silver, zinc, and coal as well, we were always on the hunt for new gold projects, and in 1994 we visited Kazakhstan with Robert Friedland to size up opportunities for exploration and development in that large country. Robert had been working on a gold deposit called Bakyrchik that had size potential, although it faced metallurgical difficulties, but we were both more interested in a major resource in the far north called Vasilkovskoye. It had been mined initially in the 1960s, but had been abandoned several times since then because of its low grade of gold, around 2 grams per tonne, as well as its location. With apparent potential for a large-scale open pit mine, it seemed to be a project worth pursuing.

We were not alone in this, with gold miners such as Placer Dome, Barrick, Dominion Mining, and LonMin, among others, having visited Vasilkovskoye and tested the Kazakhstani waters, but Robert was said to have a special relationship that would be helpful.

We flew from Frankfurt to the capital city, Almaty, landing around midnight only to find the airport completely dark, with nobody around to deal with any customs or immigration niceties. There was also no obvious way to get transportation to our hotel in town. However, we somehow managed to find something, and arrived groggily at the hotel around 4 a.m., devoid of immigration papers.

Three fitful hours of sleep later, Robert and I went over to the Cabinet offices to meet the premier, one Akexhan Kashgeldin. On hearing his name, I had visions of a tall hero from a western novel named Cash Geldin, perhaps wearing one of those Stetson hats, but the reality was slightly different. We were standing in the boardroom waiting when a door suddenly opened behind me. I turned around and saw nobody until I looked down a bit. There was Cash, the premier, with no Stetson, and rather shorter than John Wayne had seemed to be.

After pleasantries, we were shown to another room where we could begin negotiations with a bevy of his people. These were proceeding as one might expect until around noon, when we were told suddenly that we had to suspend the meeting because there was a serious football game scheduled between the government and Parliament that afternoon, and half of them were playing in it.

So Robert and I went over to the soccer stadium to have a look. It wasn't very crowded, and we were walking along a centre field row to our seats not far above the field when a voice from a box much higher up shouted: "Hey Robert. How are you doing?" It was President Nazurbaev himself.

Robert had said he had good connections.

In fact, shortly after that we were invited to meet Nazurbaev in the palace. While we waited in the anteroom outside his office, we studied a very large painting of a warrior in full dress standing on a small hill, with two other warriors in some form of obeisance at its base. We were told that this represented the three main Mongolian tribes or hordes when, in 1726, they agreed to stop fighting each other and instead focus on the common enemy, whoever that might have been at the time. From the looks of them, I wouldn't have put great odds on the enemy's success.

The leader of the Great Horde was a direct descendant of Ghengis Khan and had assumed the appropriate stance over those of the two Lesser Hordes. We were told that President Nazurbaev was a direct descendant as well, and the current Great Horde Leader. As you can imagine, in a strange country and with our complete dearth of papers to prove our legitimacy, we were properly respectful.

We did manage to secure a period of exclusive negotiations for the Vasilkovskoye property, but after two years, this had expired without an agreement being reached. By then we were involved in other, more interesting projects elsewhere in the world, and our interest in this one had diminished. The property was eventually developed and was recently producing a respectable 350,000 ounces of gold a year. Currently owned 70 per cent by Glencore, it is reportedly up for sale, with an asking price of US$2 billion.

Oh yes, the football game. It turned out that the government beat the stuffing out of Parliament. Why should we be surprised that such things do happen there too?

On Robert the Magician

As an aside, while we had known Robert Friedland as a sometime-Vancouver-based entrepreneur for years, this was the first away visit we had made with him. Robert was and is a supreme promoter, but in the final analysis is most interested in finding great mines for their own sake, and somehow pretty good at it.

In 2016, as he was about to be inducted into the Canadian Mining Hall of Fame, Robert told me a story about Murray Pezim. Murray, on being introduced to Robert for the first time, said: "I understand you're the world's second-best promoter. I'm the best of course, but we should get together and see if we can really dominate. I have this shell company called Radcliffe. Let's jointly fund it and see what we can do?"

So they both put up some money at 14 cents a share, before Robert left town. He watched it from afar as it went up to 30 cents, and then 50 cents and higher for a while before it started falling. It went back down to Robert's original 14 cents, then 12 cents, then 10, and then got delisted. The next time Robert saw Murray he asked what happened. Murray laughed and said: "Well, I sure got you that time!"

San Nicolas, a Teck Geophysical Discovery in Mexico

We would look at known deposits like Vasilkovskoye when they cropped up, but it was always more exhilarating, and often productive, when our exploration teams discovered new deposits that had been completely unknown.

Teck hadn't been active in Mexican exploration since a few property examinations we'd made in the 1960s, during which time I had had the pleasure of meeting the world-class promoter Mariano Lara and his sidekick and serious mining engineer Jesus Garcia Gandara, and of visiting prospects with our regional geologist, Harvey Sobel, who kept pet tarantulas in bottles in his room, just in case. I'd never forgotten when a gold property salesman talked Harvey and me into climbing 40 metres down a slippery 70-degree shaft with missing ladder rungs and no safety stations, only to find there was no gold there. It turned out that the salesman-owner, scared stiff, had never even gone down the shaft himself. He was waiting for someone like us to do it and tell him what was there. Checking out the tarantulas might have been safer.

In the 1990s, we began to explore in Mexico more systematically under the direction of geologist Joe Ruetz, based in Reno, Nevada. This resulted in a significant gold discovery called Los Filos that was eventually sold to and developed into a successful mine by Goldcorp, as well as a large copper-zinc discovery that remains in Teck's inventory of undeveloped properties.

This latter deposit, San Nicolas, came about after Joe negotiated an agreement with a small Zacatecas-based company to generate gold and base metal prospects for Teck. In 1994, it acquired a property called El Salvador on which trenching had exposed some interesting oxide copper, and the claim was presented to us for consideration.

Joe's team, with the help of Bob Quartermain, soon realized that it wasn't the usual type of Mexican copper prospect, but might actually be part of a volcanogenic massive sulphide deposit. These are common in Canada's Precambrian Shield, with the important Texas Gulf, Mattagami, and Noranda's Horne mine being classic, major examples, but they are rare elsewhere in North America, and were definitely unknown in that part of Mexico.

Drilling soon confirmed this insightful interpretation. Although the particular El Salvador deposit did turn out to be small, only about 1 million tonnes, it gave us an entirely new geologic model and region in which to explore for more of these VMS things.

We acquired additional claims a few kilometres to the west, where the geologists had noted anomalous copper on surface, and decided to run an IP (induced polarization) geophysical survey from the discovery zone west to test that new area. The result was a strong, 500 x 500 metres bull's-eye anomaly.* Drilling began in late 1997, and one of the first holes encountered an impressive 180 metres of massive zinc and copper sulphides, beginning at

---

* Such bull's-eye anomalies are rare in the experience of geoscientists, with most anomalies being much subtler and difficult to interpret. It's even rarer when one actually reflects an ore deposit, but this one did.

a depth of 200 metres. Follow-up drilling over the next two years delineated a substantial mineral resource, which is currently estimated to contain 111 million tonnes grading 1.23 per cent copper and 1.5 per cent zinc, along with significant gold and silver credits.

It was the first discovery of a major VMS deposit in Mexico, and a real credit to Teck's whole project exploration team. It was also satisfying to once again come up with a good geophysical discovery, which was how we had gotten our start in the business some years earlier.

Interestingly, the deposit as known to date is substantially larger and contains more copper and zinc, expressed as copper-equivalent, although it is lower grade, than the Mattagami mine that was so instrumental for Teck Corporation early on, and was a key mine for Noranda Mines for many years. San Nicolas was not developed back in the late 1990s as Teck had become active in other potentially larger prospects, including Friedland's Voisey's Bay nickel, Petaquilla copper in Panama, and then Antamina copper-zinc in Peru. Now owned 79 per cent by Teck and 21 per cent by Goldcorp, San Nicolas remains a significant part of Teck's inventory of potential new mines.

The Petaquilla Copper Deposit

Also in 1994, Teck acquired an interest in the large Petaquilla copper project in Panama. In a handshake agreement with Murray Pezim back when we had done the Hemlo deal, Murray had promised us the first chance to farm in on projects located by any of the companies in his stable. One of these was Adrian Resources, managed by Chet Idziszek, who, along with Murray, had been named BC's Mining Man of the Year for the discovery and development of the Eskay Creek gold mine a few years earlier.

Adrian owned 52 per cent of the Petaquilla property, with Inmet Mining of Toronto holding the balance.* Teck agreed to fund ongoing exploration and development to cover Adrian's share of costs, with the right to receive half of its interest in the property, or 26 per cent, if we arranged both our and

---

* Inmet was the successor company to Metall Mining, a Canadian company that had been spun off by Metallgesellschaft to hold its mining interests. After Metallgesellschaft encountered financial difficulties, it had sold its shareholding in Metall Mining and its name was changed to Inmet. Headed by Klaus Zeitler, it would play important roles in advancing both Petaquilla and the Antamina mine in Peru.

Adrian's share of senior financing to put a mine into production. This was the same structure we had agreed on with Aur in developing the Louvicourt copper-zinc mine, and with Corona in developing Hemlo gold. Inmet would be responsible for its own share of financing.

We were welcomed with open arms by the country, and I was made an honourary member of the Panama Chamber of Mines, a welcome honour despite the fact there were then no mines of any significance in the country. The Minister of Trade and Development, Raul "Bebe" Arango, invited me to his home on the opposite coast and provided his military helicopter to fly me across to our "new mine," which looked more like a diamond drill sitting on a lone rock outcrop, surrounded by jungle.

Fortunately, that helicopter didn't actually crash until the next week.

Our geologists were enthusiastic about the potential to extend the known copper mineralization substantially, and that indeed proved to be the case as we carried out surveys and drilled over the next couple of years. However, our mining team of the day was less enthusiastic about the challenge, partly because of other opportunities in Peru and in coal, so we put Petaquilla on the shelf for a while.

We would return to the property, by then renamed Cobre Panama, and resume work 10 years later as the continuing growth in the Chinese economy began to be widely recognized, but Teck would have to abandon the project in the aftermath of the global financial crisis of 2008. Inmet would carry on and begin mine development, before being acquired by First Quantum. The latter company is now in the midst of a construction program on what is expected to be a US$6 billion copper mine on our old Petaquilla property.

White Earth Titanium

Also in 1994, which turned out to be an extraordinarily successful year for acquiring major, still-dormant properties, Teck acquired 100 per cent of the large Powderhorn titanium prospect in Gunnison County, Colorado. Prior exploration work by Buttes Oil and Gas and the US Geological Survey had outlined an estimated 350 million tonnes of 11.5 per cent titanium dioxide contained in a calcium titanium oxide mineral called perovskite. Teck's drilling and test work focused on a higher-grade portion of the large complex and indicated some 40 million tonnes of 13.2 per cent titanium dioxide within a preliminary open pit layout.

The project, renamed White Earth, has been dormant in recent years, but it contains the largest known resource of titanium in the United States, as well as rare earth elements and niobium, and may become important strategically as and when titanium metal or pigment markets are developed further.

Interestingly, just as we had done earlier with the Sugarloaf ranch around the Afton mine, Teck acquired two historic ranches in the vicinity of the potential mining operation, intending to operate them alongside the mine. The combined Howard and Sammons ranches own some 10,000 acres of rangeland and hay production, and currently run some 650 head of cattle.

Pebble Copper

Meanwhile, Cominco continued to be active in exploration independently during the 1990s, and discovered what would turn out to be the very large Pebble copper-gold deposit in Alaska. By 1992, it had established a resource of approximately 500 million tonnes of apparently ore-grade copper, with potential for expansion after more exploration. However, with copper and zinc prices trending downwards and debt depressing Cominco's financial capacity, this remained a relatively dormant prospect for some years. Finally, in 2001, it was farmed out to Northern Dynasty, a junior exploration company that was part of the entrepreneurial Hunter Dickinson Group.

I recall John Thompson, Teck's chief geoscientist, worrying that we were giving up an opportunity to extend the initial discovery into a major new mining district many times the size that had been drilled off at that point. In this, he was like Spud Huestis of Bethlehem, but with a scientific pedigree, and, like Spud, he turned out to be right. Northern Dynasty raised a huge amount of speculative funds and spent heavily on further exploration, reaching some US$730 million by 2015, and expanded the resource to over 6 billion tonnes of potentially economic copper-gold mineralization.

Cominco had retained a back-in right when it farmed out the property. This entitled it, at the feasibility study stage, to reacquire a majority interest and take back management after reimbursing a multiple of Northern Dynasty's expenditures.

This type of deal sounds good when said quickly, letting the junior company and speculative market take the next, risky phase of expensive and uncertain exploration work. However, the problem is that, after additional exploration and development expenditures, and with the premium reacquisition cost added in, these projects often continue to appear marginal for the senior company, even though the underlying stand-alone economics improve. Cominco never did exercise its back-in right, and Northern Dynasty is now the sole owner.

The property holds one of the largest and most interesting untapped copper resources in the Americas, but remains undeveloped due to opposition from some local interests. Given Cominco's good name in Alaska, as a result of the success at Red Dog, one wonders if we could have managed to overcome that opposition and develop another successful mine had we retained the property instead of farming it out.

The Pogo Gold Discovery in Alaska

In the early 1990s, Watts, Griffiths, and McOuat had carried out reconnaissance stream sediment geochemical exploration in Alaska for several parties, looking initially for base metals like copper and zinc, but also for gold. In the course of the work, they discovered anomalous gold indications in an area 145 kilometres southeast of Fairbanks.

Sumitomo Metal Mining and its associated trading company, Sumitomo Corporation, acquired claims in the area of the gold anomalies and began a small diamond-drilling program to explore them. They encountered interesting gold assays in core from seven holes, and the results were written up in an obscure trade journal. If the same results had been obtained by a publicly traded junior company in Canada, they would have been reported as newsworthy in mining publications such as *The Northern Miner*, generating interest from other gold mining companies. However, coming from a large Japanese company not closely followed by such publications, they were not widely known in Canadian exploration circles.

Fred Daley, our head of mining exploration at the time, was an avid reader of obscure journals and came across the results. He immediately wrote me suggesting we should follow them up and try to get an option from SMM to explore the property. I did nothing about it. Possibly we were preoccupied with bigger things, or maybe it just didn't ring a large enough bell for me.

Finally, in early 1997, Fred raised it again, and I agreed to visit Sumitomo when I was in Japan for the annual Canada-Japan Businessmen's Conference the coming May. Coincidentally, this was to be held in Fukuoka at the north end of the island of Kyushu, and the lone gold mine in SMM's portfolio was the Hishikari mine at the south end of the same island.

I had arranged to travel from Kyushu to Tokyo after the conference was over to talk about Pogo with Moriki Aoyagi, the SMM president, but while we were on Kyushu, my wife Joan and I went south to pay a visit to Hishikari. We were driven there by Ueno-san, who had overall responsibility for the mine's operation, and met by Takashi Kuriyama, a young geologist who was in charge of keeping its ore reserves in good shape. Coincidentally, the relationship between Sumitomo Metal Mining and Teck would blossom further and both men would later become directors of Teck.

Hishikari is one of the mining wonders of the world. It is not a large mine, but is very high grade, with production at times assaying as much as 50 grams of gold (almost 2 ounces) per tonne of rock. That is many times the grade of most of the world's gold mines.

The mine is located not far from the active Kirishima volcano, and the groundwater in the underground workings is extremely hot, reaching 65 degrees Celsius (150 Fahrenheit). The gold ore is related directly to volcanic activity in the area, although the deposit itself seems to have been emplaced about a million years ago, recently, as geological time goes. I used to kid Takashi that the secret to maintaining ore reserves at Hishikari had to be to mine it slowly, so that new gold ore would be being formed just as fast as the older ore was being mined. That would be the ultimate in sustainable mining.

Equally fascinating, the mine had no conventional milling facility to upgrade the gold ore to a higher-grade concentrate. Instead, as with the first high-grade copper at Temagami years earlier, the production was what miners call direct-shipping ore, sent directly to a smelter without much further processing.

In the case of Hishikari, the smelter was Sumitomo's own Toyo copper smelter on an adjoining island. The copper smelting process requires the addition of silica as a flux, and of course quartz is the primary source of such silica. The gold at Hishikari occurred in quartz veins, as is normal, so both the gold and the quartz host rock had value, and could be shipped by barge directly to the smelter.

It was still necessary to separate at least some of the white, gold-bearing quartz rock from the black, barren rock that was mined with it. The process used to do this was probably unique in our modern mining world. The mined rock was put through a crusher to break it down into smaller pieces. These were then fed to a conveyor belt a few metres long, with lines of five or six local Japanese women standing on either side. The ones on the left would grab the dark rocks and throw them aside, while the ones on the right would take the white pieces and throw them into a shipping container. When it was full, it would be set aside for barging to Toyo. The process was simple, but worked well (see colour page 13).

Finally, the water emanating from the mine was of course very hot, and we were told that part of it was being used in hot spring spas downstream from the operation, with the rest disposed of into the local river. I'm not sure I want to know exactly how that worked environmentally, although the water was completely natural, just hot.

Joan and I were given a good tour by Ueno-san and his team, and she took her place at the conveyor belt to help separate a few pieces of white, gold-bearing rock from the black ones. We went underground to look at the mine and came away suitably impressed with the difficulties of mining at such high rock and water temperatures (see colour page 12).

We then went on to Tokyo where I met with our old friends Shinozaki-san and Aoyagi-san, chairman and president of Sumitomo Metal Mining, as well as mining engineer Ken Sudo. We worked out a development contract on Pogo under which Teck would continue exploration to follow up the seven existing drill holes. If we were successful in proving up enough gold ore to make a mine, we could arrange to put the property into production and earn a 40 per cent joint venture interest in it.

Interestingly, the gold intersections in those initial seven holes had confused most observers, including us, because we were all used to Canadian gold-bearing vein systems that were more or less vertical, or at least steeply dipping. We had tried to interpret the results using that model, and they hadn't lined up easily. It had looked as though there might be a series of steep en echelon (parallel but separate) veins within the system. As it turned out, after further drilling, the veins were unusually flat, almost horizontal, and the exploration program and mine layout had to be designed to accommodate that.

Exploration at Pogo was a real pleasure. The base camp was in a valley through which an idyllic stream ran, so clear that one could see every pebble on the bottom, over 3 metres down, and several tiers of fish swimming both ways in it. The drilling was at higher elevation, generally treeless, and with lots of rock exposed.

Dr Moira Smith did a great job of managing the exploration project, which was successful in establishing enough gold ore to justify building a mine. Ken Sudo and Ichiro Abe, a solid Sumitomo geologist, took pleasure in visiting the exploration camp periodically, as did Klaus Zeitler and I. Ken and Klaus became particularly adept at finding and consuming magic mushrooms that seemed to grow where the underlying gold content was strongest. Was this yet another exploration tool in the making?

Fred Daley's persistence had paid off. We proved up a nice ore body and put the Pogo mine into production in 2007. Representatives from the NANA, our partners in the Red Dog mine, joined Sumitomo and Teck people at the Pogo mine opening in July. It was the time of the midnight sun, and the Annual Mine-Opening Golf Tournament followed a dinner at an Alaskan gold dredge and a trip by a riverboat, with an 11:30 p.m. tee-off time.

Players encountered moose, bears, and a wolf during the round and, as the sun dipped slightly below the treetops for a few minutes before rising again, the temperature plummeted. The greens, which for the first three holes had been soft and wet, froze to the hardness of a billiard table. Sumitomo's new president, Fukushima-san, and I were seriously thinking our hands might freeze and drop off. Then on the ninth and final tee, a server came out with plastic cups of something piping hot. We never drank it, but just grasped the cup with our remaining fingers, savouring the warmth. It was the most interesting mine-opening tournament of them all.

Our interest in Pogo would be sold back to Sumitomo two years later as part of a refinancing following the global financial crisis of 2008. It was a modest mine, compared with a giant like Highland Valley or Antamina, but, perhaps not surprisingly, each new one generates the same sense of achievement for us geologists and engineers.

Epilogue

Each of these could have turned into one of Teck's mines today, but didn't, although we still have the San Nicolas and White Earth properties.

One wonders how much we, somewhat inadvertently, had been changed as a result of the Cominco acquisition. Whether that was a major inflection point, or a minor one, is debatable, but we were naturally different than during the years we were single-mindedly developing new mines.

For too long, we had been trying to ride two separate horses at the same time, one of which was dragging a heavy debt load. Our best entrepreneurial miner had been assigned downstairs to run Cominco, which may have lost us some of our edge. Would Bob Hallbauer have found a way to make good, operating mines out of Teck prospects like San Nicolas or Petaquilla? Or would he have found a way to get Pebble Copper into production within Cominco, had it had the financial strength and perseverance? We will never know.

Teck did manage some major winners in the 1990s as well, expanding our steelmaking coal side by acquiring, out of bankruptcy, a major resource that became the Elkview mine. And by taking a chance when we invested in Robert Friedland's Voisey's Bay nickel discovery in Diamond Fields. We were bought out by someone who wanted it more, but turned the profits into a share in the major new Antamina copper-zinc mine in Peru. We will see these tales in chapters 33 and 36.

Bob's successor, Mike Lipkewich, was instrumental in reopening that Elkview coal mine successfully, and in encouraging us to take on both both Voisey's Bay and Antamina. Maybe the engineer in me knows that you can't do everything at once, but the geologist part wonders why not, and is never happy when a good discovery goes to waste.

CHAPTER 32

BOB HALLBAUER, A LEADER GONE

Operating issues can be fixed, but capital mistakes stay with you a long time.
Robert E. Hallbauer

In 1995 we saw the passing of a man who had been a major part of Teck's success for the preceding 27 years.

Bob Hallbauer had been open pit superintendent at the Craigmont mine when I worked there in the early 1960s. In the years after I left and went back to Toronto, Bob moved up to mine manager and was destined for great things at Placer Development, where he was a leading member of one of the best engineering teams in the mining business. He had chosen instead to join us in Teck Corporation in 1968 as vice-president, mining, and never looked back.

Bob had quickly assembled a superb engineering team, drawing upon people we had known at Craigmont as well as from other cutting-edge organizations, and together they would go on to build more new mines in a shorter time than anyone else had in Canadian history. Their mantra was "on time and under budget," and most of his nine new mines met that target easily. The last, Quebrada Blanca, ran somewhat over budget since it was breaking new ground in the High Andes Mountains. But, as we shall see, the lessons learned there would be put to good use in later years with another high elevation project.

Their modus operandi involved doing a large majority of the design engineering for each new mine and its processing facilities in-house, on the premise that the ultimate operating success of any new mine depends heavily on how the facilities are laid out at the start. They would make use of outside engineering firms to do the detailed nuts and bolts drawings, once the conceptual design had been established, but never too early in the process. And they would draw upon consulting firms to help manage the procurement part of building a new mine, but always with strong oversight from Bob's own team, including people like Charlie Lightall and Lee Bilheimer.

Figure 32.1
Robert Hallbauer, miner extraordinaire

Like their mentors at Placer Development, their style was always to design "a good workable Ford, rather than an extravagant Cadillac." A plant that worked well from the start could always be gussied up or expanded later.

Bob's last new mine at Quebrada Blanca was completed and the first cathode copper produced in 1994. Sadly, Bob was unable to attend the official opening, after his leukemia relapsed and he was unable to travel to the high elevation at the site. Bob passed away shortly after, having made an indelible impact on the company in his years with Teck, as a mining operator, a professional, a mentor, and a thoroughly decent person. He had earned the respect of the entire Canadian mining community, culminating in his induction as a member of the Canadian Mining Hall of Fame. He was clearly one of the best ever.

Bob was a sportsman. After moving from the mines in the Interior, he always lived as close as he could to the water in Vancouver, and used to say there was no greater place to be. On the mid-May holiday weekend: "Where else would we be able to golf one day, ski the next and go fishing on the third?"

And he was a true friend to me and to all of us at Teck.

CHAPTER 33

THE SAGA OF DIAMOND FIELDS

Fortune favours the bold.
Pliny the Elder

In 1993, two prospectors were exploring for diamonds in Labrador for Diamond Fields Resources, a junior exploration company. Instead they discovered a copper-nickel prospect that would eventually become the significant Voisey's Bay mine. It would vault mining entrepreneur Robert Friedland into front-page prominence again, involve Teck as the putative mine development partner, feature a bidding war for control between Falconbridge and Inco, and see Teck reap a large profit that would later be redeployed into a key interest in the Antamina mine in Peru.

Jacquie McNish has written an entertaining and well-researched book on the Voisey's Bay saga called *The Big Score* that is, as far as we can see from its telling of the parts in which we were involved, right on.

An Unexpected Discovery

Diamond Fields Resources (DFR) had been co-founded by Robert Friedland and Jean-Raymond Boulle, primarily to explore for and develop diamond mines in Africa. However, in 1993 it financed two prospectors, Albert Chislett and Chris Verbiski, who spent much of the summer flying from site to site in the wilds of Labrador, looking for signs of diamonds. Apparently, the grizzled prospectors and the canoes, foxes, and rabbits that led to discoveries in the times of chapter 1 had been displaced by a new breed that rode from rock outcrop to outcrop by helicopter. The new breed would prove similarly successful, at times.

By September, the two had encountered little success, but while helicoptering back to the Inuit community of Nain, where they had been camped for the past month, they scanned the surroundings for signs of mineralization. Chislett noticed something that struck him as odd and asked the pilot to circle back. They hovered over a hilltop with rocks that looked like a fairly large area of gossan, a weathering feature sometimes associated with sulphide mineralization. There are many such gossans in Labrador, but this one looked a bit different.

Five days later they returned and landed. They kept the helicopter engine running so they could take a quick look and take off again if there was nothing of interest. As McNish tells it, suddenly Chislett realized this one might be for real. He began to flap his hands wildly over his head and yelled into the wind: "Shut it off, shut it off."

Almost every piece of rock they broke open with their prospector's picks proved to contain copper. They paced out the dimensions of the observed mineralization and concluded it continued for at least 400 metres by 40 metres. That was a pretty good size for the start of any discovery. "We may have a copper mine here," said Chislett, "and at least it will get us funded for another field program in Labrador next year."

Unbeknownst to them, Diamond Fields was in difficult financial straits, and it had only one experienced base metal geologist on its board: Richard Garnett. The company was most interested in diamonds and in its stock price, and to most of the directors, an undrilled copper prospect promoted by a couple of raw prospectors was of little interest. Its president urged the board to get out of Labrador, but Garnett managed to wring a modest $220,000 drilling budget out of them.

Modest is in the era of the beholder. In the days of Terry Patrick and Moriarty, that amount would have returned 220 lobsters for a feast at Temagami.

Further surface sampling and assaying the next summer showed that, in addition to copper, the rocks contained interesting amounts of cobalt and nickel. The prospectors carried out magnetic and electromagnetic surveys to help them try to define the limits of the mineral deposit. It seemed to have quite discrete boundaries, compared with many large mineral deposits that have gradually reducing grades as one moves away from the higher-grade core. This would be proven true later, and have interesting implications for us. In the end, the prospectors managed to complete four drill holes in 1994, the second of which returned an exceptionally good 33 metres of massive sulphides grading close to 3 per cent nickel. This was a good start for any drilling program on a new prospect.

Robert Friedland and Our First Meeting on Voisey's Bay

Robert Friedland is one of the most articulate, smartest people on the planet. He is also one of the best salesmen out there, and when it comes down to a serious negotiation he can be expected to know, or seem to know, more about the subject than many of the professionals on the other side. He had been responsible for the discovery of a successful gold mine in Alaska, developed by Amax Gold, and the project's name, Fort Knox, was something only he could have come up with.

We had known Robert for some time, although not through any extensive business dealings other than the abortive visit to Kazakhstan. He had been resident in Vancouver for years and was, like us, part of the small mining community that works out of there. He had moved to Singapore in the fall of 1994, before the good drill results from Diamond Fields' Voisey's Bay discovery began to come in. Having grown tired of the company's Namibian diamond play he was planning to concentrate on new prospects in Indonesia and the Far East. However, once it became clear that Voisey's Bay could be an important discovery, he returned to Vancouver and took charge with a vengeance.

It was in November of 1994, shortly after drill hole 2, that Bob Hallbauer and I trotted over to see Robert in his penthouse office in Vancouver's historic Marine Building. It was literally across the street and once again, as with Hemlo years earlier, proved the value of our being in the same town where so many of Canada's junior exploration companies were then being financed. We took the elevator to the twentieth floor, one below the penthouse, and then huffed up a flight of stairs to find Robert in his lair.

Slightly winded, we congratulated him on his discovery, and said we hoped that one day we could find a way to work together with him in developing it into a mine. I think he genuinely admired what we had done in building new mines successfully, but wasn't likely prepared to do "the ultimate deal" at that early stage, to quote Chester Millar once again.

Nor for that matter were we. One good drill hole doesn't make a mine, but it was an impressively good start. The trick for us would be to stay close to Robert and his people, monitoring what happened with the next round of drilling. Furthermore, Bob Hallbauer was more skeptical about it, as he usually was. As Jacquie McNish told it, Hallbauer was "a blunt, no-nonsense mining operator" and Friedland the "smooth-talking mining promoter," so it was like trying to mix oil and water.

Bob and I both believed in our strategy of trying to be close to and dealing fairly with those junior exploration companies that have, historically, made many of the important mine discoveries in Canada. Our objective was to be the partner of choice in such situations. For me, as a geophysicist always on the hunt for opportunities, I think it was instinctive; for Bob Hallbauer as an operator, and particularly for David Thompson as a CFO, it would always be a bit of a mental stretch.

Friedland asked what he should do next, and I answered him frankly: "Robert, if it was me and I had a drill hole this good, I'd keep on drilling to get a better idea of what I had before thinking about dealing it off." That was of course what he was going to do anyway, so why fight it? We left wishing him luck, asking him to call any time if he wanted geophysical or engineering help in the interim, and all of us agreeing to keep in touch.

The "Ovoid" Nickel Deposit Takes Shape

And luck Robert had.

Drilling continued into January and the next results were disappointing, but then drill holes 7 and 8 once again encountered substantial lengths of high-grade mineralization. Drill hole 7 contained 104 metres of almost 4 per cent nickel, an exceptionally thick intersection of ore by any standard. Instead of just a few million tonnes of mineralization, nothing to get particularly excited about, Diamond Fields geologists could now point confidently to a potential 20 to 25 million tonnes of good-grade ore, should infill drilling continue to be successful. Given the geophysical results, this seemed a reasonable bet.

For the next while, every hole encountered good nickel values and the outlines of the deposit began to take shape. It was soon given the unusual name of an ovoid, because it looked as though the developing nickel ore body was shaped like a buried egg that started at the surface and extended down below it. In some respects, it resembled our original Temagami discovery, although there the top half of the egg had been eroded away over the millennia. The egg at Voisey's Bay looked to have been mostly preserved, and of course was much larger.

It would make for easy, initial mine development as an open pit, with no need for a shaft to go underground, at least at the start. Again, this was just like Temagami, although the grades weren't as high and development would require a mill, or concentrator, whereas at Temagami the first, near-surface ore bodies were so high-grade that the mined ore could be shipped directly to smelters without further concentrating. And, to further the similarities, both were in a combined copper and nickel geological environment.

At Temagami there had proven to be many small spheres, lenses, or ovoids of ore discovered after the initial two deposits were mined out. There was an obvious potential for Voisey's Bay to have similar success in expanding the resource, and this was now a compelling reason to see if we could negotiate a development contract. It was time to act.

Bob Hallbauer was by then again suffering from a recurrence of the leukemia that he had come down with a few years back, but Mike Lipkewich, an equally conservative mine operator who would succeed him, picked up the ball. Mike supported the idea that this would at the very least make a small, high-grade mine, the minimum size of which we could now calculate, and that it had the potential to grow through more discoveries on the property. The market price, while it had skyrocketed already, was fully justified by our calculations, and in fact our own internal evaluation was even higher than the market's. This was a rare situation for a junior company discovery, since in most cases the stock market quickly overvalues reality at any given stage in the drilling.

Teck Deals In on Voisey's Bay

So one Friday afternoon in April 1995, we approached Diamond Fields with a serious offer, initially through Ed Mercaldo, an ex-BMO banker who Robert had installed as Diamond Fields' president. After the market closed, Robert and his lawyer, David Huberman, joined us.

We would have preferred to negotiate a final development contract, earning a significant equity by financing and managing the new mine through to production, as in the case of Hemlo. However, this wasn't going to be in the cards with Robert, any more than it had been with Chester Millar early on in the case of his Afton discovery. We needed either to gamble on a first step or just stand and watch. Given that judgment call, we offered to simply buy shares from the treasury, providing the company with funds to carry on working, and take our chances that by being an early supporter we could eventually negotiate a development contract when the dust had settled. I offered verbally to buy "a 5 or 10 per cent position" in the company, and this sparked some serious interest on their part.

Reaching agreement on price proved to be a bit of a challenge, because Robert demanded a premium over the market price of the shares, which had already appreciated from a few dollars to $30 in the previous five months. Normally, when there is a change in control there is some justification and precedent for the buyer paying a premium, but this wasn't the case here. On the contrary, Robert was demanding that we vote any shares we bought with him in the event of a third-party takeover bid, so it was he who was cementing control rather than us gaining it.

Regardless, we finally agreed that we would pay $36 a share, or a 20 per cent premium over the already-hyped market price, and we accepted Robert's condition on voting with him in certain circumstances. Our internal lawyer at the time, George Stevens, said: "Norm, you can't pay a premium price for this; it's already gone up more than tenfold." Friedland recalls my saying: "George, I'm over 21. Give me a pen."

By Saturday night we had the structure and price largely worked out, and the lawyers were putting together a short formal agreement. Friedland and I were sitting in my office trading stories while this went on, both aware that, just occasionally, lawyers may find a way of messing up a deal. They certainly were taking their time. Finally, George came in and asked to see me alone, saying there was something we had to settle. I had this sense that something had gone wrong.

But all George said was: "Norm, you have to tell me what it is. Is it 5 per cent or 10 per cent we're buying?" I laughed and said: "Make it 10 per cent." And in fact we rounded it off to 3 million shares, which was 10.4 per cent. So the deal was that we bought 3 million shares at a price of $36 a share, for a total of $108 million. That, choosing 10 per cent rather than 5 per cent off the cuff, was one of the most successful three seconds of my career. With 10 per cent, we would find ourselves in a position to do another important deal to acquire and build the Antamina mine in Peru a couple of years later, and that would become one of our best mines. Had I picked 5 per cent, I think we might have had to pass on Antamina. We might also have seen Diamond Fields taken over the next day by a third party, which we will come to.

This was an unusual deal. We were taking a chance we could parlay it into a direct interest in and management of the mine when things cooled down. If not, we felt the underlying asset value was already worth about 50 per cent more than we were paying, so holding onto the shares would not have been a particularly risky fallback position.

Once we were signed up, subject to the approval of both companies' boards, we had to call a telephone meeting to ratify the agreement, and we did this late on Sunday, the next day. Retired investment banker Brian Aune had just joined our board and, as with Karl Gustaf Ratjen years earlier, was introduced to our regular "new director's big deal by telephone" gambit. Unlike Karl Gustaf though, Brian thought this was great, and at the end of the meeting he said: "I like this deal; this is my kind of company."

I think it was getting there again. It's fair to say that, after several years of wrestling with the unwieldy attempt to run both Cominco and Teck, sometimes together and sometimes separately, we had gotten our mojo back.

Making the case for the deal was a bit tricky though, because none of us in Teck had actually been to visit the property yet. Mike hadn't. I hadn't. Nobody had. However, the consulting firm of Watts, Griffiths, and McOuat had been responsible for some of the work, and Jack McOuat was an independent director of Cominco at the time. So we had asked Jack to join our telephone meeting and express his opinion, which he did. He described the work done by Watts and Griffiths and supported the assays. I believe he used his favourite expression to describe the potential: "We know how small it is. We just don't know how big it is." This time, Mike and I actually agreed with him. That was exactly how we saw it.

The deal was approved, signed, and announced on Sunday 16 April 1995.

Although it didn't come out right away, we learned later that Falconbridge had been closeted with investment bankers BMO Nesbitt Burns over the same weekend, readying a full takeover bid for the next day, but when our agreement was announced, they downed their tools and abandoned their bid. It appears that we had been both right and lucky in taking a share position then, rather than sitting and waiting. If Falconbridge had bid, they might have won it early on or, more likely, it would have brought Inco out of the weeds with a counter-bid.

Why our purchase of only 10 per cent of Diamond Fields should have stopped Falconbridge is a mystery, but it worked out well for us. If we had bought just 5 per cent instead of 10 per cent would that still have deterred them? Who knows? Did Robert have a suspicion that Falconbridge was about to bid? I have never asked him.

The next week, Robert, Jack McOuat, and I helicoptered in together to visit the property and look at the drill core, and it was spectacular. I was not surprised that it was Robert's first visit to the site as well. I was a bit surprised that it was Jack's, but then I hadn't asked at the board meeting the week before whether he had really been there. He was in fact just relying upon reports from his fine staff. Nobody else had asked either (see colour page 13).

Within a month after buying the shares for $108 million, we did a bought deal with Jimmy Connacher, issuing a few Teck B shares for $100 million. By doing this, we largely covered what cash we had at risk in the thing. One of Len Watt's many adages had been "Every rat needs a second hole," and whatever he had meant by that odd statement we had often taken it as advice to cover risky ventures where practical with a bit of a fallback position.

As part of the DFR deal, we had also agreed to provide management talent on call and free of charge, including engineering services and community relations. In the latter connection, we asked Cominco's Doug Horswill to help Diamond Fields manage relations with both the Inuit community around Voisey's Bay and the government of Newfoundland, and Doug would devote much of the rest of the year to that. It was his forte, and he made a real contribution to Diamond Fields and the eventual Voisey's Bay mine. By September, we would be asked by DFR to begin the feasibility study and plant design necessary to secure financing to bring the project into production, and we would get this well under way. Things seemed to be going according to plan, but that was just an illusion.

Interlopers Emerge, or Are Enticed In

Often after the euphoria of a new discovery, the market dies down, and there is a lull of several years before the mine reaches production. This would not be the case with Robert Friedland in charge. He has been called a charming rogue, and it has been said he could sell a comb to a bald man. He could convince the chickens to invite the fox for dinner. He could sell iceboxes to the Inuit. He is also single-minded when it comes to completing anything he's started, such as optimizing and closing a deal.

Whether or not Robert ever planned to see Diamond Fields develop the mine itself, he was determined to create that impression, which led other mining companies to try to be even more creative in finding a way to participate. Naturally, this would include the two main nickel players in Canada, Inco and Falconbridge. It would also include other nickel miners like Western Mining of Australia, Sumitomo Metal Mining of Japan, and Outokumpu of Finland, as well as most of the large diversified mining houses in the world.

The stage was set for the games to begin in earnest.

It was clear from the start that we might not be the final player in that game. I had a cartoon drawn up by one of our draftsmen showing a sacrificial goat tethered to a stake, presumably on top of a buried fortune. The goat was Teck, and looking hungrily at it from the surrounding jungle were a number of hungry lions and other animals. One of the lions had a head that was recognizable, that of Inco's Chairman, Mike Sopko, but he was not the only predator (see figure 33.1).

Perhaps a bit breathlessly, shortly after our deal was announced, Friedland had authorized Ed Mercaldo to meet with Sopko and offer him the chance to buy up to a maximum of 25 per cent of Diamond Fields. Mike was obviously disappointed because he wanted a majority stake, but this was all that was on offer. I was disappointed, but not surprised.

Mike and I were good friends, and we had a discussion about Voisey's Bay at the annual meeting of the Canada-Japan Businessmen's Conference in Victoria in May. I had been co-chairman of the Canadian side for a couple of years, and had quietly arranged that Mike would be included in our foursome in the annual golf tournament. We didn't talk about Voisey's Bay as we golfed, winning $5 and pride being more important, as usual.

But Mike and I were smokers at the time, and during a break in the official proceedings, we found ourselves outside on the deck. Mike confided to me: "I don't know what to do, Norm. Half of our directors want me to make a deal on Voisey's Bay, and the other half don't. I'm dead either way." That uncertainty is often the nature of deals that turn out well. If they were obvious at the start, they wouldn't be easily available.

It was interesting that he would say this, given Teck's clear interest in being the winner ourselves, but I have to admit I was already beginning to wonder which side I would be on in the end. If we could get the ultimate deal as originally planned, great, but if not I would be on the same side as Robert Friedland, seeking top dollar. It was not our style, but as Flip Wilson was wont to say, "The devil made me do it."

In June, the two announced that Inco would buy a 25 per cent stake in a new DFR subsidiary, Voisey's Bay Nickel Company. Inco would also buy a 7 per cent share interest in DFR itself. Inco had picked up a little bit more than a net 25 per cent, but not control, no more than Teck had. And Diamond Fields still controlled the subsidiary with its 75 per cent holding. It was Friedland at his finest.

Figure 33.1
The Voisey's Bay jungle, complete with lions and a tethered lamb

Work on the property continued, with both Teck and Inco now providing technical input as the drills rolled on.

The games were not over. Friedland would play Inco and Falconbridge, by now lured back into it, as though he were using a Stradivarius. In this, he would use the siren of potentially much more nickel in a new, lower-grade, but possibly extensive zone that had been discovered trailing down from the ovoid. This he imaginatively labelled "the Eastern Deeps," recalling some of the famous deep mines of South Africa. It didn't matter that the African ones were gold, and completely unrelated geologically. The game was in the name. Robert described the new zone in his favourite way, as "extending to the centre of the earth."

Don Lindsay, whose first mine visit had been to Temagami, was by then heading up the global mining group for investment bankers CIBC Wood Gundy. He had been following the Voisey's Bay saga and, with the exciting news about the Eastern Deeps, he approached Falconbridge's CEO, Frank

Pickard, and convinced him there was now an opening for Falconbridge to bid. Inco held 25 per cent of the downstairs company owning the nickel deposit, but with a decent premium Falconbridge could stand a good chance at getting DFR itself and full control. Falconbridge could trump its old nickel rival in spades.

Robert had set that up nicely.

One morning the next December, Robert asked me to come to his presidential suite at Vancouver's Pan Pacific Hotel for breakfast. We had a nice conversation about all sorts of things, since by this time I was not even thinking about any realistic prospect of negotiating our own way into control of DFR, and eventually there was a knock on the door. It was Mike Sopko. Robert opened the door a crack, told him he was tied up in a meeting and asked him to wait outside for 15 minutes or so. Robert winked at me and asked me to wait with him for a while. Then, when it was timely, I left and went down the hall, turning right into the elevator lobby for that floor. Sitting in one of the two waiting chairs there was Mike Sopko, and his jaw dropped. What was Keevil doing in there?

By now Mike was not the lion of my cartoon. The lion was back there in the hotel room and Mike was potentially another tethered goat. Teck was becoming an animal of uncertain parentage, invented by Robert the Magician.

Mike went in to meet the lion, well prepared to present and defend his new offer of an all-share acquisition valued at $28 a share (the shares having been split four for one since our initial purchase at $36). This valued the company at $3 billion, a far cry from the $1 billion just over a year earlier. It would be a tax-free rollover to DFR shareholders, which for some time is something that Robert and his associates had said they would prefer.

Predictably, Robert replied that $28 wasn't good enough, and that he was "looking for something over $30." He sent Mike away with instructions to better his proposal or walk for good.

Not one for walking at the best of times, Sopko soon came back to Diamond Fields with a "final offer" of over $30, as Robert had asked. He proposed a stock swap valued at $31 a share, or close to $3.5 billion, provided Robert would agree to a lock-up, agreeing to tender his and his group's shares at that price. According to Jacquie McNish, Friedland said he wouldn't agree to the lock-up. "I'm accepting the price, but not the lock-up. If you give me $35, I'll give you the lock-up."

Meanwhile, back at Falconbridge, Frank Pickard had convinced his board and major shareholder Noranda to support an offer valued at $4 billion, consisting primarily of Falconbridge shares and a new equity instrument that would give Diamond Fields shareholders additional upside should more high-grade ore be discovered at Voisey's Bay. Such things are sometimes called widgets.

At the suggestion of Noranda's leader, Jack Cockwell, who realized it was likely that in the end the smaller Falconbridge would be outbid by Inco, the offer would include a significant break fee, payable by DFR to Falconbridge should that happen. Don Lindsay was authorized to present this to Ed Mercaldo and did so in early February 1996. Mercaldo called Robert in South Africa, and he confirmed that it was acceptable. The next day, trading in the shares of both Falconbridge and Diamond Fields was halted, although no news report was put out for hours.

Sopko was furious. Robert was still playing his Stradivarius. I was just becoming bemused by it all.

The game was still not over, and readers interested in pursuing the saga much further would enjoy reading the McNish book. It may read like fantasy fiction, but I think she got it right. Suffice it to say here that, through mysterious circumstances, there was some discussion at this stage about Inco and Falconbridge joining forces and splitting up Diamond Fields between them, which might have made countless litigation lawyers happy. Friedland got wind of it, and the whole thing was called off quickly.

The litigation community was furious. How could this one get away?

Inco was not about to let the prize go to its rival, and in April it raised Falconbridge's bid by 21 per cent, which was 40 per cent over its own, latest "final offer" of a month earlier. None of the offers were all cash, and because of the mix of securities involved, it is hard to establish a precise value on each, but the Inco offer was valued at about $4.5 billion. It was now game over, and Inco had won, or had it?

Epilogue

While we had not made our initial investment for any reason other than to have a chance at being the eventual mine developer, which would have been our eleventh new mine in just over 20 years, we had always assumed that we might get outfoxed. Our in-house valuation of Voisey's Bay at the time we paid $36 a share for a 10.4 per cent interest in DFR was in the $50 range, for a total of $1.4 billion, so we hadn't been too concerned about the downside.

By the time Inco made its final offer 16 months later the value of our $108 million investment had quadrupled which, while it was second prize, was quite acceptable. Our cash position was stronger by over $500 million as a result of these events, and we took advantage of it by redeploying the funds into an interest in the Antamina copper-zinc project in Peru, a new joint venture with Noranda and Rio Algom. That was to become one of our most important mines, and we wouldn't have been able to consider it without the Diamond Fields gain.

Sometimes one thing leads to another, and as Yogi Berra said: "When you come to a fork in the road, take it."

CHAPTER 34

STRANGER STILL, THE BRE-X TALE

We observe a lot, just by watching.
Yogi Berra

About the same time that we were playing, and being played, in the Diamond Fields saga, another newsworthy story was developing. This one involved an apparent discovery of a different metal and an even more spectacular stock market run-up, but with a different result.

If we'd found that the zinc business lacked a certain element of discipline, it was nothing compared with the new lack of discipline in the gold business. I thought we knew gold well, having mined it through the fixed $35 years, the Emergency Gold Mining Assistance Act in Canada, the freeing up of gold by President Nixon, and the frenetic rise in 1979 to over $800 an ounce, followed by the inevitable fallback. Having seen it all, what we really knew was that we knew nothing about what the price might be the next year, but we did know a little bit about ore deposits, ounces, tonnes of reserves, costs, and even the risk of rudimentary salting.

Then along came Bre-X.

The Story

A lot of good books have been written about this escapade as well. Among the best are *Bre-X: The Inside Story* by Diane Francis, and *Gold Today, Gone Tomorrow*, by Vivian Danielson and James Whyte of *The Northern Miner*. All we can add here is a bit of colour about our own involvement.

The story is fairly well-known, although details about who knew what and when are still missing and rumours abound. Bre-X was the largest gold salting fraud ever devised by man, although as it turned out it was not all that sophisticated. Nevertheless, it fooled a great many analysts and investors, and led otherwise sound mining companies to chase that illusory pot at the end of the rainbow.

Salting is an age-old trick of fraudulent gold promoters, usually with bits of gold added to rock samples sent in for assay. The reported assay results are thus much higher than the gold content of the original rock, sometimes leading to a feeding frenzy of would-be buyers of the property. There are various other ways to salt, including even just doctoring of the assay certificates. In this case, it was the old-fashioned way, with gold being added to the samples. As it turned out, it was not even the right kind of gold.

Who actually led the salting at the Bre-X property has never been determined. Most people think it was a geologist named Michael de Guzman, who may have jumped out of a helicopter in Borneo when in danger of being found out, or may have been thrown out, or may still be around.

It had all started innocently enough, with the general knowledge in the mining industry that sporadic amounts of gold occurred in rocks near the Busang River in Borneo. Several junior mining companies out of Australia had explored properties there in the 1980s, but by the early 1990s Borneo gold wasn't uppermost in investors' minds and the properties became dormant. Some of those Australians asked a geologist named John Felderhof to try to find a buyer for the claims.

Meanwhile, a Calgary promoter named David Walsh was looking for a gold prospect for his new company, Bre-X Minerals. The only person he knew in Indonesia was Felderhof, so Walsh called him to see if he knew of any good exploration ground he could acquire. Felderhof said he did, and Bre-X picked up the old Busang property in 1993. Felderhof then introduced Walsh to de Guzman, who came with good references for gold exploration in the region. Guzman had done some of the early work for the Australians on what would become known as Bre-X's Central Zone.

Renewed exploration began quickly, and it was remarkable how, with good Calgary know-how, the property suddenly become more valuable than it had been in the hands of those Australians.

The Northern Miner reported on the Bre-X acquisition in August 1993, saying "recent sampling returned values ranging from 2.19 to 114.0 grams of gold per tonne." The sampling, coupled with a reinterpretation of existing data, including 19 shallow, old drill holes, "suggests the property could contain about 20 million tonnes at 2 grams of gold per tonne, mineable by open pit." That sounded like a reasonable start, and the story had begun.

With its fine new property, Bre-X began exploration drilling, but early results in the Central Zone were just about the same as the Australians had found earlier. They were low grade in gold, erratic and discouraging. Funds to continue work were hard to come by, and Bre-X shares lay low.

So far, this is a familiar story about prospecting for gold. All of us involved in mineral exploration have drilled prospects for which we had high hopes, only to have them dashed by the drill and assay results.

A Feeding Frenzy

But soon Bre-X began to report better news, and stories began to circulate that there might be something good there after all. When crumbs are thrown into a fish tank, the little denizens will throng around in a feeding frenzy. So it is with rumours of gold. "Investors" can develop the frenzied habits of sharks, or perhaps it is of lemmings.

Walsh didn't know much about mining, but he did know something about what would catch the attention of speculators. He took steps to build up the perception of a quality team, and in early 1994, Dr Paul Kavanagh joined the Bre-X board of directors. Recently retired as head of exploration for Barrick, a major gold producer, and with a long, respected career behind him, Kavanagh lent a new aura of credibility to Bre-X. To many of us who had known him well over the years, he was "Mr Straight Arrow."

Teck geologist Wayne Spilsbury, then based in Australia and our eyes and ears on Asia, visited the property in early 1995. He was given a good show and tell on site by de Guzman and Felderhof, and saw a few quartz veins that carried a bit of gold, as was well-known from previous work. Walsh proposed that Teck buy some shares to provide ongoing funding and become Bre-X's strategic partner in Indonesia. Wayne declined. At that time, Bre-X was trading at around $2 a share, a normal level for a speculative prospect that just possibly might work out.

According to Danielson, shareholders were soon being told that resources in the Central Zone would be "about 3 million ounces, once assay results of nine more holes were in hand." Walsh took it a step further, using visual estimates on drill core from a newly named southeast zone, and said: "Based on extremely encouraging data to date from assays and visual results, Bre-X continues to be confident that six to eight million ounces of gold, in various resource categories, will be achieved by November." By the summer of 1995, the share price was up seven times to $14.

We had agreed with Wayne's assessment when he turned down the opportunity to invest, but were getting increasingly impressed as the reported gold content soared with more time and exploration work. The supposed resource had started at around a million ounces, not particularly noteworthy, but as work went on and news came out, it seemed that there might be up to 10 million ounces of gold there. This amount, if valid, had to be of major interest to any gold mining company, and of course was. It was becoming watched more closely within the industry, as well as by market speculators.

By the following February, Bre-X was able to report: "An independent evaluation of our drilling results pegs recoverable reserves at 16 million ounces of gold." Around that time, Bre-X also announced the appointment of a respected financial expert, Rolando Francisco, who had worked at Goldcorp and Lac Minerals, as chief financial officer and director. This added further credibility to "the management team." By then the shares were trading at $140, up another tenfold in the space of about six months.

The Indonesian director-general of Mining told reporters that Busang is "one of the world's largest gold finds and could contain 40 million ounces." At the Bre-X annual meeting, John Felderhof said: "All I can say is that I think we have 30 million ounces, plus, plus, plus."

A number of well-known mining analysts had visited the Busang property and generally given it a thumbs up. Nesbitt Burns' Egizio Bianchini, considered by many as Bay Street's top gold analyst at the time, at one point estimated total resources to three significant figures at 42.6 million ounces. He was hardly alone.

A unit of the famous engineering firm Kilborn SNC Lavalin was retained to provide an estimate of the size of the resource. This was reported in July 1996 as a "measured and indicated resource of 93.8 million tonnes averaging 2.17 grams per tonne," (or 6.57 million ounces) with "a further 20.79 million ounces classified as inferred." Now we were up to even more significant figures. We used to be taught "the law of significant figures" in Engineering 101, but then we were usually working with slide rules in those good old days. That law seems to have been forgotten in the mists of time and with the advent of computers.

By this time the Bre-X market had climbed to $250 a share.

In September, Paul Kavanagh made a presentation on the project to *The Northern Miner's* Southeast Asian Mining Conference. The Busang discovery was the biggest news of the day, and at the symposium. Paul presented some maps showing dozens of drill-hole locations and very good assays. The holes were generally spaced at intervals along a series of parallel lines, as is normal in the business, with the odd hole off-line where topography made a consistent pattern difficult or impossible. The maps were hand-drawn and not what one would expect from a polished show and tell, but in fact this may have augmented their credibility. Surely a first-rate, pure promotion would have been done with more style and panache, one might have thought.

I was at the presentation and took it all in, with only one suspicion. I noticed that every line of holes contained assays that were remarkably consistent. Each hole on one line would have gold assays that clustered closely around an average grade of, say, 2.1 grams per tonne. The next line of drill holes would show a set of similarly consistent assays, but this time clustered closely around a different number. And results from the next line would be different again, but also clustered around one number.

That should have been my first clue that something was fishy because, as a geoscientist used to analyzing data, I knew that in real life numbers seldom worked that way. Mineralization, whether gold or copper, is usually more erratic. The same applies to stock price charts, which should never follow a perfect sine wave if they are to be believed, as Cliff Rennie should have known when Hallbauer and I tricked him back at Craigmont.

However, like Cliff, being a natural optimist and becoming more than willing to believe at that point, I rationalized it by thinking the holes might have been drilled in the wrong direction, and that a different drilling pattern might have given more varied results, as was common. That doesn't make sense, in hindsight, but I have to admit that a major salting fraud was the last thing in my mind at the time, or in the minds of most in the business. The shares continued to trade at about $250.

Earlier, as Busang seemed to be getting bigger and better, John Morganti, head of gold exploration for Teck, had written to David Walsh with a tentative offer for us to join with Bre-X in the ongoing exploration. The offer was subject to due diligence, including drilling by Teck of new, confirmatory holes in some key parts of the discovery area. Morganti was also intrigued but skeptical from day one. We were determined to make any investment decision subject to careful checking, probably twinning some of the discovery holes, just as Cyprus Amax had done in Chile after it had acquired the El Abra copper property from Codelco.

In this case, Walsh wrote back saying that Bre-X would not be considering any joint venture proposals for the time being. He wanted to do more work to see just how big this thing was.

John Willson, who had been managing a steel plant on Annacis Island for Cominco when we bought into that company, was by then CEO of Placer Dome, the combined company after Dome Mines had taken over Placer Development. He too decided that Busang was too exciting to ignore, and contacted Walsh in early 1996. According to Danielson and Whyte, Walsh gave the same response: "We're drilling, have plenty of money to drill, and no difficulty in raising more." He told Willson they would keep drilling until fall, and then have an auction to find a senior mining partner.

This sounded eerily familiar and actually made sense, being similar to the advice Bob Hallbauer and I had given to Bob Friedland after his Voisey's Bay nickel discovery a year earlier. Friedland had asked us what we thought he should do, and I had replied that he should keep on drilling for a while longer, to find out just how large the nickel deposit really was. Of course, it might also have made sense to Walsh if he knew the thing was a fraud, wanted the game to continue, and didn't want any mining company to have a chance to test drill and verify the data. To this day, I'm not sure what he knew and didn't know at the time. I actually suspect he knew nothing of the fraud until right about the end, but others have a different view.

At this point, both Teck and Placer had finally made approaches to Walsh. We were both still skeptical, but unable to resist the possibility, indeed probability, given the independent support by analysts and engineers who had visited and studied the property, that this really was something uniquely valuable in the gold business.

By then, Barrick, which had not seemed interested earlier as Paul Kavanagh was retiring, was becoming excited about the growing resource and was rumoured to be going after it full bore. Whether we were skeptical or not, the apparent size of the Busang prospect was becoming something that any major gold company had to take a hard look at. And in the macho world of competitive mine hunting, nobody with any gumption wants to be left the hindmost. The stage was set for a fight.

Let the Games Begin

At the time, Barrick was one of the leading gold producing companies in the world. Newmont was the biggest American gold company. Teck operated the two Hemlo mines, arguably the best recent gold discovery in North America, and Placer Dome had decided to become a pure gold company, casting aside years as a successful diversified company when it was Placer Development. All four were determined to have a go at Busang, with whatever doubts they may have had earlier seemingly dissipated.

In the summer of 1996, two senior Barrick people met with Felderhof and Francisco in Jakarta and began talks about a joint venture. Barrick founder Peter Munk soon went over to present his case personally, reportedly attempting to talk directly with President Suharto. President George Bush and former Prime Minister Brian Mulroney, both members of Barrick's advisory board, wrote glowing letters in support of the company.

Late in 1996, Munk was invited to a meeting in Jakarta with Bre-X and government officials. Walsh, Felderhof, and Francisco were there for Bre-X. Mines Minister Sudjana represented Indonesia and began the so-called negotiations. He instructed the two companies that the deal they would do would end up with Barrick holding 75 per cent and Bre-X 25 per cent of the "foreign content" of the new mine. There would be some additional portion set aside for Indonesia and friends. The two mining companies were left to go away and work it out, but along these lines.

Most mining industry people were outraged, not only by the government apparently dictating the terms, but in selecting the senior operating partner as well. Rumours abounded as to how that could have happened. Placer's Willson reportedly said: "We don't think this is right. We think Bre-X should be allowed its natural right to conduct an auction and find a partner of choice, rather than have a partner imposed upon it." My old friends at Placer had always been annoyed at our coining the phrase "partner of choice," feeling that this should have been their own slogan, and here they were using it as well. The little devils.

I was quoted too, comparing this perfidy to our recent, positive experience with Diamond Fields in Newfoundland, where the government had left the dealings to us in the private sector and had not interfered.

Bre-X and Barrick resumed this purported negotiation as instructed but, not surprisingly, failed to agree by a government-imposed deadline. The uncertainty of how much had to be set aside and for whom in Indonesia may have been a factor. As well, the situation was becoming complicated after a third, private Indonesian party attempted to claim a contractual interest in the property from Bre-X, or from whoever actually might have thought they owned it.

By this time, the other obvious suitors in the game were getting itchy fingers. I'd met Wayne Murdy, president of Newmont, when we were touring Europe as part of an RBC Dominion Securities investor road show a couple of years back. Jim Bob Moffett of Freeport was the third member in the tour. In those events, we were all competing for investor interest, but tended to see ourselves as part of the action team, and we'd hit it off as miners do in such times.

Wayne called me at home one night to ask what we were doing about this fiasco. We commiserated a bit and agreed we should talk about it further in the next few days. I'm not sure whose idea it was, but we agreed we should bring our mutual friends at Placer, also apparently wallflowers in this dance, into the conversation.

We convened a conference call to review the status, and what we might do about it. I was by then in Chile, Wayne was in Denver, and John Willson was in Vancouver. After a bit of telephonic wailing and gnashing of teeth about the way in which the competition seemed to be handling it, we got down to the nitty gritty. What could we do? Was there any merit in putting together a joint venture between the three of us to try to counter Barrick? It was an interesting conversation among old acquaintances in what is generally a close industry of like-minded people. We were all straight arrows, or considered ourselves that. But in the end, we couldn't see how to put together a joint effort. Willson said he was going to go it alone. We agreed we would too. Wayne Murdy said he'd probably stand aside.

So off I went to Jakarta, along with my intuitive wife, Joan, to see if we could find out something more about what was going on. It was quite a merry-go-round. We were all there, somewhere. Willson and I were in the same hotel, exchanging old war stories as we ran across each other in the lobby. Peter Munk was in another hotel. For all we knew, Wayne Murdy might have been somewhere in town after all, and South African gold producers Anglo American and Goldfields could have been anywhere. Were we the lions or the gladiators? Or perhaps it should have been the foxes or the hens?

By that time, President Suharto had become interested personally, and had asked an Indonesian industrialist and old friend, Mohammed "Bob" Hasan, to get involved. He was told to see if he could work out something that was fair, not only to the private players but to Indonesia. That seemed to be an interesting, novel concept in the circumstances.

Willson and I each went to visit Bob Hasan separately. He had a beautiful home in Jakarta, with a large, idyllic garden that included a putting green. He had been an avid golfer and had regularly played in the Bing Crosby and other pro-am tournaments in California. Hasan and I shared a really nice lunch at his home, as well as a small putting contest, which in the spirit of customer golf I attempted to lose but didn't.

He asked me, if we weren't chosen as the mine developer, who I thought it should be. I replied I understood it was a difficult decision. We were experts in gold mining and milling, as were the other two known players. We had also built the kind of very large-tonnage mining and milling operations such as that envisaged here, which some of the others had not, so we should have an edge. But if we didn't get it, Placer probably should, since it had built larger base metal mines of this size before. Barrick's gold mines were all good, but much smaller in terms of plant size. There may have been an element of sour grapes in my advice, but it was correct.

Danielson and Whyte later reported: "Hasan had talked with Placer Dome and Teck; he was greatly impressed with the idea that Teck, with its experience with big base metal projects, gave it a better handle on how to run Busang's proposed giant open pit, and was the best choice." They also wrote: "Had events taken a small turn here or there, Teck might have emerged as the victor in the Battle for Busang. David Walsh confessed after it was over that it would have been his choice as well. He liked Teck and its low-key approach to doing business, saying it was fair and always helpful."

We also thought by then that there really might be gold there!

John Willson was quoted in the same book as saying: "We went down a road with Hasan, who was presumably the delegate of the President, and continued negotiating. But there were other companies involved. For a time, it appeared we and Barrick were the front runners, but in the end he turned to Freeport." Hasan would later say that the notion simply came to him that he knew someone in the mining business who ran a big project in Indonesia. He prevailed upon Freeport's chairman, Jim Bob Moffett, to make a proposal to develop it.

Back in the Jakarta hotel, Joan and I had gone upstairs to the cafeteria to have lunch with David Walsh and Roly Francisco. It was a strange meeting and Joan said to me afterwards: "There's something wrong here. Both Walsh and Roly seemed really nervous, and Walsh looked like he'd just seen a ghost. He couldn't even look us in the eye. Let's get out of here." Perhaps that should have been my next clue.

I recall Bob Hasan asking after our lunch at his home: "Do you think this Busang thing is for real? Is the gold really there?" They were good questions, and I don't know to this day if he had begun to suspect something wasn't quite right. Bob was wired in closely to the Indonesian military, and it was a military helicopter that de Guzman later was said to have jumped out of. Possibly that question was the third clue, after my doubts about the validity of the data Paul Kavanagh had shown at *The Northern Miner* symposium and Joan's observations. But doubts take second place when you're on the hunt.

As it happened, we didn't win the beauty contest. Neither did Placer, nor Barrick. In the end, Freeport was handed the right to arrange financing and manage Busang, and earn an interest in the "mine." Bre-X would retain a holding, and there would be certain Indonesian interests involved as well. The deal was announced on 17 February 1997, and Freeport began the due diligence the rest of us as suitors had always intended to do and, just possibly, some in Bre-X might have hoped could be avoided for as long as it could.

Freeport retained Graham Farquharson of Strathcona Minerals to manage this, and it was a good choice. His introduction as a member of the Canadian Mining Hall of Fame reads: "He has earned a reputation as a senior statesman of Canada's mining industry by demonstrating a commitment to integrity, fairness and technical excellence."

The first thing Strathcona did was to begin twinning seven holes adjacent to some of the important, gold-bearing Bre-X drill holes. These showed the presence of only insignificant amounts of gold, nothing close to what Bre-X had been reporting.

How could that be? How could it have escaped the notice of many of the deans of Canadian mining analysts, independent engineers, investors in the Canadian stock market, and leaders of some of the largest gold companies in the world? There appeared to be nothing there, as we say in the business when there is not enough of it. The answer may be that lemming behaviour is not confined to major oil companies. Or just that, when the chase begins, it's human nature not to want to be left behind.

What had really happened?

Farquharson's investigation continued, and he discovered that the bags of pulverized drill core sent to the independent assay labs actually did contain significant amounts of gold. The assays seemed to have been accurate. The only trouble was that the gold hadn't come from the rocks on the site, but had been added to the sample bags somewhere between the drill site and the assay lab.

That wouldn't have been the first time this had been done. Salting of samples has occurred from time to time for as long as people searched for gold. It had just never been done on such a scale and for so long, and fooled so many people.

Furthermore, it hadn't even been done that well. Farquharson saw, as soon as he opened a few sample bags and looked at the ground rock under a microscope, that the gold in it was in rounded grains, just as we have all seen with pebbles in fast moving streams, and could only have come from alluvial, or placer gold in river beds. There is no way that gold from drilling solid, hard rocks could have been rounded in that way.

Evidently, whoever had run the scam hadn't had access to the right kind of gold, but had found a place somewhere in Borneo where he could pan gold from a stream. Then he carefully opened the bags of crushed drill core and added measured amounts of this wrong kind of gold to them, before sending them on to the labs. That would explain the strange assay pattern in Paul Kavanagh's maps. It seems the salter had been very careful in measuring out just the right amount of gold to be credible, but had done it so well that all the results from each line of drill holes assayed almost the same amount of gold, with remarkable and incredible results. The next line was similarly consistent, but with a different gold content. Perhaps the salter had forgotten to put the right numbers in his notebook.

Rudimentary? Yes, but the scam had worked for quite a while. One can imagine the perpetrator getting sucked further and further in as it went on, probably wondering frantically what he was going to do for an exit strategy. Was it just to go sailing out of a helicopter into the jungle?

One final anecdote completes our role in this odd story. Not being one to give up the hunt too easily, one Friday late in the game, after Freeport was granted the deal but before the results of the due diligence work had been announced, I decided on the spur of the moment to call up Freeport's Dick Adkerson, who had succeeded Jim Bob as CEO. I congratulated him on getting the Bre-X deal and said how interested we had been. I asked that he keep us in mind if it ever turned out they wanted a partner to help develop the mine. His response, given in a high-pitched, quavering voice unlike his normal tone, was: "Have you ever been on the property? Have you ever sampled it?" and so on. Perhaps that should have been my fourth clue.

Two days later, on 4 May, the Farquharson report came out. There was no gold there after all, at least to speak of. The market for the shares collapsed and the game was up, although who did what, who knew what, and how anyone involved expected to have a decent exit strategy remains undetermined to this day. As Winston Churchill said in a different context: "It is a riddle, wrapped in a mystery, inside an enigma."

CHAPTER 35

THE SUMITOMO CONNECTION

Respect will open doors. A lack of respect will shut them.
John Bragg

As we have seen, the early years for Teck Corporation and the Keevil Mining Group had coincided with boom years in the Japanese economy and an increasing need for that country to import raw materials to feed its growing industrial base.

It was a nation with an educated and diligent labour force and high aspirations, but its geology was such that it was chronically short of essential commodities like oil, copper, and steelmaking iron and coal, without which many useful secondary products could not be made.

Japan had actually been a producer of mined copper for some 250 years, going back to the start of Sumitomo's Beshi mine at Niihama in 1691, but that mine was small relative to Japan's 1960s consumption needs and in any case was due to close soon. The leading Japanese copper smelting and refining companies were Sumitomo, Dowa Mining, Nippon, Mitsui, and Mitsubishi, and following the Beshi closure, only Dowa would continue to mine any copper in the island nation.

So, Japan had needed to locate and procure copper concentrates and other raw materials from offshore to fulfill its growing needs. The smelting companies and their related international trading companies began an aggressive search for such opportunities, often by offering financing to encourage the development of new mines in other countries. This would be replicated in coal procurement with financial and purchasing support for new coal mines in southeastern BC in the late 1960s, and again in northern BC 10 years later. It was a good plan for Japan, and necessary.

Canada was an obvious candidate in this quest to develop new copper mines, and one of the first significant investments by the Japanese in this area had been Sumitomo Metal Mining's agreement to finance Bethlehem Copper's project in 1960. The leader on the Japanese side was Mr Kenjiro Kawakami, who is known as the father of Japanese overseas copper investing.

The pattern would continue with larger and larger investments, including Sumitomo's backing of Cerro de Pasco's Rio Blanco copper project in Chile, and financings by various Japanese smelting consortia of projects in Papua New Guinea, Indonesia, Peru, and Zambia over the ensuing 10 years. In Canada, Cominco had been deeply involved with a Japanese financing consortium negotiating the possible Valley Copper development around 1970, but in the end didn't proceed with it.

Back in 1966, we had agreed to sell copper concentrates from our Temagami mine to Sumitomo, although this was an indirect contact since we were actually selling through Phillipp Brothers, then a major metal trading company.

Around the same time, we had arranged to bring in two partners to help finance our ongoing research and development costs for our DIGHEM airborne geophysical system. One was SOQUEM, the Quebec Crown Corporation, and the other was Dowa Mining. Doug Fraser and I hit up a good friendship with its Canadian representative, Minami-san, and we would go on to deploy the new technology to discover the Montcalm nickel deposit in a joint venture with Dowa.

Our personal relationship with SMM began in 1970, after its protege, Bethlehem Copper, had announced plans to issue a large block of treasury shares to a third party. This in turn had prompted our attempt to compete with a higher bid, to try to buy that block ourselves, but we were turned down. As noted earlier, I had visited Kawakami-san in Tokyo shortly after, and it was evident that he had been as disappointed as we were in the outcome, and would have preferred that Teck be the purchaser of those shares. We had shared a few stories, thus beginning a relationship that would continue for decades.

We would visit Sumitomo every time we were in Japan, and the successive SMM chief executives would visit us each time they came to Canada, both sides looking for opportunities to work together but also building up warm personal relationships.

Sometimes it would end up with amusing mishaps, such as the time my father and I took Kawakami-san's successor, Akira Fujisaki, to dinner and had plans to attend a Maple Leafs hockey game in Toronto. My father was back into one of his favourite Cadillac cars at the time, and as we drove from the restaurant to Maple Leaf Gardens he ran out of gas. I'll never forget how the three of us trudged up the hill in deep snow trying to find a downtown gas station that would lend us a can of fuel to get going again. From then on, Fujisaki-san tended to make his visits in the summer months. His successor,

Masamichi Fujimori, may have heard the story because he too would tend to visit us in the summer months, although by that time we were based in balmier Vancouver.

Fujimori-san's successor was Akihiko Shinozaki, who in turn was succeeded by Moriki Aoyagi, each of whom we would become quite close to, continuing an association that would lead eventually to SMM acquiring a significant shareholding in Teck. The strong relationship has continued through Moriki's successor Koichi Fukushima, Nobumasa Kemori, and the current president, Yoshiaki Nakazato.

The Canada-Japan Businessmen's Conference

The annual Canada-Japan Businessmen's Conference, started by Alcan's David Culver and Hisao Makita in 1976, became a forum I would attend every year along with Bob Hallbauer, Keith Steeves, and others from Teck. Alternating between Canada and Japan in successive years, the conference was held in places like Halifax, Toronto, Ottawa, Victoria, Vancouver, and Banff in Canada, and Tokyo, Yokohama, Kyoto, Osaka, Fukuoka, and Karuizawa in Japan. The participants were CEOs and senior managers of companies from both countries, from as many as nine different business sectors.

Golf was often an unofficial part of the social agenda, and we would commonly meet for games with our Nissho-Iwai coal partners and with people from other companies we were working with. This included games with successive SMM presidents Shinozaki-san in Vancouver, Aoyagi-san in Japan and Toronto, and, long after the CJBC program had been disbanded, succeeding SMM CEOs Fukushima-san in Japan and on Vancouver Island, and Kemori-san in Japan.

I was co-chair of the CJBC Metals Sector for several years, and my associate chair at a 1993 session in Banff was Sumitomo's Shinozaki-san. This was one of the better sessions for entertainment outside of the business sessions, with fake rivers set up in the convention centre where participants could pan for gold. There were Klondike dancing girl sessions at Lake Louise, joined on the stage by such Canadian side luminaries as Keith Steeves and Cominco's Ted Fletcher.

As it happened, Mr Shinozaki's son was due to get married in Banff the following week, and at the close of the business sessions it was customary for each co-chair to stand and thank his counterpart. So I thanked my co-chair for his good work in drawing out all of the important business points, and then announced: "Congratulations are in order. Mr Shinozaki's son is getting married in Banff next week."

The interpreter duly translated this important piece of information, and the entire Japanese side burst out laughing. It seems she had misunderstood, and announced: "Shinozaki-san is getting married in Banff next week." Of course, most of their side understood enough English to know what I'd really said, and caught on pretty quickly (see colour page 14).

In 1996, the conference moved to Fukuoka on the southernmost major Japanese island of Kyushu. After the meeting, Joan and I visited Sumitomo's Hishikari gold mine at the south end of the island, following which we went on to Tokyo to meet Aoyagi-san privately to negotiate a joint venture interest in Sumitomo's Pogo gold prospect in Alaska. It was a successful meeting, and we would go on to build a new gold mine on the property some years later.

The business dealings around the CJBC were serious and the frivolities just that. It was a great way to build relationships between the key players of two major trading nations. We made many friends in a number of the Japanese trading, smelting, and coal companies, but those from Sumitomo Metal Mining seemed destined to stand out. Perhaps it was because so many of its executives were working geologists and engineers, like us.

Unfortunately, the Canada-Japan Businessmen's Conference no longer exists, having been abandoned in the early 2000s after more than 25 successful years. It is missed by those of us from both sides of the ocean who attended and developed many lasting friendships.

Metallgesellschaft Decides to Sell Its Temagami Position

Meanwhile, Metallgesellschaft, the German company that had held a 49 per cent partnership interest in Temagami Mining Company, had transferred that holding to Metall Mining Corporation, a new public Canadian subsidiary formed to hold its international mining assets. Shortly after that, Metallgesellschaft made an unfortunate speculation in oil futures that almost bankrupted the 150-year-old company. As a result, it found it necessary to sell its interest in Metall Mining, which then became an independent public company, renamed Inmet Mining Corporation.

With no more German shareholder connection, Klaus Zeitler eventually retired from the presidency of Inmet, although he remained a valued, independent director of Teck. Inmet's board appointed the renowned Bill James, who years earlier had been a director of Teck and CEO of Falconbridge as well, as its new president. If all of this sounds a bit incestuous, it really wasn't. Just the way things worked in a small mining world.

James decided there really wasn't much point in Inmet, which had its own major investments on the drawing boards, continuing to own a minority, illiquid, non-controlling interest in Teck, no matter how valuable it might be or not be. So in early 1998 he gave us notice that he intended to sell his 49 per cent of Temagami and, gentleman that he always was, gave us plenty of time to find a friendly buyer.

That we would do, but first we tried to explore an alternative solution, which was to find a way to have those Class A shares held by Inmet converted to ordinary Class B shares, gradually reducing the number of Class A shares outstanding under our dual share structure. This was something the investment community seemed likely to want to see done eventually.

Our plan was to have Teck make an offer, including a modest premium, to all of its Class A shareholders to convert part or all of their holding into Class B shares. The idea was that Inmet would turn in its A shares, both those held directly, and, through its 49 per cent interest in Temagami, replacing them with ordinary B shares.

Temagami was prepared to tender enough of its own A shares as well, so that its effective control position would remain at the same percentage, no higher and no lower. The idea was to end up reducing the number of Class A shares outstanding, but not to use that arrangement to increase (or decrease) its existing control position. This would allow Inmet to get out without requiring us to replace it with a new partner, and seemed to be a fair and sensible solution for all.

There was one potential problem. A large Canadian pension fund had long held a fairly substantial block of Class A shares as well, and if we proceeded with the plan and many of the other A shareholders turned in their shares but the fund didn't, we might have inadvertently handed control of the company to the pension fund, or whomever it might sell to. That was not part of the plan, so we decided to ask the fund to agree to tender its Class A shares to the offer, either all if it preferred, or at least, like us, a sufficient number to maintain the status quo, rather than increasing its voting position. It all sounded pretty reasonable.

First, though, we asked two major investment banks to give us a fairness opinion on the appropriate premium, since presumably those Class A shareholders would require some consideration to encourage them to tender their shares. Each advisor said that the proper ratio would be 1.15 Class B shares for each Class A tendered, or a 15 per cent premium.

So Teck director Brian Aune and I went over to see the pension fund to make our proposal. After some discussion with our usual contacts that seemed to be going well, they left us alone while they sought approval from senior colleagues. They soon came back with a vice-president who said he would agree to tender as proposed, except that he wouldn't do it for just a 15 per cent bonus. He wanted a 30 per cent premium. His actual words were: "We don't believe in multiple voting shares in principle, but since we own them, we want a bigger premium to turn them in."

That did seem a bit inconsistent to us. Naturally, we couldn't accept it, but he was adamant and refused to negotiate. We left saying we'd have to go to Plan B, but we didn't really have one. I think he knew it, and expected us back.

And Sumitomo Metal Mining Buys It

So we had to develop a Plan B, and I suggested we go to Tokyo to visit our old friends at Sumitomo Metal Mining to see if they'd be interested in buying Inmet's position. We had never discussed this with them before and had no particular reason to think they would be interested, but decided it was worth a shot.

The Japanese style was often said to be decision-making by developing a consensus, taking time to reflect on matters thoroughly, rather than deciding on the spot, but Bill James had given us enough time that we could live with that, even if it took months. So I called to say I'd be in Tokyo shortly and would like to make our usual courtesy call on SMM. I outlined briefly the opportunity we would like to discuss, so as not to take them by surprise.

A few days later, I showed up at their office. By this time, Aoyagi-san was president and Shinozaki-san had moved on to chairman. As was customary, Aoyagi-san sat across from me and Shinozaki-san sat on his left. With them were Ueno-san and Ken Sudo, whom we knew well and who had "stayed over from a prior meeting," as well as Yokoyama-san, general manager of corporate planning.

We exchanged a few pleasantries and stories, and then I popped the question. It went like this, without much elaboration.

Keevil: "Would you like to buy the Inmet position and be our new 49 per cent partner?"

Aoyagi-san glances at Shinozaki-san, and says: "Yes."

Well, it wasn't quite that quick, but pretty close. Decisiveness and support of their old friends seems to be characteristic of Sumitomo Metal Mining, which is probably why we get along with each other so well.

Aoyagi-san turned the conversation to details of the proposed investment and asked a few general questions. He asked about succession, and I told him it wasn't cast in stone. He replied that was okay because he didn't know who his successor would be either. It became clear that they had decided they wanted to do the deal, hence the large group that had pre-cleared the consensus, and the discussion turned to tactics. Did I think the seller was ready or was it waiting for the market to improve? They asked me if I would do the price negotiation for them.

The next day, I met to follow it up with Yokoyama-san, Goto-san, and Mura-san from their legal department, and Nakazato-san, then from Mr Yokoyama's department.

The purpose of this second meeting was to flesh out some of the necessary detail and raise questions that needed to be answered, such as whether there was there any need for government approvals. There would be other details to be resolved by lawyers to get an actual agreement, but by and large it was a done deal.

So much for long negotiations and time spent building consensus. Even given our long friendship, corporate and personal, and relationship as suppliers of high-grade copper concentrates out of Highland Valley Copper, this surprised me. Like Brian Aune and Keith Steeves in different parts of our history, my reaction was confirmation that these really are my kind of people. As each had said about Teck at those times, I too could say about Sumitomo: "I like this company."

And we have had the pleasure of having two Sumitomo people serve on our board of directors ever since. They've included Ueno-san and Kuriyama-san, both of whom we had met at the Hishikari mine; Abe-san, who is an accomplished geologist and expert on Pogo gold; Sudo-san, a long-time respected miner; Mochihara-san, who'd come over from Mitsibishi after Ken Sudo took ill; Kubota-san, whose calm knowledge has been invaluable; and Fukoda-san and several others. Each has made a real contribution during his tenure.

Ironically, when we had selected Metallgesellschaft as partners over Messina, back in 1977, it had been because of its long, 150-year history in the business. That history had ended with an unfortunate speculation in oil futures. Our new Sumitomo partners trumped that long Metall history in spades, having been in the mining business for more than 250 years, and having grown into one of Japan's major metals producers.

Moriki Aoyagi retired after a few years and was succeeded as president by Koichi Fukushima, he in turn by Dr Nobumasa Kemori from the Niihama nickel refinery, and most recently by Yoshiaki Nakazato, who had been part of the SMM team when Aoyagi-san and Shinozaki-san had agreed to purchase the Teck A shares previously held by Metall. The friendship has stood the test of time and grown, and hopefully will evolve into many opportunities for both companies to work together in the coming years.

CHAPTER 36

FINDING ANTAMINA, A JEWEL
IN THE ANDES

No bird soars in a calm.
Wilbur Wright

Around the same time, we would enter into another agreement with Inmet that would lead to the major new Antamina mine in Peru, one of our most important mine-building projects yet.

The first recorded reference to copper in the area is in an 1860s report by Italian explorer Antonio Raimondi. He had climbed into the upper Ancash region, 4,000 metres above sea level, where he was told of an old mining camp with copper diggings put down years earlier, probably by the Incas. By the 1960s, copper and zinc mining had become an important industry elsewhere in Peru, with most of the key properties owned by three major companies: Cerro de Pasco Corporation, run by Bob Koenig, a friend whom we encountered in earlier stories; the Marcona Mining Company; and Southern Peru Copper.

But by the early 1970s Peru had been stricken by the same urge to nationalize resources that had affected Chile, Mexico, and others, including even some parts of Canada. After three years of recurring strikes by the "proletariat of mine workers," Cerro found it necessary to capitulate to the trend. Its properties, including the major Cerro de Pasco mine and smelter and a copper prospect it held called Antamina, were taken over by the government and put into a state firm called Centromin. Marcona was nationalized in 1975. Only Southern Peru Copper remained under private ownership.

Time passed, and by 1991 Peru had encountered a severe recession and rampant inflation and had embarked on a program of privatization, or reprivatization to be more accurate.

Centromin was by then, not surprisingly, the country's biggest state-owned copper, zinc, silver and lead mining company. It was announced that it would be sold, with Credit Suisse First Boston and a local investment bank retained to evaluate it and conduct the process. They proposed an auction for all of the company's assets in a single transaction, with a base price of US$340 million and an additional commitment to invest US$240 million in its operations over the ensuing three to five years.

At least 28 firms signed up for the auction, including companies from Canada, China, Japan, and the United Kingdom. Excitement prevailed until April 1994 and the first call for bids, when none of them submitted a proposal at all. It seemed that a series of news articles mysteriously appearing in US journals just weeks before the bid date had raised concerns about environmental issues at some of the older Centromin mines and smelters, pointing out that the liability for ameliorating this was not defined in the bidding process.

However, these problems were resolved over the next while, and by 1996 some specific Centromin assets were being offered for sale separately. Among these was Cerro's old Antamina copper prospect.

Antamina, a Different Kind of Copper Deposit

For readers not fully versed in the geology of copper deposits, Antamina is not like the large, low-grade deposits found at Highland Valley and most of those that have been developed in Chile and the United States. The latter tend to be of a class known as porphyry coppers, with mineralization widely disseminated in an igneous host rock, usually granitic, which had intruded the surrounding rocks ages ago and solidified as a rock containing small amounts of copper, in some cases enough to be economically mineable.

Those same hot intrusive granites often affected parts of the surrounding rocks into which they were being intruded, in a process called wall-rock alteration. In cases where those earlier rocks were particularly susceptible to being chemically changed, such as limestones, they may form what are called skarn deposits, containing exotic new minerals like calcium silicates and, in some cases where the hot fluids were metal-bearing, minerals containing copper or zinc.

Skarn deposits are generally much smaller and more erratic than disseminated porphyry copper ones, but can be much higher grade in copper, zinc, and other metals. Craigmont was a skarn deposit, smaller at some 30 million tonnes compared with many billion tonnes at the Highland Valley porphyry copper deposits only a few kilometres to the north, but with five times the ore grade in copper.

Antamina is another skarn deposit, although much larger. Peter Laznicka, in the textbook *Giant Metallic Deposits*, called it the world's largest continuous copper-zinc skarn.

Privatization by Centromin

When the Antamina property was put up for auction in 1996, it had reported proven and probable reserves of 129 million tonnes at an average grade (combining copper and zinc values) of 2.2 per cent copper-equivalent. Interestingly, this was about the same grade as Craigmont, but the deposit was already said to be four times bigger. It was also about the same size and grade as our recent San Nicolas discovery in Mexico.

This was still not a large tonnage by modern open pit standards, but the ore grade was good, and there was obvious geological potential to extend the resource. However, with the known copper deposit being primarily under a lake, at an elevation of over 4,000 metres, and surrounded by high mountain walls that would have to be dealt with, it seemed that development would present difficult topographical and engineering issues.

Teck didn't put in a bid at the initial auction. It was obviously a good prospect, although hardly a slamdunk operationally. The size of the resource as advertised was similar to the more easily developed San Nicolas discovery, with both having potential to become larger with more exploration. As well, we were actively exploring the low-altitude Petaquilla property in Panama, and were concentrating on becoming the developer of Diamond Fields' Voisey's Bay nickel prospect in Newfoundland.

However, two Canadian companies close to us, Inmet Mining and Rio Algom, grasped the upside potential, did enter the auction, and beat out the two main competitors, Noranda and Rio Tinto. Inmet and Rio Algom had each considered bidding independently, but concluded that if a mine was to be built on the remote property, it would have to be so large and expensive that neither company could do it alone, so they decided to join forces and bid as a partnership.

Once again Peru's Centromin, on Credit Suisse First Boston's advice, had defined how the bidding should proceed, and how the winner would be selected. Bids had to include an upfront cash payment of at least US$17.5

million and a commitment to spend a set amount in exploration and engineering work over a two-year option period. The bids would also include an amount the winner would commit to spending in the ensuing five years on mine development, the "investment amount," if it wished to continue with the project and develop a mine. If the winner walked away after the initial two-year option, the property and all data would revert to Centromin. An interesting wrinkle in the bid rules was that if the winning company did make the development commitment after the two-year option, and then spent less on mine development than its "investment amount," it would only have to pay Centromin a penalty of 30 per cent of the shortfall.

The winner of the auction would be determined by adding up the cash payment plus the two-year work commitment plus 30 per cent of the investment amount. Obviously, the higher that final number, even though it was optional, the better chance the bidder had of winning the auction.

The lead entrepreneur on the Inmet side was our good friend Klaus Zeitler, then still its CEO. As he recalled about his first visit to the property and the realization of how big it could be:

> I am not sure anymore whether it was the extensive copper mineralization we saw during that trek to the camp, the hallucinations caused by the thin air while trying to sleep at night in the freezing cold, or the scientific explanations of my geologist colleagues led by Ian Pirie that convinced us. But after walking the whole Antamina bowl, visiting some accessible underground exploration tunnels, studying some geological maps and making reasonably conservative estimates, we were convinced we were standing, walking and sleeping on one of the largest mineralized karst (a.k.a. skarn) deposits in the world.
>
> From there it did not take long to come to the conclusion that, if we are at all serious, we should assess this project on the basis of an ore body of half a billion tons and be prepared to risk some $20 million to prove up the monster. Then we could decide whether we should develop the project or sell it to one or two of the big fish in the mining industry for a decent profit.

Klaus and Peter Rozee, Inmet's in-house lawyer and later a valued Teck executive, both recognized the potential to expand the resource significantly with further drilling and were determined to win the auction.

They realized that the bid structure would encourage interested parties to bid even more on the final investment amount than they ever expected to spend to actually build the mine, since the penalty was only 30 per cent of any shortfall. The penalty would in effect just be the cost of purchasing the property. A smart bidder would be able to increase his chances of winning by putting in the very highest final payment imaginable, within reasonable limits.

Inmet figured it out quickly, but as Peter Rozee recalls it, Rio Algom and particularly Ulli Rath, who was the promoter of the project internally, took some convincing that it was proper to make an investment commitment substantially in excess of the anticipated real cost to build a mine. Fortunately, Inmet prevailed, and the two bid accordingly.

At the time, the expectation in the marketplace was that a mine, if the indicated reserves could be confirmed, might cost about US$1.2 billion. In the end, there were three bidders: Rio Tinto, with a final investment amount of US$900 million; Noranda, with US$1.9 billion, a pretty aggressive number I'm sure they thought would win, being well over the expected construction cost; and the Inmet/Rio Algom team, at a mind-boggling US$2.5 billion.

Naturally and ingeniously, Inmet/Rio Algom had won it. Their bid was for US$20 million upfront, a commitment to spend at least US$13.5 million on exploration and development, and the optional US$2.5 billion investment amount. It was an aggressive, imaginative bid, and a credit to Klaus Zeitler of Inmet and Lawrie Reinertson, then CEO of Rio Algom.

The bids were opened and the winner determined one Friday in July 1996. Klaus and Lawrie held a press conference in Toronto to announce that they had won the auction and to outline their plans. As Klaus described it, they were brimming with pride and happiness. Unfortunately, it did not last long in Rio Algom, because two days later Reinertson died of a heart attack. He was succeeded by American miner Pat James.

Klaus soon left Inmet and the project as well. As he recalls: "When they saw our bid for $2.5 billion, some of Inmet's shareholders did not understand the strategy and thought that I suffered from megalomania. So, soon after we won the bid together with Rio Algom, Inmet and I parted company and I joined Teck as senior vice-president." Klaus would, as we shall see, eventually become involved with the project again.

At this point, Rio Algom and Inmet had a tiger by the tail, but a good one if the exploration worked out and financial conditions continued to be reasonable. They had two years to explore and decide, with the final commitment required by September 1998. That seemed far enough off.

They went to work on the property almost immediately, with a major program using five drills to confirm the size and grade of the deposit. By early 1998, they had increased the size of the indicated resource fourfold to 500 million tonnes grading 1.2 per cent copper and 1.0 per cent zinc, with values in silver and molybdenum as well. The combined metal grade was equivalent to 1.66 per cent copper, which was exceptionally high for such a large deposit.

At the same time, Inmet and Rio Algom carried out environmental baseline studies and, along with engineering giant Bechtel, completed preliminary engineering studies for the proposed mine and mill, or concentrator. The planned facility would have a production capacity of 70,000 tonnes per day, or 25 million tonnes per year, sufficient for an initial mine life of 20 years. The construction cost was estimated to be US$1.6 billion, before preproduction interest and working capital.

The two companies had begun financing negotiations with their banks and Japanese consumers, led by Mike Parrett of Rio, but whether these could be completed successfully and on time was becoming debatable as economic conditions worsened.

The Asian Crisis Intervenes

Everything was apparently going as planned technically, but "the best-laid schemes of mice and men gang aft agley," as Robbie Burns wrote. Or, as Murphy's Law says: "If anything can go wrong, it will."

While Rio Algom, Inmet, and Bechtel were completing the engineering and design work on the project, financial events in some Asian countries began to unravel. It started with the collapse of the Thai currency in July 1997, but soon spread to South Korea and engulfed much of the region, other than China. The "Asian Crisis" began to affect other parts of the world as far away as Brazil and Russia. Within a year, Russia had defaulted on its debts, and even in the US, highly rated funds like Long-Term Capital Management were failing. In mid-1998, major investment indices in Canada and the US fell by as much as 30 per cent. Investors, fearing the worst, as they will from time to time, rushed to safety.

This was starting to happen just as Inmet and Rio Algom were approaching that fateful September 1998 when they would have to fish or cut bait – to actually commit to build it or walk away from the project. Under the circumstances, it seemed highly unlikely that they would be able to find the capital to build the planned mine, the expected construction cost of which by then was closer to $2 billion, including pre-production interest. Yet, they had been remarkably successful in proving up a much bigger, more attractive copper deposit, one that would make an important mine if it could possibly be financed into production. It was a major geological and engineering success story (see colour page 14). ·

Inmet and Rio considered a plan under which they would each reduce to a 40 per cent interest, and bring in a Japanese company or consortium for a 20 per cent equity, but it was debatable whether Inmet could handle even that level of commitment, and as well there didn't seem to be a lot of enthusiasm on the Japanese side at the time. So, early in 1998, Inmet announced that it would be seeking buyers for its interest. It asked potential bidders to sign confidentiality agreements, which Teck and some others did.

Gary Jones, our main evaluations engineer and vice-president of corporate development, was en route back from working on our Lobo-Marte gold exploration project in Chile when this was announced. I caught up with him in Miami and asked him to divert to Toronto to take a look at the data room. As Gary tells it: "I only had a sports jacket with me and it was minus 30 degrees in Toronto, so after half a day in the data room I took an hour off to buy a winter overcoat."

Teck was in especially solid financial condition, including the $500 million in additional cash we'd come out of the Diamond Fields adventure with. Because the Antamina copper-zinc deposit had by then grown about four times in size and actually looked very attractive, despite the financial crisis, we came to the conclusion that we should make a serious offer. However, 50 per cent of a $2 billion construction cost was more than we were prepared to handle given our size and general economic conditions at the time, so we decided we should seek a third partner to share the risk and opportunity.

By this time, Bill James had been appointed CEO of Inmet and Klaus Zeitler had joined the management team of Teck. Interestingly, particularly in light of later events, and at Klaus's prompting, we considered making a friendly offer to acquire Inmet for Teck shares. At least some Inmet shareholders had indicated they would support this, and using our cash together with Inmet's, and some Inmet asset sales, we thought we probably could have financed the full 50 per cent of Antamina.

Where we would be now had we been able to pull this off will be forever unclear. It was an interesting idea, but was impractical in view of the time it would take to gain all necessary approvals and close such a deal, and given the need for Inmet and Rio to make a firm commitment to Peru's Centromin by the coming September, just a few months away.

So we were back to looking for a third-party partner. Unfortunately, the confidentiality agreement we had signed contained a clause that prevented us from talking to other companies about joining forces. We knew Rio Tinto was still interested, and was looking at the data. We surmised Noranda would be as well, since it had been one of the earlier bidders when Inmet and Rio Algom had won the auction.

We told Bill James we wanted a release so that we could talk to some of the other interested companies and perhaps form a consortium so we could make a good bid. Bill refused, and would hold firm for some time. It appeared that he didn't want the limited number of interested parties (if indeed there were many others in the middle of that Asian Crisis) ganging up on him and jointly lowballing the bidding. That was understandable, although we had concluded that without a partner we were unlikely to bid at all.

Still, we had signed the confidentiality agreement and had sent our "team" of Gary Jones into the data room to begin studying the detailed work the two companies had carried out since the initial auction. As we learned later from Peter Rozee, Inmet actually had two identical data rooms a few floors apart in its Toronto office building. One floor was being used for Rio Tinto, which had a huge team of engineers and financial types, at least a dozen people, poring over the data. In the other room was Teck's team, initially just Gary alone, but later joined by Mike Lipkewich and two others after Gary had called for help.

Gary was enthusiastic, as he often was about good opportunities, and his enthusiasm spread to the others, as well as back to our head office. We decided we really did want to be a player, but were still not able or prepared to go for the full 50 per cent interest Inmet had for sale.

As it happened, Rio Algom was just as interested as we were in encouraging Inmet to be reasonable and let us find a partner since, if Inmet failed to find a good buyer, Rio Algom might end up having to fund 100 per cent itself, which would have been a non-starter as well. So Pat James' project man Ulli Rath became our new best friend, trying to encourage Bill James to release us, but it seemed not to be working.

One day though, I was talking to David Kerr, Noranda's president, about something completely different, and it turned out they had not signed a CA after all. They were permitted to talk to anyone they liked. We were not, but it didn't take long for us both to figure out that the CA didn't say anything about our listening – just not talking. So we listened, and it was evident that Noranda was in exactly the same boat we were in. They were equally interested in getting involved with the project, but also didn't want to be exposed to a full 50 per cent in view of the Asian Crisis.

Now the lawyers reading this may conclude quickly that our listening proactively was not permitted any more than talking, but it did get things going. It evolved that Rio Algom was also prepared to move down from its 50 per cent interest, and there was room for a three-way deal, if we could convince Bill James to let us do it.

In one further indicator of how small the mining world is, who should have been advising James? Sure enough, Don Lindsay and his CIBC band of merry men.

With Ulli Rath's help, we finally managed to convince Bill, got our release to talk to Noranda, and we agreed quickly on the outlines of an agreement. Noranda and Teck would each buy 25 per cent from Inmet, Rio Algom would reduce down to 33.3 per cent and assign 8.3 per cent to each of us, so that the end result would be a simple three-way partnership, with each of us holding a 33.3 per cent interest. The total purchase price for Inmet's share: $70 million plus a royalty.

The agreement was signed in May 1998, giving us about four months to get any necessary financing in line, and then either make our joint US$2.5 billion investment commitment to the Peruvian government or abandon the project. Obtaining the financing would be a tall task even in the best of times. It was a particularly audacious move in those uncertain times and, unfortunately, would be seen as such by many in the investment community for several years.

At the deal closing, there was a strange scent of myrrh and frankincense in the air, although the market's olfactory senses seemed less advanced than our own. That may be inevitable, because sometimes the best moves are the risky ones that are, for a time, unpopular. Deal-making 101 still holds that, if they were obvious, they wouldn't be available at a reasonable price.

Teck Offers Part of the Deal to Cominco

In taking on this commitment, I had in mind from the start that we would invite Cominco to participate as a partner on our side. The newly expanded Antamina was by then obviously an exceptional project, the kind most mining people dream of discovering and would be grateful to be offered. Since Cominco was primarily a zinc company, already experienced in Peru with the Cajamarquilla lead-zinc refinery, and was a partner with us in the similarly altitude-challenged Quebrada Blanca mine, it seemed to make complete sense.

So we offered Cominco the opportunity to take a third of our interest, or 11.1 per cent of the Antamina partnership, leaving Teck at 22.2 per cent. This was a financial level we in Teck would find comfortable, and if as many envisaged our two companies might eventually be merged, the combined Teck/Cominco would still be an equal one-third partner with each of Noranda and Rio Algom in the project. There was also some symmetry, in that in QB, Cominco as the sponsor had held a slightly larger interest than Teck and here that would simply be reversed.

Why do things that make so much sense turn out to be so difficult? Is it Finnegan's Law?

Unfortunately, there seemed to be no buy-in from Cominco's mine operating people, who may have been still smarting from their construction cost overrun at QB, and in fact would even argue in favour of selling that mine a year later. Their geologists were more interested, quite naturally, given the size and grade of the ore deposit, but seemed reluctant to stick their heads up lest they be chopped off. This, we had found, was considered to be a clear and present danger in the Cominco of the day.

David Thompson had voted for it at the Teck level, but was reluctant to press the issue at Cominco, perhaps because of its ongoing debt issues. With no sponsor willing to raise his head, it was hard to see how the independent directors could be expected to grasp the ball.

In fact, one well-respected independent asked: "Why would we consider taking a minority interest in a mine?" The obvious answer was that Teck had shown the way to grow value and had done extremely well with less than 100 per cent interests in a number of new mines as it overtook Cominco and much of the Canadian mining industry. Opportunity does not exist only in 100 per cent lumps.

Also, Antamina was potentially a very good mine, and other well-established companies like Noranda had already taken a minority interest in this very project. Unfortunately, that argument didn't sway non-mining board members in the absence of a strong supporter from management.

We gave it one last shot with a couple of the more knowledgeable independent directors, meeting in David Thompson's conference room. David Sinclair had been the head of Coopers Lybrand, later PwC, for Western Canada. A canny Scot who had never spent a dollar foolishly and knew quite a bit about both investing and the mining business, he argued cogently for the deal. Also in the meeting by telephone from Toronto was director Don Worth, who had been the primary mining advisor to the Canadian Imperial Bank of Commerce for years, as well as David Thompson and me. Thompson had two aides present, Bill Armstrong, a top geologist who was an ore reserves specialist, and Cominco's top smelting man from Trail, Roger Watson.

Thompson was Cominco CEO, but remained silent the whole meeting. Armstrong raised a question about whether there should be more drilling to be absolutely sure of the ore reserves (yes, obviously, but not important), and Watson said the zinc concentrate was of no interest to Cominco since the route to the coast would not pass by Cominco's Peruvian refinery at Cajamarquilla (true enough, but irrelevant).

David Sinclair kept up the good fight for as long as he could, but without support was running out of steam. It was not going too well. Then Don Worth finally spoke up and drawled: "Waaa'll, I remember back in the early 1980s when our bank lost a lot of money in Peru." Quite true. It had been tough back then, under entirely different government and security conditions. Silence. Nobody spoke up further in support, and David Sinclair, having shot his bolt, folded his cards, as did I.

What to do now? I'd told our directors that with our strong cash position we could easily justify a 25 per cent investment in the joint venture on our own, but that 33 per cent could be a bit of a stretch. The plan of letting Cominco have a third of our position meant we would be committed only to 22 per cent in Teck, but would have an additional interest indirectly through Cominco. Now, with the embarrassment of it being rejected by our own associated company, we would be exposed to a full 33 per cent, which was more than I'd said we should easily handle.

Reluctantly, I had to call David Kerr and Pat James and admit to them a bit of what had happened, saying that in view of our inability to bring our own supposedly controlled affiliate along to the party it seemed as though we ought to reduce our interest to a level more in keeping with our financial position in Teck, the "parent company" of Cominco. Some kid that was. Rebellion is natural at some stages in life, but usually at a younger age.

Kerr and Pat James both thought the outcome was as ludicrous as I did, but were quick to agree to a change in our partnership ratios to 25 per cent Teck and 37.5 per cent Rio and Noranda. Given the strength of the new partnership, both were quite happy to have more. We had to modify the management committee agreement slightly, and the change was done.

This all occurred late on a Thursday, and as it happened we were having our first ever joint strategic planning meeting with Cominco at Semiahmoo in Washington State that weekend. Saturday morning, Cominco director Don Worth arrived from Toronto and saw me in the hotel lobby. His first words were: "I really think we should have done that deal!"

I could have throttled him, old friend that he was, but the damage had been done. We'd had to give away a serious chunk of one of the best ore deposits discovered in decades.

I learned later that Bill Armstrong had actually had no real concerns about the drilling density and thought Cominco should have taken the deal, but didn't feel comfortable in sticking his neck out to support it. Then a few months later, Roger Watson came to us and demanded that we arrange to sell some of the zinc output to Cajamarquilla. It seemed it no longer mattered that it wouldn't pass by Cominco's refinery on the way to the coast after all.

Zounds!

Arranging the Financing

It was still necessary for the three of us, Teck, Noranda, and Rio Algom, to raise the financing for what had by now grown into a major mining project and would take over $2 billion to build. While as a group we were stronger than the Inmet/Rio Algom partnership had been, the world was still transfixed by the Asian Crisis, and bank financing was far from a sure thing.

Key to our plans, as with many major projects at the time, was to get the Japan Export-Import Bank (JEXIM) in as a lender. This lead commitment would help us to get a reasonable amount of additional financing on decent terms from other sources, including the main banks each of us used.

So, one of the first things we did was travel over to Japan to try to line this up. It was Mike Parrett of Rio Algom returning, along with David Bumstead of Noranda, and with Richard Mundie and me on the Teck side. Parrett was the financial guy who'd been trying to deal with this for months, Bumstead because as the chief sales and marketing guy for Noranda he would have known the Japanese buyers, and Richard and me because we knew most of the Japanese players from our CJBC days.

We managed to get some meetings set up with Mitsubishi Corporation, which had been the trading company assigned to Antamina from past dealings.

On arriving in Tokyo late the first day, we went to a Japanese fast food restaurant. It was a noisy setting with food flying all over the place and hearty Japanese hooting and hollering as each piece was delivered, accompanied by saki or beer. The next day, we visited Mitsubishi for the official business. One of the keys to getting JEXIM financing had always been that there had to be a Japanese company participating in the consortium. The rule of thumb was that this had to be at least a 15 per cent interest, and that they had to be purchasing a reasonable amount of the metal output.

Having had our interest reduced already by what had happened at Cominco, we didn't want to have to give up that much, and had hoped to keep the group dilution at no more than 10 per cent. David Bumstead pointed out that Noranda would prefer to give up no interest at all, and could place the concentrate elsewhere than Japan if necessary. Since Noranda was in the concentrate purchasing business for its own smelters, and this was actually Bumstead's job, we could see they might have a different idea, but Mike Parrett was with us that JEXIM financing was critical.

As it turned out, the Mitsubishi team wasn't keen on taking even a 10 per cent participation. In fact, what they really wanted was something more like zero, which would of course dash any hope of JEXIM participation. As one of them said, the most recent big copper project in the world to have been financed was "the last of the current generation of new copper mines." Once again the world didn't need more copper. They assumed there would be no need for more big new mines for a while, and they would prefer to decline, politely of course.

This was a serious problem. The investment community was already crucifying us. Teck's share price was in the penalty box, big time, despite what we still believed was a very good deal. The market was really concerned on three grounds.

First, how could we possibly arrange over $2 billion in financing with the Asian Crisis unresolved? Second, how could we expect to build the proposed mine on budget when nobody in the entire world had ever done that for any project and any product at such an altitude in the High Andes? That included Cominco's recently completed mine at Quebrada Blanca. Finally, metal prices were still weak, and weakening, so why should investors support someone building a new mine in that economic environment, even if it had been at sea level and simple to build? These were actually all pretty good points, and if Japan wouldn't play ball it could have been game over.

Meanwhile the rest of the industry was grumbling about low prices, low profitability, and the general need to restrain production. Doug Yearley, the CEO of Phelps Dodge at the time, told the Annual CIBC Mining Dinner in Toronto that the trouble with the copper business was that there were always "rogues" who would flood the market with new production at the worst time. He didn't mention us by name, but we three amigos knew exactly whom he meant. So did the market.

But we replied confidently to Mitsubishi: "Actually, this is not the last of the previous generation of big, low-grade copper projects. It's a special case, a high-grade skarn ore deposit and not one of those old-style, low-grade porphyry coppers. It's really the first of the next generation of better copper mines."

Never ones to ignore a good response, or to miss a good opportunity, Mitsubishi relented, and agreed to participate as a partner in our consortium, but only as to 10 per cent. They would undertake to try to convince JEXIM to provide financing, despite the Japanese interest being below the prescribed 15 per cent. As a result, if the financing could be completed, the ongoing partnership interests would be Noranda 33.75 per cent, Rio Algom 33.75 per cent, Teck 22.5 per cent, and Mitsubishi Corporation 10 per cent.

With Mitsubishi agreeing to participate, the partners exercised their option to make the $2.5 billion investment commitment on schedule in September 1998, even though it would still be months before it was clear the project could actually be financed. The reality was not quite as daunting, since the penalty for not performing would amount to only $750 million, or $170 million to Teck, but it was still daunting enough. It was, in 1998, an aggressive use of the word "only."

By this time, the expected cost to complete the new mine had increased to US$2.4 billion. Five months later, in February 1999, Compania Minera Antamina S.A. (CMA), the group's operating company, announced that "in view of the current international financial crisis," completion of the financing had been delayed by four or five months. Investors, quite understandably, were getting no less skittish. We were finding it was hard to skate smoothly up the ice from a seat in that penalty box.

Engineering and Managing the Project

Meanwhile, work on the site and re-engineering by the new ownership group continued. One of the key questions still to be determined was whether the copper and zinc concentrates should be transported some 300 kilometres to the coast by truck or by pipeline. There were hearty disagreements among the parties on this fundamental question. Bill James for Inmet had been a vocal proponent of the road alternative, and with the respect due him for his years in the business, this was still being taken seriously.

In fact, Bill had actually taken the keys to a large truck and personally driven the entire existing route from the mine to the coast, on available existing roads such as they were, to prove it could be done. He was that kind of guy.

Others were vehement that a pipeline was the safest and best solution, despite the higher construction cost. In May 1998, as we were finalizing the acquisition agreements, Teck's senior vice-president, mining, Mike Lipkewich, had visited the property and quickly reached the conclusion that access to and from the mine could become a fatal flaw. The road Bill James had driven at the time went through a UNESCO World Heritage Site, and there was no certainty it could be used to transport equipment and concentrate through the park. Even in the unlikely event this could be negotiated, it would not be clear for some time and we had to make decisions then.

The team did find an alternative route that could be developed at a cost of some $30 million, small relative to the total cost of the mine, so trucking continued to be an option, and Bill James continued to argue for it as only he could, considering that he had already sold out of the project.

Mike was pressing for a pipeline but there were some concerns, since there had been a similar 200 kilometres of concentrate pipeline built from the new Alumbrera copper mine in Argentina a short while earlier, and it had failed, shutting down the entire operation for a time. Mike decided to walk the main parts of that Alumbrera pipeline himself to see just why it had failed, and it became clear that it had traversed a dry riverbed that, at times, wasn't at all dry and could wash out any pipeline. It was a minor engineering problem that could be dealt with.

In the end, the partners decided to switch to the pipeline alternative, even though it would add $140 million to the capital cost. One determining factor against the road plan was that it would have meant an exceptionally long line of trucks leaving and returning to the mine, running past any given point along the mine road every six minutes. Lower down, on roads closer to the port, they would be joined by traffic from other mines as well. That, along with some pretty harrowing terrain, just seemed to be an accident invited to happen, and given the number of accidents already occurring on those lower roads, it was the right thing to do.

One small concern about the pipeline alternative had been that the concentrates would flow downhill easily from the mine at 4,200 metres elevation, but then have to go uphill over a substantial mountain range between the mine and the sea before eventually starting downhill again to the coast. There was a good chance that the energy created flowing down the first leg would be sufficient to push those concentrates up over the second range, after which it was downhill again. That was the theory, supported by engineering calculations. As it turned out, it actually did work that way, much to the relief of all the non-engineers.

This uncertainty as to the ultimate route and cost didn't help in speeding up the financing, but negotiations progressed and in June, nine months after the project commitment, Teck, Rio Algom, and Noranda were able to announce that they had obtained US$1.32 billion of project financing from a consortium of commercial and EXIM banks. It was the largest project financing commitment ever for a greenfields mining project. The partners would provide the rest directly.

The project was already moving along at the site as financing negotiations progressed. The new partners had continued to retain Bechtel to assist in engineering design and procurement, and had assigned engineers from each of the mining companies to provide owner management.

Usually in a mine development program there is one company designated as operator, and it provides management supervision. Difficulties can crop up where there is more than one capable operating company with an ownership position and no clearly assigned operator, but in this case the construction program went extremely well under a three-way co-management system.

For one thing, it had been agreed that each one of the three mining companies would appoint the head of the Management Committee for a yearly term, in succession.

Second, as it happened, many of the engineers with each of the three had worked closely with some from the other two in previous joint ventures. Noranda and Teck engineers had cooperated on the site in building Louvicourt, for example, and Teck and Rio Algom engineers had cooperated at Bullmoose and Highland Valley. Rio also had just come off a successful new high-elevation mine development at Cerro Colorado in Chile.

To a great extent, the engineers knew who the stars from each other's companies were and in which disciplines, so it was easier than with strangers for a consensus to be reached that "this job is best suited to a Noranda guy, that one to a Teck engineer, and let's let a Rio guy do the third one." Pride of who was in charge could, ideally, take second place to getting the best job done most effectively.

We also set up a weekly CEO meeting by telephone between David Kerr of Noranda, Pat James of Rio Algom, and me. Everybody in Lima and on site knew these calls were happening, and the last thing they wanted, quite naturally, was for us to interfere in technical decisions at the operating level. They didn't want us trying to pick the trucks, nor of course did we. So they had a really good incentive to get along and keep us quiescent. We CEOs were happy to play the game as long as it seemed to be working, and in fact it actually did work out really well. As Milton said: "They also serve who only stand and wait."

Epilogue

The Antamina project was completed and achieved commercial production, as defined in the lending agreements, in October 2001. Naturally, the price of copper hit a 15-year low of 60 cents a pound just as we achieved full production, and times were still tough for the whole copper industry. Teck's share price had sat in the penalty box for three years while we were acquiring, financing, and building the new mine – one of our best ever as it turned out. Two years later, copper had recovered to over a dollar a pound and our shares got right back on track with our long-term value-building trend. The penalty box was an understandable but uncomfortable hiatus we had to go through to get there, another stepping stone along the way.

There was some shuffling of partners while construction was progressing. In mid-2000, with the Asian Crisis a distant memory, Noranda announced that it had quietly acquired 9 per cent of Rio Algom, and, with Chile's Codelco, launched a joint takeover bid for the company. Gordon Gray, Rio's chairman, flew off to London in the company's new private jet to be wined and dined by Mick Davis, the mover and shaker behind Billiton, a growing mining company from South Africa. Davis agreed to act as a "white knight" and to top the Noranda/Codelco bid.*

He was successful, and we had a new partner in Antamina, even before completing construction of the mine. Then, the next spring and still before we completed construction, BHP and Billiton agreed to merge, so that we had another, bigger partner.

It was interesting, and proof once again that most successful mining companies realize the fundamental importance of good ore reserves to their corporate future and should see and grasp bargain opportunities at the low point in the cycle. This is usually well before the investment community, with its shorter time horizon (long term these days being a synonym for the next quarter), will recognize the value.

It confirmed what we had believed for years. Without the protection of our dual share structure, Teck would have been swallowed up, just as Rio Algom was. This was true not only in 2000 but probably would have occurred in several earlier times when we were building new mines that were largely unrecognized or unappreciated by shorter-term investors.

And the world goes round. Mick Davis would leave BHP Billiton shortly after engineering the merger of those two into what became the world's largest mining company. An entrepreneur rather than an administrator, he started a new mining company named Xstrata and, with a series of well-timed acquisitions just as the China super-cycle was about to be recognized, managed to build it into another major mining company. Naturally, Xstrata would eventually take over Noranda, and once again introduce a new partner to the Antamina story. Not to be outdone, Xstrata would then be taken over by Glencore, so that at the time of writing in 2017 the partnership consists of Teck, Mitsubishi, BHP Billiton, and Glencore.

Are we builders, or are we all just chips in a game we don't understand? Or maybe we do.

---

* Some knights are born white and others black, and some are just ambidextrous, as the universe unfolds.

In 2010, the partners began a major expansion of the Antamina mine to increase daily processing capacity to 130,000 tonnes, at a capital cost of US$1.3 billion. Antamina has become one of the great mines of the world.

Klaus Zeitler, Ulli Rath, Lawrie Reinertson, Bill James, Mike Lipkewich, Pat James, and David Kerr are no longer involved, and Noranda and Rio Algom no longer exist, but all deserve full credit for their vision in helping to create this major mine under very difficult economic and construction conditions.

EPILOGUE, PART FIVE

The 1990s turned out to be the second decade in what has been called "the 20 years of declining commodity prices in real terms" or, as Rio Tinto's retired chief economist, David Humphreys, termed it, "the barren years." And the penultimate three years also saw the "Asian Financial Crisis," a trying time to be popular while building a major new mine under risky financial and construction conditions.

In addition to Antamina, Teck and partners had built two other new mines in the 1990s, at Quebrada Blanca and Louvicourt, and had put a fourth, Elkview Coal, back into production successfully after a previous owner had gone into receivership. As well, we had negotiated participation in what would become the new Pogo gold mine in Alaska, and had discovered or helped prove up mineral deposits that could eventually develop into significant new mines at San Nicolas in Mexico, Pebble Copper in Alaska, and Petaquilla in Panama.

But the low-price environment and the penalty box years while we started to build the large Antamina mine held us back from our previous growth rate in adding shareholder value, and we would not get back onto our historic track until Antamina was completed and commodity prices began to recover once again early in the next decade.

It is the nature of the mining business that no one is immune to the effect of cyclical prices, or extended periods during feasibility studies, permitting, and construction when the value of new ventures is largely unrecognized by the market. However, carefully executed creation of new wealth through mine-building can, over the long run, increase shareholder value reasonably consistently in spite of those ups and downs in commodity prices. Resting on one's old ores, and simply being a cyclical player, is not likely to.

PART SIX

BEFORE THE BOOM

In 2001 we completed construction at Antamina, on time and within the $2.4 billion budget, which may have been a world first for a major project at over 4,000 metres elevation in the High Andes. It was a credit to the combined construction and operating teams of the three partners, with Teck's side led by Mike Lipkewich, that we could pull it off against what had been all expectations in the market.

It was also the year when we finally tied the knot with Cominco, seemingly having first exhausted all possible alternatives. David Thompson took on the presidency of the merged company and I moved up to chairman.

We would complete two additional deals during the first five years of the twenty-first century, both of which would prove important for the future. These would be the timely acquisition of the remaining 34 per cent of Highland Valley Copper from BHP, just before copper prices finally began to recover; and the consolidation of all of the major Canadian steelmaking coal mines into a single partnership under Teck management.

The continuing growth of China's economy had been remarkably consistent since Deng Xiaoping announced, in 1980, his challenge to quadruple its size within 20 years, but this had remained largely unnoticed in the West. That was not surprising, since China had started from a relatively small GDP base. However, it began to have a larger and larger impact on the rest of the world as it continued its remarkably steady growth. During my visits back in 1980, I had seen it as an intriguing place in which to explore, develop, mine, and then export metals from. Instead, by early in the twenty-first century it would become the major consumer of some 40 per cent of the mined commodities that we in the rest of the world produced, leading to an unprecedented boom in the prices of many commodities. This would have huge ramifications for our business as the super-cycle flowed, and later ebbed.

Would we see these changes coming? Perhaps in a way, as we will show, but we would not act upon this as quickly as we should have. Observing opportunities, and acting upon them, are two quite different things.

By mid-decade, there would be a changing of the guard again, bringing in new blood to carry on the Teck tradition. Don Lindsay, whom we have seen in so many different places earlier in the book that he seemed either to be James Bond or The Shadow, would come over from CIBC World Markets to become our president and CEO in 2005. I would continue as chairman, although less actively, and David Thompson would soon step aside. He would be missed.

CHAPTER 37

NOODLING STRATEGY

It reminds me of the way we used to navigate on the coast of Peru. Close-in sailors would navigate by keeping an eye on the coast, then farther-out sailors who navigated by watching the boats that were watching the coast, and so on. Somehow you got very far away from the coast.
Hernando De Soto

By 1999, we were well into construction at the new Antamina mine, and the market was well into keeping us in the penalty box for the second year of what would be a four-year term. Even Tie Domi didn't get put there that long. As well, we were still subject to that dreaded holding company discount markets sometimes give to parent companies that control another similar company. Ironically, the controlled affiliate is usually not subject to that same discount. It was becoming clear that we had to do something other than the status quo with our investment in Cominco. It was time to fish or cut bait.

It has been said that Genghis Khan's forces could ride two horses at the same time, but one wonders how well and for how long. It definitely was not the best way to run a mining business for any length of time, with seeming conflicts of interest being inherent and divided focus and loyalties inevitable. In dealing with this situation we certainly could not have been accused of acting hastily, and students of successful takeover history might well argue that more deliberate action a little sooner would have been in order.

Phillips, Hager and North Opine on Teck

That June, we held our annual strategic planning meeting of the Teck board, this time at Whistler Mountain in British Columbia. Interested in how and why the market perceived what we were doing, we invited Ian Mottershead, the senior investment manager of Phillips, Hager and North, to speak to us. PH&N had been one of our most loyal investors for years, and, in Ian's words, we were considered a core position. At times, we had been their only mining holding when the sector was out of favour.

Ian was eloquent, incisive, complimentary, and called a spade a spade, all at the same time. It was quite a feat. He said PH&N liked Teck's multi-commodity approach, although they weren't keen on gold, it being not like other metals. "We have liked Teck's strong balance sheet. We have admired management's skill in contra-cyclical asset purchases and sales. We have admired Teck's intelligence gathering ability," he said, referring to our relationship with junior explorers.

"We were particularly excited by the opportunities that we thought would be presented to the company with a strong balance sheet when the resource stocks severely underperformed interest sensitive and technology stocks over the last 2 or 3 years. We were however disappointed with the selection of Antamina."

Ian was aware that Shell Canada had been seeking a partner for its Alberta oil sands project at the same time, and that we had considered it as an alternative major investment. He wished we had done that one rather than taking on Antamina. He even said he "admired the contra-cyclical aspect of the purchase, buying copper when it was out of favour rather than just chasing the flavour of the day. We like the huge, high-quality ore body, but we can't make the numbers work using a long term copper price of $0.90 a pound." Of course the facts – that we would eventually build Antamina on budget and that the Shell oil sands project would overrun its budget by $5 billion – were not known to either of us then. Nor was the fact that copper prices would surge in a few years as the steady growth in China turned supply surpluses into deficits for a time.

Ian's view was the market perspective at the time, even by our oldest fans. It was what it was.

He concluded by saying: "We think that Teck has the skills necessary to reward long-term shareholders. We think that your long-term focus on employing capital, whether on new capital spending, deal-making or exploration, should result in Teck achieving a return on equity that is significantly superior to its competitors."

Fred Daley, our exploration vice-president, asked Ian's opinion on our exposure to coal. He said he had no opinion. Fred then asked if Ian had any examples of other mining companies that were making the kind of contra-cyclical moves that appealed to him. Ian's answer was interesting. He said: "No. I think that Teck does this extremely well. Frankly, I've been listening to you talk about this for years and I've looked at other companies and I don't see very much of it. Rather, more often I see rising interest in copper as the price of copper rises, and so on."

Interestingly, Ian's comments reflected an investor who looked for good long-term strategies and results, as did we, rather than the short-termism that has perverted much of the market in the years since. Unfortunately, Ian has retired, as have many like him, Bob Hager passed away, and PH&N has become a division of a large bank.

Jim Gill and His Wild Idea

After Ian left, we spent a couple of hours noodling about what he had said, and exchanging ideas on where we should be heading. We had done well by our Diamond Fields foray and were getting along nicely with Antamina, fully committed, but our eternal question was what should we do next?

We had asked several management people, including Mike Lipkewich, chief geoscientist John Thompson, and Gary Jones, as well as Jim Gill, the Aur Resources founder and a Teck board member, to present their thoughts on what Teck should look like in five years.

The most entertaining and perhaps perceptive presentation was from Gill. He started by saying that we had a good base from which to grow – 11 operating mines, an active exploration and development team, several quality development projects, and a controlling interest in Cominco. He referred to our market capitalization of $1.2 billion putting us in the third tier of world mining companies, and said that he "saw Teck in five years as a large, global mining enterprise, with a market capitalization in excess of US$4 billion."*

He went on to say:

> This will provide Teck with the liquidity and critical mass demanded by the investment community, greater access to capital markets and greater ability to be competitive in the acquisition area. I would like to put forth a hypothetical scenario that would allow my vision of

---

* The numbers were quite different not that long ago. Realization of the impending China boom was still out there in the future, and the big three of Rio Tinto, Anglo, and BHP were each worth about $20 billion at the time, with the next tier being eight companies in the $2 billion to $8 billion range. For a time recently, BHP Billiton's market cap was 10 times that, and Rio Tinto's 5 times, both as a result of the huge increases in demand generated by China's growth.

Teck in 2005 to become a reality. First thing we do is merge with Rio Algom on a NAV for NAV (net asset value) basis. We sell off coal, industrial minerals, their uranium project and their metals distribution business. We should be able to monetize that at about US$450 million in this poor economic environment, and then we merge with Cominco.

The discussion went on, with some expressing concern about increasing our exposure in Peru, considering that Cominco's difficult Cajamarquilla plant was already there, and others worried that if the dual share structure had to be eliminated with such a three-way merger, it would likely end up with the newly merged company being taken over by one of the international majors, and Canada could lose three of its best mining companies in one fell swoop.

But, as Jim Gill also pointed out: "Teck's stock price is $7 and the Net Asset Value about $13, whereas Cominco and Rio Algom are not discounted nearly as much. Is there a way you can get these companies to acknowledge that this is true? They have to accept your stock price being $11 rather than $7. It's not going to happen, but you have to find a way that the gap isn't so big."

That was certainly a concise assessment of why the great idea wasn't about to happen easily, and a good challenge to rectify it, if we could and had the time.

Rio Algom's Pat James Had a Similar Idea

Interestingly, by that time Rio Algom was a quite different company from the days when we had tussled over that unfortunate gentleman's agreement 14 years earlier.

By 1999, Lornex had been privatized, with Teck and Rio Algom splitting up its assets, primarily Highland Valley Copper and Bullmoose coal, pro rata. George Albino was gone, and parent company Rio Tinto of the United Kingdom had finally sold its controlling shareholding in 1992. Rio Algom had started up Cerro Colorado, a new copper mine in Chile in 1994, not far from our Quebrada Blanca project, and acquired the interesting Spence copper prospect in the same region. It was doing well, but now as a widely-held company without a founder's influence, it had groped its way through a number of management and strategy changes, much as Placer had some 15 years earlier.

Gordon Gray, retired after a career running the real estate company A.E. LePage, had become chairman. He and his board had hired a couple of presidents who had come and gone. The latest, for the last few years, had been Pat James, an American miner with a good operating track record and a head on his shoulders. We had gotten to know each other well as a result of our existing joint operations as well as the regular CEO meetings on the Antamina construction project.

In one of our conversations shortly after Jim proposed his hypothetical plan, Pat had suggested a similar but even more far-reaching wild idea of his own. Saying "Size matters," his idea was to put all of Teck, Cominco, Rio Algom, and Noranda together in one friendly mega-merger, on a simple net asset value basis with no premiums. He called it The Great Canadian Mining Company. Whether or not he had ever raised it with Noranda as well was not clear.

It might have worked, in this or another parallel universe.

However, it was about then that Noranda announced it had bought 9 per cent of Rio Algom and launched a hostile bid for it. One thing led to another, Gordon Gray jetted off to London to have that dinner with Mick Davis, and Rio Algom was instead acquired by Billiton. That part of the Gill/James wild ideas was gonzo, as far as we were concerned.

I was impressed with Noranda's nimbleness in seeing and grasping a good opportunity. Unlike the market, they (and we) knew how well construction at the Antamina project was actually going. They recognized the value of Cerro Colorado and perhaps Spence, not to mention Rio Algom's 34 per cent of Highland Valley Copper. With no leading shareholder and its good development assets being discounted by the market, it was a sitting duck. It fit John Bradfield's dictum about Noranda's need to add new mining assets to augment those being used up. It was something we would have done in an earlier time, or perhaps then, had we the financial capacity and/or fairly valued share currency.

As Jim Gill had said, we had to find a way to make sure the gap between our net asset value and market price wasn't so big. It really had to start by dealing with our holding company problem, a.k.a. the Cominco problem. It seemed it wouldn't go away on its own, and it was high time we resolved it.

CHAPTER 38

BITING THE BULLET ON COMINCO

Mongolians do not always do what foreigners think they should. Ghengis Khan's warriors pinged arrows from a distance at adversaries who had pencilled "pitched battle" into their day planners. This was unsporting but effective.
Jonathan Guthrie, *Financial Times*

What was Teck doing about Cominco, anyway? That was a good question, and one that had been preoccupying us from time to time ever since our consortium acquired effective control in 1986.

At the time, we had been concerned about the Cominco valuation. Was it really worth the price the market was putting on it? As George Albino had said when we bought it: "I didn't think Teck used discount factors." We did, but we were also prepared to take a chance on investing step by step in things where there was optionality, or the chance to try to make something better out of it. That was why we had refused to buy CP's full 53 per cent holding, only taking 30 per cent, and even at that level, had brought in two minority partners, Germany's Metallgesellschaft and Australia's MIM.

We had started with just a 15 per cent interest, using no bank borrowings to achieve that. We had put our foot on the company, as the Australians say, and the next step was to see what we could do with it. We could test the waters and then either sell, hold, or buy more? There would be time to work that out. But by then, in 2000, it had been 14 years since we had bought that first stake. Few could have accused us of acting hastily in this.

For the first three years after buying out CP, we had been preoccupied with getting to understand the company, helping to build its Red Dog mine, and of course looking after our own Teck business as well. We were comfortable having Bob Hallbauer downstairs running the show there, probably, in a way, more comfortable than Bob was himself. He had to deal with a management group that had, for the most part, been accountable to nobody but themselves in the later CP years. He also had to deal with Cominco's chronic debt problem and consider selling assets, which no red-blooded miner really likes to have to do.

For the next four years, things hadn't gone as well. The Red Dog mine encountered metallurgical problems at start-up, some of which we should have foreseen. And the price of zinc began to fall back once again. The profitable fertilizer division had to be sold, but Cominco's debt continued to increase regardless.

The new QSL lead smelter that Cominco had committed to install, before we came onto the scene, had proven to not be working as advertised. The engineering firm responsible happened to be Germany's renowned Lurgi, which was a unit of Metallgesellschaft, and Bob Hallbauer had to skate between charges of conflict of interest by old Cominco people on the one hand, and Metall people on the other, all the while just trying to do what was right. In the end, he threw Lurgi out and switched over to an entirely new smelting process called Kivcet, one that had been designed and proven in, of all places, Kazakhstan.

We had entered into two potential new mining ventures together, with Teck and Cominco each investing in Aur Resources' new Louvicourt base metals discovery in Quebec and the Quebrada Blanca copper project in Chile.

But Metall's interests changed: it began to see no real option value in Cominco, and decided to get out. It sold its Nunachiaq interest to MIM in 1992. We were getting more entwined, and the partners less so. MIM itself began to tire of the holding two years later. By then Bruce Watson, who had done the deal with us originally, had moved on and Norm Fussell, a taciturn financial guy, had become CEO. We got along well with Norm, and were always amused by a habit he had of coming into my office or David Thompson's and just sitting there. He could sit in silence for minutes on end, which may have been a good negotiating tactic, because the other guy would usually get impatient and start talking. It was, as David called it: "He who speaks first, loses." However, it did make for awkward silences when there was little business to be done, and the encounters were just to say a friendly hello.

In 1994, we learned that MIM had decided to sell its 50 per cent Nunachiaq position (by then a net 17 per cent of Cominco). One of Fussell's new confidantes, Phil Wright, was after him to get rid of that non-working holding. MIM wanted us to buy them out, so we agreed to meet with Norm and one of his staff on neutral ground in Honolulu. David and I wore shorts and golf shirts to show our devil-may-care attitude and exude confidence. Norm and the aide showed up in full suits in the Hawaiian heat.

David and I had agreed beforehand that we would out-wait Fussell, so we entered the room, shook hands, and just sat there. We sat, and sat, and sat, with nobody saying anything for what seemed like half an hour but might have been 10 minutes or so. Eventually, Fussell's sidekick piped up and began talking. We'd won. We settled on a price and bought MIM's position. So, after seven years, Teck had gone from the original 15 per cent net interest to 34 per cent, but that was just by taking out the partners, and nothing else had really changed.

Bob Hallbauer passed away the next year, and David Thompson agreed to go down to run Cominco. This he did ably, but it meant that another of the key players from our strongest growth years was less available to us upstairs in Teck. We would still meet and brainstorm regularly, but a divided focus is never quite as effective as single-minded attention to a common purpose.

In Cominco's four-year period under David, the new Kivcet smelter had its own start-up problems, but eventually reached design capacity. However, capital expenditures in Cominco continued to exceed cash flow, just as they had since 1990. Debt hit a 10-year high of $830 million in 1998, despite more asset sales in the continuing attempt to deal with it. In the circumstances, Cominco had found it easier to turn down the Antamina opportunity we had given it than to work with us on it, much to our consternation.

Particular operating issues aside, the simple fact of two similarly sized companies in the same business cohabiting in part, but not fully, led to inevitable tensions at both the board and management levels as well as costly duplications of management and overhead.

In hindsight, we should have decided to fish or cut bait a lot sooner. It would probably have been better for all concerned, whichever way was chosen. We needed to get on with it.

Toward a Solution

The problem was front and centre in the months following that June meeting at which Mottershead and Jim Gill had spoken. Gill had raised his bold and intriguing idea, one which he had admitted wasn't going to happen unless we fixed the market discount from NAV.

The rest of the industry was not standing still and there had been other M&A activity going on, including the recent acquisition of Cyprus Amax by Phelps Dodge. Noranda had just made its hostile offer for Rio Algom, and been trumped by Billiton. We were becoming concerned that if we continued to accept a deeply discounted share price without doing anything about it, others might decide to try to do something about it for us.

In our papers for a management strategy session the next February we noted that, until two years earlier, the value of Teck's shares had grown at a compounded 11 per cent for over 15 years since 1980, second among established miners only to Rio Tinto's 12.5 per cent (in both cases without adjusting for dividends). We wrote: "The engine of this growth was new mine development, and at this point Teck currently has as good an inventory of projects as at any time in its history, so a resumption of internal growth from projects on hand can reasonably be anticipated, other things being equal." That would in fact happen once we completed Antamina and escaped the penalty box, but as we wrote that optimistic statement we were still in the box, and not that comfortable.

A holding company discount hadn't seemed too relevant a factor during our earlier years, even though we did have subsidiaries or affiliates from time to time, but it was now being said by some investors as a reason not to own Teck shares. As well, Teck was sometimes being seen as too diversified, in an investment climate that had developed a fancy for pure plays, in which investors who wanted to own zinc, for example, might prefer to own Cominco rather than Teck. Likewise, in coal, they might prefer a pure play like Fording, rather than Teck, and so on for other commodities. It was the investment flavour of the day, at least until it was not, a while later.

These reasons not to own us hadn't been raised in any material sense until recently, and were arguably just add-ons to the biggest reason, which were concerns about whether or not we could pull off construction at the large high-elevation Antamina project on time and on budget and whether copper prices would recover in the near term. However, they all added up to a difficult situation. As the numbers we showed at the February strategy session proved, our undervaluation was about 40 per cent. There was what we called hidden value there of a billion dollars, some of which we might recover if we could resolve "the Cominco question."

For discussion purposes, we tabled 14 different options to fix the situation. Some were permutations on the Gill/James ideas, and some were more likely to be effective than others. They included:

Option 6: The sale of Cominco for cash, eliminating the holding company discount and providing cash for Teck to concentrate on building value directly once again. This would take Teck back to the roots that had made it quite successful on its own, and was attractive to some of us.

Option 8: A joint takeover bid for 100 per cent of Cominco, with Teck first buying enough to reach 50 per cent, and then inviting a third party to acquire the remaining 50 per cent. Thereafter, Cominco's operations would be operated as a private partnership by Teck and the third party.

Option 9: Cominco itself to buy back Teck's 50 per cent shareholding in it, in exchange for 50 per cent of Cominco's assets and liabilities. Those operations would then be run as a partnership between Teck and the newly freed up, smaller Cominco. This was somewhat similar to Option 8, but via an internal transaction rather than bringing in a third party.

Option 12: Teck to buy additional Cominco shares to reach 50 per cent and then fully consolidate Cominco's results. This was considered but rejected as a final solution, since it was just a way of accounting, and in reality we would still not have direct ownership of the underlying operating assets and access to their cash flow.

Option 13: The status quo.

Option 14: Teck to distribute all or a majority of its Cominco shares to Teck's shareholders via a dividend in species, giving them each the choice to hold or sell. It would remove the distraction upstairs in Teck of what to do about all this, and was similar to what BCE (Bell Canada Enterprises) had done recently with its Nortel holding.

These were all possibilities, but we focused in fairly quickly on the preferred one, which was Option 8. This was the most appealing for two reasons.

First, while we would have to buy a few more shares to reach 50 per cent, we wouldn't have to pay a premium to buy out the remaining 50 per cent we already controlled. The third party would pay whatever premium was necessary, but not Teck.

This was similar to the plan we had come up with when we arranged to buy out the 27 per cent minority shareholding of Afton in 1981. We didn't want to pay the necessary $55 a share then either, sensing that it was well overpriced, but Metallgesellschaft did want to own a piece of it. So, we had arranged that Metall would buy out the minority instead of us, after which we would convert Afton from a company to a 73/27 per cent joint venture and would then hold our interest equity directly, rather than downstairs through a subsidiary.

Second, with the right international partner, we might be able to develop some synergies, particularly if they brought zinc assets, prospects, or added expertise to the table.

A Potential Partner

We soon hit upon Anglo American, the South African mining conglomerate controlled by the Oppenheimers, as a logical partner.

Interestingly, Anglo American had been considered a likely buyer when Canadian Pacific had first revealed it wanted to sell its controlling shareholding 14 years earlier. Cominco's management, then headed by Norm Anderson, had been anxious to find a compatible company to take over the position.

It hadn't happened back then, but by 1999, Anglo had its potential new Skorpion zinc mine in Africa on the drawing boards, and a strategic alliance combining it with Cominco's zinc assets and experience seemed to be worth considering. James Campbell, then an executive with Anglo, had made contact with us about looking for joint opportunities and took an immediate shine to the idea of joining in a takeover bid to take out the minority shareholders of Cominco. We began exchanging data, and things were progressing well.

As it happened, Julian Ogilvie Thompson, the CEO of Anglo American, was due to address the annual CIBC Mining Dinner in November 1999, and we arranged to get together for two days of discussion and negotiations in Toronto just before it. It seemed as though this was an opportunity both he and I really liked, as did Campbell, and we made arrangements to continue discussions in the ensuing weeks. At the CIBC dinner that night, I was actually sitting beside Julian at the round head table. Since we had been talking together for most of the last day and a half, we didn't talk much at the dinner, each conversing more with whoever was sitting on the other side.

It's funny, but at another CIBC dinner two years earlier, the Australian mining financier Robert de Crespigny was the keynote speaker, and I happened to have had dinner with him the night before about some project we've both long forgotten. Sure enough, at the formal dinner I was placed beside the speaker, and having already had our own lengthy meeting we both seemed to largely ignore each other and converse primarily with the person on the other side of us. I've concluded that if someone wants to get the inside scoop on who is doing a deal with whom at CIBC mining dinners, one should take note of who is *not* talking to someone it would seem he should be, not the other way around.

Anyway, Teck and Anglo had a series of follow-up meetings in Vancouver and London, and I would have given it a probability of well over 50 per cent that the deal would go through. It would have been a real coup for us, ending the long years of tensions and holding company discounts, and bringing our half of the assets directly into Teck at little or no further cost.

However, it was not to be. Julian Ogilvie Thompson soon retired as CEO, and was succeeded by Tony Trahar. The new guy was a chartered accountant with little interest in the mining business, and was more interested in pursuing a deal to unwind the complex cross-holdings between De Beers, an affiliated diamond company, and Anglo American. Our little dream project suffered rigour mortis very quickly, and we were back to Square One.

We had concluded by that time that we weren't going to stick with the status quo any longer. We still weren't inclined to sell because, as David Thompson was by then saying from his new perch: "Where else could you find such assets?" Or, as Hallbauer had always said: "Real miners don't sell good mines." Red Dog and Highland Valley were good mines, despite HVC's low ore grade and the low price of copper at the time.

Moving to 50 per cent of Cominco

Meanwhile, with Bob Hallbauer gone, some people downstairs had concluded that they had little ongoing interest in owning the Quebrada Blanca copper mine, and Cominco advised us that it was prepared to sell its 38 per cent interest. Cominco was still in its perennial debt reduction mode, and could use the proceeds for that purpose. As well, when I asked its chief operating officer of the day, responsible for all three of Cominco's mining operations, why he would be prepared to sell, he replied: "If I've got a problem at Red Dog and another problem at QB in Chile, you know where I have to put my attention." That wasn't our way of reasoning, but we all do think differently.

Naturally, we looked at Teck buying Cominco's QB position, but with our much larger Antamina project still not finished, I thought we should pass on this one. We were aware of the possibility of deep sulphide copper ore beneath the current supergene open pit, having drilled five deep holes to confirm this, but with the copper market as it was in 2000, that mineralization was too low grade to consider mining, at least for the foreseeable future.

I was a director of Aur Resources at the time, and Jim Gill was a director of Teck. This was an arrangement we had made when Teck had first invested in Aur, and it continued after we did a development contract to help build its Louvicourt mine. I knew Jim was interested in expanding Aur's mining operations and had his eye on Chile, so I let him know about Cominco's interest in selling QB.

In March 2000, we put together a deal that fit the objectives of all three parties nicely. Aur would buy out Teck and Cominco's interests for $304 million, with $129 million going to Teck and $175 million to Cominco. It was one of those rare win-win-win situations. Gill had the additional mine he had been looking for, and an expanded base from which to try to build a new Teck himself, as he had often said he wanted to do. Cominco had divested an operation some of its people seemed not to be keen on, and had $175 million to apply against its debt. And Teck had additional funds to invest in some interesting way.

Late in 1999, Teck had bought 7.9 million more shares of Cominco at a cost of $179 million, bringing our holding up to 44 per cent. In June, Teck used its share of the QB proceeds to buy an additional 5.1 million Cominco shares in the market, of which 4 million were bought under a tender offer to all Cominco shareholders. At that point, Teck owned 49.8 per cent of Cominco. A short time later we bought an additional 100,000 shares, bringing our ownership to 50.1 per cent.

The following March, after several months of negotiations, Teck and Cominco announced an agreement to merge the two companies. It was finally over.

Negotiating the Name

Not a lot needs to be said about the financial and legal negotiations. Once we owned over 50 per cent of the company one could almost hear the air being let out of the balloon on both sides. For some in Cominco, and perhaps even in Teck, there was no more hope or illusion that Teck would go away. For us in Teck, we knew we'd missed out on Option 8, and for that matter Options 6 and 9, and would have to pay too much, but there was a sense of relief that it was over, and we could all get on with the next stage of our lives peacefully.

At the end, there was one last thing that had to be agreed on – the name of the ongoing company. David Sinclair had been head of the independent negotiating committee for Cominco, and he was sent upstairs with his marching orders. "Norm," he said, "I'm here to tell you that the Cominco special committee will approve the deal but on one condition. The new company has to be called Cominco Teck."

I replied: "David, old friend, let me think about that a moment. I've thought about it. The answer is no. It's going to be Teck Cominco."*

"Okay," he said equally quickly, "but can we correct a little rounding error in the share exchange ratios?" I gave him that win and, old Scottish accountant that he was, he has lorded it over me for that ever since. He had won his and I'd won mine.

We had to decide who would have what title in the proverbial corner offices. I had never held myself out as an administrator – it just isn't my forte or even interest – so I was happy to take on the role of chairman of the board. David Thompson was appointed president and CEO, and for the next five years until David retired, we made a pretty good team.

Epilogue

Was merging, effectively paying up to buy the 50 per cent of Cominco we didn't already own, the right thing to do?

Certainly, our Teck shares were undervalued because of the holding company perception as well as still being in the stock market's Antamina penalty box until it could be proven that that project was a success. Issuing undervalued shares to pay a premium for fully-valued Cominco shares meant that Teck shareholders lost on both sides of the equation. Having just come off good deals in Diamond Fields and Antamina, we could easily have waited rather than pressing ahead to resolve the Cominco situation. However, after 14 years it seemed time to get on with it.

Was it my biggest mistake? I've often wondered what has happened in one of those alternate universes in which we did Option 9 instead, once Option 8 had failed? This was the idea to split Cominco into two separate companies, each holding half of the assets in joint venture with the other under agreed management contracts. It would have meant Teck holding half of the mining and smelting assets outright, and a newly independent company,

---

* Not too many years later the name was changed to Teck Resources, and so it remains as this is being written in 2017.

"New Cominco," the other half. New Cominco would simply have replaced Anglo American from the Option 8 plan.

It would have been doable, less expensive for Teck, and attractive to management at Cominco as well, since it would have freed them up to run an independent company once again. We each would have been half the size, but large enough that this would have been irrelevant. Where would each company be now, had we done that instead? One can never know, but perhaps each would have excelled in their different ways, just as Agrium had done when it was spun off as an independent public company.

CHAPTER 39

CONSOLIDATING CANADIAN COAL

Happiness is like a butterfly. You can chase it all over the field and never catch it.
But if you sit quietly on the grass it may come and land on your shoulder.
Family saying, after Henry David Thoreau

As Teck Cominco entered the new millennium, marked by the successful completion of the new flagship copper-zinc mine at Antamina, there were new opportunities to pursue in metallurgical coal.

For years the Canadian steelmaking coal business had been fragmented, with a number of mines in BC and Alberta held by a number of different companies, unlike their major customers in Japan, where the various steel companies were coordinated under a single buying organization for Canadian coal. It was not a level playing field and there was an argument for some kind of consolidation on our side of the water.

The old competition for coal sales between northeast and southeast British Columbia producers had diminished. In the northeast, the Quintette mine had closed after years of difficulties. The profitable Bullmoose mine had almost mined out its limited coal reserves at the South Fork deposit and was due to close soon, although there was still potentially mineable coal across the valley at West Fork. Meanwhile, Teck had become a major player in the southeast, with its rehabilitated Elkview mine (see colour page 15).

The largest producer in the Elk Valley continued to be Fording Coal, a division of CP Limited. Fording operated the Fording River and Greenhills mines north of Sparwood, having picked Greenhills up from Westar at the same time that we acquired Elkview. The third significant producer in the area was Luscar Ltd, which recently had taken over the Manalta family mines, including Line Creek, in a hostile bid in 1998. In 2001, it in turn was taken over by the Sherritt Coal Partnership, a partnership between Sherritt International and the Ontario Teachers' Pension Plan.

Rationalizing the Canadian Met Coal Industry

There was a growing sense that the time for rationalization had come. David Thompson and I had talked about the possibility of buying Fording River and Greenhills from CP, which had been the subject of rumours that it might break itself up or demerge, creating new companies out of a host of unrelated businesses.

In May 2001, a month after the Sherritt takeover of Luscar, I was in Calgary for the annual Canada-Japan Businessmen's Conference, and took the opportunity to visit David O'Brien, the head of CP. I asked him if he would consider selling the Fording division, and he seemed quite interested in the idea. He asked for an indicative offer, which I said we would give him. On returning to Vancouver, we noodled the pros and cons further, and got back to O'Brien with our offer, which was for a cool one billion dollars. That was a lot of hay in 2001, and it definitely got his attention. He promised to consider it seriously.

Unfortunately, when he did respond it was to say that CP might well have accepted the offer in normal times, but that it was considering splitting the company into four or five units, as had been speculated, and there were tax reasons why he couldn't sell Fording at that time. Apparently, a breakup such as the one they were contemplating could be done tax-effectively under an arrangement called a butterfly, but it was only available to them if CP had not sold any of its major assets in the prior year. In fact, CP did break itself up later in the year, spinning off its hotels and shipping divisions as well as its coal as separate public companies, and the Fording Coal division became Fording Inc.

Fording Inc. was now able, to quote Mohammed Ali, to "float like a butterfly, and sting like a bee."

Fording Inc. as a Public Company

Over the next while, we had a few brief conversations with Jim Gardner, formerly a CP vice-president and now the CEO of Fording Inc. We had known him for years through the CJBC meetings, and we talked about putting our coal operations together, now that he was a free man.

Unfortunately for us, the newly freed Jim had the idea that Fording should be the bee, acquiring Elkview, rather the other way around. We could understand that. Overall, his set of mines was bigger than ours. On the other hand, we were comfortable with our own Elkview mine, which we naturally thought was the best. We agreed to keep in touch, and every few weeks over the next year I'd ask David what new ideas he'd been working on. He'd say: "Fording, but we can't seem to figure out how to come to a deal."

It would take something external to move this off dead centre, and in October 2002, one year after the spinoff of Fording Inc., that happened. Sherritt International Corp's Coal Partnership with the Ontario Teachers' Pension Plan surprised the market with a hostile $1.5 billion takeover bid for 100 per cent of Fording. At $29 a share, it was $6 higher than the price the shares had been trading at. The Fording board, evidently having seen something coming, announced on the same day that it would convert the company immediately to an income trust, a fancy structure that in its day had some tax advantages for shareholders.

If Sherritt had been successful, it would have gained control of four of the five metallurgical coal mines in the Elk Valley. This was a rationalization that Fording and Teck had each seen the advantages of for some time, but done between us rather than through an interloper. Furthermore, from our perspective, Elkview would have been left as something of a hanging chad.

David Thompson spoke to Jim Gardiner, offering our assistance as a white knight, but Jim was convinced that their income trust gambit would work as a practical defence. David was not so sure, so flew to Toronto to meet Sherritt's CEO Ian Delaney. David proposed that we participate with Sherritt in the bid, and combine all of the Canadian metallurgical coal mines into a stronger player on the world scene. Knights can, after all, be white, black, or any colour they choose, and sometimes even be ambidextrous.

That offer and $1 would get us a cup of coffee, and was more or less politely declined.

Meanwhile, Jimmy Pattison, Canada's wealthiest businessman, took an interest in the situation. He controlled Westshore Terminals, Canada's largest coal port, through which both Fording and Elkview exported their coal. Fording was his biggest customer and he was concerned about who would be running its coal business. David and I talked with Jimmy about his participating in a counter-offer, and he was enthusiastic about trying to work something out with us.

On 26 November, Jimmy and I called Dick Haskayne, Fording's chairman and a well-known Calgary businessman, to tell him we were prepared to counter Sherritt's offer in a friendly deal. He said we'd better act fast because they had an important meeting arranged with Delaney's group in Calgary the next morning.

The Players Joust

David, Jimmy, and I flew off to Calgary in Jimmy's plane a few hours later to meet Haskayne alone, Fording management seemingly still thinking they could succeed in maintaining their new-found independence. The meeting went well, as we outlined our idea of a partnership between Teck and the Fording Income Trust. Dick was receptive to working with us, but thought our plan was too complicated and suggested instead that Teck and Westshore invest in the Fording Trust. Having once been invited to buy some shares in Afton, done so, and seen where that had led, we were hoping for a little more concrete assurance.

The next day Haskayne, Gardiner, and Allen Hagerman, Fording's CFO, met with Delaney and his CFO, Jowdat Waheed, as planned. The meeting began badly before deteriorating, and, as Dick Haskayne wrote in his book *Northern Tigers*: "I basically booted them out."

Teck and Westshore began preparing a counter-offer, with David Thompson, our CFO John Taylor, our internal lawyer Peter Rozee, and Michael Korenberg from Jimmy's team taking up residence in a Calgary hotel. We had investment banking advice from CIBC and were co-operating where possible with Fording's lawyers and advisors. A week later, on 4 December, we announced our bid.

It was basically the same plan we had outlined to Haskayne. We would roll our Elkview mine plus $200 million into a new coal partnership to earn a 38 per cent interest, with the Fording Trust holding the balance. Westshore and Teck would each buy a 13 per cent interest in the Fording Trust for $170 million as well. The bid was valued at $1.7 billion, well above that of Sherritt/Teachers, and was seemingly supported by the Fording Trust. Our offer was well received by the market, which loves a bidding war, and of course assumed Sherritt would quickly counter.

David flew off to Maui for a Christmas break with his family, but that was abruptly shortened. He was called back for a Calgary meeting between all parties, to be held on 11 December. He took the overnight flight back to Vancouver and joined Jimmy, Korenberg, and me on Jimmy's plane to Calgary again that morning.

As David later wrote: "The purpose of the meeting was to see if any common ground could be reached between the two sides. It was useful that I met Brian Gibson of Teachers for the first time. Quite a lot of information on various assets was exchanged in several sub-group meetings, but there was no agreement." David may have been too humble in this, because my sense was that he and Gibson had hit it off quite well, which would be important as the situation evolved.

David flew back to rejoin his family in Maui, and a week later Sherritt and Teachers published a 340-page formal offer document. In his own formal response as chairman of Fording, Dick Haskayne stated: "In my 25 years as a corporate director in Canada I have never been presented with a more questionable document than the new Sherritt offer. It is a smoke and mirrors offer." He wrote directly to Brian Gibson outlining his concerns, as Teachers had held itself out to be an outspoken advocate of good corporate governance.

In early January, Sherritt and Teachers upped their offer, with an increased cash component we would have difficulty matching. Teck was hurting from the very low metal prices of the latest recession, and Westshore, despite Jimmy's backing, was a much smaller company.

According to David:

> Dick Haskayne called to say that Sherritt and Teachers were prepared to hold a final round of discussions with the Fording Trust the next day in Toronto. The choice of location was indicative of the relative strengths of the two parties.
>
> Michael Korenberg and I discussed a possible solution. Metallurgical and thermal coals served completely different markets. Met coal served the international steel industry whilst thermal coal supplied local utilities. Only the Fording River mine serviced both markets. If Luscar took the thermal coal and Teck the met coal it would be a natural division of the assets. The only problem was that the thermal assets were smaller than the met ones. The ambitious Delaney would want a major position in both of them.

The Toronto meetings began on Tuesday as planned and went well into the night. Delaney had to leave Wednesday for a scheduled dinner with Fidel Castro, but said he would return late Thursday to see where things stood.

As David recalled:

> One of the commitments Sherritt and Teachers had made was that they would maintain the cash distributions from the Fording Income Trust to the shareholders, even if there were insufficient earnings in the Trust to pay for the distribution. Teck was in closer contact than they were with the world met coal market, which was dominated by Japan, and the indications were that the price would fall in the new "coal year" beginning April 1, 2003. Our analysis indicated that this would mean a shortfall that would have to be covered by Sherritt, which did not have enough earnings itself, and by Teachers.
>
> Early on Wednesday morning I asked to see Brian Gibson privately, together with John Taylor. John showed him the numbers, which would be particularly large losses if the coal price declined as predicted. Brian became quite concerned.
>
> The conversation broadened as to how Teck managed its mines and markets, and to the problems that Luscar had had in its metallurgical coal assets. Teck had always made it clear that we wanted the management role in the met coal assets, even if we had a minority interest. This position had never been fully accepted by Gardiner and the Fording board.
>
> Brian then suggested a division of the assets exactly along the lines Michael Korenberg and I had discussed. He asked if we would be prepared to sell the thermal assets in Fording at a reasonable price. We responded that we would certainly support it if both bidders agreed, and the overall price to the Fording shareholders was satisfactory to the Fording board so they could accept it too.

Hopefully, Ian Delaney's dinner with Fidel Castro was going as well.

Under the Teck-Westshore offer, Teck would have had a 38 per cent share of the coal partnership, including the thermal coal. Brian, John and I calculated that if Teck reduced its position to 35 per cent it could

reduce its cash payment. I stated that the 38 per cent was very important to Teck, and that in negotiations with Fording we had asked for
40 per cent. Brian's next idea was very attractive. He replied that if
Teck would waive all management fees on the partnership, but was
able to increase the cash flow of the partnership by reducing operating costs over a three-year period, then he would agree that Teck could
recover up to 5 per cent of the whole partnership, increasing our ownership from 35 per cent to 40 per cent.

Since our argument that there would be a benefit to the Trust if Teck
would provide operating management of the whole partnership had been
the reason for demanding a 40 per cent interest, this seemed reasonable and
we agreed. We would have to earn what we had said we were contributing,
just as we had done with the Quintette mine under our agreement with the
creditor banks a few years earlier.

David asked Brian to outline his proposal to Dick Haskayne and then to
an inner group of the negotiators, excluding the investment bankers. He did,
and it was clear that Jowdat Waheed was disturbed by the idea, but we decided to begin a redraft of the proposal, including a fair price for the thermal assets. This continued through the night and next morning, and the
lawyers began drafting portions of the agreement as points were agreed on.

Delaney arrived back late in the afternoon, having been briefed by Waheed but not by Gibson. He was not pleased, but in the end said he would
accept the deal if the terms were fair to Luscar. Work on the agreements continued over the weekend, and there were the usual number of clangers that
had to be resolved, some larger than others. The agreement was announced
at a press conference on Monday morning.

Each participant made a short address. David complimented Brian
Gibson and Ian Delaney for consolidating the Canadian metallurgical coal
industry, "a task that many managers in the business had tried to do but
failed to achieve during the last twenty years."

David Thompson had pulled off a coup, once again demonstrating why
we had been intent on eventually getting him to our side of the table back
in the days when his Messina and Metallgesellschaft were duking it out. He
had used his whole arsenal of patience, knowledge of the opponents, more
knowledge of the business than some of them had, and a tad of divide and
conquer when the Teachers' representative began to realize the risks.

Teck was now the clear manager and a substantial owner of the second biggest metallurgical coal mining group in the world, after the BHP-Mitsubishi Alliance in Australia.

As part of the agreement, and with a significant equity interest in the Fording Trust as well, Teck was entitled to nominate two trustees. Dick Haskayne retired and was replaced as chair by Michael Grandin. The remaining trustees were others from the old Fording board.

David summed up the operating terms:

> The Partnership agreement specified that Teck was the manager of the Partnership and that the Fording Coal Trust, although owning 65 per cent of the Partnership, did not play any active role in management. Jim Gardiner was appointed Trust CEO, Jim Popowich COO and Ron Millos from Teck as CFO. Gardiner reported to Mike Lipkewich, Teck's senior vice-president for mining, and to myself as president of the Managing Partner. This arrangement might have worked if there was a consensus on the objectives and a spirit of co-operation, but this turned out to be not the case.
>
> Even when we reached agreement on a course of action, Mike was frustrated by the time it took to achieve the objective. In fairness, we were integrating the cultures of three different companies: Fording, Teck and Luscar, and the coal price was falling as John Taylor had predicted to Gibson and Waheed. Teck had a separate incentive and that was to achieve the cost reductions necessary to earn the extra 5 per cent of the Partnership.

There was some shuffling of Fording management, not surprising given the golden parachutes they had negotiated for themselves during the fray. Gardiner was let go, and Jim Popowich took on his role, being quite supportive and helpful to us, but in the end he too would have no choice but to retire when it came time to exercise his own golden parachute or lose it.

And while some trustees on the Fording Trust did have that spirit of co-operation, it's fair to say that one or two from the old Fording board of directors had exactly the opposite attitude. Some even seemed determined to see to it that we didn't make enough savings within the three years to earn that extra percentage, since that would be forever. There was a conflict of interest on this matter right from the start.

It was a situation calling for patient and careful management, and frustrating at times.

Fortunately, Jim Popowich was an engineer's engineer, as interested in controlling costs and doing the right thing as anyone. Mike Lipkewich's group, with Jim's full support, did in fact achieve the planned synergies by June 2004, a full year and a half earlier than had been targeted, and Teck's direct interest in the partnership, by then christened the Elk Valley Coal Partnership, was increased by 5 per cent to 40 per cent as planned.

Epilogue

As with Highland Valley before, we had pulled off a regional mining consolidation from prior diverse ownership interests, leading to much more efficient operations under a single Elk Valley Coal Partnership, albeit with an income trust partner whose interests would at times be in conflict with ours as an operating mining company.

When Fording Inc. had converted itself into the Fording Trust it had been in large part as a defensive move, to ward off potential raiders such as Sherritt, or perhaps even us, although we would have defined the term a bit differently. As we have seen, black and white knights can change colours quickly, as do other forms of chameleons.

The operating managers of the old Fording Inc. might have considered the adage: "Be careful what you wish for" when they did the Trust conversion. There are times in many businesses when the wisest path forward is to reinvest much or all of cash flow in sustaining or growing the business, and this can certainly be said of mining companies. And when an operating, growth company like the old Fording Inc. or Teck is in partnership with a dividend maximizer like a Trust, it clearly is a recipe for ongoing conflict.

The good news is we had put together the world's second-largest producer of seaborne metallurgical coal, under our management control, by contributing a key asset rather than having to borrow heavily to buy it. David Thompson's talent at poker had taken advantage of an opportunity to give us a new and improved hand when Sherritt reared its head, but there were still cards to be played.

We would either have to deal with the inherent conflicts of purpose through persuasion or, if that proved impractical, by buying out the Trust, either completely or in cooperation with some friendly miner who had objectives similar to ours. It was a situation not unlike what we had experienced earlier at Afton and Cominco. With a contract to manage the partnership, we had, as the Australians say, put our foot on it, and the next step would be up to Teck.

In hindsight, we should have insisted that the Trust convert back to a company like the original Fording Inc., on closing the deal. This would have removed the structural conflict of interest from the start. Or, had that proven impossible to negotiate, we should have expanded the agreement that gave us management control to give us clear carriage over long-term business growth decisions in the same way it did short-term mine operating ones.

It was a great deal that would move Teck well forward, but the fact that we didn't resolve the underlying conflict of objectives at the start would cost us heavily a few years later.

CHAPTER 40

DENOUEMENT

Lack of forbearance in small matters upsets great plans. We must pay attention to the situation.
Mao Zedong

In addition to achieving full production at Antamina and rationalizing the Canadian metallurgical coal business, the first five years of the new millennium saw Teck Cominco acquire the minority interest in Highland Valley Copper that had previously been in Rio Algom, as well as several sales and shutdowns of older mining operations, all part of the inevitable ebb and flow that must occur in revitalizing the mining business.

It also saw, finally, the end of the prolonged period of declining commodity prices in real terms, or the barren years, that had plagued the industry for too long. By 2005 this had transitioned into the newly-christened "super-cycle" with China's continuing economic growth.

Teck's previous years of building and assembling a number of strong operating mines had put it in an enviable position to benefit from this emerging new era.

Increasing Teck's Interest in Highland Valley Copper

The ownership of HVC had been stable since the mid-1980s when the previous Lornex, Bethlehem, Valley Copper, and Highmont mines had been consolidated into a single partnership, much as we had just done in the coal patch. Each of those mines had been very low grade by the standards of the day, and without the efficiencies gained by that earlier consolidation, it is unlikely they could have lasted until things began to turn around in the new millennium.

Despite the merger, it had often been touch and go for the new HVC. Operations were suspended in early 1999 because of low copper prices, and the mine was able to resume production four months later only with the support of temporary wage concessions from its unionized workforce, as well as power rate concessions from BC Hydro. In November 2001, the price of copper hit a 15-year low of 60 cents a pound, once again the lowest in constant dollars since the Depression. Were David Thompson's worst fears about to come true, and would the price actually reach zero in the foreseeable future? Not likely, but they were trying times.

HVC had extensive known copper resources in the ground, but with the low grades and the incremental capital cost required to develop them they would remain uneconomic at the copper prices the mine had been experiencing as it hung in over the previous decade. Unless there was a major price improvement, HVC was scheduled to exhaust its developed resources and close in 2009.

By 2003, Rio Algom had long ago been acquired by Billiton, which in turn was acquired by BHP, and its 34 per cent interest in HVC was now a minor holding in that much larger company. With the mine's short life and marginal economics, BHP put its share up for sale. It approached Teck Cominco to see if we would make an offer, but we declined. Having a right of first refusal under the original agreements, we could wait and see what price BHP might be able to secure from third parties and decide then.

With the price of copper still low throughout most of 2003 there was little interest, but finally Macquarie, an Australian merchant bank, managed to get a Canadian company, Quadra Mining, to offer BHP $73 million for its interest. This valued the whole of HVC at only $220 million. In early December, we received formal notice under our first refusal, and had 60 days to respond.

If this had happened six months earlier we likely would have passed, but copper prices were starting to recover nicely, reaching $1.03 a pound by the end of December. David Thompson, although generally disinclined to spend money where there was any possible alternative, grasped the nettle and agreed to buy it.

It was a brilliant decision. In 2004, that 34 per cent interest alone earned Teck Cominco a pre-tax cash flow of $134 million, in 2005, $204 million, and in 2006, $337 million, all for a purchase price of $73 million. In 2004, we announced an extension of the HVC mine life by four years to 2013, and further work since has extended it to 2023, with every likelihood that it will be extended again as we move on. David has called it "one of the best deals we ever did." It was certainly one of them.

Miscellaneous Sales, Shutdowns, and a New Discovery

In mid-2000, we had learned that an entrepreneurial Quebec company was lobbying for government financing to help it bring a new niobium deposit near Oka into production, in direct competition to our long-established Niobec mine. That could have disrupted the market in which we had been tolerated by the huge Brazilian miner for years as a small, stable, alternative source of niobium supply. With bigger fish in the pan, we agreed to sell our 50 per cent position to those same Quebec interests for $48 million. Built 24 years earlier for only $18 million and profitable from the start, Niobec had been one of the early drivers in Teck's growth, but it was time to move on.

At the same time, Teck Cominco sold its 70 per cent interest in the Los Filos gold deposit, discovered by Joe Ruetz's Mexico exploration team in 1995, to Wheaton River Minerals for $48 million. Wheaton River eventually became part of Goldcorp, which put the property into production successfully in 2008.

A Peruvian exploration team led by Manuel Montoya was responsible for a program that discovered the small but good-grade Zafranal copper-gold prospect in Peru in 2004, now being considered for mine development.

David Thompson arranged to shut down the Trail and Cajamarquilla zinc refineries in BC and Peru for one and three months respectively, taking 55,000 tonnes of zinc that might otherwise have gone to inventory off the market. He obviously hadn't read this book's chapter 28, of course yet to be written, but these shutdowns had the same negligible effect on the surplus inventories as we'd achieved some years back. Where was Ted Fletcher and his baleful stare when we needed him? Or did I just forget to tell David?

In 2004, we sold the Cajamarquilla refinery to Votorantim Metals for US$183 million, plus a conditional payment should the price of zinc rise above a set figure. Such price participations are designed to give the seller some feeling of happiness but seldom have any actual value. However, as it turned out, the price of zinc did rise, generating a good amount of additional revenue for us.

The Bullmoose coal and Polaris lead-zinc mines shut down, each after producing for 20 years. Intel would have to find a new source for all that nice low-alpha lead that the Polaris mine had been supplying to Trail for a song.

And Cominco's historic Sullivan lead-zinc mine at Kimberley finally closed. It had run successfully for 90 years, a Canadian record. It had been the inspiration for and the main supplier to the Trail smelting and refining complex, and without them the Consolidated Mining and Smelting Company, later Cominco, would have been a very different animal.

It turned out that the Sullivan ore deposit was cut off by a fault at the bottom of the mine. Geologists could pretty well project where it was offset to, and where drilling might be able to prove up more lead and zinc of similar metal grades. The problem was that, even if more of the same grades could be proved up, the cost of sinking a new, deep shaft and trying to develop deep mineralization at great depth didn't seem to be economically viable. This was particularly so given the steep geothermal gradient in the area, with the rocks already uncomfortably hot at the lower mine levels. So it was decided that there was no alternative but to finally close the mine, after all those good years.

Interestingly, this was, on a larger scale, the same problem we had encountered at the Temagami mine in the 1970s, with the ore horizon cut off and displaced by a major fault in the lower parts of the mine. In both cases, we will likely never know for sure what treasures lay below.

The End of the Barren Years and a Super-Cycle Emerges

The new millennium saw the emergence of China as a major force in the world economy and a dominant consumer of much of the world's natural resources output, and the gradual realization by much of the investment and business community in the rest of the world that this was happening.

As we have seen, the mining industry had experienced slow growth in world demand for most of the past two or more decades, leading to sustained periods of oversupply and generally declining prices. At the start of this period, few realized it was coming. By the end of it, human nature being what it is, few thought it would ever end. Declining real prices for commodities began to be seen as the new norm, at least until they didn't.

It is well-known that growth in metal consumption per capita in emerging countries, particularly of widely used ones like copper, is often fairly rapid as people's living standards improve. Then, as economies mature, that increase per capita slows to a lower, steady state. In much of the 1960s and into the early 1970s there had been a surge in demand from the expanding economies of Japan and South Korea, in particular, and metal prices tended to be strong. Then, when that subsided and with no major emerging regions to take their place, the western world entered a period of over 25 years of sluggish consumption growth. This was exacerbated by the mining industry's innate tendency to create excess new production every time there was a modest price improvement, soon ending it, and perpetuating the long secular decline.

Chapter 42 includes a telling graph of the price of copper from 1963 to 2015, expressed in constant (1975) dollars to adjust for the effect of inflation. There were a number of brief peaks and valleys along the way, but we can see now that there were three broad secular trends: an earlier super-cycle of the late 1960s, induced by Japanese and South Korean growth; the 25 to 30 barren years between; and the recent China-induced second super-cycle.

The excess of supply over demand in any one of the barren years was often quite small, but the effect was cumulative. Inventories of most metals built up and prices reacted accordingly, staying low for the most part. It was not an easy time for the mining industry, nor for short-term investors, who began to view miners as "destroyers of capital." That description may have been valid for some companies in that era, but not for all.

But now, by the early 2000s, there was once again a major new source of demand, largely from China but to be augmented from some other emerging countries, and the dynamics of the business were about to change dramatically.

When Did China's Boom Really Begin?

The impact on prices for copper and many other commodities started to attract attention around 2004, but in fact the huge rate of growth in China had been in place for years, ever since 1980 when Deng Xiaoping had described his plan to quadruple China's GDP by the year 2000. As Hu Yaobang had calculated, achieving that would mean an annual growth rate of 7.2 per cent, which was a challenge for any country, but which China would actually exceed in many years.

Growth from a small beginning may happen at a high rate, but for a time it doesn't have a great impact on the scheme of things elsewhere. It can easily pass unnoticed by decision-makers in the West, such as us. But if growth keeps going at or near that pace, it can eventually become hugely important. It's an industrial example of the well-known miracle of compound interest.

When did we notice its growing importance to our business? Certainly it was not in 1980, when I was making several visits to China looking for mine development opportunities. Deng Xiaoping was just starting on a major new direction for the country, and I was still looking at it as potential virgin exploration ground, from which we might build mines and produce metals to ship out to the developed world, not the other way around. Well, 25 years is a long time, isn't it?

For me, it was probably when I was asked to address Roundup, a major Vancouver Mining Conference, in January 2003. The subject was "Mining in the Next 20 Years," which was a bit of a mug's game to try to deal with, but I gave it a shot anyway. Some of my projections were more or less on target and some way off, but one in particular sticks in my mind.

China was beginning to be recognized as an increasingly important consumer of some metals, and I had looked back at its consumption of several of them (copper, zinc, and nickel) in 1990, 1995, and 2001, the most recent year for which I had data.

The growth in copper consumption (figure 40.1) was typical and remarkable, with China's consumption having doubled in the five years from 1990 to 1995, and then more than doubling in the next six years. If that trend continued at even close to the same rate, China's consumption would surpass that of the US within a year, and be far ahead of it within the next five years. In fact, that did happen, and it continued to grow at a similar rate for some time.

The reality is that China's copper consumption had shown a similar steady rate of growth for a 30-year period. The trend I had noted at Roundup had been there for a long time, and would in fact continue for a while at very much the same pace, with profound consequences for the world's mining and other industries.

Now, early in the twenty-first century, there was not only rapid growth in consumption per capita once again from a developing country, as earlier in the 1960s, but it was at such a large rate, and on an increasingly high population base, that it was bound to have a huge effect on world metal consumption if it continued.

While I was as late as much of the industry in realizing just how far-reaching this would become, one of my predictions at the 2003 Roundup Conference had been that, within 10 years, at least one of China's mining companies would be among the world's major mining houses. Privately, I argued that we should make contact once again with some of the ones that might turn out to be that major, perhaps our old friends at CITIC, and

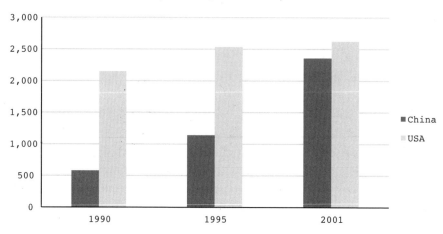

Copper Consumption – China vs. USA
(thousands, metric tonnes)

Figure 40.1
China's copper consumption grew steadily for 1990 to 2001. If it continued apace,
China's would soon pass that of the United States. (From a speech to the Roundup
Mining Conference in Vancouver, BC, in 2003)

develop new relationships that could lead to joint venture mine developments, here or in the third world. It seemed a natural opportunity to develop some sort of mutually beneficial, symbiotic association.

A new era had definitely emerged, after several trying decades in which our growing mining company had managed to do fairly well in spite of slow prices. The question was how should we now position ourselves to take full advantage of the new reality?

Built to Last

As 2005 ended, Teck was in exceptional shape after 30 years of reasonably steady growth. We had interests in 11 mines producing coal, copper, zinc, and gold. This included our 40 per cent-owned, and Teck-managed, Elk Valley Coal Partnership, the second-largest producer of seaborne metallurgical coal in the world. We had a twelfth mine, Pogo Gold in Alaska, ready for development, and two interesting undeveloped base metal properties, Petaquilla in Panama and San Nicolas in Mexico, on the drawing boards.

Teck was in its strongest financial position ever, with over $3 billion in cash and no net debt. Our gross operating profit, before depreciation and amortization, was a record $2.2 billion, with the biggest contributor being copper, followed by zinc and coal.

Teck had grown 500-fold, from a market capitalization of $25 million in 1975 to $12.6 billion, and with its mining base and China boom upon us was certain to grow further.

Our share price had increased reasonably consistently over the years in spite of the inevitable ups and downs of the commodities and economic cycles, and was at a new record level. In fact, $100 invested in Teck B shares in 1975 would have grown to $8,900, assuming dividends had been reinvested. This represents a compounded rate of return on investment of just over 16 per cent, and was at or near the top of that achieved by established world mining companies over the period. This was satisfying for our whole team that had set out to build something strong and lasting, particularly considering the secular decline in most metal prices the industry had experienced over much of the time.

As figure 40.2 shows, there had been ups and downs along the way, some externally induced as the business cycle waxed and waned in the early 1970s and early 1980s, and some self-induced, as during the Antamina penalty box years in the late 1990s. While the latter had been uncomfortable for a time, it is a natural part of a mining business in which, if we are to survive and grow, we need to make significant capital investments on projects whose outcome will be uncertain for a number of years, and which may appear risky when times are tough. Antamina did turn out to be a very good mine, and we had gotten right back on track when that became more widely evident.

It has happened before, and it will happen again.

Time for a Change

David Thompson and I were pretty proud of what we had been a part of creating, along with the team that included my father, Bill Bergey, Ed Thompson, Bob Hallbauer, Keith Steeves, Mike Lipkewich, and others too numerous to name. Those of us still in the saddle could ride it out and enjoy the good times ahead, which was certainly tempting.

However, my father and Hallbauer were gone, and Lipkewich and Steeves had retired or were about to. Thompson and I were both in our mid to late

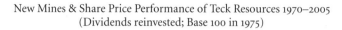

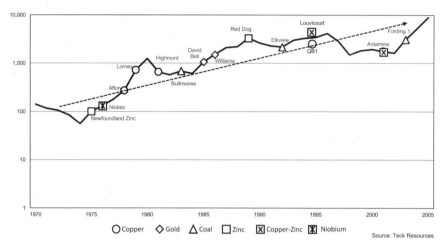

Figure 40.2

The share price of Teck Corporation, assuming reinvestment of dividends, from the major consolidation of Keevil Group companies in 1970 through 2005. The dotted trend line represents a compounded rate of return on investment of 13 per cent.

60s, and I was mindful of the fact that, for many of us, our most productive years had tended to be when we were in our 40s and early 50s. That does seem to be a peak time for people in our business, when youthful vigour is augmented by years of experience, and before one can become jaded by too much of either success or failure.

It was time to contemplate a change, handing off to someone who could take the company to greater things in the coming decade, and we began a quiet search, both internally and externally.

CHAPTER 41

THE CHANGING OF THE GUARD

If I seem unduly clear to you, you must have misunderstood what I said.
Alan Greenspan

Getting succession right is a tricky thing, particularly at or near the top. Is it best done from within, or by recruiting from outside? Should a new CEO be someone who has been a part of the company's best years and shares the same values, or is new blood preferable as part of creative destruction?

There is obviously no right answer to these questions, except to acknowledge that it is tricky, especially if one has to go outside.

We in Teck had recruited from outside many times, which was necessary simply from the staffing requirements when growing from a $20 million to a multi-billion dollar company. This included many strong engineers, miners, and geologists as well as numbers men, including Bob Hallbauer, David Thompson, Keith Steeves, and Mike Lipkewich. Each had filled important roles and were leaders, but none had come in to start at the top, as CEO.

So when Hallbauer went down to run Cominco, he had been with Teck for 16 years and was already part of our culture. In fact, he had helped create it. Similarly, when Bob passed away and Thompson went down, he had been with Teck for about the same amount of time. They had each been part of the team that had built Teck, and the moves had given them and their successors new challenges, while staying within the Teck Group.

The question was whether we could succeed internally again or whether we should go outside. The executive committee of Bob Wright, David Thompson, Brian Aune, David Sinclair, Tak Mochihara, and me became an ad hoc succession committee and, with considerable input from other board members, decided to look in both directions.

We interviewed a number of internal candidates, some of them self-identified and others we saw as having particular potential. It was interesting that some of those who were apparently more qualified professionally were reluctant to take on the job, much as David had been when we first asked him to go over to run Cominco. There were others who may have wanted it more, but didn't seem, to us, to be quite right.

Meanwhile, we were looking outside as well, and retained professional help to locate candidates.

Keith Anderson, then with Spencer Stuart and now with Russell Reynolds Associates, took on the task, and began to work with his own team to sort through possible candidates.

At the same time, several of us had once again encountered and were considering Don Lindsay, whom we have seen in these stories a few times already. Don was a miner by education and initial training, having been inspired by a piece of copper ore he'd seen as a 12-year-old visitor at our Temagami mine. He had worked as an engineer at the Labrador iron mines before going on to become an investment banker with Wood Gundy, and by then was heading up its successor, CIBC World Markets.

David Sinclair had been on the annual CIBC Fishing Derby hosted by Don for visiting miners from around the world and, after sitting with him in a small boat for four hours, called me to say he thought Don was due for a change from working at the bank and would be a good candidate. Coincidentally, both Bob Wright and I had also spoken with Don again recently, in different circumstances, and it also seemed to us like an idea whose time had come. We asked Anderson to put Don on his list and interview him, in addition to his own list of candidates.

Bob, David Thompson, and I met with Don in Toronto several times, and were impressed with his depth of knowledge of the players in the industry. I had learned from experience that it really paid to be close to your peers in other companies, because you never knew when one might become a valuable partner, whether in a time of need or of opportunity.

We were also looking for an individual who combined, to the extent possible, many of the various talents that had gone into building Teck, including geology, mining engineering, and finance. My father, Bob Hallbauer, and I had come from the science or engineering side. David Thompson, as a numbers man, was adept at managing existing assets and caring for the dollars, yet could optimize major deals like the HVC acquisition from BHP and the Elk Valley Coal consolidation.

With 11 producing mines and a smelting-refining facility at Trail, we were complex enough that we needed a person with the administrative capacity to manage these ongoing operations well. With the strategic objective of continuing to build value among the best in our industry over the longer term, we were looking for someone who could also instinctively see and take advantage of new opportunities. It was an interesting challenge since, apart, apparently, from Ghengis Khan's horse men, there are few people who can ride two such steeds with any degree of perfection.

In the last definitive interview that Bob Wright, David, and I had with him in Toronto, Don said that, in his opinion, the measure of a mining company CEO would lie with how many good new mines he was able to bring to the company during his tenure. We talked of a lot of things, but not too surprisingly, that would stick in my mind. The last thing we needed was someone who would rest on our existing ores. This was an important part of what we needed to hear and know.

Keith Anderson interviewed Don privately as well, and his report and accompanying references were very positive. Keith felt that Don stood out above the other potential candidates he had brought forward, which is not always easy for an executive search consultant to say. It is one of the things I have admired about Keith in working with him, then and since.

So we made our decision, and in November 2004 it was announced that Don Lindsay would be appointed president of Teck Cominco Limited, effective 1 January 2005. This would give him a few months to work under David Thompson, and learn where the gremlins were before taking over completely. On 27 April 2005, after the annual meeting, David retired as CEO and Don was appointed to succeed him.

For almost 40 years, Teck had enjoyed, or perhaps persevered through, having a Keevil as president and CEO. For the last five, it had had David Thompson, who had been a major part of the team for so long he could have been considered one of the co-founders of the company. This time we would be appointing new blood directly to the presidency. Teck would have new leadership as it entered another new era and the evolving super-cycle. David would remain on the board for a while to offer any help he could as time went on and the new team took hold, as would I.

Thompson and Lindsay Spoke on the Transition

A reading of a Jane Werniuk *Northern Miner* interview with Don and David at the time is interesting, showing why we all seemed to be of common mind. Excerpts include:

Don Lindsay: "You're never smarter than the cycle. There's a very good commodity cycle right now, because of the economy in China. But one thing you know for sure is that there will be a down-cycle. You have to manage the company and your assets with that in mind all the time."

And, on the unpopularity of the industry over the down years: "I would hope that people have a renewed appreciation of just how essential the mining industry is. It should be self-evident that, 'If you can't grow it you have to mine it,' but we probably have to invest even more in educating the public about how important it is to their daily lives."

And: "In our lobby you can see drill core from the Temagami copper mine, discovered 50 years ago. Ironically it was the first mine I ever visited. I was on a canoe trip with my father, and it was just a coincidence that we ended up there, but something about that makes me feel this is the right place to be."

And Don said: "The key now is to build from where it is, to do whatever we must do to find or acquire new mines. That's the most important job for the company. Although David Thompson is retiring, he is remaining on the board, so he will be close by and I will be consulting him frequently. Plus, my office is right next to Norm Keevil's."

And David Thompson chimed in with his natural modesty: "I joined Teck because it was a young, exciting company and I hoped it would work out. Bob Hallbauer [then senior vice-president] and Norm Keevil [then executive vice-president] had already started growing the company, and all I did was join the team. The highlight of my time here has been that we successfully grew the company from a very small base to a very sizeable company now. If you look at it deal-by-deal you miss the point; really the consistent organic growth of the company is much more important."

And David added what we all know or learn from experience: "This is a cyclical business. We all know it, but people often don't behave that way. At the top everyone wants to spend as much money as possible. At the bottom everybody feels that we've had it and should go somewhere else. If you keep a level head, and realize that triumph and disaster are really two sides of the same coin, then you just ride it through."

Ian Mottershead couldn't have said it better.

EPILOGUE, PART SIX

Reflecting on our story through 2005, it had been a great 50-year ride for a whole host of people who played key roles in building Teck into a major force in Canadian mining. New to the business during the early events covered in part 2, we began by feeling our way, but over the next 30 years we evolved from prospector/geoscientists into serial mine developers, adding 12 new mines over a span of 25 years – almost one every two years – culminating with our participation in Antamina, completed in 2000 and our largest project yet. Not all the new mines were major ones by industry standards, but each was material to Teck in its day. We'd become Canada's fastest-growing diversified mining company, with mines in gold, niobium, copper, zinc, and metallurgical coal.

Having built most of these projects from the ground up, we'd been able to create new wealth for the communities and countries in which we operated, our employees, and our long-term investors. With each of these, we had tried to be the partner of choice, and we had generally succeeded. It had been a satisfying experience for all of us involved, a close-knit group of geologists, engineers, entrepreneurs, lawyers, and accountants that truly did function as a team from the C-suite down.

Antamina had been the last and largest of these new mines, but in the next five years we had begun construction on the new Pogo gold mine in Alaska, in joint venture with Sumitomo; we had acquired the minority interest in Highland Valley Copper previously held by BHP; and we had used our Elkview coal mine and equity funding from Teck and Jimmy Pattison's Westshore coal port as the keys to consolidating all the major Canadian steelmaking coal mines into a single partnership, managed by Teck.

As 2005 ended, our major operations included Red Dog in Alaska, Highland Valley Copper in BC, Antamina in Peru, the Hemlo gold mines in Ontario, the Trail metallurgical zinc-lead complex in BC, and control of the Elk Valley Coal Partnership in western Canada. Important prospects for future development included Pogo gold, the Petaquilla copper-molybdenum property in Panama, the San Nicolas copper-zinc property in Mexico, and the Zafranal copper property in Peru. This had been the result of a simple but successful strategy over 30 years. Discover the discoveries, design, build and operate the mines, and do it again and again.

And the new China-driven super-cycle was a welcome change after some 30 years of gradually declining commodity prices in real, inflation-adjusted terms. Teck's established mines had led us to the strongest financial position in our history as 2005 ended, with a record $3.1 billion in cash, more than offsetting $1.7 billion in debt, and a market capitalization of $12.6 billion.

But leadership must change with time. With my father, my brother Brian, and Bob Hallbauer long passed away and with David Thompson and me approaching the time to hand over the leadership baton, we sought out and appointed a successor in Don Lindsay, a young investment banking executive with a graduate degree in mining engineering and 19 years with the Canadian Imperial Bank of Commerce and its predecessor company. He succeeded David as president and CEO in May 2005, with me continuing as chair and both of us staying on the board to help in the transition. As Don said at the start: "The key now is to build Teck from where it is, to do whatever we must do to find or acquire new mines. That's the most important job for the company."

PART SEVEN

A ONCE-IN-A-LIFETIME PHENOMENON

The China super-cycle was the dominant event of the early twenty-first century, as the "opening-up" movement begun by Deng Xiaoping in 1978 had resulted in China emerging as one of the major economies in the world.

Slow but steady exponential growth from relatively modest beginnings can go unnoticed for a long time, but there comes a point at which observers begin to recognize and react to it. That happened for the mining industry generally around 2005, although there were some outside of China who saw it coming earlier and some who reacted later. As the country became increasingly important and even dominant as a consumer of the world's mineral and other products, this led to a boom in worldwide demand for the products we miners produce, whether copper, iron ore, coal, zinc, or even oil, and a corresponding rise in their prices.

The result was recognition in the mid-2000s of a new "China super-cycle," expected by many to be "stronger and longer" than normal industrial cycles.

Chapter 42 describes some of the broader mining industry's responses to this new era, while chapter 43 recounts stories of some of Teck Resources' main ups and downs as the boom waxed and waned. It features one acquisition that set the company back for years, as well as another project that resulted in the development of a large new copper mine, expected to be a core operation of Teck for decades to come.

This section ends in 2019, after which the Covid-19 pandemic created major dislocations in the world's economies. Volatility continues as this is being written in mid-2022, and the stories of this decade remain to be seen, let alone told.

CHAPTER 42

LIFE IN A SUPER-CYCLE

Men, it has been well said, think in herds; it will be seen that they go mad in herds,
while they only recover their senses slowly, and one by one.
Charles Mackay, *Extraordinary Popular Delusions and the Madness of Crowds*

The China super-cycle had its genesis in 1978 in Deng Xiaoping's reform and opening-up program as he announced his goal to quadruple China's gross national product within two decades. Deng's colleague Hu Yaobang calculated that this would require a compounded annual growth rate of 7.2 per cent for 20 years. As it happened, rates varied from year to year but were generally at or above this level. China's economy and share of world trade had been modest at the time, so growth of 7 to 10 per cent had little noticeable impression on Western observers for much of those 20 years, but the miracle of compounded annual growth can be dramatic if sustained at that level, and for much of the time it was.

The result, as we noted in a 2003 address to a mining industry conference, was that China's consumption of copper, a bellwether industrial metal, had grown steadily from 1990 through 2001, doubling every five years. We said: "If that trend continues, China's consumption of copper would surpass that of the US within a year and be far ahead of it within the next five years." In fact, it accelerated, and by 2020 China was consuming over 50 per cent of the copper produced in the world. China's impact on many other commodities was equally dramatic, one of the defining features of the early twenty-first century.

By 2005 the mining industry in the West had recognized this new China super-cycle, had predicted it would be "stronger for longer," and had begun aggressively responding to it. By the cycle's end in 2016 the industry had learned or relearned some of the lessons of previous boom times.

Refined Copper Consumption (kt) in China and the World

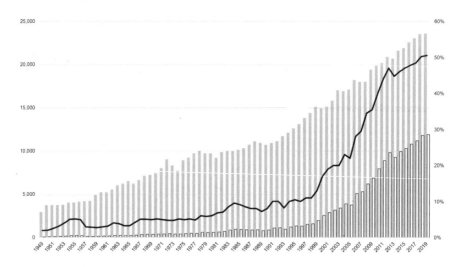

Figure 42.1
Refined copper consumption in China and the world. China's share began rising around
1980, accelerating in 2000 and again after 2006

Dr Copper

We have two classes of forecasters. Those who don't know,
and those who don't know they don't know.
John Kenneth Galbraith

Copper has been called "the PhD of metals," a bellwether of pending growth
or decline because of its widespread usage across much of the world's economy. A rising price due to increasing demand is often a signal that other
commodities and the economy in general can see good times ahead. Dr Copper may not be quite as good at predicting the downside, but that has yet to
sully its pedigree.

Fig. 42.2 tracks 56 years of copper prices, from 1963 through 2019, adjusted for inflation, using 1975 as a base. To some, this chart may appear
nothing more than a series of "squiggles" up and down. To others, the short-
term ups and downs can be seen as noise on top of three distinct eras: the
strong China super-cycle of 2005–19; an earlier, similarly strong but less dra-

Copper Price – 1963 to 2019 (constant 1975 dollars, $/lb)

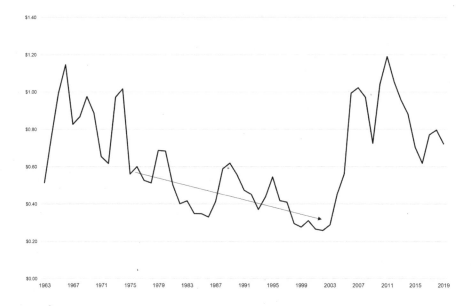

Figure 42.2
The inflation-adjusted LME price of copper, 1963–2019. The China super-cycle was like
an earlier one in the late 1960s, each based upon surging Asian demand growth. The two
eras were separated by 30 years of generally declining prices in real terms, as shown by
the arrow.

matically named cycle, 1964–74; and the 30 years of generally declining prices
in real terms in between.

While there were a few blips up during those barren years, such as around
1990, the increases were soon wiped out as new supply more than offset
growing demand. The arrow illustrates the seemingly inexorable trend during those 30 years, leading Teck's CFO David Thompson to suggest facetiously
in 1999 that the price of copper could soon hit zero. It wouldn't, of course,
but something significant had to occur for it to escape from the trend.

That something was the continued strong growth of the Chinese economy, with increasing use of copper per capita on top of its very large population.

Sir Andrew Mackenzie, the CEO of the world's largest miner, BHP, from
2013 to 2019, has said of the recent super-cycle that it was a "once-in-a-lifetime phenomenon." In fact, older miners had experienced a similar "once-

in-a-lifetime" event years earlier. Like the recent China boom, it too resulted in large part from the emergence of major new markets for commodities in some emerging Asian countries, notably Japan and South Korea.

The long secular decline following that earlier super-cycle was a difficult time for the mining industry, leading *Business Week* magazine in 1984 to print its infamous cover story "The Death of Mining." It was followed, curiously, by the so-called barren years in which Teck Corporation had its best-ever years of growth in both size and value. Go figure.

One investment fund manager and shareholder told me a few years ago: "I've been a student of the mining industry since 2005." Such limited experience would clearly give a student of the industry a different perspective than those of us who had lived through either of the earlier two eras. On the other hand, many older industry managers, cautious after the 30 barren years, may have been too slow to react to the surprisingly steady growth of China's commodity consumption until it became obvious to all by the mid-2000s.

Viewers of figure 42.2 might wonder whether the mining world is due for another long, secular decline like the one following the earlier super-cycle. The straight answer is that we never know. That said, as this is being written there is a strong push towards vehicle electrification as part of the response to climate change, and that cannot occur without a major impact on copper needs. On the other hand, producers of oil and thermal coal are under scrutiny, part of the response to climate change as well. Demand for the two commodity types seems likely to diverge.

The present pandemic will likely subside, but its long-term impact on the economy is unclear. And there are always other unknowns, such as the risk of surprise wars and inflation, each of which is rearing its head as this is being written. As always, sound management over the next decade will be management that keeps in position to respond to several eventualities, rather than risking everything for any single outcome.

Changing Management as the Boom Began

Energetic young CEOs ... with a remit to grow.
David Humphreys

Interestingly, many of the world's established mining companies had fared reasonably well during those barren years. There were laggards, as there always have been, but some of the diversified companies from established majors like BHP, Rio Tinto, and Anglo American down to newer ones like Teck Corporation showed double-digit compounded annual growth in shareholder value over much of the 30 years of declining commodity prices between 1975 and 2005 (Fig. 40.2). There were good opportunities to be taken, and these miners managed to grow despite the apparently difficult times.

But with the new China super-cycle era upon us, many of those successful companies decided they would need new management blood. As David Humphreys puts it in *The Remaking of the Mining Industry* in 2015: "By 2007 three of the largest mining companies had appointed energetic young CEOs (all of them under 50) with a remit to grow. Marius Kloppers came in at BHP Billiton (replacing the seasoned Chip Goodyear), Tom Albanese at Rio Tinto and Cynthia Carroll at Anglo American. Vale already had a sub-50-year-old at the helm, Roger Agnelli. These companies began to think bigger and to look with predatory interest at each other."

As well, Teck had just appointed 40-something mining engineer turned investment banker Don Lindsay as president and CEO. Mick Davis, a financial entrepreneur of similar vintage, had left BHP Billiton and was in charge at Xstrata.

Whether this "remit to grow" was articulated or just assumed, it does seem to be a natural inclination of ambitious new executives. And whether it was a remit to grow value or just size – merely getting bigger for its own sake – could lead to dramatically different outcomes.

Those who think like long-time owners will lean towards increasing value steadily over the years, irrespective of quarterly or annual ups and downs. The legendary Warren Buffet has said: "Our favorite holding period for an investment is forever." As I have said many times, "Size may be the result of success; it is seldom the reason for it." In fact, it can even be an impediment, as Chip Goodyear once observed.

On the other hand, for the odd corporate manager with an edifice complex, size may seem more important than value and quick increases through mergers or acquisitions much more attractive. It is easy to think some of these energetic new CEOs may have leaned towards the latter remits.

Casting Predatory Eyes

Are we to feast, or be feasted upon?
The law of the jungle

One can imagine a question like this unfolding at many of the established mining companies as demand from China surged. A few anecdotes suggest this may have been the case.

Management at Brascan (now Brookfield), which had controlled Canada's large Noranda Mines for over two decades, was for the most part as young and enthusiastic as the executives at BHP, Rio Tinto, or Teck. Nevertheless, perhaps by then more fully aware of the cyclicality of the resources business, Brascan put its 42 per cent shareholding in Noranda up for sale in 2004. Absent a good bid, the next year they decided to merge Noranda with its subsidiary Falconbridge, reducing its controlling shareholding in the combined company (now named Falconbridge) to a more marketable level of about 20 per cent.

Teck's new CEO Don Lindsay approached Brascan about buying it, but David Thompson, still on the Teck board, was lukewarm. In any case, two weeks later Xstrata moved quickly to acquire 19.9 per cent of Falconbridge for $2.1 billion, "getting its foot on it," as the Australians say. Brascan feasted by selling out, while Xstrata did so by buying in. With different perspectives, the hunger of each was satisfied.

The prize was thought to be Falconbridge's Sudbury nickel mines, which, while smaller than Inco's dominant position in that district, were still significant. As well, the price of nickel, which had languished between $2 and $4 a pound for 15 years, was beginning to skyrocket with the super-cycle. It would in fact flare momentarily to over $20 before crashing back down to its historic range, almost identical to the pattern we had seen first-hand with molybdenum prices in the early 1980s (chapter 22).

Inco, sensing it might also be destined to be somebody's supper and working on the premise that the best defence can be a good offence, made its own bid for all of Falconbridge in late 2006, touting the value of obtaining long-sought operating synergies in the Sudbury camp after years of talk but no action by the two main companies.

Teck and Xstrata then seriously contemplated trumping this with coordinated bids for Inco and Falconbridge respectively, expecting that with our new cooperative management we might finally achieve those synergies at Sudbury, but this joint initiative was shelved when Canada's minority Liberal government called an early election. Rightly or wrongly, I concluded that this proposed takeover of two historic Canadian mining companies would have become a top wedge issue in the election, affecting its outcome, and our planned takeover attempt would have been toast. Others differ, but that is what makes a market.

A few months later, when the election was over and the government had changed, Xstrata bid for Falconbridge and, independently, Teck made a $17.8 billion cash and shares bid for Inco. Inco, still wanting to dictate who ate it, then approached American miner Phelps Dodge, which was interested in avoiding its own last supper – perhaps in the jaws of Grupo Mexico. They agreed on a three-way merger of Inco, Falconbridge and Phelps Dodge, to be called Phelps Dodge Inco, and of course based in Arizona. This initiative was necessarily contingent on Inco successfully acquiring Falconbridge.

Xstrata then upped its bid for Falconbridge and Phelps Dodge backed away, itself soon to be eaten in a friendly merger with Freeport. Inco then turned to CVRD (now Vale) of Brazil, which trumped Teck's bid and feasted on Inco, while the latter's shareholders enjoyed their newfound cash bonanza. Teck walked away with its balance sheet intact.

Meanwhile, it seems Marius Kloppers, the young new leader of the world's largest miner, BHP Billiton, had been eyeing number two, Rio Tinto, which was apparently reluctant to become a meal.

Back in America, major aluminum producer Alcoa had been eying Canada's Alcan off and on for years but had always withdrawn when rebuffed by its respected CEO, David Culver. However, by early 2007 Culver had retired, replaced by Dick Evans, and Alcoa mounted a hostile US$27 billion offer for it.

Alcan, which had already sensed something lurking out there in the forest, had taken a hard look at making itself less attractive by buying Inco a year earlier, but had decided not to. Evans came up with a better defence, approaching Rio Tinto with an offer it couldn't refuse. He would let it make a friendly US$38 billion bid for Alcan. Rio Tinto graciously accepted the offer, perhaps eyeing BHP and thinking it needed a good defence too. It was a deal that Evans himself would later describe as "one of the worst decisions ever, the largest metals and mining transaction in the history of the world at the high point in the commodity cycle."

As David Humphreys further reports: "Any hopes the Alcan acquisition would put Rio Tinto beyond the reach of BHP Billiton were dashed when, a month following approval of the Alcan deal by Rio Tinto shareholders, BHP Billiton made an all-share bid for the company. After rejection by the Rio Tinto board, BHP Billiton took its bid hostile in February 2008." Rio Tinto managed to hold them off for a time, and BHP Billiton would formally withdraw its bid when the global financial crisis arrived seven months later.

You can't make this stuff up. And this was just a sample. Slow and steady, incremental growth had seemingly been supplanted by the attempted quick fix. As I said wryly in Teck's 2008 annual report: "In such matters, the winners and losers are never fully apparent until some years after the fact."

The Global Financial Crisis

More money has been lost reaching for yield than at the point of a gun.
Raymond F. DeVoe Jr

The economic surge in China that began to be widely appreciated in late 2005 was interrupted in 2008 by a deep global financial crisis (GFC), said by many observers to have been the worst since the Great Depression of the 1930s. Those of us who had experienced the recession of the early 1980s might differ, but each resulted in material damage to the unprepared.

As Humphreys reports: "The GFC, which arrived in full force following the crash of Lehman Brothers in September 2008, brought the 2½-year commodity boom to an abrupt halt. Prices across the board tumbled as did the share prices of mining companies. Those companies worst impacted were the ones who were most indebted and whose repayments were going to be most affected by reduced cash flows. Among the Global Diversified Miners, Xstrata and Rio Tinto suffered most while BHP Billiton suffered least, although even its share price halved during the second half of 2008." Teck Resources was one of the former, as we will see in the next chapter.

Unlike the 1980s recession, this one was deep but relatively short-lived. Humphreys again: "Largely due to resurgent demand from China, commodity prices staged a remarkable recovery in the second half of 2009, and during the next two years many commodities, including some of the most important mined minerals, copper, iron ore, and gold, went on to attain new price highs."

The boom continued. The mantra as the super-cycle became apparent in 2005 had been that the upsurge would be "stronger for longer." Perhaps few really thought longer meant forever, but hope springs eternal, and it was easy to act as though it would. In fact, as with the earlier super-cycle around 1970, it would last about ten years, peaking in 2011 before declining for five years through 2016.

Nature Abhors a Vacuum

Show me the incentive, and I'll show you the outcome.
Charlie Munger, Berkshire Hathaway

The mining business lives on the battlefield of the age-old war between Dr Copper and Aristotle, who coined his law that "nature abhors a vacuum."

A sharp rise in the price of a cyclical commodity presents an irresistible opportunity, and myriad prospectors, mining executives, and investors will rush in where even angels may fear to tread. Sometimes these rises are major, such as the Japan-based boom of the mid-1960s or the recent China-based one. At other times they end up as smaller blips on the long trend, such as the one that peaked in 1989 (figure 42.2), but in almost all cases they result in substantial investment decisions by mining companies, whether to build new mines or to invest in capacity increases at older ones. The resulting new supply often arrives just as the increasing demand that prompted it starts to sputter and can lead to the downward leg of the cycle, until some years later it all begins again.

Earlier I described Rio Tinto CEO Sir Alistair Frame's concern in 1984 that the company's large Escondida copper prospect in Chile would never be-come economically sound in his lifetime. Copper was trading at around 63 cents a pound and he felt it needed a sustainable price of at least 85 cents a pound to justify a construction decision. By 1988, the price of copper was over $1 a pound, and a decision was made to put the mine into production.

Timing is everything and Escondida did very well, in part because it is an exceptional copper deposit. But it was joined or followed in short order by other large new copper mines including Grasberg in Indonesia; OK Tedi in New Guinea; Olympic Dam in Australia; Collahuasi, our Quebrada Blanca, Radomiro Tomic, and El Abra in Chile; and the expansion of Cerro Verde in Peru. That was a lot of new copper for existing markets to absorb, and the price inevitably resumed its secular decline.

Catching the Wave

History doesn't repeat itself, but it often rhymes.
Attributed to Mark Twain

With demand finally starting to outstrip supply in 2005 after all those lean years, it was inevitable that prices would rise dramatically and new supply would come on stream to fill the vacuum – and perhaps overfill it again.

Soon every mining executive and investor had noticed China's long-increasing copper consumption, and the resulting boom led to record levels in the size and apparent value of most world mining companies. All were king of the castle for a while, until following the global financial crisis of 2008 one was reminded more of Humpty Dumpty. But that severe collapse was short-lived and was followed by a strong rebound through 2011, after which the mining world entered a five-year decline.

Even as the acquisitive predators were eyeing and chasing each other, by 2005 the operating side of the industry was responding to the new shortages in the old-fashioned way. Every prospector and mining company dusted off any shovel-ready expansion or new mine development project on its books. Many of these had been idle for good reason, considered marginal under previous price scenarios, but with the new stronger-for-longer mood they became too attractive to resist.

Humphreys summarizes the result, beginning with a major increase in capital expenditures as the industry sought to expand. This started in 2005 and continued through 2008, when it was interrupted by the global financial crisis. "Despite stalling in 2009, capex in the mining industry began once more to climb steeply and in 2011 and 2012 reached new record levels. Annual capex levels (in 2014 dollars) had ranged from US$25–40 billion from 1978 to 2004 but peaked at over $120 billion in 2012."

An increase in capital spending of that magnitude, more than 300 per cent, could not help but lead to a major increase in supply. Humphreys continues: "Having managed modest growth of 1.7% a year from 2001–2011, global copper production grew 4% in 2012 and 8.5% in 2013, according to the International Copper Study Group. Chile, which had seen almost no growth in copper output for a decade, saw production grow 6.5% in 2013."

And aggressive production increases were seen elsewhere as well. "As a result of massive investment in Australia and Brazil, production of seaborne iron ore surged almost 10% in 2013 and was forecast to grow a further 6% a year over 2014–2016."

The iron majors were widely criticized, by us and others, for fighting over sales volume rather than profitability, but many of us in in metallurgical coal and other commodities tended to think the same way, until we didn't.

Aristotle's vacuum had nearly been filled by 2011 when the London Metal Exchange copper price averaged $4 a pound, almost five times the price in 2003. It began to decline through 2016, when copper averaged only $2.21 a pound, before gradually beginning to recover modestly over the next three years.

Humphreys reports on the industry's contemporaneous rediscovery of moderation. "Not coincidentally, late 2012 and early 2013 saw the replacement of many of the CEOs who had presided during the boom years, including those of Rio Tinto, BHP Billiton, Vale and Anglo American. These management changes brought with them a marked shift in the language of the industry. Gone were the visionary statements and bullish claims about long-run growth in commodity demand. The new CEO of BHP Billiton, Andrew Mackenzie, sought to bring perspective to China's recent development, calling it 'a once-in-a-lifetime phenomenon.'"

It was as though an entire industry and investment community had developed collective amnesia, forgetting almost everything that had been learned about cycles. But there is one thing that seems a constant. At their nadir, almost everyone in the business becomes conditioned to the worst being here for the foreseeable future, and cost cutting becomes the watchword. Conversely, as the peaks approach, almost everyone expects good times to last indefinitely, mergers and acquisitions and share buybacks become the rule, and caution is thrown to the wind. With such crowds, the mantra seemingly becomes a dyslectic "Buy high, sell low."

PricewaterhouseCoopers on the Boom and Bust

The "stronger for longer" thesis had given way to what many now saw
as the "weaker forever" phase.
Jim Rutherford, Anglo American

The auditing firm PricewaterhouseCoopers produces an annual review covering financial results of the world mining industry. In its report for 2015 it noted that the top 40 world mining companies had experienced their first ever collective net loss, and financial leverage had reached new heights.

PwC reported:

The Top 40 companies were *faster* in their pursuit of production. Rampant Chinese demand led to a fierce race to increase capacity at any cost. Business models were adapted to accommodate short-term decisions and production junkies emerged.

The market climbed *higher*, reaching dizzying levels. Production records were smashed, and the industry was awash with cash. Big licks of the prize money [were] then plunged into new projects (and acquisitions), leading to bulging balance sheets, prepared to take on escalating demand.

And the belief was *stronger* for longer!

If that sounds a lot like Yeats's classic "The Second Coming," someone at PwC deserves compliments for a poetic bent. PwC continued:

The Top 40 had impairments of $53 billion in 2015 and have now written-off the equivalent of 32% of [capital expenditures made] since 2010. It is no wonder that inertia prevails …

The market capitalisation of the Top 40 dropped 37% in 2015, a drop disproportionately greater than that in commodities prices. Investors were concerned by liquidity and punished the Top 40 for … squandering the benefits of the boom.

It has been said that a rising tide lifts all ships, and a falling tide the reverse. PwC's words may have been melodramatic, but they were right in concluding that individual companies' results depended not only upon the rise and fall of prices but on how they managed through this once-in-a-lifetime opportunity.

Each of BHP, Rio Tinto, Anglo American, and Teck had proven to be good investments for their long-term owners over the 30 barren years that preceded the super-cycle. Assuming reinvestment of dividends, three of them had produced double-digit returns on their shareholders' invested capital, and the fourth was not far behind. Surprisingly, none generated returns even close to that in the next 14 years up to and including the pre-pandemic 2019. All had flattened their own growth curves, despite the obvious opportunity to match or better them.

Reasons certainly varied and it is not for us to generalize about other companies, but we can review how Teck sought out and pursued opportunities over the super-cycle, how this differed from previous practice, the results, and what it might take from all that as it plans its strategy for the next 15 years.

CHAPTER 43

TECK RIDES A ROLLER COASTER, 2006–2020

*The three keys to a successful, sustainable mining company are its ore reserves,
its people, and its financial strength.*
Teck annual report, 1980

Approaching the Super-cycle

Those three keys, identified over 40 years ago, remain unchanged. There is an important fourth as well – a culture of respect for those with whom we do business: our employees, our investors, junior and senior mining companies, and the communities in which we operate. This we have long described as "being the partner of choice."

A successful mining company must have a cadre of executives at the top who combine a variety of complementary talents: strong mine operators to manage its mines well; exploration specialists to make the discoveries that will precede the establishment of those mines; engineering and construction teams experienced in building new mines; and financial professionals who can manage risk and maintain the kind of strong balance sheet that makes it possible to add value through opportunities that often appear in the deepest of down times. This describes the C-suite at Teck in the three decades leading up to 2006, headed by Bob Hallbauer, David Thompson, and two Keevils, with the contribution of many others too numerous to name.

We closed the first edition of this book reflecting on what a great ride it had been for the people – mentors, colleagues, friends, and family – who played key roles in making Teck a major force in Canadian mining. It had been onward and upward from 1975 through 2005 as we built or acquired a long series of new mines, creating jobs and new wealth for the communities where they were located. Figure 40.2 tells the story in a nutshell, a story of cyclical ups and downs as well as a few years in some investors' penalty box until we completed Antamina, but creating ever more value for our shareholders with each cycle.

As 2005 ended Teck had the strongest financial position in its nearly 100-year history. Its legacy producing interests, mines at Antamina in Peru, Red Dog in Alaska, and in Canada Highland Valley Copper, Hemlo gold, the consolidated Elk Valley Coal Partnership, and the Trail metallurgical complex, were all profitable as super-cycle prices crept in.

The company had $3.1 billion in cash against only $1.7 billion in debt, for a net cash position of $1.4 billion. Teck's share price (Class B shares, adjusted retroactively for a two-for-one split that occurred in 2007), $21 when new CEO Don Lindsay took office in May, closed the year at an all-time high of $31. A year later in 2006, net cash produced by those same legacy assets had increased to $3.8 billion, operating profits again hit a record level, and the share price closed at $44.

Teck was preparing for the future. Construction at the new Pogo gold mine in Alaska was well underway, and Teck and partner Inmet Mining were exploring the large Petaquilla copper property in Panama. The stage was set for Teck to be stronger for longer.

Teck in the Super-Cycle

Some years are better for planting seeds. Others are better for harvesting.
Rarely are both exceptional at the same time, in the same place.
Bruce Flatt, CEO Brookfield

How did Teck do in the super-cycle, widely expected to be stronger for longer? Former BHP CEO Sir Andrew Mackenzie referred to the boom as a "once-in-a-lifetime phenomenon," although perhaps he might have said a "once-in-a-lifetime *opportunity*" for Teck and its peers in the mining business.

Figure 43.1 tracks Teck's share performance in the super-cycle from 2005 through 2016, when it hit its nadir, and on through 2019* as more normal conditions again took hold.

---

* The three years after 2019 included significant, abnormal downturns for the whole world economy as the Covid-19 pandemic erupted, leading to labour shortages, supply chain disruptions, construction cost overruns, fears of inflation taking hold again as it had in the 1970s, and a war between Russia and its old ally Ukraine. At the same time, concerns about the potential impact of climate change led to new initiatives to reduce the world's carbon footprint, with potentially negative impacts on producers of oil and coal and positive impacts on copper and other "metals of the future." Teck shares traded as low as $9 in March 2020,

TECK.B Share Price (C$/sh)
(Year-end, 2008–2019)

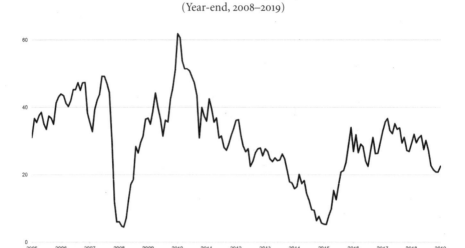

Figure 43.1
The market price of Teck shares from year-end 2005 through 2019

This chart uses a conventional stock trader's style rather than the 30-year exponential growth chart of Figure 40.2. The recent results are like a roller coaster, in sharp contrast with the preceding years during which Teck share value had grown steadily at a double-digit rate despite regular ups and downs in the business cycle. As a general rule, after a frenzied ride, roller coasters end up about where they began.

The stories of this era can be broken down into four phases. First, there were three years of merger and acquisition activity, the results of which set the stage for the rest of the 15-year period. Second, we saw a dramatic fall with the global financial crisis, followed by recovery and a ride to the top as the boom part of the super-cycle continued for a while. Third, there were five long years of decline as the cycle waned, and fourth, three years of relative calm as economies recovered before the dramatic ups and downs during the Covid-19 pandemic and its aftermath.

in the $30–$40 range for most of 2021, and as high as $56 with strong coal and copper prices in June of 2022, before falling back to the mid-30s a month later. Given the volatility and many uncertainties, the tales of these years should be left for future historians.

New Management as the Super-Cycle Begins

Long-term planning in Italy is comparable to the life span of a fig.
Eric Reguly

In his first strategic planning meeting after being named president and CEO Don Lindsay started off with an eloquent "eat or be eaten" challenge. His observations included:

- Ten of Australia's leading mining companies were consumed by acquirers in the last five years.
- A powerful trio of super-majors rules the industry, Rio Tinto, Anglo American and BHP, a group known as the werewolves of London.
- If Australia could produce a global powerhouse like BHP through a series of takeovers, so could Canada.

David Thompson cast me a baleful glance as Don presented this pitch: David and I had different but complementary backgrounds, had worked together closely for 25 years, and each knew first-hand how the company had been built. This, growth through a series of major corporate takeovers, was not the way.

Clearly, like Placer Development, the great Canadian mining company that had been an early model for Bob Hallbauer and me as well as many members of our engineering team, we had been much more successful discovering new mine development opportunities* and acting upon them through solid engineering than we had been in acquiring large companies. The prolonged Cominco experience detailed in chapters 25, 28, and 38, which had slowed us down if not setting us back as we struggled to manage and assimilate it, had not changed our minds one bit.

---

* Exploration geoscientists would all like to make important, virgin mineral discoveries from grassroots programs of their own design. That can be most satisfying, but in a world where fewer than one in a thousand prospects turn out to result in an economically sound mine, success runs against the odds. We learned early on that our role in coming up with mine development opportunities was as well to *discover the discoveries*, whoever had made them, and act upon these by becoming the discoverer's partner of choice and helping to turn them into real mines. It was a plan used successfully by Placer Development earlier and adopted successfully by Teck in its own strong growth years.

But Don was one of the most persuasive people I have ever met, capable of selling refrigerators to polar bears. It was his greatest asset, if well controlled, and a possible liability, if not.

This newly popular acquisitive bent was probably a sign of the early super-cycle good times Humphreys later described as a parade of "energetic young 40-something new CEOS ... with a remit to grow" who "began to look with predatory interest at each other." Interestingly, our own team of Hallbauer, Thompson, and me had accomplished some of our best growth years while in our mid-40s to mid-50s, albeit aided by the availability of wise old owls like my father and some experienced board members.

We had been actively looking for ways to grow ever since Teck Corporation had been created, but our eyes had been focused on potential mineral development prospects that would create new wealth and value, not just corporate acquisitions for the sake of size alone. That was how we had grown from a $25 million to a $12.6 billion company, seeking out and acting upon mine development opportunities one after another. I liked to say that size was the result of success, not the primary reason for it.

But in this new era, as China continued its rapid economic growth, an economy promising to be "stronger for longer" was a welcome change after those 30 barren years, as Humphreys had called them. There would be new opportunities to grasp, new ideas to try, and we were willing to listen.

And we still had a phalanx of board members who had been with Teck for enough years to understand what had worked and what had not as we had built the company. David Thompson and I were still on the board, along with seasoned executives Keith Steeves, Robert Wright, Warren Seyffert, Norman Keevil III, and Brian Aune, a highly successful investor. All had been Teck directors long enough to understand the strategy and culture that had built the company. More recent additions included Hugh Bolton, a highly regarded professional director; Derek Pannell, recently retired as CEO of Noranda Mines; and Chris Thompson, previously CEO of Gold Fields of South Africa.

This balance between experience and enthusiasm seemed to auger well for a successful future in the revolutionary "stronger for longer" era of opportunity.

Think Differently, to Build or to Buy?

We all look at everything, let's be honest about that. If the competition doesn't show up, that's because they aren't the best buyer for the asset. And when you buy, you will pay the highest price that anybody else would be willing to pay.

Chip Goodyear, retired CEO of BHP

It was not unexpected that Don would think differently than I did as a geoscientist, Bob Hallbauer did as a mine builder and operator, or David Thompson did as a long-time mining financial executive. Don had spent the previous 19 years as a deal broker with CIBC World Markets and its predecessor, advising mining companies to buy or sell themselves or their assets. Success in that field is measured by short-term results, often characterized as "you eat what you kill." The main rewards are for finishing deals one starts, not for dropping them as the price gets more difficult to justify.

For years to come, in almost every annual Teck strategic planning meeting, Don would lead a session called "Build versus Buy?" He would observe quite correctly that building a new mine might take five or ten years, and that such a commitment entailed all sorts of risks such as construction cost overruns and material changes in the markets for the product over such a long time. Our later foray into developing an oil sands mine, described below, drove this home. When buying existing producing assets, on the other hand, one would likely see what Don called "cash on cash," or an early return on the investment. There is also an element of instant gratification involved in a quick buy.

I might counter with Chip Goodyear's words about the cost of buying in a competitive market. Buying at the top of the cycle and in a hotly competitive market seems unlikely to add real value, unless the buyer can see significant upside potential that is either unseen by or not available to the pack.

On the other hand, earning an interest in a good development prospect with serious upside potential by providing engineering and construction management and arranging financing can turn out a lot better than paying full value for a producing mine or company. And it is more likely to create new jobs and wealth for society. It had worked for Placer Development and Teck for years and had been one of the keys to the success of both companies.

In the end, "Build versus Buy?" is the wrong question to ask.* A good build can be much better than a bad buy, and vice versa. It's really a matter of doing the right thing at the right time, and not the wrong thing at any time.

In fact, as we shall see, the venture for which Don will be remembered longest was the discovery and development over many years of the major hypogene copper deposit underlying the original Quebrada Blanca mine. It had been part of the upside potential when Teck recovered the Quebrada Blanca property in the acquisition of Aur Resources. It was a combination of buying and building that worked out exceptionally well.

Phase One: Three Years That Set the Course, 2006–2008

Returning to Oil, Bidding for Inco, Re-acquiring the QB Property, and Fording2

When the Prince kisses a new project, he has no idea whether it will turn out to be Cinderella or remain a toad.
Paraphrasing the Brothers Grimm

Despite his thesis about acquisitive werewolves, Don's first significant move as CEO was another conventional "Teck-style deal," as he agreed to participate in building a substantial new mine from the ground up. Said quickly, it sounded right up our alley. Only thing was – it was developing an oil mine, rather than our usual copper, zinc, gold, or coal.

It was not widely remembered by 2005, but Teck Corporation had begun largely as an oil company 42 years earlier when oil discoverer Canadian Devonian Petroleums and gold miner Teck-Hughes had merged to create it. At the time 80 per cent of our combined income had come from producing 4,000 barrels of oil a day from the Steelman field in Saskatchewan. For several years we ploughed many of the profits back into the ground, vainly hoping to discover more oil, as told in chapter 9.

---

* The question would never entirely disappear: 17 years later, in his final conference call with shareholders, Don said, "It's a classic build versus buy. I think most of us would rather buy because as the big deal closes, you're starting to get cash returned right away. I think most of the industry has a bias to do that."

Eventually it occurred to us that we knew much more about mining than the oil business, everything being relative, of course. After a few years, as we had successfully beefed up our mining side to overtake the income from the Steelman field, we spent the next decade trying to find a good way to exit oil.

But by 2005 it seemed a good idea to return to it. Some of our largest operations by then were open-pit coal and copper mines, and with the mining technology of oil sands production making up a significant part of the total operating cost, it seemed logical for a solid mining operator to partner with an oil company that had the necessary processing and marketing capacity as we jointly developed a new producing operation.

As well, the resource on offer was in nearby Alberta and had potential to give us many decades of production once developed successfully. That all fitted nicely with our historic strategic objective of participating in long-life mineable resources where we had expertise, in safe jurisdictions, and with important products the world needed that would be valuable over the years to come.

So in 2005 we agreed to acquire 15 per cent of the Fort Hills oil sands partnership, led at the time by Petro-Canada, a major Canadian oil company with no experience mining oil sands. It seemed like a good complementary partnership, one to which each side could contribute meaningfully. We also acquired some nearby lands on which we hoped to develop a 100 per cent owned oil sands mine we called Frontier; we would use our newfound oil expertise to develop it after Fort Hills had been completed successfully. It was a plan that made sense at the time.

Things happen. By 2009, Petro-Canada had been acquired by Suncor, an experienced oil sands operator, so that Teck's mining expertise, while helpful, was no longer necessary. Total Petroleum of France also became a partner, and Teck increased its interest to 21.3 per cent. The commodities super-cycle was still in a rising phase in 2009 and would not begin to slip until 2012 for metals, and somewhat later for oil.

By 2013, as the super-cycle at large was showing signs of age, Suncor, Total, and Teck announced plans to build a $13.5 billion oil sands mine at Fort Hills, fully supported by Teck's board of directors. Don Lindsay announced: "With an expected mine life of at least 50 years, Fort Hills is one of the best undeveloped assets in the Athabasca region and is a natural fit with our business strategy of acquiring and developing long-life assets in stable jurisdictions. With Fort Hills and our other oil sands assets, we are building a new division within Teck that will create value, significant cash flow and diversification for our business for decades to come."

The price of oil was still strong, with West Texas Intermediate (wTI) selling at close to US$100 a barrel as the project was sanctioned. There was sufficient new pipeline capacity on the drawing boards to get Canadian oil to market, and the economics looked good.

But things kept happening. Within two years the wTI price had dropped to below $30 a barrel. The expected new pipeline capacity failed to materialize, and landlocked Alberta crude has since sold at consistently high discounts on the posted wTI price. Environmental concerns related to climate change risks continued to increase, with the long-term future of oil markets becoming less clear than earlier thought. To top it off, the actual capital expenditure by the time Fort Hills reached production in 2018 had increased to $17 billion.

In 2020 Teck cancelled plans to build the nearby Frontier mine and wrote off its $1.1 billion investment. At the same time Teck and Suncor each wrote down their investment in Fort Hills, Teck by a further $1.2 billion.

Unfortunately, this did not become the success story we had expected it to be, and we could have made better decisions along the way – but that is hindsight. As this is being written, oil prices have once again started to rise as parts of the world begin recovering from the pandemic and with Russia's invasion of Ukraine, but in a new era in which the impact of carbon emissions on our earth's climate has begun to be felt more strongly around the world, the future for Canadian oil is less clear than when we began. As Don Lindsay has said: "Would we do it again the same way if we knew what we know now? The answer is no." Teck sold its interest in Fort Hills for $1 billion in late 2022 and wrote off its remaining investment.

Casting Predatory Eyes on Nickel

In individuals, insanity is rare, but in groups, parties, nations, and epochs,
it is the rule.
Friedrich Nietzsche

Sure enough, while Fort Hills was a historic Teck-style deal, by early 2006 Teck had joined the parade of predator-eyed players. We began chasing major nickel producer Inco as the market price moved up, eventually making a top-of-market bid of $17.8 billion in cash and shares for it, as described in the previous chapter. This led to defensive moves by Inco and higher bids from several others. After a few months of ever more ambitious chess moves by various predatory companies, CVRD (now Vale) of Brazil appeared to have "won" Inco with an all-cash offer of $19.4 billion. We thought it was all over.

Investment bankers hate to lose a deal once they start pursuing it, and will bend every effort to keep it alive. Teck was not going to win by adding more of its own shares to try to top CVRD's all-cash offer, but Bob Dorrance, CEO of TD Securities, called Don with a novel idea. He thought there would be a market for Teck to quickly sell $6 billion of its own shares to Canadian and international institutional investors in an overnight "bought deal" and then use the cash to top CVRD's offer with a surprise $20 billion counterbid.

Don agreed to try, but the overnight issue proved to be a hard sell, and the next morning Don and the Teck board decided to down tools and drop the whole thing. It was truly over.

The price of nickel had languished between US$2 and $4 a pound for the previous 15 years, flared to $20 as the bidding war raged, and then immediately fell back to earth. Why as chair I had let Teck get drawn into this one escapes me, except that we had begun with almost $4 billion in cash on hand produced from our existing mines, our own shares had soared along with the target company, and our offer was partly in Teck shares. So, in the end, while it was a large deal, we probably weren't betting the company. But it bore no resemblance to anything in our history that had made the company great. It was a deal well lost.

The Return of Quebrada Blanca

I believe everything we do in life is part of a plan. Sometimes the plan
goes as intended, and sometimes it doesn't. That's part of the plan.
Matthew McConaughey

It wasn't all hostile acquisition attempts in those first three super-cycle years. In mid-2007, Teck used its record cash position, still in the bank after the failed chase for Inco, to acquire Aur Resources for $4.1 billion. It was a friendly deal that recovered the remaining supergene copper resource at Quebrada Blanca and the underlying deep hypogene copper prospect now known as Project QB2. Also included was another Chilean copper mine under construction at Carmen de Andacollo, an interesting property we had attempted to acquire for exploration when we were first working for ITT in Chile back in the 1960s.

As described earlier on page 306, most economic copper mineralization in Chile and elsewhere is in the form of copper sulphides, in ores that require crushing, grinding, and flotation in a costly mill before the copper concentrate is shipped to a smelter for further processing. With deep weathering in northern Chile's arid regions, these original near-surface copper sulphides are often oxidized and leached, the copper mobilized and redeposited above or near the original "hypogene" sulphides. This secondary copper mineralization is referred to as "supergene." In some places it is higher grade and relatively easily processed using a solvent extraction and electrowinning process (SX-EW) to produce high-purity cathode copper at the mine site, bypassing conventional smelters and producing copper plate that can be sold directly to consumers.

Cominco Resources CEO George Tikkanen, who had been part of the team responsible for acquiring the important Red Dog prospect in Alaska some years earlier, recognized a similar opportunity at Quebrada Blanca in the early 1990s. The mine was built and put into production in 1994 by Cominco and Teck, based upon that near-surface, enriched supergene ore. As we mined it, we drilled a few deeper holes and did indeed encounter low-grade sulphide copper, the original hypogene mineralization. But with a grade around 0.4 per cent copper and a metal price of 80 cents a pound, the time when it might become economic to mine seemed far into the future.

By 2000, Cominco's management had decided it should sell its 38 per cent interest in Quebrada Blanca and use the proceeds to reduce its chronically heavy debt (page 412). Teck, with our smaller 28 per cent interest, seriously considered buying Cominco's share and keeping control of the property, but with the low copper price and construction not yet finished at our own landmark Antamina project, we decided to pass on it.

Earlier, Teck had been in partnership with Aur Resources as we jointly developed the Louvicourt copper and zinc mine in Quebec. I had been on the Aur board of directors for eight years and Aur's CEO Jim Gill was on Teck's board, so when it became clear that Teck and Cominco were prepared to sell QB and Aur wanted to expand its copper exposure in Chile, it was an obvious step and a simple matter to negotiate a transfer price acceptable to all three companies. Cominco's in-house lawyer playfully accused me of having had a conflict of interest for seeing to it that the property remained in friendly hands, although everyone was equally happy with the outcome. It was the closest I ever came to being a real investment banker.

And having it in friendly hands turned out to be one of the best backup plans we ever made.

As shown earlier in figure 42.1, the copper market had changed materially between 2000 and 2007. By 2000, China's economy had been growing steadily since Deng's commitment to quadruple it within 20 years, but it still accounted for only 10 per cent of world copper consumption. In the next seven years this would continue to grow exponentially, and by 2007 it had reached 30 per cent of world consumption and was still rising.

In 2007 the price of copper leaped above $3 a pound, four times what it had been in 2000, and the super-cycle was on the move. Jim Gill decided he and his team wanted to sell Aur and retire, and with our strong cash position still intact after the Inco episode we were able to reach a friendly deal that once again satisfied all parties. We had the Quebrada Blanca mine back in our camp.

The limited immediate attraction of buying Aur was that it would quickly augment our annual copper production through what remained of the QB supergene deposit, as well as through a partially completed plant designed to process hypogene ore from Chile's historic Andacollo copper property. This near-term increase in copper output was of interest to Don and stock market players given the recent surge in the price of copper.

The upside potential was the possibility of discovering an economic copper deposit under or near that QB supergene deposit we had been mining for 15 years. This was obviously a long shot, as any exploration geologist knows. Classifying ore as economic is not only a matter of the grade being adequate but also of the tonnage of the deposit being large enough to support building a new mine and concentrator at that location, along with the necessary infrastructure. It is rare that a few early drill holes will stand up to further work and lead to a major new mine, although hope springs eternal for most geologists. But I've often felt that good luck is one of the best geoscientific methods any explorer could have in his or her toolbox, and in this case, as we shall see, we had it.

There was competition for Aur, which we thought at the time was most likely to come from Anglo American with its interest in the nearby Collahuasi mine. As we would learn years later, the most serious of the other bidders was Phelps Dodge, whose president, Tim Snider (now a valued director of Teck), had also been struck by the upside potential of the deeper hypogene mineralization and had recommended the acquisition to his board. He was turned down.

This proved to be one of the best deals Teck had made in years. We will return to Project QB2 later, but first we need to deal with an intervening acquisition that, unfortunately, coincided with the onset of the 2008 global financial crisis and put Teck in serious financial jeopardy.

Doubling Down, the Second Coal Deal

We always aim to be the partner of choice, for prospectors, junior and senior mining companies, and for employees, investors and the communities in which we operate.
The Teck code

While we were completing the Aur acquisition, managing the Elk Valley Partnership was proving to be frustrating. As described in chapter 39, under the 2003 agreement, Teck had 40 per cent ownership and was the managing partner of the newly consolidated coal mines, with the Fording Trust owning a non-operating 60 per cent. Teck also held 20 per cent of the trust, but when it came to reinvestment decisions there was room for differences of opinion between Teck, as a miner interested in the long-term success of the mines, and the trust, primarily interested in maximizing near-term cash flow and annual payments to its unitholders.

We might have resolved this better back in 2003 when we put together the coal partnership in the first place, but those negotiations were done under some competitive stress and the inherent conflict was left to be worked out as the partnership went on. Ideally, it ought to have been settled through a friendly working agreement between the partners, but unfortunately the relationship began to deteriorate rather than improve with time. By 2007 it began to look as though a Teck buyout of the trust was the easiest solution – provided we could agree on a satisfactory price.

Potential buyout discussions with the trust began in early 2007, several months before the Aur acquisition. Metallurgical coal was selling at $100 a tonne and the Fording Trust units were trading at about $25. By June 2007, when a presentation was made to the Teck Board in Tokyo, the units were trading between $28 and $33. The total market value of the trust was around $4 billion, and the chance of negotiating a reasonable agreement seemed good.

How this progressed over the next year from Tokyo onwards is an interesting story of the perils of chasing what might initially have seemed a potentially good deal upwards in the face of a rising market, ignoring clear signs of impending global financial difficulties, with management recommending acquisition without a safety net at or near the top of that market and a board ratifying it for all the wrong reasons. It should be told and understood if future leaders are to avoid the same mistakes.

After receiving our initial offer, the trustees were determined to canvas the world to see if there were alternative buyers at a better price. This process dragged on for the better part of a year while they kept Teck's interest in their back pocket and during which they received no other serious offers. So, a year later, in June 2008, they indicated to us they were finally prepared to negotiate a deal.

The thing was, by then the price of coal had tripled to $300 a tonne. This major increase was in large part the result of seasonal floods in Australia, but it was also a time when price enthusiasm was rampant in the commodity world. In hindsight, it was like the Roaring Twenties before the Great Depression. The price of oil had climbed to $140 a barrel, and CIBC World Markets chief economist Jeff Rubin, in an Icarus moment, was predicting that oil would soon reach $225 a barrel. Fording units traded as high as $96 that June, almost four times what they had been valued at when we had started talking about a buyout.

This deal we had begun working on a year earlier had become substantially more expensive, but once again there is a natural tendency among investment dealers not to give up on a deal once started. At a point, someone should be the wise old owl, prepared to say no.

If one believed such commodity price inflation was going to continue building up "stronger for longer," as some still did, one might have thought it was a good time to buy. If one thought it less likely, or that there were serious economic risks on the horizon, it may have seemed wiser to be patient and wait it out.

Signs of Potential Trouble Ahead

Markets can stay irrational longer than you can stay solvent.
John Maynard Keynes

And in fact, there were clear signals of potential trouble ahead well before the collapse of historic investment bank Lehman Brothers in September 2008 and the ensuing global financial crisis (GFC) that wreaked havoc on the unaware.

The GFC came as a surprise to many who were reveling in the good times, but not to all. Countless learned books have been written about it, some by those who foresaw it and many by those who missed it completely.*

One of the root causes of the GFC was the years of extraordinarily low interest rates that preceded it. Low rates led to a chase by investors and savers for high interest or dividend yield, increasingly available in the riskiest investments such as sub-prime mortgages and exotic financial instruments. Financial engineers and major investment banks began packaging these riskiest loans together with other less risky ones in a massive sales effort, one that eventually backfired as the whole market collapsed in September 2008.

There had been signs of financial excess on the horizon a year earlier, beginning with the failure of some offshore Bear Stearns hedge funds and a scary run on the UK's Northern Rock bank in the summer of 2007. I was in Scotland at the time and the lines of frightened depositors hoping to recover something from their bank accounts reminded me of scenes from the Great Depression of the 1930s. It left me concerned enough to begin watching what was going on in that financial world, even though that was beyond my pay grade as a simple geophysicist.

Two months later, still in 2007 and a year before the GFC exploded on the world, long-time investment banker Merrill Lynch wrote down its holdings in subprime mortgage securities by $7.9 billion, announcing a net loss of $2.3 billion, and its CEO was soon gone. The mood of one who saw a crisis

---

* Retired Bank of Canada governor Stephen Poloz, in his 2022 book *The Next Age of Uncertainty*, is critical of the extent to which political economists have bought into the concept of "black swans," the idea that many world-altering events are random and, therefore, unpredictable. "When an economist declares that an economic or financial event (such as the 2008 GFC) is a black swan, they are essentially absolving themselves of any responsibility for not foreseeing it."

coming but played on was captured by the CEO of Citibank, Chuck Prince, who famously said: "When the music stops, in terms of liquidity things will get complicated. But so long as the music is playing, you've got to get up and dance." He too was soon gone.

Just as Teck's David Thompson had seen a major recession coming in 1980 and had taken appropriate action to avoid the worst of it (chapter 21), retired banker Charles R. Morris forecast a similarly major financial markets crisis ahead with *The Trillion Dollar Meltdown*, published in February 2008, only seven months before the worst of it happened.

Morris noted: "The coming crisis is often compared to the Long-Term Capital Management debacle which rattled global finance in 1998. But that involved about $100 billion in positions, with no more than $10 billion or so at risk in a worst case. It was settled when New York bankers met in the New York Fed's boardroom and agreed to cough up $3.6 billion. Today, the at-risk values are 100 times higher. There is no room big enough for a meeting and no list of who should be at the table." He observed about the Nobel Prize winners who ran Long-Term Capital Management: "As a general rule, only the very smartest people can make truly catastrophic mistakes."

Morris's book was a compelling read, and I immediately gave a copy to each of Teck's directors, although it is unclear how widely it was read, if at all. In the euphoria of a rising market, Cassandra has few listeners. It is easier to keep dancing.

In March, a month after Morris's book was published, major New York investment bank Bear Stearns collapsed. It was quickly bailed out for pennies on the dollar by JPMorgan Chase, after pressure from the US Treasury Department and the New York Federal Reserve Bank, each highly concerned about the situation spreading further.

In a 2019 post-crisis book by US bankers Ben Bernanke, Hank Paulson, and Timothy Geithner, *Firefighting: The Financial Crisis and Its Lessons*, the authors said: "We knew that Bear wasn't the only overleveraged and inter-connected nonbank at risk of a run. Seven months into the crisis (March 2007) the Bear drama was a sobering reality check about the frailty of the system, the limits of our powers, and the potential for catastrophe in the near future."

But the party continued. By June 2008, as the market peaked, all risks seemed to have been forgotten again. In an eerie reprise of the Club of Rome days before a major financial collapse 27 years earlier, the ever-bullish Don

Quixote was assembling a new resources investment fund to capitalize on the latest "new era of resources scarcity" and even I thought about buying into it. Luckily, I didn't.

That same June, a year after the Tokyo board meeting and with both coal and Fording unit prices more than tripled, the Fording trustees were, not too surprisingly, finally ready to deal, and the Teck board met again to consider a much larger, multi-billion-dollar bid for Fording Trust's 60 per cent of the Teck-operated Elk Valley Coal Partnership.

The Anatomy of a Mistake

Boards, at the very least, should act in the classic sense like a governor on an engine that measures and regulates the machine's speed and, if necessary, turns it down to keep it from blowing up.
David Zweig

This bid would prove to be a near-disaster for a historic Canadian mining company and many of its shareholders. I'm embarrassed to have let it happen under my watch as chair, but the tale should be told as a caution to future managers and boards that may be inclined to chase acquisitions past their "best by" date and into the top of a fragile market.

The meeting began with a presentation by a representative from Australia's Macquarie investment bank, who had been asked by management to advise the Teck board on the proposed deal. As noted, the price of steel-making coal had tripled from $100 to $300 a tonne over the course of the year since we had first considered making an offer, and the price of the Fording Trust units had risen even more. It was not lost on most of us that this was due in large part to seasonal flooding in Queensland, but Macquarie played this down and suggested we might be into a new, secular high-price environment for coal for some time. Perhaps, and perhaps not, but it was an essential part of the pitch.

I argued against the proposed offer, based upon the unprecedented size of it in what clearly were financially precarious times, as described in the Morris book, and reminded the board that the much larger Noranda Mines had twice nearly gone under by borrowing heavily to buy at the top of the market. New Teck director Derek Pannell, recently retired as Noranda CEO, was sitting beside me and muttered, "I remember that," but few at the table heard or listened.

I argued as well that the proposed deal would create too big an imbalance between our base metal and coal operations. I suggested that if the buyout was indeed thought necessary to eliminate our uncooperative partner, we bring in another coal-mining company with similar mining business interests to Teck for about a third of the deal, making it more manageable financially and leaving us better balanced.* Don Lindsay acknowledged that this was a good idea but urged the board to approve the deal immediately, saying, "we can look for a partner on even better terms after the closing." Enthusiasm at a market top can trump wisdom any day.

The pressure to close early was on, and as Lindsay wrote later: "We wanted the deal to close sooner rather than later while the coal price was still at $300. At that price the cash flow per month was going to be very substantial."

After the discussion had gone on a while longer, and with little being offered in the way of caution by the other directors, one said she had to leave soon to catch a plane and moved approval of the bid since it could be "transformational" for the company. As it would turn out, it certainly would transform us, although not in the direction she apparently expected. Senseless change just for the sake of change makes no sense, and the word should never again be used at Teck.

Next, professional director Hugh Bolton said, "Well, we have to support management," and he seconded the motion.* The proposal was put to a vote, and everyone but me voted for it. We were ready to make the Fording Trust an offer it couldn't refuse.

In July, Teck announced its offer to purchase all the issued Fording Trust units for a net cost of $12 billion. While a high price at what was quite likely

---

* We had done something like this once before when we wanted for structural (tax) reasons to eliminate the minority 27 per cent public interest in Afton Mines but were reluctant to pay the market price, which had in our view become too high. The solution was to find a compatible industry partner (Metallgesellschaft), interested in owning a part of the mine as a partnership, and that would fund the purchase price to acquire it. It had worked (see page 258). There are often other ways to skin a cat.

* Bolton later apologized, admitting that the proper role of a board is to be the "chamber of sober second thought," like a properly functioning Senate, and not to act as a rubber stamp for management's wishes. Chris Thompson apologized as well, although he said I should have pounded the table more. Several other board members said they had been influenced by the fact that the jury was still out on management and it needed to be supported at this time, since it had not been supported clearly enough during the Inco bid. One, when asked later why he had voted for the deal, said, "Well, Don wanted to do it."

near the top of the market, it might have been manageable if the latest thinking about a "new era of resources scarcity" had lasted for a while longer. Bank financing had been arranged, including a US$5.8 billion bridge loan due to be repaid in one year, and a term loan for the balance of US$4 billion. The Fording unitholders were to vote on the offer by 30 September, and the purchase would close on 31 October. Teck's plan had been to do a substantial bond issue in October before the closing and while the market was still strong, using that funding to replace the bridge loan and some of the term loan.

Management had also agreed to offer a minority 20 percentage points of our newly acquired 60 per cent of the coal partnership to a compatible mining industry partner, if one could be found, after the purchase was concluded. Said quickly and forcefully, it might have sounded to some like a good deal all around, and Bob's your uncle.

But that's not what happened.

When the Music Stopped

We like to blame bankers and financial markets, as if their reckless lending
was to blame for our reckless borrowing.
Niall Ferguson

The Lehman Brothers collapse occurred in mid-September and markets finally crashed. The global financial crisis was upon us, just as Charles R. Morris had predicted and Bernanke, Paulson, and Geithner had fretted about six months before. The world, which had been "awash in liquidity" two years earlier, suddenly encountered a credit freeze unlike anything seen in living memory.

In major risk initiatives such as our commitment to buy out the Fording Trust, particularly in perilous times, it is usual for the purchasing partner to insist on a "market out" clause under which it can terminate the deal in the event of major, unexpected changes in the financial environment, sometimes referred to as "acts of God." The banks, more fully aware of the risks that had surfaced over the previous year than Teck management, had insisted on that perfectly normal market out clause in their undertakings with Teck.

Inexplicably, though, come October the banks did not exercise their market out and instead put up all the funds, apparently intoxicated by the large fees that were on the table if the deal was completed. Teck management, which equally inexplicably had itself *not* negotiated a market out* with the Fording Trust, was advised by some counsellors that it was legally bound and had no choice but to accept the bank loans and close the deal on schedule at the end of October.

As a result, Teck, which had finally retired the last of Cominco's debilitating historic debt load and had been completely debt-free two years earlier, suddenly had an unheard-of $12 billion in debt. The market price for our shares collapsed, falling from $35 to $4. The total market value of the company (its market capitalization) had dropped to $2 billion. There were concerns amongst investors and employees alike that this 100-year-old company would collapse. The "transformational" acquisition was almost fatal.

It was, as the British footballers say, an "own goal." Don Lindsay's first words to me were "I blew it," as he asked for the chance to stay on as CEO and help us try to work our way out of it.

Digging Out of a Deep Hole

Creation is a struggle. It takes imagination. It takes energy. It takes years.
Destruction is the breathless work of moments.
Michael Tobert

What to do? Shareholders, both short- and long-term ones, were angry and threatening. Innocent employees throughout the company's operations were worried about their jobs and pensions. But the situation was what it was, and we had to do our best to recover from it.

Unfortunately, David Thompson had been removed from the board at the annual meeting earlier in the year. Had he still been there, he doubtless would have joined me in arguing and voting against the Fording Trust offer. Together we might well have carried the day, or at least helped put the proposition on hold for further review. Either way, the ensuing years would have been much different for Teck, but it had happened.

---

* As Don Lindsay later wrote, in 2016: "In the original negotiations I had pushed hard to have a market out for Teck in the transaction. However, I ran into a lot of resistance and was pushed by my own team and counsel to drop it on the theory that the other side would never accept anything less than a firm deal. My compromise was to ensure the banks had the market out and if markets suffered, we would rely on them to do the right thing. With the benefit of hindsight, we should have stuck with our original position." Yes.

One way forward would have been to bring David Thompson back to manage the workout, and there were many in and outside of Teck who argued for it. But David was even angrier than I was and couldn't understand how our directors, let alone management, could have let it happen. To come back he insisted on carte blanche, or absolute control of the recovery program. He certainly could have done it and done it well, since when one is in a deep hole there are only so many ways to dig out of it. How different would Teck have looked today? It's impossible to know.

It was not an easy choice, but after a couple of sleepless nights punctuated by dreams of polar bears I decided to back Don Lindsay's request that he be allowed to try to clean up what he had done. We called a special board meeting and I began to explain why I thought Don was the right person to fix things, with weekly if not daily input from Teck's executive committee and various board members.

Meanwhile, Don and Len Manuel, our in-house legal counsel, kept sliding in and out of the meeting, Len with a worried look. Len then told us that CIBC, Don's old employer, had called the loan he'd used to purchase Teck shares. I told Len I'd phone Gerry McCaughey, the bank's new CEO, after the meeting and ask him to rescind the call. Meanwhile, the board agreed with the proposal that we ask Don to work with us to fix what had been done.

I didn't even know McCaughey personally, but when I phoned to tell him Don would be in charge of rectifying things he was pleased. He said he'd been unaware of the called loan and would be sure to reverse the call.

With the help of Teck's executive committee and its newly appointed director Jack Cockwell, who met with him weekly for six months, Don developed and executed a "12-step plan" and pulled off a recovery by the middle of 2009. The boom years of the super-cycle resumed for a while, and Teck shares reached a new record level in early 2011 before once again beginning a long, slow decline, as illustrated in figure 43.1.

But the own goal and recovery were not without a heavy cost in people, mines, and future development prospects.

As part of the 12-step plan, in January 2009 we had to reduce headcount by some 1,300 employees and contractors, none of whom shared any responsibility for the situation. It was a tough decision but necessary for the company's survival. We were able to claim a tax refund of over $1 billion, and through the efforts of our tax specialists we received much of it promptly. We had to sell part of the hydropower dams that supplied the Trail refinery complex, plus three gold mines – the two at Hemlo and the just-completed Pogo mine in Alaska – as well as future byproduct streams at several mines that would increase future operating costs and could lower their future viability in the event of another downturn.

And we had to give away our valuable partnership interest with Inmet Mining Corporation in the major Petaquilla copper development project in Panama, on which we had jointly announced the start of a feasibility study only a few months before this ill-fated second Fording deal.

Inmet was soon taken over by First Quantum, which put our lost Petaquilla property into production in 2021 as the new US$6 billion Cobre Panama mine. This major but lesser-known loss hurt particularly for a company like ours that had succeeded as a serial new-mine developer by seeking out just such opportunities in weak times and making good mines out of them.

Teck, wounded as it was, could have been the target of an opportunistic takeover and a long-time Canadian mining champion lost to foreign hands had it not been for our dual share structure.* It was a scary winter but by April the recovery was well underway, and it was cemented in June when Teck issued 100 million treasury Class B shares, representing 17.2 per cent of the company, to China Investment Corporation (CIC).

Teck survived, but with the loss of some important assets, with substantial dilution after the issuance of so many shares to CIC, and with a debt load that would inhibit the company's ability to capitalize on opportunities for a decade to come.

Post-mortem

The painting in figure 43.2, by artist David Lee, hung behind my desk for years and is now hanging behind that of Teck's new CEO, Jonathan Price. It is shown in full colour facing page 231 and is an important reminder to always combine risk-taking with wisdom.

---

* In February 2009, Roger Agnelli, the CEO of Brazil's Vale mining company, approached me and kindly offered to take Teck over for a nominal premium over our collapsed $5 share price. Fortunately for all shareholders I, representing the largest Class A shareholder, was able to politely reject that offer. Agnelli, always a gentleman, walked away equally politely. By the end of the year Teck's Class A and B share prices had recovered to over $35, on their way to $60 two years later, and Teck survived as an important independent Canadian mining company.

Figure 43.2
The meaning of the owl:
Everyone could use a wise old owl looking over his or her shoulder.
Even a wise old owl may go out on a limb sometimes.
But if the limb breaks, a wise old owl has wings that allow it to fly away safely.

Business lessons learned include:

1 Never bet the company without an appropriate safety net.
2 Never blindly ignore clear danger signs on the horizon.
3 Always work to be the partner of choice, not an adversary.
4 Never chase what might earlier have been a good deal well past its "best by" date.
5 Never forget the story of the wise old owl.

Phase Two: The Boom Continues, 2009–2010

Never confuse genius with luck and a bull market.
John Bogle

The super-cycle boom continued for a few more years after recovery from the GFC, with the average copper price peaking at US$4.00 a pound in 2011 and still strong at $3.61 in 2012.

Teck reported unprecedented financial results in 2011, with revenues of $11.5 billion, gross profit before depreciation and amortization of $5.8 billion, and cash flow from operations of $4.6 billion. Its shares closed 2010 at a record high of $61.79, with the low of $4 in 2008 being long forgotten by many.

That predatory acquisition frenzy era of the early super-cycle years was behind us, and perhaps much of the industry, as emphasis turned to managing and expanding existing operations. In 2011 alone Teck announced a $475 million mill modernization project and expanded life for its Highland Valley copper mine, progress on a major mill expansion at Antamina, and a modest mill expansion at Carmen de Andacollo.

Additional drilling on the deep hypogene copper prospect under the original Quebrada Blanca mine had continued over the previous three years, and reserves and resources at this important prospect had continued to grow.

In coal, Teck produced 22.8 million tonnes and announced expansion plans at its six producing mines as well as the restart of its old Quintette mine. It said in its annual report, "We expect to reach a production rate of approximately 31 million tonnes of coal per year by 2014, subject to permitting."

In oil, Teck announced its 21 per cent participation in the planned $13.5 billion Fort Hills oil sands project in Alberta.

The continuing boom had allowed Teck to work its debt load down nicely from the unprecedented $12 billion it had reached in 2008, and by 2011 net debt had been reduced to a manageable level of just under $3 billion (Figure 43.3).

It seemed the best of times – but this was about to change once again.

Phase Three: The Second Half of the Cycle, 2011–2015

I've never been certain whether the moral of the Icarus story should only be,
as is generally accepted, "don't try to fly too high," or whether it might also be thought
of as "forget the wax and feathers and do a better job on the wings."
Stanley Kubrick

The nature of such large cycles is that boom times tend to be followed by down times, often as increasing supply encouraged by the former meets steady or slowing demand. This began happening for many commodities around 2012 and metals, oil, and coal prices began falling substantially from

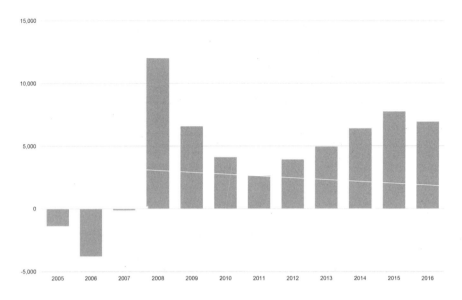

Teck net debt, year-end ($millions)

Figure 43.3
Teck's untenable net debt position of $12 billion in 2008 had declined to under $3 billion
by 2011 as the boom continued, but soon began rising again with the down-cycle to
$8 billion in 2015, just as we hoped to begin developing the deep extension of the
Quebrada Blanca mine.

their peaks. That was the situation when PwC put out its scathing report on the global mining industry's travails through 2015, referred to in the last chapter. The downturn was compounded by rampant concerns about a hard landing in the important Chinese economy, reducing demand even more.

With metal and coal prices falling over the four years after 2011 and with major expenditures on oil sands construction as well as too many unnecessary, top-of-market share buybacks, debt began climbing again to reach almost $8 billion in 2015. And that was before committing to any major construction costs on the important QB2 expansion project, potentially the next core operation of the company, but not yet permitted and financed. Teck shares had once again plummeted to under $5, market capitalization was once more less than $3 billion, and net debt at $8 billion was more than double that. We had come full circle from financial strength to weakness for the second time as the cycle progressed.

We were in a difficult position from which to try to build a US$5 billion new mine at QB2, let alone do much else to secure the new ore reserves essential for the company's future.

It's not hard for a company to become profligate in good times, and there may have been some of that during and after the peak of the commodity price cycle. That is when a CEO needs to be a wise old owl and to have a good chief financial officer with the stature David Thompson had while CFO with me in Teck's best years. He sat at the board table as an equal director, as did Bob Hallbauer as chief operating officer. Each was unafraid to speak up when I or anyone else might propose something daft, and it worked well.

But luckily, the scary scenario of a hard landing in China did not materialize, and commodity as well as share prices began to improve again in 2016. The net debt was reduced to $7 billion by year-end and, importantly, Teck's finance team of Don Lindsay, Ron Millos, and Scott Wilson – with the help of director Laura Dottori-Attanasio – succeeded in rescheduling much of the near-term debt into the future. With an improving economy, developing QB2 began once again to seem a realistic opportunity.

Phase Four: Recovery and New Beginnings at Quebrada Blanca, 2016–2020

A pool begins with many drops of water.
Xi Jinping

Following our reacquisition of the Quebrada Blanca property in 2007, an expanded drilling program had shown that the underlying hypogene deposit did in fact extend beyond the area of our previous drill holes, and in Teck's 2008 annual report we announced an inferred resource of 1 billion tonnes grading 0.5 per cent copper and 0.02 per cent molybdenum. Work began on a scoping study. It was a very good start.

Substantial drilling programs in 2009 and 2010 had continued to expand the size of the known deposit, and by the end of 2011 reserves and resources at QB2 were estimated to be about 4 billion tonnes grading 0.44 per cent copper, with 0.017 per cent molybdenum as a potential byproduct. This major increase in tonnage showed promise of QB2 becoming a significant mine. The copper grade was low compared with most Chilean mines, but this was offset by low waste-to-ore ratios, which could keep operating costs competitive. A feasibility study for a potential deeper mine was completed in 2012, and a social and environmental impact assessment (SEIA) was filed with Chilean authorities.

Then a major hiccup occurred when it was found that some parts of the earlier supergene operations at Quebrada Blanca had violated the mine's obligations under its original SEIA permit. Teck was forced to withdraw its proposed new SEIA for QB2 while regularizing the situation at QB1, hopefully within a year.

But the price of copper continued to fall as the super-cycle waned and Teck's debt load began to surge upwards again. The sense of urgency to make a major construction commitment tends to diminish in such times. Teck's 2013 annual report stated: "Design work on the Quebrada Blanca Phase 2 project continued, although at a slower pace because of the permitting issues. The level of future engineering activities and associated costs [is] under review, with a further slowdown in activities anticipated in 2014." The pendulum of business cycles continued.

The new SEIA for QB1 was received in 2016, and despite this being near the low point of the market cycle Teck resubmitted the SEIA for QB2. It was approved in 2018, 39 years after the Quebrada Blanca property was first acquired by Teck, and 11 years after it was reacquired with the Aur purchase. Perseverance pays, but it can take a long time.

With the world mining economy recovering to a more normal level after the industry's 2015 problems, work accelerated at QB2 once again, and by 2018 when a construction decision was being contemplated the total of reserves and resources had increased further to over 6 billion tonnes. Two years on, by 2020, this had increased to over 8 billion tonnes grading 0.39 per cent copper plus byproduct metal, a major increase from the 1 billion tonnes announced in 2008 (Figure 43.4).

But Teck's debt load was still uncomfortably high, and there were questions internally and externally about whether Teck should proceed with the projected US$5 billion development of QB2 on its own or reduce some of the risk by taking on a partner to help in funding it.

My natural instinct was that major mine development opportunities like this are rare and should be grasped to the fullest possible when they occur. In fact, a significant part of Teck's earlier growth had resulted from being the partner brought in to earn interests in new mines by providing financ-

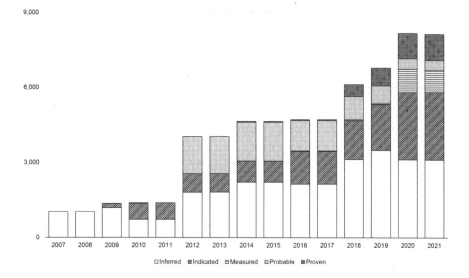

QB Hypogene Resource and Reserve Tonnes (millions of tonnes)

□ Inferred   ▨ Indicated   ⊟ Measured   □ Probable   ■ Proven

Figure 43.4
The increase in combined reserves and resources at QB2 over 15 years

ing and mine development assistance. As a rule, we had not given away interests in them, although we had done so with the Bullmoose coal project as
we prepared for the 1981 recession.

Others argued for bringing in a partner, perhaps for a variety of reasons.
In the end we all agreed to pursue that, in my case not just for financial reasons but because it had been almost two decades since Teck people had participated in the construction of a new mine of this magnitude at Antamina.
An ideal partner would supplement our lost years of on-the-job development experience and bring discipline to the process, in addition to funding.

As with Antamina, Quebrada Blanca is in the Andes Mountains at an elevation of over 4,000 metres. In addition to the new mill, or concentrator,
we would need to build a new tailings dam, a 165-kilometre pipeline to deliver copper concentrate down to the coast, and a new port from which to
ship that concentrate to market. Mines require a lot of water in the processing facilities, and Teck had committed to using desalinated water from the
ocean rather than tapping the limited fresh water supplies in northern Chile.

This meant building a desalination plant near the coast and a second 165-kilometre pipeline to pump water up to the site 4,000 metres above sea level. In all, construction at QB2 would be six or seven major projects rolled into one, requiring more than 14,000 people working on the various components at peak times.

So, in 2018, as we received the final SEIA, Teck began a quiet auction process with a select number of companies expected to be compatible partners. One of these was our long-time shareholder and even-longer-time business friend, Sumitomo Metal Mining. Its chair Nakazato-san expressed strong interest when I visited him in Tokyo in mid-2018. Because of our personal as well as corporate relationship it was thought that I should stay out of the bidding process, and I did. When SMM's President Nozaki-san visited Teck in Vancouver late in 2018 as the final negotiations were to take place, I welcomed him in my office but under the watchful eye of our amused lawyer, who was there to be sure I said the right things and nothing else. For a moment I missed the good old days when men were men and …, but good governance rules.

All is well that ends well. Sumitomo won the deal fairly and squarely and became a 30 per cent partner in QB2. Teck is now a 60 per cent partner and manager, and the Chilean government company ENAMI, from whom we had acquired the property back in 1989, retains a 10 per cent carried interest.

In December 2018, Teck and Sumitomo announced plans to build a mining and milling operation at QB2 with a capacity of 143,000 tonnes per day, at an expected ongoing capital cost of US$4.8 billion, excluding working capital, escalation, and interest. The first copper concentrate production was expected to take place in the second half of 2021.

Things happen, as I've said many times in this book, but 2020 presented a big one as the Covid-19 pandemic spread throughout an unprepared populace. It set many of the world's economies back for over two years until the development and distribution of new vaccines as well as acquired immunity began to lessen its impact. As this is being written in late 2022, its severity seems to have diminished in much of the world.

The pandemic had an immediate impact on construction schedules everywhere, and QB2 was no exception, as to both costs and timing. Covid-19 required a temporary suspension of construction and a restart with preventative requirements including a reduced workforce that could be accommodated on the site. Construction slowed and costs increased.

As of July 2022, construction at the project was over 90 per cent complete and the first copper production was scheduled to occur by the end of the year, approximately 18 months behind the original schedule announced before the pandemic.

This expanded Quebrada Blanca is expected to be a core mining operation for Teck for many decades, as was Antamina, and is a credit to the perseverance of Don Lindsay and his colleagues, who persisted with QB2 through 12 years of ups and downs between recovering the property and the sanctioning of mine development, as well as the further bumps in the road as construction proceeded during a pandemic.

Teck's Alex Christopher, Amparo Cornejo, and Dale Andres, along with many others, did a tremendous job working with Teck's project director, Karl Hroza, and our construction manager, Bechtel, as construction progressed.

Since mid-2020 the project has also benefited materially from Harold "Red" Conger's operating and construction experience with Phelps Dodge and Freeport. Red, like the iconic Bob Hallbauer before him, joined Teck as chief operating officer after a long, successful career building and operating large mines, and was named president and COO of Teck Resources as part of our new C-suite in July 2022.

EPILOGUE, PART SEVEN

The China super-cycle really was a once-in-a-lifetime experience for many people currently in the mining business, although a similar cycle had occurred 40 years earlier. Each began with rising demand from emerging or re-emerging Asian economies, and each led to much the same results, including significantly higher prices, increased supply, increases in "resources nationalism," eventual overcapacity, and declining prices until the boom ended. The two super-cycles were separated by some 30 years of declining commodity prices in real terms, an era that economist David Humphreys called "the barren years," with the former cycle now remembered by only a few of the more experienced miners still around.

As the recent boom began, many large mining companies found themselves with young, ambitious new CEOs without any experience of cycles this strong, and they began looking at each other with predatory eyes. Results of the ensuing takeover battles were a mixed bag, with few clear winners and losers.

And most companies in the industry, large or small, began dusting off every shovel-ready expansion or new mine development project on their books. Over the first four years of the boom, capital expenditures reached unprecedented levels, and by 2012 as supply overtook demand the inevitable began happening once again. Commodity and share prices began a long decline until they reached a bottom in early 2016. PriceWaterhouseCoopers reported that the 40 largest miners in the world saw their stock prices fall by 37 per cent in 2015 and "investors punished [them] for squandering the benefits of the boom."

Teck Resources experienced the same internal and external pressures over that 15-year period, including growing its own set of predatory eyes, with mixed results. Figure 43.1 tells the story from an investor's perspective. Three years of frenetic acquisition activity were followed by a nearly fatal collapse, after which we saw recovery for two more years as the boom continued. Then it peaked, to be followed by five years of prolonged decline to the same low point as in 2008. By 2019 it had recovered to about where it was when the super-cycle began in 2005.

The thing about roller coasters is that after a frenzied experience of ups and downs they usually end up about where they started.

In this most recent "new era," Teck participated in the development of an oil sands mine, sold as this went to press; the completion of construction at the Carmen de Andacollo mine; breaking ground on the hypogene part of Quebrada Blanca, now in construction and potentially a core asset for decades to come. On the other hand, after the untimely Fording Trust purchase, Teck was forced to sell three gold mines, give away an important development project that subsequently became the US$6 billion Cobre Panama mine, and sell 17 per cent of the whole company to CIC of China.

The $12 billion debt load from the Fording deal inhibited the company for some time, although as figure 43.3 shows it was worked down to a manageable $3 billion by 2011 before beginning to rise again. By 2015, with capital expenditures at Fort Hills and other projects as well as untimely share buybacks, it had once again soared to an unmanageable $8 billion, just as metal markets collapsed for a second time. As a result, when it came time to sanction its flagship deep Quebrada Blanca mine development in 2018, Teck had to sell 30 per cent of it in order to "de-risk" the project.

But the stage had been set for growth as Teck eventually renewed its long-held commitment to never rest on its ores. The deep QB2 mine is expected to achieve first production in 2023, and Teck has a portfolio of several other copper and zinc properties from previous exploration activities, some of which it will be able to develop in sequence in the coming years.

Teck was not responsible for the global financial crisis. It was destined to occur irrespective of our actions. But it's interesting to think where Teck would be today if more of its managers and board had seen it coming and it had kept its powder dry instead of buying at the top of the market without the safety valve of a market out. We would have been able to act upon opportunities during the GFC, as we had done in acquiring the Hemlo gold prospects during the 1980s crisis or Antamina in the 1990s one, each to become key mines for us. Today in some alternate universe, Teck and our partner Inmet might well have retained and built the Petaquilla ore deposits into the major Cobre Panama mine and still have QB2 underway as our next new mine, perhaps having retained our 90 per cent interest.

It is a lesson future mining company management and boards might well keep in mind. Opportunity will knock loudest at the doors of those who have kept their powder dry at or near the top of the cycle, able to deploy it wisely at or near the bottom.

But it was what it was, and the future will be what we make of it.

Don Lindsay had said, as he was interviewed for the CEO position, that "the measure of a mining company CEO would lie with how many good new mines he was able to bring to the company during his tenure."

It took a long time for QB2 to get there, but the mine is in the final stages of construction as this is being written. All the Teck people who worked on it, including Don, Alex Christopher, Dale Andres, Karl Hroza, Amparo Cornejo, Marcia Smith, Red Conger, and many others, should be proud of their achievement.

PART EIGHT

REFLECTIONS MOVING FORWARD

In September 2022, Don Lindsay retired after 17 years as CEO, to be succeeded by Jonathan Price, a metallurgical engineer who had joined Teck in 2020 after 14 years in executive mining roles with BHP Billiton.

Harold "Red" Conger joined Teck at the same time after 40 years of successful mine operating and development experience with Freeport-McMoRan and its predecessor company Phelps Dodge, and he was named Teck's new president and chief operating officer. Jonathan and Red are key parts of Teck's new C-suite of senior executives, and each was appointed to the board of directors. They, along with other ongoing members of Teck's senior management team, will lead the company as it builds for the future, responsibly producing the mined products that society needs, and never resting for long on its ores.

Each new management team develops its own characteristics and culture, based upon its members' past experience and on the economic environment in which it finds itself.

An earlier C-suite led by two Keevils, David Thompson, and Bob Hallbauer during the company's strong growth years in the late twentieth century became serial new mine developers out of necessity as well as choice. There is nothing that sharpens the minds of miners so much as realizing that their limited ore reserves will eventually run dry. Hence the admonition that is the title of this book.

The next regime under Don Lindsay began in an unprecedented boom as the China super-cycle took hold, leading to new highs and new lows as commodity prices rose and fell. It often questioned whether buying or building was the best strategy for growth, leading to one seriously damaging buy and a relative dearth of mine-building until that resumed near the end with QB2.

It was a materially different culture from that which had prevailed earlier, and likely an interregnum between that earlier culture and the new one that will be established by the new C-suite appointed in 2022.

I am confident that the new team will continue to build the company based upon the best practices of previous cultures, keeping it a strong Canadian-based company with international operations – one of which its employees, founders, and shareholders can be proud.

Some of these practices that have stood the test of time include:

- Think like a long-term owner, not a short-term trader. Never focus primarily on the next quarter or year, but on the future of the company.
- Seek value over size for its own sake. Remember that size can be the result of success, but it is seldom the reason for it.
- Always deal respectfully with partners, including junior or senior mining companies, employees, communities in which we operate, and infrastructure companies that carry our products to market. Work hard to deserve a reputation as the partner of choice.
- Remember to promise less, deliver more. In the end, respect will be earned by what you do, not what you promise.
- And never rest on your ores.

I hope that after another 10 years Norman Keevil III, Jonathan Price, Red Conger, and their colleagues will be able to add several more exciting chapters of progress in a new edition of *Never Rest on Your Ores*.

The following chapters, "Crossing the Stream by Feeling the Stones" and "Riding into the Sunset," are modified slightly from those of the first edition. They include reflections on our experiences as the company was being built, some thoughts on the importance of mining to the world's people, and general advice for those who hope to build the new mining companies of the future.

CHAPTER 44

CROSSING THE STREAM BY FEELING THE STONES

During times of less capital availability… those with more capital,
more opportunities come to them.
Bruce Flatt

Reflecting back, it's been a great ride for a whole host of people who played key roles in building Teck into a major force in Canadian mining: mentors, colleagues, friends, and family, many of whom know who they are. Together, and often with helpful partners, we were able to build a long series of new mines, creating jobs and new wealth for the countries and communities where they were located.

If there was a grand plan it evolved over time. Early on, we were explorers for our own account and for others, as much to enjoy the chase as to profit from it. Then, after some success, we began to try to build a sustainable mining company, one that would stand the test of time and make us proud. We became engineers as well as explorers. And we became mine builders, with a steady sequence of new mines that created new wealth for our shareholders and communities where we worked. It ended up as the Teck Resources of the twenty-first century, one of Canada's most influential mining companies.

While the plan had evolved, the underlying premise never did. It was always to execute it professionally, as well as we could, and aim to be among the best in the business. We tried to balance our natural optimism with a dose of reality checks, willing to consider (if not always follow) the sage advice of our more conservative colleagues. As John Thompson, our chief geoscientist, once said: "Optimism is a wise life tactic. Optimists are disappointed no more often than pessimists, but they feel a lot better during the time between life's tragedies."

Plus ça change, plus c'est la meme chose

If we learned anything along the way, it is that times change. Old eras are followed by new ones, which in turn may become old ones as they are again replaced. One has to respond to change, taking the best learnings one can from history and adapting them to the new realities of the day. That said, there are some lessons about the business that seem to stand the test of time.

1. *The world will continue to need mined resources.*

As most people go about their daily business, they seldom stop to think how essential the products of mining are to their everyday lives, not only for those of us living in the developed world, but also for those in less-developed countries who aspire to better lives.

The products we mine contribute quietly to the everyday lives of people. Copper is essential for most things electrical, including the ubiquitous cell phone. Coal and iron are necessary to make the steel we take for granted, and zinc to help prevent corrosion of it. Niobium is essential for the magnetic resonance imaging machines used in hospitals, and the list goes on. Most of the metals of the future, which will help us approach a net-zero-carbon world, will not be there without mining.

From the miner at the rock face underground to the shovel operator in the open pit, and to the technician tending her fire in the smelter, all are working quietly to produce the things so many people take advantage of. More power to them all.

2. *The vast majority of mines have finite lives.*

Each will eventually deplete its resources and need to be replaced. Unless society is to go back to horses and buggies instead of horseless carriages, and smoke signals instead of cell phones, a world with expanding populations and natural expectations will continue to need new mines, not only to replace but to augment existing supply.

It's not just mining companies that can never rest on their ores. It's the economies of a busy world that rely upon the industry's products.

3. *Good mines are hard to find.*

Good opportunities to find and build new mines are rare, as any geologist or prospector with a few years of experience has learned. When good ones appear they must be recognized, analyzed, and (if warranted) grasped without delay.

Being rare, the good ones are not generally there on demand. Our own experience over decades has been that ones that made a difference turned up on average some two or three years apart, sometimes in bunches and sometimes after more than two or three years. So, as important as it is to recognize and act when the good ones appear, it's equally important to be patient, and keep one's powder dry in the periods between those rare good opportunities.

4. Don't focus so much that you limit those opportunities.

If good mine development or purchase opportunities are few and far between, then it doesn't make too much sense to restrict your horizons to a single commodity.

The reason Teck has been diversified has nothing to do with evening out the cycles of different commodities, which generally are much the same anyway. It is because a mining company *prepared* to build mines in a variety of commodities within its expertise will naturally have more opportunities to choose from, or between which to allocate resources, than a company with a narrower, single-product focus.

We didn't set out consciously to find niobium, for example, or to get into coal, but grasped the opportunities when they arose. We are miners, and a good mine is a good mine, irrespective of commodity. The opposite is equally true.

5. Work hard to be the partner of choice in the business.

Many good mining prospects are discovered by junior exploration companies but in the end are developed by majors with the necessary financial and operating strength to bring them into production. Positioning yourself as the preferred developer, and walking the walk, can pay obvious dividends if it encourages people to bring good new projects through the door.

Treat the person across the table as you would want to be treated. Don't try to optimize every deal to the last pound of flesh. What goes around comes around in a small mining world, and a reputation for fair dealing is everything.

Partnering can be important with other major companies as well. When we acquired the option to participate in the large Antamina development project, it started with a few telephone calls and meetings between Teck, Rio Algom, Inmet, and Noranda, all previously partners in one or another mining venture, and we knew each other well. In addition, building that mine successfully resulted in part from the fact that the onsite engineers for each party had worked with some from the other parties on those earlier projects and were comfortable sharing responsibility rather than hoarding it.

6. *Avoid being weighed down by the anchor of debt.*

The most obvious problem is that too much debt can put a person or company under when things get tough, as so many have found to their chagrin. But almost as important is that lack of financial strength at cyclical bottoms can make it difficult to take advantage of the increased opportunities that will always appear there.

The wise among us put something away at the tops of cycles and have it available to capitalize on opportunity at the bottom. It may be that a little "whoa" at the top can save much "woe" at the bottom.

7. *What you pay, acting reasonably, is less important than how you pay for a long-life asset.*

When Joe Oppenheimer was whining about how he left something on the table in his bid for the Collahuasi copper mine, I told him not to worry. It was a long-life mine and in five years nobody would remember what he had paid for it. That was true.

On the other hand, negotiating the purchase of anything at what seems to be a good price is irrelevant if it risks putting you or your company under. It pays to cover your downside, as our wise old owl knows, and not "bet the company." Once again, putting together a long-life asset with the financial staying power to withstand unexpected downturns beats betting it all on a quick gain anytime.

8. *Size matters.*

Being too small, below "critical mass," it may be difficult to be sustainable in this business. But being too large, companies and other organizations will have a natural tendency towards bureaucracy. In our experience there is a Goldilocks size somewhere in the middle that will avoid both of those problems, and chasing size for its own sake is best left to those with an edifice complex.

But staying in this mid-range is also a way of maximizing opportunity. Very large companies will naturally try to focus only on the very large projects that can make a difference to them, thus often ignoring mid-size projects that would be quite important to mid-size companies. The Goldilocks company can look seriously at both the mid-size and very large projects, the latter by joint venturing with other mid-size companies as we did at Antamina. Just as being prepared to be diversified gives one more opportunities from which to choose than a single-product company has, so being in a position to partner on large-scale projects as well as benefit by building mid-size ones directly should naturally mean exposure to more opportunities for success.

9. *Mine life matters.*

We have seen how uncertain future price forecasts are, but it is easier to come close to being right over the longer term, when the laws of supply and demand have time to reach an equilibrium. It is too easy to get it wrong in the short term.

So, building or buying a short-life mine can go terribly badly, whereas with a long-life mine, and a reasonably knowledgeable assessment of likely future supply and demand, one has a better chance of getting it right. Short-life investments should be left to those who feel compelled to maintain annual ounces of gold or tonnes of copper production, which is irrelevant to a long-term investor.

10. *Remember that good opportunities are rare, and not always available when you want them.*

It pays to be patient and wait out the slack times, rather than just leap for the sake of leaping. Warren Buffett once compared investing to baseball, except he noted that that investing is a game where you can stand at the plate indefinitely waiting for the right pitch.

11. *Remember that designing and building mines is an art as well as a science. Maintain the talent.*

Placer Development became very good at this in its heyday, not only because it had great engineers from bottom to top, but also because it had grown by building a succession of new mines quickly and well. Placer had developed internal engineering, construction, and operating teams with current hands-on experience that could be taken on to the next project. We found this for ourselves in Teck's most active mine-building years from 1975 through 2000, as each time we built a new one we got better at it.

Such up-to-date, hands-on experience is a huge asset, and the lack of it a potential liability. It is an edge one can lose quickly by not keeping up, and I've argued for years that it can be good practice to keep development teams working actively on designing, permitting, and building smaller mines in those intervening years while waiting for the big ones to be ready for them.

12. *Don't take no for an answer too easily* when pursuing opportunities.

Sometimes the first and most obvious approach fails, but a second way can succeed, as illustrated by three examples that were important to us.

When we asked Neil Ivory, Ivory and Sime's Montreal-based Canadian representative, if its shareholding in Yukon Consolidated was for sale, he said no. We were going to drop the idea until Norm Rudden, our treasurer, asked why we didn't call head office in Scotland to be sure. We made a cold call there and bought control of Yukon from them the next week, and it gave us an important interest in the soon-to-be-expanded Lornex mine, about to become a core part of Highland Valley Copper.

When we tried to negotiate a development contract with the directors of Afton Mines, we were told they weren't ready to do the ultimate deal. So we went out and bought 50 per cent of the company's shares on the open market, and we covered our bet by selling enough of our passive shareholding in Mattagami Lake Mines to offset the cost.

When Robert Friedland wasn't ready to negotiate a development contract on Diamond Fields' Voisey's Bay discovery, we offered instead to buy a 10 per cent interest in the company as an interim move, getting our foot in the door. While the other foot never made it through, we ended up with a very large profit that we were able to redeploy into participation in the larger and very successful Antamina mine instead.

13. *Most importantly, manage well but think like an owner.*

Commit to building value over the longer term, in spite of the inevitable cycles with which we live. Never accept just being a *cyclical metal company*, taking the plaudits with every rising tide and blameless when the cycle reverses and the tide goes out. Such companies may be good trading vehicles and even popular in the good times but are hardly investments with which a Warren Buffett or a Jimmy Pattison would have been comfortable.

CHAPTER 45

RIDING INTO THE SUNSET

Anybody who does things makes mistakes. If, after my death, people say that what
I did was 70% correct, that would be quite good.
Deng Xiaoping

What we have accomplished has been the result of a strong team effort, with different colleagues as time passed. Each would have told parts of the story with their own particular emphasis and nuance, but with the same dedication to "doing it right" that has been a hallmark of this group and this company.

One of my friends asked me to reflect upon the three or four key lessons I could take from all of this. Perhaps the first is to always be listening and learning. As Ray Dalio of Bridgewater Associates has said: "People think my success is due to what I know. It's more to do with how I deal with not knowing."

Another is the importance of working closely with people with like values, ones like Bob Hallbauer and the Thompsons, Seyffert, Wright, Lipkewich, Steeves, Zeitler, Bergey, Frantz, Sibbald, and the many others who played key roles. Our secret was that there were no silos and little hierarchy. Each of us had our day jobs, but for all of us the avocation was looking for the next real opportunity. Achieving success for the business was everybody's challenge, and we never let anyone get away by saying "It's not my job."

I've not forgotten Herb Hawkes, the geochemist from Berkeley. Herb was a treasure trove of ideas, an occasionally absent-minded, entrepreneurial scientist who never stopped thinking, and who was eager to share his new thoughts with anyone who would listen. One of his doctoral students asked him why he didn't take more care to protect these ideas, and his memorable reply was: "If I ever get to the point where my latest one is my last, you guys should put me out to pasture." It's worth remembering. The willingness to pass ideas and information freely back and forth can often lead, synergistically, to people coming up with even better ones. I can't say it too often because it may be one of the most important observations in any organization: *hoarding ideas and information is the dystopian habit of the bureaucrat.*

And importantly, it is crucial to keep all hands on top of a major, company-building project and not let it slide away. We learned a lot about perseverance and staying on it with Bullmoose, even when everyone and everything seemed to be conspiring to make us accept delays or give up. In that respect, chapter 18 may well be worth rereading occasionally.

Doing a few things very well with your nose to the grindstone always beats spinning wheels on too many things. Challenges and delays are just that, meaning one needs to put in even more effort to get past them. One should never accept easily that it is so much harder this time. It was seldom as easy as, looking back, it may now seem.

Another is that there are times when, if we are to add real value, we must do things that are right but not particularly popular in the short term. Building Antamina was one of them, putting us in many investors' penalty box while we built it in difficult times, only to see it become one of Teck's core assets when it had been completed.

We learned that it is important to aim for the best, and wait for it. We tried to ask about every proposed deal: "Will it make us a better company?" Or in life: "Will it make us a better person?" If it won't, don't do it.

And we learned generally to follow the sage advice "Promise less, and deliver more." It's admittedly hard to remember this in these modern days when we are expected to provide guidance for the next quarter or two at the drop of every hat, but it's a reputation worth having, especially when compared with the opposite.

Well, three or four can turn into six or seven, can't it?

It's an uncertain world, and that may be what makes the mining business so fascinating. There are discoveries to be made, and there is nothing like the elation from a good diamond drill hole. And the opening of a new mine – that's what makes it all worthwhile. One regret is that John Simpson never told me earlier about the Stetson that had ridden on his head while he attended 23 mine openings. We didn't have quite that many openings, but were closing in on it, and I would have liked to have done something the same, maybe wearing one of the old Keevil hats from before Stetson took over the Keevil Hat Company.

I've had the pleasure of working with many great people in our company and with our many partners, and meeting all of the characters, the prospectors, engineers, geologists, promoters, family – including my father and Alan Keevil, brothers Harold and Brian, my sons Scott and Norman, and my wife

Joan – and all the others who make up the mining world, including even Moriarty. It's a small world, as we have seen, and full of characters of the highest order.

We have "lived in interesting times" for years, and we still do. The ongoing job for those who follow is to learn what they can from it and continue building a great Canadian company, for our shareholders, our employees, our communities and country, and for our own satisfaction. That, as a general rule, is what drives progress.

Thanks to those who blazed the trails. Hopefully these words will help blaze a few for the next generation of miners, for entrepreneurs at large, and for readers young and old. And hopefully as well, Teck will never again rest on its ores but will keep growing them through new mine development, and will still be a strong, vibrant Canadian mining champion 10 and 20 years from now. Most of my many great-grandchildren will be reaching maturity by then; each will have received a copy of this book and a few shares of Teck, and some may be inspired to make deep footprints of their own.

BIBLIOGRAPHY

Barnes, Michael. *The Scholarly Prospector*. General Store Publishing House, 2006.

– *More Than Free Gold*. General Store Publishing House, 2008.

Bernanke, Ben, Hank Paulson, and Timothy Geithner. *Firefighting: The Financial Crisis and Its Lessons*. Penguin Books, 2019.

Cohan, William D. *House of Cards*. Doubleday, 2009.

Crowson, Phillip. *Inside Mining: The Economics of the Supply and Demand of Minerals and Metals*. Mining Journal Books, 1998.

Danielson, Vivian, and James Whyte. *Bre-X: Gold Today, Gone Tomorrow*. *Northern Miner*, 1997.

Dunbar, W. Scott. *How Mining Works*. Society for Mining, Metallurgy & Exploration Inc., 2016.

Eliot, T.S. "The Love Song of J. Alfred Prufrock" in *Poetry: A Magazine of Verse*, 1915.

Francis, Diane. *Bre-X: The Inside Story*. Key Porter Books, 1997.

Fukuyama, Francis. *The End of History*. The National Interest, 1992.

Grayson, C. Jackson. *Decisions under Uncertainty: Drilling Decisions by Oil and Gas Operators*. Harvard Business School, Division of Research. Bailey and Swinfen, 1960.

Green, Lewis. *The Gold Hustlers*. Alaska Northwest Books, *1977*.

Grescoe Paul, Richard Haskayne. *Northern Tigers: Building Ethical Canadian Corporate Champions*. Key Porter Books, 2007.

Grove, Andrew. *Only the Paranoid Survive*. Profile Business, 1998.

Humphreys, David. *The Remaking of the Mining Industry*. Palgrave Macmillan, 2015.

Keevil, Ambrose. *The Story of Fitch Lovell*. Fletcher and Son, 1972.

Kissinger, H. *On China*. Penguin Canada, 2012.

Koller, T., M. Goedhart, D. Wessels. *Valuation: Measuring and Managing the Value of Companies,* 6th ed. Wiley, 2015.

Laznicka, Peter. *Giant Metallic Deposits.* Springer, 2010.

Lefolii, Ken. *Claims.* Key Porter Books, 1987.

Lewis, Michael. *The Big Short.* W.W. Norton & Company, 2010.

Lonn, George. *The Mine Finders.* Pitt Publishing Co., 1966.

McNish, Jacquie. *The Big Score.* Doubleday Canada, 1998.

Meggs, Geoff, and Rod Mickleburgh. *The Art of the Impossible: Dave Barrett and the NDP in Power, 1972–1975.* Harbour Publishing, 2012.

Mine 2016, PricewaterhouseCooper, 2016.

Morris, Charles R. *The Trillion Dollar Meltdown.* Perseus Books, 2008.

Poss, John R. *Stones of Destiny.* Michigan Technological University, 1975.

Python Mining Consultants. *History of Mining in Kirkland Lake.* 2010.

Shulman, Morton. *The Billion Dollar Windfall.* William Morrow, 1970.

Tennyson, Alfred, Lord. "The Charge of the Light Brigade," 1854.

Thompson, Edward G. *A Boy from Utterson,* 2015. Private publication.

Vogel, Ezra F. *Deng Xiaoping and the Transformation of China.* Belknap Press, 2013.

Yeats, William Butler. "The Second Coming." 1919.

INDEX